WHY CIVIL RESISTANCE WORKS

COLUMBIA STUDIES IN **TERRORISM AND IRREGULAR WARFARE**

COLUMBIA STUDIES IN **TERRORISM AND IRREGULAR WARFARE**
Bruce Hoffman, Series Editor

This series seeks to fill a conspicuous gap in the burgeoning literature on terrorism, guerrilla warfare, and insurgency. The series adheres to the highest standards of scholarship and discourse and publishes books that elucidate the strategy, operations, means, motivations, and effects posed by terrorist, guerrilla, and insurgent organizations and movements. It thereby provides a solid and increasingly expanding foundation of knowledge on these subjects for students, established scholars, and informed reading audiences alike.

AMI PEDAHZUR, **THE ISRAELI SECRET SERVICES AND THE STRUGGLE AGAINST TERRORISM**
AMI PEDAHZUR AND ARIE PERLIGER, **JEWISH TERRORISM IN ISRAEL**
LORENZO VIDINO, **THE NEW MUSLIM BROTHERHOOD IN THE WEST**

WHY CIVIL RESISTANCE WORKS THE STRATEGIC LOGIC OF NONVIOLENT CONFLICT

ERICA **CHENOWETH** & MARIA J. **STEPHAN**

COLUMBIA UNIVERSITY PRESS   NEW YORK

*The views expressed in this book
do not represent those of the United States Government.*

COLUMBIA UNIVERSITY PRESS
Publishers Since 1893
NEW YORK   CHICHESTER, WEST SUSSEX

COPYRIGHT © 2011 COLUMBIA UNIVERSITY PRESS
Paperback edition, 2013
All rights reserved

Library of Congress Cataloging-in-Publication Data
Chenoweth, Erica, 1980–
   Why civil resistance works : the strategic logic of nonviolent conflict / Erica Chenoweth and Maria J. Stephan.
      p. cm. — (Columbia studies in terrorism and irregular warfare)
   Includes bibliographical references and index.
   ISBN 978-0-231-15682-0 (cloth)—ISBN 978-0-231-15683-7 (pbk.)—ISBN 978-0-231-52748-4 (e-book)
   1. Civil disobedience. 2. Nonviolence. I. Stephan, Maria J. II. Title. III. Series.
JC328.3.C474   2011
303.6'1—dc22   2010037567

COVER & INTERIOR DESIGN BY **MARTIN N. HINZE**

FOR MY FAMILY
—E. C.

TO MY PARENTS AND BROTHER
—M. J. S.

CONTENTS

LIST OF ILLUSTRATIONS IX
LIST OF TABLES XI
ACKNOWLEDGEMENTS XIII

PART I **WHY CIVIL RESISTANCE WORKS** 1
ONE THE SUCCESS OF NONVIOLENT RESISTANCE CAMPAIGNS 3
TWO THE PRIMACY OF PARTICIPATION IN NONVIOLENT RESISTANCE 30
THREE EXPLORING ALTERNATIVE EXPLANATIONS FOR THE SUCCESS OF CIVIL RESISTANCE 62

PART II **CASE STUDIES** 85
INTRODUCTION TO THE CASE STUDIES 87
FOUR THE IRANIAN REVOLUTION, 1977–1979 92
FIVE THE FIRST PALESTINIAN INTIFADA, 1987–1992 119
SIX THE PHILIPPINE PEOPLE POWER MOVEMENT, 1983–1986 147
SEVEN WHY CIVIL RESISTANCE SOMETIMES FAILS: THE BURMESE UPRISING, 1988–1990 172
CASE STUDY SUMMARY 192

PART III **THE IMPLICATIONS OF CIVIL RESISTANCE** 199
EIGHT AFTER THE CAMPAIGN: THE CONSEQUENCES OF VIOLENT AND NONVIOLENT RESISTANCE 201
NINE CONCLUSION 220

EPILOGUE 229
APPENDIX 233
NOTES 243
REFERENCES 261
INDEX 279

ILLUSTRATIONS

FIGURE 1.1 FREQUENCY OF NONVIOLENT AND VIOLENT CAMPAIGN END YEARS 7
FIGURE 1.2 NUMBER OF NONVIOLENT CAMPAIGNS AND PERCENTAGE OF SUCCESSES, 1940–2006 8
FIGURE 1.3 SUCCESS RATES BY DECADE, 1940–2006 8
FIGURE 1.4 RATES OF SUCCESS, PARTIAL SUCCESS, AND FAILURE 9
FIGURE 1.5 SUCCESS RATES BY CAMPAIGN OBJECTIVE 9

FIGURE 2.1 THE EFFECT OF PARTICIPATION ON THE PROBABILITY OF CAMPAIGN SUCCESS 40
FIGURE 2.2 THE EFFECT OF PARTICIPATION ON SECURITY-FORCE DEFECTIONS 50

FIGURE 3.1 PERCENTAGE OF CAMPAIGNS BY LOCATION'S POLITY SCORE 67
FIGURE 3.2 PERCENTAGE OF CAMPAIGNS BY LOCATION'S RELATIVE POWER 72
FIGURE 3.3 RATES OF CAMPAIGN SUCCESS BY REGION 74

FIGURE 8.1 THE EFFECT OF RESISTANCE TYPE ON PROBABILITY OF DEMOCRACY 215

TABLES

TABLE 2.1 TWENTY-FIVE LARGEST RESISTANCE CAMPAIGNS, 1900-2006 33
TABLE 2.2 THE EFFECT OF NONVIOLENT RESISTANCE ON NUMBER OF PARTICIPANTS 34
TABLE 2.3 THE EFFECT OF NONVIOLENT RESISTANCE ON MECHANISMS 48
TABLE 2.4 THE EFFECTS OF MECHANISMS ON THE PROBABILITY OF SUCCESS 51

TABLE 3.1 THE EFFECTS OF STRUCTURAL FACTORS ON CAMPAIGN OUTCOMES 70
TABLE 3.2 DISTRIBUTION OF VIOLENT AND NONVIOLENT CAMPAIGN OUTCOMES BY CAMPAIGN OBJECTIVE 73
TABLE 3.3 THE EFFECT OF VIOLENT RESISTANCE ON CAMPAIGN SUCCESS 81

TABLE II.A CASE SELECTION 87

TABLE 4.1 THE NONVIOLENT AND VIOLENT IRANIAN CAMPAIGNS COMPARED 117

TABLE 5.1 PALESTINIAN DISTURBANCES IN THE WEST BANK AND GAZA STRIP, 1988-1992 120
TABLE 5.2 THE NONVIOLENT AND VIOLENT PALESTINIAN CAMPAIGNS COMPARED, 1987-1992 145

TABLE 6.1 THE NONVIOLENT AND VIOLENT PHILIPPINE CAMPAIGNS COMPARED 157

TABLE 7.1 THE NONVIOLENT AND VIOLENT BURMESE CAMPAIGNS COMPARED 185

TABLE II.B CASE STUDY SUMMARY OF NONVIOLENT CAMPAIGNS 194

TABLE 8.1 THE EFFECT OF RESISTANCE TYPE ON POSTCONFLICT DEMOCRACY 214

TABLE 8.2 THE EFFECT OF RESISTANCE TYPE ON PROBABILITY OF POSTCONFLICT CIVIL WAR ONSET 217

TABLE A.1 NONVIOLENT CAMPAIGNS 233
TABLE A.2 VIOLENT CAMPAIGNS 236

ACKNOWLEDGMENTS

IT IS IMPOSSIBLE to recollect all the people from whom I received inspiration, assistance, and unwavering support while researching and writing this book. But I wish to recognize a few, with additional thanks to those not mentioned here.

First are my colleagues at the International Center on Nonviolent Conflict—Peter Ackerman, Jack DuVall, Hardy Merriman, Althea Middleton-Detzner, Maciej Bartkowski, Daryn Cambridge, and Vanessa Ortiz—all of whom have believed in and supported this project from the very start. They introduced me to the topic and to Maria, and I gratefully acknowledge the financial support that made the study possible. I also thank Stephen Zunes, Doug Bond, Cynthia Boaz, and Kurt Schock for their comments on the research.

The cohort of scholars I met during two years at the Belfer Center at Harvard's Kennedy School of Government helped the project take off. To Ivan Arreguín-Toft, Boaz Atzili, Kristin Bakke, Emma Belcher, Nik Biziouras, Tom Bielefeld, Jonathan Caverley, Fotini Christia, David Cunningham, Kathleen Cunningham, Erik Dahl, Alexander Downes, Ehud Eiran, Emily Greble, Kelly Greenhill, Mike Horowitz, Matthew Kocher, Sarah Kreps, Matthew Kroenig, Adria Lawrence, Jason Lyall, Steve Miller, Assaf Moghadam, Jonathan Monten, Harris Mylonas, Wendy Pearlman, Phil Potter, Scott Radnitz, Elizabeth Saunders, John Schuessler, Tammy Smith, Monica Toft, and Stephen Walt: your brilliance continues to awe and humble me.

Matthew Fuhrmann gave up four days of his vacation during July 2009 to fly across the country and help me resolve seemingly intractable problems from data structure to simultaneous equations. I can only hope to emulate his selflessness and clarity of mind as my career progresses.

I also appreciatively acknowledge the continued support of colleagues at the University of Colorado. Colin Dueck, Steve Chan, David Leblang, and Jennifer Fitzgerald are excellent mentors. Special thanks go to Susan

Clarke. Everyone lucky enough to know Susan is familiar with her dedication to mentoring young scholars and the enthusiasm with which she challenges us intellectually while simultaneously advocating for us professionally. My classmates at the University of Colorado have also proved to be some of my most valued colleagues. I owe Jessica Teets, Orion Lewis, Michael Touchton, Helga Sverrisdóttír, and Marilyn Averill a great debt for helping me mature intellectually, and I look forward to our continued collaborations. Thanks also to my earlier mentors at the University of Dayton, including Margaret Karns, David Ahern, Jaro Bilocerkowycz, Gerald Kerns, and Mark Ensalaco.

The Institute of International Studies at the University of California, Berkeley, provided me with a scholarly home away from home from 2007 to 2009. I am especially indebted to Ned Walker, Regine Spector, and Brent Durbin, who provided useful feedback at various stages of the project.

I also thank my colleagues at Wesleyan University. Don Moon has been a relentless advocate of the project, and a fellowship at Wesleyan's Center for the Humanities, under the headship of Jill Morawski, provided me with useful feedback and time to complete the manuscript. I also thank my colleagues in the Government Department for their friendship and support, especially Mary Alice Haddad, Peter Rutland, Mike Nelson, Erika Fowler, and Doug Foyle for commenting on various versions of the manuscript. I am indebted to several terrific students, especially Jeremy Berkowitz for helping with data collection and Nicholas Quah for his assistance in proofreading the manuscript. Elizabeth Wells, at American University, provided research assistance during the early stages of data collection.

We benefited from outstanding feedback from seminar and panel participants at Georgetown, Rutgers, Yale, Harvard, Wesleyan, the University of Dayton, the United States Institute of Peace, and King's College, as well as at meetings of the International Studies Association, the American Political Science Association, and the World International Studies Committee.

Our editor at Columbia University Press, Anne Routon, has been extremely helpful throughout the preparation of the manuscript, as has her assistant Alison Alexanian. We thank them both for their responsiveness and guidance and for securing top-notch reviews that helped us to improve the manuscript. We also thank Mike Ashby for his stellar copyediting.

My family's generosity is what has made everything possible. All the Chenoweths and Abels have inspired and encouraged me throughout my life and career. My parents, Richard and Marianne, have been my most persistent advocates, and even read and commented on draft chapters. My sister Andrea and her fiancé Phil are terrific friends and brilliant communicators; I thank them for their support and inspiration. I also thank my brother, Christopher, and his wife, Miranda. In the past year, Christopher and Miranda have blessed us all with William, my only nephew, whose few months on this earth have made me even more dedicated to helping to end violent conflict wherever it is unnecessary. I also thank the Petty family—Kathy, Linda, Mattie Jean, and Warren—as well as Tyler, Elizabeth, Stephanie, and Adam for supporting me through various stages of this project. I owe a debt I can never fully repay to Kathe, Angi, Joyanna, Melody, Kathy, George, Tommy, Scott, Rachel, Vic, Marc, Nadia, and Gelong Tashi for all that they have given to me. And finally, there is Allison. The daily joys of sharing our lives together have kept me afloat through this and many other endeavors. I thank her for her wisdom, patience, kindness, humor, and enduring eagerness for adventure.

ERICA CHENOWETH
OAKLAND, CALIFORNIA

I did not expect to write a book on people power with a domestic terrorism expert who takes delight in running regression analyses! But after our chance meeting at Colorado College four summers ago, Erica and I realized that we needed to bring together our respective expertise to produce this book. And it has been a great ride together. I would like to thank first my mentors from the Fletcher School, including Richard Shultz, Eileen Babbitt, and Hurst Hannum for supporting my initial foray into the study of civil resistance. Professor Shultz and Steve Miller, from Harvard's Belfer Center for Science and International Affairs, recognized the weighty international security implications of popular struggles involving different weapons and enthusiastically encouraged me to pursue this line of research.

Dr. Peter Ackerman, one of the world's leading experts on strategic nonviolent action, became my Fletcher dissertation adviser, mentor, and friend. Peter understood, when writing his own doctoral dissertation four decades ago with Gene Sharp, a pioneer in the field of nonviolent action to whom we all owe a great debt of gratitude, that eventually the academy would catch on to the remarkable albeit underappreciated track record of popular nonviolent struggles around the world. As the founding chair of the International Center on Nonviolent Conflict (ICNC), Peter, along with his partner, Jack DuVall, have shepherded the global expansion of knowledge and practical know-how about the waging of nonviolent struggle. During my tenure at the ICNC I had the opportunity to interact with some remarkable and courageous nonviolent activists from all over the world. Their determination, bravery, and will to win using nonviolent methods have been a source of profound inspiration for me.

I thank Peter and Jack, along with the incredibly dedicated people at the ICNC and at Rockport Capital, including Hardy Merriman, Shaazka Beyerle, Vanessa Ortiz, Berel Rodal, Althea Middleton-Detzner, Nicola Barrach, Maciej Bartkowski, Jake Fitzpatrick, Daryn Cambridge, Suravi Bhandari, Deena Patriarca, Ciel Lagumen, and Kristen Kopko for their hard work, support, and friendship. Hardy Merriman, in particular, has been an editing rock star. The ICNC's diverse team of academic advisers, including Stephen Zunes, Kurt Schock, John Gould, Mary Elizabeth King, Larry Diamond, Doug McAdam, Les Kurtz, Cyndi Boaz, Janet Cherry, Howard Barrell, Roddy Brett, Kevin Clements, Barry Gan, Scott O'Bryan, Lee Smithey, Victoria Tin-bor Hui, Brian Martin, Senthil Ram, April Carter, and Howard Clark have provided Erica and me with good advice and prompt and thoughtful feedback on earlier iterations of this work. Mubarak Awad and Michael Beer, from Nonviolence International, have also been great supporters over the years. Through their own interdisciplinary work, the aforementioned scholars and scholar-practitioners have made significant strides to advance the study and practice of civil resistance.

Some of my most enjoyable and amusing moments at the ICNC were spent in the company of "the Serbs"—the young guns who formed Otpor and helped mobilize the Serbian population to nonviolently oust "the butcher of the Balkans" in 2000. Srdja Popovic, Ivan Marovic, Slobo Djinovic, and Andrej Milojevic went on to found the Center for Applied Nonviolent Action and Strategies, a Belgrade-based NGO that trains nonviolent activists throughout the world. May they continue to grow a global cadre of nonviolent conflict veterans and help transfer skills and hope to a new generation of civic leaders.

Ambassador Mark Palmer, who has been a great mentor of mine, showed me a different side of the U.S. State Department and encouraged me to be a friend of nonviolent-change agents from within the U.S. government. Through his work with the Council for a Community of Democracies, Mark is helping institutionalize global solidarity with those who are fighting against huge odds to defend basic rights and freedoms. I greatly admire Mark and hope to follow in his footsteps.

I would also like to extend thanks to my Pol-Mil colleagues at the U.S. embassy in Kabul, particularly the Civ-Mil Plans and Assessments team. Phil Kosnett, JoAnne Wagner, Melanie Anderton, Jen Munro, Emilie Lemke, and Tammy Rutledge have listened to me expound on the virtues of civic mobilization while supporting my efforts to engage with Afghan civil society and speak publicly about civil resistance in Afghanistan. I hope that organized civic action led by Afghans will help transform this war-torn society and lead it to a more peaceful future.

Finally, I would like to thank my parents, Marianne and Phil, and my brother Peter, whose love, encouragement, and insistence that I maintain a sense of perspective (and humor) while working on this book helped see me through. A girl could not ask for a more supportive and caring family. I am also grateful for the friendships of those in Vermont who continue to serve as my "prayer warriors." They know who they are.

MARIA J. STEPHAN
KABUL, AFGHANISTAN

PART ONE
Why Civil Resistance Works

CHAPTER ONE **THE SUCCESS OF NONVIOLENT RESISTANCE CAMPAIGNS**

Nonviolence is fine as long as it works.
MALCOLM X

IN NOVEMBER 1975, Indonesian president Suharto ordered a full-scale invasion of East Timor, claiming that the left-leaning nationalist group that had declared independence for East Timor a month earlier, the Revolutionary Front for an Independent East Timor (Fretilin), was a communist threat to the region. Fretilin's armed wing, the Forças Armadas de Libertação Nacional de Timor-Leste (Falintil), led the early resistance to Indonesian occupation forces in the form of conventional and guerrilla warfare. Using weapons left behind by Portuguese troops,[1] Falintil forces waged armed struggle from East Timor's mountainous jungle region. But Falintil would not win the day. Despite some early successes, by 1980 Indonesia's brutal counterinsurgency campaign had decimated the armed resistance along with nearly one third of the East Timorese population.[2]

Yet nearly two decades later, a nonviolent resistance movement helped to successfully remove Indonesian troops from East Timor and win independence for the annexed territory. The Clandestine Front, an organization originally envisaged as a support network for the armed movement, eventually reversed roles and became the driving force behind the nonviolent, pro-independence resistance. Beginning in 1988, the Clandestine Front, which grew out of an East Timorese youth movement, developed a large decentralized network of activists, who planned and executed various nonviolent campaigns inside East Timor, in Indonesia, and internationally. These included protests timed to the visits of diplomats and dignitaries, sit-ins inside foreign embassies, and international solidarity efforts that reinforced Timorese-led nonviolent activism.

The Indonesian regime repressed this movement, following its standard approach to violent and nonviolent challengers from within. But this repression backfired. Following the deaths of more than two hundred East Timorese nonviolent protestors at the hands of Indonesian troops in Dili in November 1991, the pro-independence campaign experienced a major turning point. The massacre, which was captured on film by a British cameraman, was quickly broadcast around the world, causing international outrage and prompting the East Timorese to rethink their strategy (Kohen 1999; Martin, Varney, and Vickers 2001). Intensifying nonviolent protests and moving the resistance into Indonesia proper became major components of the new strategy.

Suharto was ousted in 1998 after an economic crisis and mass popular uprising, and Indonesia's new leader, B. J. Habibie, quickly pushed through a series of political and economic reforms designed to restore stability and international credibility to the country. There was tremendous international pressure on Habibie to resolve the East Timor issue, which had become a diplomatic embarrassment, not to mention a huge drain on Indonesia's budget. During a 1999 referendum, almost 80 percent of East Timorese voters opted for independence. Following the referendum, Indonesian-backed militias launched a scorched-earth campaign that led to mass destruction and displacement. On September 14, 2000, the UN Security Council voted unanimously to authorize an Australian-led international force for East Timor.[3]

The United Nations Transitional Administration in East Timor oversaw a two-year transition period before East Timor became the world's newest independent state in May 2002 (Martin 2000). Although a small number of Falintil guerrillas (whose targets had been strictly military) kept their weapons until the very end, it was not their violent resistance that liberated the territory from Indonesian occupation. As one Clandestine Front member explained, "The Falintil was an important symbol of resistance and their presence in the mountains helped boost morale, but nonviolent struggle ultimately allowed us to achieve victory. The whole population fought for independence, even Indonesians, and this was decisive."[4]

Similarly, in the Philippines in the late 1970s, several revolutionary guerrilla groups were steadily gaining strength. The Communist Party of the Philippines and its New People's Army (NPA) were inspired by Marxist-Leninist-Maoist ideologies and pursued armed revolution to gain power. State-sponsored military attacks on the NPA dispersed the guerrilla resistance until the NPA encompassed all regions of the country. The Philippine government launched a concerted counterinsurgency effort, and the NPA was never able to achieve power.

In the early 1980s, however, members of the opposition began to pursue a different strategy. In 1985 the reformist opposition united under the banner of UNIDO (United Nationalist Democratic Organization) with Cory Aquino as its presidential candidate. In the period leading up to the elections, Aquino urged nonviolent discipline, making clear that violent attacks against opponents would not be tolerated. Church leaders, similarly, insisted on discipline, while the National Citizens' Movement for Free Elections trained half a million volunteers to monitor elections.

When Marcos declared himself the winner of the 1986 elections despite the counterclaims of election monitors, Cory Aquino led a rally of 2 million Filipinos, proclaiming victory for herself and "the people." The day after Marcos's inauguration, Filipinos participated in a general strike, a boycott of the state media, a massive run on state-controlled banks, a boycott of crony businesses, and other nonviolent activities.

A dissident faction of the military signaled that it favored the opposition in this matter, encouraging the opposition to form a parallel government on February 25 with Aquino at its head. Masses of unarmed Filipino civilians, including nuns and priests, surrounded the barracks where the rebel soldiers were holed up, forming a buffer between those soldiers and those who remained loyal to Marcos. President Ronald Reagan's administration had grown weary of Marcos and signaled support for the opposition movement. That evening, U.S. military helicopters transported Marcos and his family to Hawaii, where they remained in exile. Although the Philippines has experienced a difficult transition to democracy, the nonviolent campaign successfully removed the Marcos dictatorship. Where violent insurgency had failed only a few years earlier, the People Power movement succeeded.

THE PUZZLE

The preceding narratives reflect both specific and general empirical puzzles. Specifically, we ask why nonviolent resistance has succeeded in some cases where violent resistance had failed in the same states, like the violent and nonviolent pro-independence campaigns in East Timor and regime-change campaigns in the Philippines. We can further ask why nonviolent resistance in some states fails during one period (such as the 1950s Defiance Campaign by antiapartheid activists in South Africa) and then succeeds decades later (such as the antiapartheid struggle in the early 1990s).

These two specific questions underline a more general inquiry, which is the focus of this book. We seek to explain two related phenomena: why nonviolent resistance often succeeds relative to violent resistance, and under what conditions, nonviolent resistance succeeds or fails.[5]

Indeed, debates about the strategic logic of different methods of traditional and nontraditional warfare have recently become popular among security studies scholars (Abrahms 2006; Arreguín-Toft 2005; Byman and Waxman 1999, 2000; Dashti-Gibson, Davis, and Radcliff 1997; Drury 1998; Horowitz and Reiter 2001; Lyall and Wilson 2009; Merom 2003; Pape 1996, 1997, 2005; Stoker 2007). Implicit in many of these assessments, however, is an assumption that the most forceful, effective means of waging political struggle entails the threat or use of violence. For instance, a prevailing view among political scientists is that opposition movements select terrorism and violent insurgency strategies because such means are more effective than nonviolent strategies at achieving policy goals (Abrahms 2006, 77; Pape 2005). Often violence is viewed as a last resort, or a necessary evil in light of desperate circumstances. Other scholarship focuses on the effectiveness of military power, without comparing it with alternative forms of power (Brooks 2003; Brooks and Stanley 2007; Desch 2008; Johnson and Tierney 2006).

Despite these assumptions, in recent years organized civilian populations have successfully used nonviolent resistance methods, including boycotts, strikes, protests, and organized noncooperation to exact political concessions and challenge entrenched power. To name a few, sustained and systematic nonviolent sanctions have removed autocratic regimes from power in Serbia (2000), Madagascar (2002), Georgia (2003), and Ukraine (2004–2005), after rigged elections; ended a foreign occupation in Lebanon (2005); and forced Nepal's monarch to make major constitutional concessions (2006). In the first two months of 2011, popular nonviolent uprisings in Tunisia and Egypt removed decades-old regimes from power. As this book goes to press, the prospect of people power transforming the Middle East remains strong.

In our Nonviolent and Violent Campaigns and Outcomes (NAVCO) data set, we analyze 323 violent and nonviolent resistance campaigns between 1900 and 2006.[6] Among them are over one hundred major nonviolent campaigns since 1900, whose frequency has increased over time. In addition to their growing frequency, the success rates of nonviolent campaigns have increased. How does this compare with violent insurgencies? One might assume that the success rates may have increased among both nonviolent and violent insurgencies. But in our data, we find the opposite: although they persist, the success rates of violent insurgencies have declined.

The most striking finding is that between 1900 and 2006, nonviolent resistance campaigns were nearly twice as likely to achieve full or partial success as their violent counterparts. As we discuss in chapter 3, the effects of resistance type on the probability of campaign success are robust even when we take into account potential confounding factors, such as target regime type, repression, and target regime capabilities.[7]

The results begin to differ only when we consider the objectives of the resistance campaigns themselves. Among the 323 campaigns, in the case of antiregime resistance campaigns, the use of a nonviolent strategy has greatly enhanced the likelihood of success. Among campaigns with territorial objectives, like antioccupation or self-determination, nonviolent campaigns also have a slight advantage. Among the few cases of major resistance that do not fall into either category (antiapartheid campaigns, for instance), nonviolent resistance has had the monopoly on success.

The only exception is that nonviolent resistance leads to successful secession less often than violent insurgency. Although no nonviolent secession campaigns have succeeded, only four of the forty-one violent secession campaigns have done so (less than 10 percent), also an unimpressive figure. The implication is that campaigns seeking secession are highly unlikely to

FIGURE 1.1 **FREQUENCY OF NONVIOLENT AND VIOLENT CAMPAIGN END YEARS**

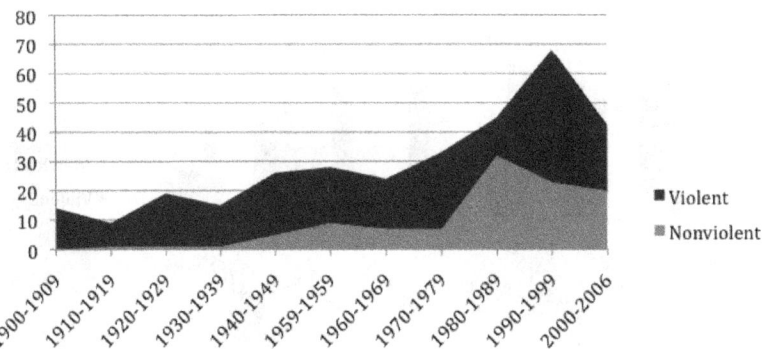

FIGURE 1.2 **NUMBER OF NONVIOLENT CAMPAIGNS AND PERCENTAGE OF SUCCESSES, 1940–2006**

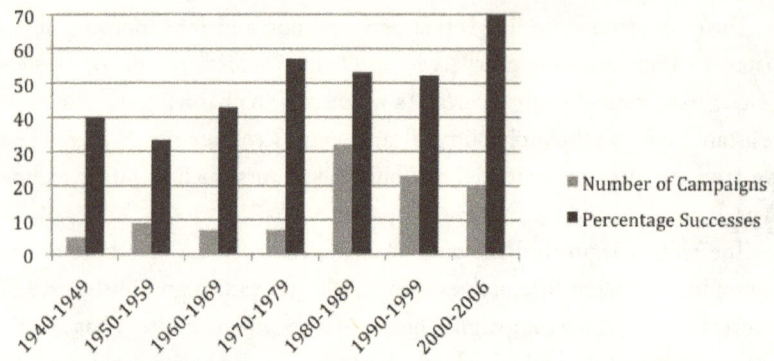

FIGURE 1.3 **SUCCESS RATES BY DECADE, 1940–2006**

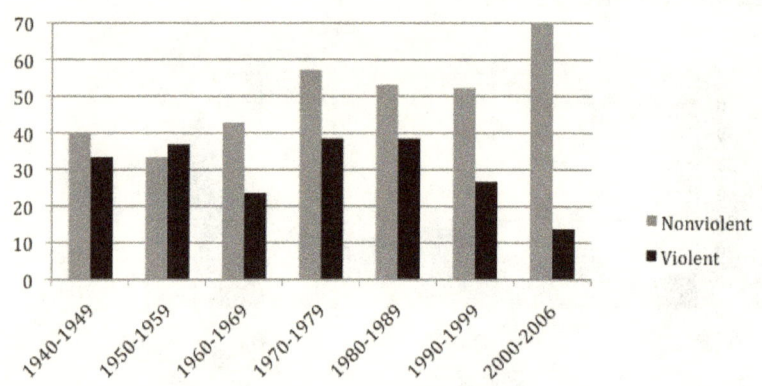

FIGURE 1.4 **RATES OF SUCCESS, PARTIAL SUCCESS, AND FAILURE**

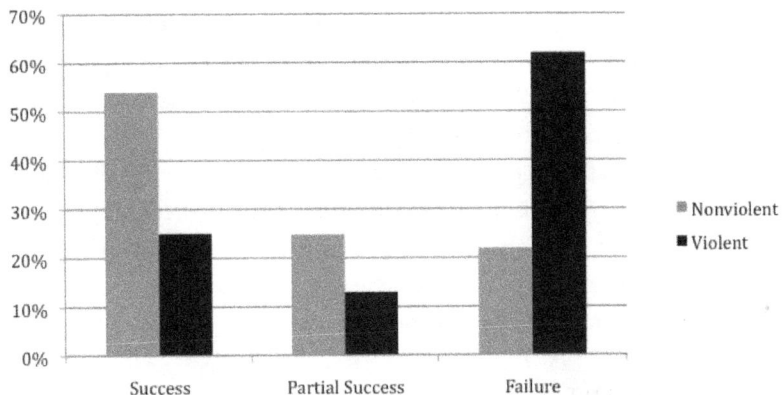

FIGURE 1.5 **SUCCESS RATES BY CAMPAIGN OBJECTIVE**

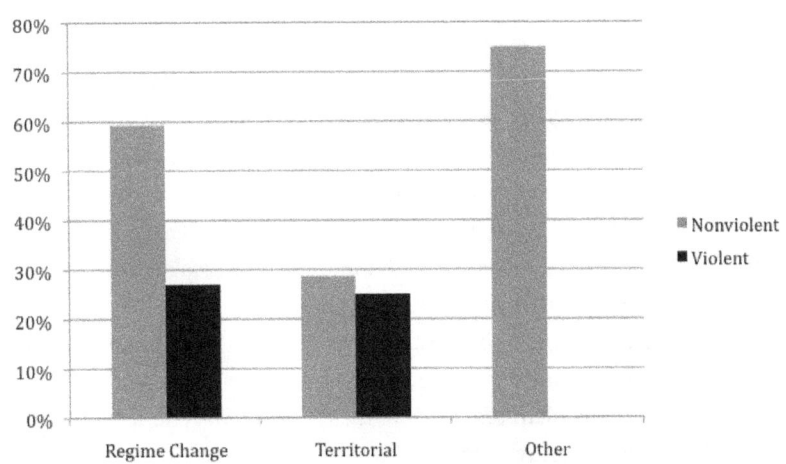

succeed regardless of whether they employ nonviolent or violent tactics. We explore various factors that could influence these results in chapter 3. It is evident, however, that especially among campaigns seeking regime change or liberation from foreign occupation, nonviolent resistance has been strategically superior. The success of these nonviolent campaigns—especially in light of the enduring violent insurgencies occurring in many of the same countries—begs systematic exploration.

This book investigates the reasons why—in spite of conventional wisdom to the contrary—civil resistance campaigns have been so effective compared with their violent counterparts. We also consider the reasons why some nonviolent campaigns have failed to achieve their stated aims, and the reasons why violent insurgencies sometimes succeed.

THE ARGUMENT

Our central contention is that nonviolent campaigns have a participation advantage over violent insurgencies, which is an important factor in determining campaign outcomes. The moral, physical, informational, and commitment barriers to participation are much lower for nonviolent resistance than for violent insurgency. Higher levels of participation contribute to a number of mechanisms necessary for success, including enhanced resilience, higher probabilities of tactical innovation, expanded civic disruption (thereby raising the costs to the regime of maintaining the status quo), and loyalty shifts involving the opponent's erstwhile supporters, including members of the security forces. Mobilization among local supporters is a more reliable source of power than the support of external allies, which many violent campaigns must obtain to compensate for their lack of participants.

Moreover, we find that the transitions that occur in the wake of successful nonviolent resistance movements create much more durable and internally peaceful democracies than transitions provoked by violent insurgencies. On the whole, nonviolent resistance campaigns are more effective in getting results and, once they have succeeded, more likely to establish democratic regimes with a lower probability of a relapse into civil war.

Nestling our argument between literatures on asymmetrical warfare, contentious politics, and strategic nonviolent action, we explain the relative effectiveness of nonviolent resistance in the following way: nonviolent campaigns facilitate the active participation of many more people than violent campaigns, thereby broadening the base of resistance and raising the costs to opponents of maintaining the status quo. The mass civilian participation in a nonviolent campaign is more likely to backfire in the face of repression, encourage loyalty shifts among regime supporters, and provide resistance leaders with a more diverse menu of tactical and strategic choices. To regime elites, those engaged in civil resistance are more likely to appear as credible negotiating partners than are violent insurgents, thereby increasing the chance of winning concessions.

However, we also know that resistance campaigns are not guaranteed to succeed simply because they are nonviolent. One in four nonviolent campaigns since 1900 was a total failure. In short, we argue that nonviolent campaigns fail to achieve their objectives when they are unable to overcome the challenge of participation, when they fail to recruit a robust, diverse, and broad-based membership that can erode the power base of the adversary and maintain resilience in the face of repression.

Moreover, more than one in four violent campaigns has succeeded. We briefly investigate the question of why violent campaigns sometimes succeed. Whereas the success of nonviolent campaigns tends to rely more heavily on local factors, violent insurgencies tend to succeed when they achieve external support or when they feature a central characteristic of successful nonviolent campaigns, which is mass popular support. The presence of an external sponsor combined with a weak or predatory regime adversary may enhance the credibility of violent insurgencies, which may threaten the opponent regime. The credibility gained through external support may also increase the appeal to potential recruits, thereby allowing insurgencies to mobilize more participants against the opponent. International support is, however, a double-edged sword. Foreign-state sponsors can be fickle and unreliable allies, and state sponsorship can produce a lack of discipline among insurgents and exacerbate free rider problems (Bob 2005; Byman 2005).

THE EVIDENCE

We bring to bear several different types of evidence to support our argument, including statistical evidence from the NAVCO data set and qualitative evidence from four case studies: Iran, the Palestinian Territories, Burma, and the Philippines.

It is appropriate here to briefly define the terms to which we will consistently refer in this book. First, we should distinguish violent and nonviolent tactics. As noted earlier, there are some difficulties with labeling one campaign as violent and another as nonviolent. In many cases, both nonviolent and violent campaigns exist simultaneously among competing groups. Often those who employ violence in mass movements are members of fringe groups who are acting independently, or in defiance of, the central leadership; or they are agents provocateurs used by the adversary to provoke the unarmed resistance to adopt violence (Zunes 1994). Alternatively, often some groups use both nonviolent and violent methods of resistance over the course of their existence, as with the ANC in South Africa. Characterizing a campaign as violent or nonviolent simplifies a complex constellation of resistance methods.

It is nevertheless possible to characterize a campaign as principally nonviolent based on the primacy of nonviolent resistance methods and the nature of the participation in that form of resistance. Sharp defines nonviolent resistance as "a technique of socio-political action for applying power in a conflict without the use of violence" (1999, 567). The term *resistance* implies that the campaigns of interest are noninstitutional and generally confrontational in nature. In other words, these groups are using tactics that are outside the conventional political process (voting, interest-group organizing, or lobbying). Although institutional methods of political action often accompany nonviolent struggles, writes sociologist Kurt Schock, nonviolent action occurs outside the bounds of institutional political channels (2003, 705).[8]

Our study focuses instead on a type of political activity that deliberately or necessarily circumvents normal political channels and employs noninstitutional (and often illegal) forms of action against an opponent. Civil resistance employs social, psychological, economic, and political methods, including boycotts (social, economic, and political), strikes, protests, sit-ins, stay-aways, and other acts of civil disobedience and noncooperation to mobilize publics to oppose or support different policies, to delegitimize adversaries, and to remove or restrict adversaries' sources of power (Sharp 1973).[9] Nonviolent resistance consists of acts of omission, acts of commission, and a combination of both (Sharp 2005).[10]

We characterize violent resistance as a form of political contention and a method of exerting power that, like nonviolent resistance, operates outside normal political channels. While conventional militaries use violence to advance political goals, in this book we are concerned with the use of unconventional violent strategies used by nonstate actors.[11] These strategies are exhibited in three main categories of unconventional warfare: revolutions, plots (or coups d'état), and insurgencies, which differ according to the level of premeditated planning, protractedness, and means of overthrowing the existing order.[12] The weapons system available to an armed insurgent is very different from that of its nonviolent analogue. Violent tactics include bombings, shootings, kidnappings, physical sabotage such as the destruction of infrastructure, and other types of physical harm of people and property. However, the cases we examine do not include military coups, since we are primarily interested in substate actors that are not part of the state. Both violent and nonviolent campaigns seek to take power by force, though the method of applying force differs across the different resistance types.

The list of nonviolent campaigns was initially gathered from an extensive review of the literature on nonviolent conflict and social movements. Then these data were corroborated with multiple sources, including encyclopedias, case studies, and a comprehensive bibliography on nonviolent civil resistance by April Carter, Howard Clark, and Michael Randle (2006). Finally, we consulted with experts in the field, who suggested any remaining conflicts of note. The resulting list includes major campaigns that are primarily or entirely nonviolent. Campaigns where a significant amount of violence occurred are not considered nonviolent.

Violent campaign data are derived primarily from Kristian Gleditsch's (2004) updates to the Correlates of War (COW) database on intrastate wars, Jason Lyall and Isaiah Wilson's (2009) database of insurgencies, and Kalev Sepp's (2005) list of major counterinsurgency operations. The COW data set requires all combatant groups to be armed and to have sustained a thousand battle deaths during the course of the conflict, suggesting that the conflict is necessarily violent.

This study makes a further qualification. Nonviolent and violent campaigns are used to promote a number of different policy objectives, ranging from increasing personal liberties to obtaining greater rights or privileges for an ethnic group to demanding national independence. However, this project is concerned primarily with three specific, intense, and extreme forms of resistance: antiregime, antioccupation, and secession campaigns. These campaign types are chosen for several reasons. First, they provide a hard case for civil resistance. Antiregime, antioccupation, and self-determination campaigns are typically associated in the literature with violence, whereas civil rights and other strictly human rights movements are more commonly associated with nonviolent methods. However, in this study we argue that nonviolent resistance can be used to achieve political objectives most commonly identified with violent insurgencies.

Success and failure are also complex outcomes, about which much has been written (Baldwin 2000). For our study, to be considered a "success" a campaign had to meet two conditions: the full achievement of its stated goals (regime change, antioccupation, or secession) within a year of the peak of activities and a discernible effect on the outcome, such that the outcome was a direct result of the campaign's activities (Pape 1997).[13] The second qualification is important because in some cases the desired outcome occurred mainly because of other conditions. The Greek resistance against the Nazi occupation, for example, is not coded as a full success even though the Nazis ultimately withdrew from Greece. Although effective in many respects, the Greek resistance alone cannot be credited with the ultimate outcome of the end of Nazi influence over Greece since the Nazi withdrawal was the result of the Allied victory rather than solely Greek resistance.

The term *campaign* is also somewhat contentious as a unit of analysis. Following Ackerman and Kruegler (1994, 10–11), we define a campaign as a series of observable, continual tactics in pursuit of a political objective. A campaign can last anywhere from days to years. Campaigns have discernible leadership and often have names, distinguishing them from random riots or spontaneous mass acts.[14] Usually campaigns have distinguishable beginning and end points, as well as discernible events throughout the campaign. In the case of resistance campaigns, beginning and end points are difficult to determine, as are the events throughout the campaign. In some cases, information on such events is readily available (e.g., Northern Ireland from 1969 to 1999); however, in most cases, it is not. Therefore, our characterization of the beginning and end dates of campaigns is based on consensus data and multiple sources.[15]

Some readers may be tempted to dismiss our findings as the results of selection effects, arguing that the nonviolent campaigns that appear in our inventory are biased toward success, since it is the large, often mature campaigns that are most commonly reported. Other would-be nonviolent campaigns that are crushed in their infancy (and therefore fail) are not included in this study. This is a potential concern that is difficult to avoid.

We adopted a threefold data-collection strategy to address this concern. First, our selection of campaigns and their beginning and end dates is based on consensus data produced by multiple sources. Second, we have established rigorous standards of inclusion for each campaign. The nonviolent campaigns were initially gathered from an extensive review of the literature on nonviolent conflict and social movements. Then these data were corroborated with multiple sources, including encyclopedias, case studies, and the bibliography by Carter, Clark, and Randle (2006).

Finally, we circulated the data set among experts in nonviolent conflict. These experts were asked to assess whether the cases were appropriately characterized as major nonviolent conflicts, whether any notable conflicts had been omitted, and whether we had properly accounted for failed movements. Where the experts suggested additional cases, the same corroboration method was used. Our confidence in the data set that emerged was reinforced by numerous discussions among scholars of both nonviolent and violent conflicts.

Nonetheless, what remains absent from the data set is a way to measure the nonstarters, the nonviolent or violent campaigns that never emerged because of any number of reasons. Despite this concern, we feel confident proceeding with our inquiry for two main reasons. First, this bias applies as much to violent campaigns as to nonviolent ones—many violent campaigns that were defeated early on are also unreported in the data. Second, this study is not concerned primarily with *why* these campaigns emerge but with *how well* they perform relative to their competitors that use different methods of resistance. We focus on the efficacy of campaigns as opposed to their origins, and we argue that we can say something about the effectiveness of nonviolent campaigns *relative to* violent campaigns. We do concede, however, that improved data collection and analysis and finding ways to overcome the selection bias inherent in much scholarship on conflict are vital next steps for the field.

WHY COMPARE NONVIOLENT AND VIOLENT RESISTANCE CAMPAIGNS?

Generally, scholars have eschewed the systematic comparison of the outcomes of violent and nonviolent movements. One notable exception is William Gamson, whose seminal work (1990) on American challenge groups discovered that groups employing force and violence were more successful than groups refraining from violent tactics (McAdam, McCarthy, and Zald 1996, 14). Not only does he seem to conflate force with violence, but also his conclusions, while perhaps pertinent to certain types of groups within the American political system, do not necessarily apply to all countries during all times.[16]

Hence scholarship on this question rightly investigates whether such generalizations are applicable to other places and periods. In attempting to understand the relationship between nonviolent and violent tactics and the outcomes of resistance campaigns, however, scholars have tended to focus on single case studies or small-n comparisons in what has become a rich accumulation of research and knowledge on the subject (Ackerman and DuVall 2000; Ackerman and Kruegler 1994; Boudreau 2004; Schock 2005; Sharp 1973, 2005; Wehr, Burgess, and Burgess 1994; Zunes 1994; Zunes, Kurtz, and Asher 1999). What has been missing, though, are catalogs of known campaigns and systematic comparisons of the outcomes of both nonviolent and violent resistance campaigns, although this trend has begun to shift (Shaykhutdinov 2010; Stephan and Chenoweth 2008).

As one might expect, there are several good reasons why social scientists have avoided comparing the dynamics and outcomes of nonviolent and violent campaigns, including their relative effectiveness. First, the separation of campaigns into violent and nonviolent for analytical purposes is problematic. Few campaigns, historically, have been purely violent or nonviolent, and many resistance movements, particularly protracted ones, have had violent and nonviolent periods. Armed and unarmed elements often operate simultaneously in the same struggle. Still, it is possible to distinguish between different resistance types based on the actors involved (civilians or armed militants) and the methods used (nonviolent or violent).[17] Scholars have identified the unique characteristics of these different forms of struggle, and we feel comfortable characterizing some resistance campaigns as primarily violent and others as primarily nonviolent. We are furthermore careful to avoid characterizing a campaign as violent merely because the regime uses violence in an attempt to suppress the protest activity.

Second, security studies scholars seem to have eschewed the study of nonviolent action because nonviolent action is not typically viewed as a form of insurgency or asymmetrical warfare (Schock 2003). Groups deliberately adopting nonviolent tactics are commonly understood as doing so for moral or principled reasons (Howes 2009). Since some key authors promoting strategic nonviolent action have also been pacifists, this characterization has not been wholly unfounded. Nonetheless, among some security studies scholars, the idea that resistance leaders might choose nonviolent tactics as a strategic choice may be considered naive or implausible. Although the topic of civilian-based defense, a type of unconventional defense involving civilian populations defending their nations from military invasions and occupations using organized noncooperation and civil disobedience, received the attention of security and strategic studies (including the RAND Corporation) during the Cold War, interest in the subject from the security studies community has waned since the fall of the iron curtain (Sharp 1990).[18] Hence the serious study of strategic nonviolent action has remained something of a pariah within security studies despite decades of scholarship on the subject.

Finally, the questions of interest in this book—whether nonviolent resistance methods are more effective than violent resistance methods and under which conditions civil resistance succeeds or fails—are by nature extremely difficult to study. It is not by accident that few authors have been able to compile large-n data sets on the subject despite important efforts to do so.[19] The measurement of effectiveness itself is difficult to gather and defend, and the independent effects of resistance methods on the outcomes are not always easy to discern given the complexity of these contentious episodes.

Despite the challenges associated with studying this subject, we argue that the theoretical and policy implications of the research questions at hand are too important to avoid. Sidney Tarrow has argued that investigating the reasons why movements succeed and fail is one of the main foci of the entire contentious politics research program (1998). Our book demonstrates that scholars can take a reasoned look at the relative effectiveness of nonviolent and violent resistance, even if the measures of such terms are imperfect. We undertake such an exploration by examining 323 cases from 1900 to 2006 of major nonviolent and violent campaigns seeking regime change, the expulsion of foreign occupiers, or secession. This research is the first to catalog, compare, and analyze all known cases of major armed and unarmed insurrections during this period. From this data, we find support for the perspective that nonviolent resistance has been strategically superior to violent resistance during the twentieth and twenty-first centuries. Because the data are highly aggregated, we provide only a first look at these trends. But our findings point to a powerful relationship that scholars and policy makers should take seriously.

SCHOLARLY IMPLICATIONS

This research is situated among several distinct albeit related subfields of political science and sociology. We are explicit in conceptualizing civil resistance as a form of unconventional warfare, albeit one that employs different weapons and applies force differently. The literature on contentious politics has long explored the relationship between methods and outcomes. Recent scholarship in security studies has explored similar questions.[20] Others in the discipline deal with the concept of strategic effectiveness in an indirect, if somewhat peripheral, way. For instance, in his seminal work on the political economy of rebellion, Jeremy Weinstein (2007) argues that activist rebellions are more likely than opportunistic rebellions to achieve their strategic objectives. Activist rebellions, which are dependent on social support, are more likely to target opponents selectively. Opportunistic rebellions target indiscriminately, thereby undermining their public support.

Wood (2000, 2003) argues that transitions to democracy are likely when insurgents are able to successfully raise the costs to economic elites of maintaining the status quo, a process that emerges when labor unions and worker parties strike over an extended period. DeNardo's work (1985) on mass movements also demonstrates that methods and outcomes of revolutions are related, with disruption and mass mobilization being key determinants of revolutionary success. However, Weinstein (2007), Wood (2000, 2003), and DeNardo (1985) all remain agnostic as to how the methods of resistance—nonviolent or violent—could affect the outcomes of resistance campaigns.

Following those who have analyzed nonviolent campaigns through the lens of strategic theory, we are similarly interested in the relationship between strategy and outcome (Ackerman and Kruegler 1994; Ganz 2010; Helvey 2004; Popovic et al. 2007; Sharp 1973). Our perspective does not assume that nonviolent resistance methods can melt the hearts of repressive regimes or dictators. Instead, we argue that as with some successful violent movements, nonviolent campaigns can impose costly sanctions on their opponents, resulting in strategic gains. We join a long line of scholars concerned with the strategic effectiveness of different tactical and operational choices (Ackerman and Kruegler 1994; Sharp 1973; Zunes 1994).

What is perhaps obvious is our voluntaristic approach to the study of resistance. In this book, we make the case that voluntaristic features of campaigns, notably those related to the skills of the resistors, are often better predictors of success than structural determinants. On the surface, this argument immediately puts us at odds with structural explanations of outcomes such as political opportunity approaches. Such approaches argue that movements will succeed and fail based on the opening and closing of opportunities created by the structure of the political order. As Tarrow has argued, "political opportunity structures are 'consistent dimensions of the political environment which either encourage or discourage people from using collective action'" (Tarrow 1998, 18). Let us briefly discuss how our perspective differs from this approach.

In our study, a political opportunity approach might suggest that nonviolent campaigns succeed so often because the regime is undergoing a transition, signaling to the opposition that the time is right to go on the offensive. McAdam argues that "most contemporary theories of revolution start from much the same premise, arguing that revolutions owe less to the efforts of insurgents than to the work of systemic crises which render the existing regime weak and vulnerable to challenge from virtually any quarter" (1996a, 24).[21]

What we have found, however, is that the political opportunity approach fails to explain why some movements succeed in the direst of political circumstances where chances of success seem grim, whereas other campaigns fail in political circumstances that might seem more favorable. Such explanatory deficiencies leave us wondering how the actions of the groups themselves shape the outcomes of their campaigns.

For instance, a common misperception about nonviolent resistance is that it can succeed only against liberal, democratic regimes espousing universalistic values like respect for human rights. Besides the implicit and false assumption that democracies do not commit mass human rights abuses, the empirical record does not support this argument. As Kurt Schock writes, the historical record actually points to the opposite conclusion:

> In fact, nonviolent action has been effective in brutally repressive contexts, and it has been ineffective in open democratic polities. Repression, of course, constrains the ability of challengers to organize, communicate, mobilize, and engage in collective action, and magnifies the risk of participation in collective action. Nevertheless, repression is only one of many factors that influence the trajectories of campaigns of nonviolent action, not the sole determinant of their trajectories. (Schock 2003, 706)

The claim that nonviolent resistance could never work against genocidal foes like Adolph Hitler and Joseph Stalin is the classic straw man put forward to demonstrate the inherent limitations of this form of struggle. While it is possible that nonviolent resistance could not be used effectively once genocide has broken out in full force (or that it is inherently inferior to armed struggle in such circumstances), this claim is not backed by any strong empirical evidence (Summy 1994). Collective nonviolent struggle was not used with any strategic forethought during World War II, nor was it ever contemplated as an overall strategy for resisting the Nazis. Violent resistance, which some groups attempted for ending Nazi occupation, was also an abject failure.

However, scholars have found that certain forms of collective nonviolent resistance were, in fact, occasionally successful in resisting Hitler's occupation policies. The case of the Danish population's resistance to German occupation is an example of partially effective civil resistance in an extremely difficult environment (Ackerman and DuVall 2000).[22] The famous case of the Rosenstraße protests, when German women of Aryan descent stood for a week outside a detention center on the Rosenstraße in Berlin demanding the release of their Jewish husbands, who were on the verge of being deported to concentration camps, is a further example of limited gains against a genocidal regime brought about by civil resistance. The German women, whose numbers increased as the protests continued and they attracted more attention, were sufficiently disruptive with their sustained nonviolent protests that the Nazi officials eventually released their Jewish husbands (Mazower 2008; Semelin 1993; Stoltzfus 1996). Of course, the civil resistance to Nazi occupation occurred in the context of an Allied military campaign against the Axis powers, which was ultimately decisive in defeating Hitler.

Regardless, the notion that nonviolent action can be successful only if the adversary does not use violent repression is neither theoretically nor historically substantiated. In fact, we show how, under certain circumstances, regime violence can backfire and lead to the strengthening of the nonviolent challenge group.

A competing approach, resource mobilization theory, suggests that campaigns succeed when resources converge around given preferences, allowing for mobilization to occur regardless of political opportunities. A resource mobilization approach would suggest that "the dynamics of a movement depend in important ways on its resources and organization," with a focus on entrepreneurs "whose success is determined by the availability of resources"

(Weinstein 2007, 47). However, this perspective does not account for the ways in which the actions of the opponent may account for the success or failure of campaigns when they deploy their own resources to either counter or outmaneuver the challenge group.

Instead of attempting to fit our explanation within one of the two prevailing approaches, we instead view our approach as an interactive one that draws on a contentious politics approach. Such a perspective can be justified by the fact that the structure of the political environment will necessarily shape and constrain the perceptions of resistance leaders, whereas the actions of resistance movements will often have distinguishable and independent effects on the structure of the system. This approach follows from a number of recent works in social movement studies and security studies (Arreguín-Toft 2005; Schock 2005; Weinstein 2007; Wood 2000, 2003).

Civil Resistance Research in Context

Readers familiar with the literature on civil resistance may wonder how our work differs from the canonical literature in this field. The seminal works on nonviolent resistance by Gene Sharp, Robert Helvey, Peter Ackerman and Christopher Kruegler, Ackerman and Jack DuVall, Stephen Zunes, Adam Roberts and Timothy Garton Ash, Kurt Schock, Mary E. King, and others have all advanced our understanding of strategic nonviolent action in important ways.

Sharp's three-volume opus, *The Politics of Nonviolent Action*, established the theoretical foundation for nonviolent action. It reads as a handbook of nonviolent resistance, explaining the theory of power and the different methods of nonviolent action and the ways that nonviolent action can affect the adversary (conversion, persuasion, accommodation, and coercion). Sharp's work is seminal; it provides a unified theory on the strategic mechanisms through which civil resistance can work.

Robert Helvey builds on much of Sharp's original foundation in his work on how to act strategically during the prosecution of a nonviolent conflict (2004). He identifies similarities between civil resistance and military strategy, providing a handbook of sorts for how to identify campaign goals, develop strategic plans, and operational problems movements face during a campaign.

Our book is distinct in several ways. First, although Sharp's and Helvey's volumes provide a theoretical gold mine, they do not attempt to test their assertions empirically. Our book is the first attempt to comprehensively test many of the ideas Sharp and Helvey have developed. Second, Sharp's and Helvey's comparisons with violent resistance are implicit; they simply present nonviolent resistance as an effective strategy in asymmetrical conflict. In our study, we explicitly compare nonviolent and violent resistance to test the hypothesis that nonviolent resistance is indeed a more effective strategy.

In Ackerman and Kruegler's *Strategic Nonviolent Conflict*, the authors develop a framework informed by strategic theory for analyzing the outcomes of nonviolent resistance campaigns. The book features multiple case studies of successful and failed nonviolent action, from which the authors generalize twelve principles of successful nonviolent action. Although the book is highly analytical, the case studies are inductive in nature: their purpose is to find patterns about why nonviolent campaigns succeed rather than to test hypotheses.

Ackerman and DuVall's book *A Force More Powerful* has been perhaps the most widely read book on nonviolent action. The book is empirical, featuring descriptive accounts of nonviolent campaigns ranging from Russia to South Africa. One of the most accessible books on nonviolent conflict, it was adapted into an Emmy-nominated documentary series. Recently the authors have sponsored the development of a video game named after the book, the purpose of which is to train scholars and activists in the tactics and strategy of nonviolent resistance. The book is not intended to be an analytical exploration of why nonviolent resistance succeeds compared with violent resistance, nor does it attempt to control for other factors that might predict the success or failure of movements. Our study expands the universe of cases, explicitly compares nonviolent and violent resistance, tests theoretical hypotheses concerning the mechanisms that lead to success, and controls for other factors that might account for different outcomes. We do, however, focus far less on the dynamics of violent unconventional warfare, such as guerrilla warfare and violent insurgency.

Stephen Zunes, Adam Roberts and Timothy Garton Ash, and Kurt Schock have all contributed to the academic understanding of the conditions under which nonviolent resistance succeeds and fails. Their works share a comparative case study approach to explaining individual cases or illuminating patterns in nonviolent resistance activity (Roberts and Garton Ash 2009; Schock 2005; Zunes, Kurtz, and Asher 1999). Much of our argument is compatible with findings in Zunes's various works, although our aim is to explain broad patterns rather than individual cases. Roberts and

Garton Ash similarly attempt to explain the dynamics of nonviolent resistance in a diverse range of cases. Other authors have examined single case studies and associated phenomena in great depth (Bleiker 1993; Clark 2000; Dajani 1994; Eglitis 1993; Huxley 1990; Martin 2007; McCarthy and Sharp 1997; Miniotaite 2002; Parkman 1988, 1990; Roberts and Garton Ash 2009; Sharp 2005; Stephan 2010; Stoltzfus 1996). The goal of these contributors, however, is not always to explain campaign success or failure but rather to explore a number of social movement problems and questions related to their cases. Thus their works demonstrate some important lessons but not necessarily about why and when civil resistance works.

In *Unarmed Insurrections*, sociologist Kurt Schock compares successful and failed nonviolent, prodemocracy campaigns against nondemocratic regimes. This work comes much closer to the analytical purposes of our book. Schock compares six nonviolent campaigns in nondemocracies to identify patterns among the trajectories of these campaigns. He challenges the political opportunity approach, and argues that strategic factors can help explain the outcomes of the campaigns. Most important, Schock's work bridges the structure-agency divide and analyzes the iterative, interactive nature of political opportunities and strategic choice. Specifically, Schock argues that tactical innovation, resilience, and the shifting between methods of concentration and methods of dispersion can help to explain the divergent outcomes of different campaigns.

Vincent Boudreau also analyzes the outcomes of prodemocracy movements in Southeast Asia, using a compelling contentious politics model (2004). However, he does not focus on the relative effectiveness of nonviolent and violent action, instead exploring the interaction between different modes of repression employed by dictators in Burma, the Philippines, and Indonesia and the impact of these forms of repression on the protestors. He is explicitly critical of the possibility of accurately representing these conflicts using quantitative analysis, instead arguing in favor of viewing each conflict as a complex system of its own (2004, 3).

Our findings are highly compatible with Schock's and share much in common with Boudreau's as well, notwithstanding methodological differences. But our argument about the primacy of participation in nonviolent resistance appears unique in this literature. Moreover, as with the Ackerman and Kruegler book, our study expands the universe of cases to include antioccupation and secession campaigns in addition to regime-change campaigns. Our study is not limited to Southeast Asia, nor are our cases restricted to nondemocratic targets. Instead, we attempt to comprehensively examine major nonviolent and violent campaigns all across the globe, against all types of targets, from 1900 to 2006.

Readers familiar with Ivan Arreguín-Toft's argument in *How the Weak Win Wars* may see some similarities to our argument. In his book, Arreguín-Toft argues that weak powers sometimes win wars when they employ indirect strategies against stronger powers. That is, if the stronger power is employing conventional war strategies, a weaker power that uses unconventional or guerrilla war will be likely to succeed. For instance, the British conventional army succumbed to the guerrilla war waged by American colonists during the Revolutionary War (though, as mentioned earlier, the armed insurgency followed years of nonviolent civil resistance). On the other hand, a weaker power that uses conventional strategies against a stronger power relying on conventional strategies will fail. The 1991 Gulf War demonstrates that point: the militarily inferior Iraqi army was unable to successfully take on Coalition forces.

Conversely, if a stronger power employs unconventional strategies against a weaker power's conventional strategies, the weaker power will win. For instance, Hitler's air bombing of British civilian targets did not force the British into compliance. Instead, the attacks emboldened the British against the Germans (Arreguín-Toft 2001, 108). But when a stronger power employs unconventional strategies against a weak power also using unconventional strategies, the stronger power will win. The Russian government has used "barbaric" strategies against Chechen rebels, effectively crushing the Chechen insurgency.

While we do not dispute Arreguín-Toft's findings, we illuminate a new dimension in his typology, which is the use of strategic nonviolent action as an indirect strategy against a militarily superior opponent. When Arreguín-Toft describes indirect strategies for weaker powers, he refers to two types of strategies: direct defense, which he defines as "the use of armed forces to thwart an adversary's attempt to capture or destroy values such as territory, population, and strategic resources," and guerrilla warfare, defined as "the organization of a portion of society for the purpose of imposing costs on an adversary using armed forces trained to avoid direct confrontation" (2001, 103). We argue that unarmed, civil resistance can be even more effective than direct defense or guerrilla warfare, both of which are armed strategies against militarily superior opponents.

Our results are also consistent with Max Abrahms's findings, which suggest that terrorist activities that target civilians are less effective than guerrilla warfare strategies that target policy and military personnel (2006). But our findings extend his thesis further, in that we argue that in most cases all types of violent campaigns are likely to be less effective than well-managed nonviolent campaigns.

What all these works, including ours, have in common is a call for scholars to rethink power and its sources in any given society or polity. Although it is often operationalized as a state's military and economic capacity, our findings demonstrate that power actually depends on the consent of the civilian population, consent that can be withdrawn and reassigned to more legitimate or more compelling parties.

Squaring the Circle: The Effectiveness of Violence?

Some scholars, such as Robert Pape, have developed recently theses on the efficacy of violent conflict. In particular, some argue that terrorism—especially suicide terrorism—is an effective coercive strategy, especially against democracies (2003, 2005). Jason Lyall and Isaiah Wilson have also discovered that violent insurgency is growing in effectiveness—against democracies in particular (2009). Given these authors' findings, there are some surface discrepancies with our findings. We address each of these arguments in turn.

First, Pape argues that suicide terrorism is an effective punishment strategy against democracies (2003, 2005). Suicide bombers convey both capability and resolve to soft targets in democracies, demonstrating to these countries that continued occupation will result in protracted, escalating, indiscriminate war against the country's civilian population. Such acts lead to a decline in morale in the democracy, which ultimately judges that withdrawal from the occupied territory is less costly than the occupation. In his study, five out of the eleven suicide bombing campaigns since 1980 have achieved at least partial success.

Pape's argument and empirics have been widely criticized (see, for instance, Ashworth et al. 2008). Yet if we take his argument at face value, we can offer yet another criticism, which could be applied to almost all scholars whose research tests the efficacy of different violent methods. Such scholars often assume or argue that violence is effective, but compared with what? In particular, Pape makes no attempt to compare the relative efficacy of suicide terrorism against alternative strategies. Even in some of his most prominent cases—Lebanon and the Palestinian Territories—we have seen mass, nonviolent resistance perform effectively where violent insurgencies have failed. In the Lebanese case, the 2005 Cedar Revolution involved more than a million Lebanese demonstrators forcing Syria to withdraw its forces from Lebanese soil. And, as shown in chapter 5, the First Intifada moved the Palestinian self-determination movement further than the Palestine Liberation Organization's violent campaign that preceded it, or the Al-Aqsa Intifada that succeeded it.

In another example, Lyall and Wilson argue that violent insurgencies are becoming more effective against highly mechanized militaries, which prove to be unwieldy in urban settings against well-camouflaged insurgents (2009). They show that since 1975 states have succeeded in crushing insurgencies only 24 percent of the time. In their study, they determine success from the state's perspective, such that complete defeat of the insurgents is considered a success, whereas a draw or a loss to insurgents is considered a failure. When one looks more closely, however, one can see that their primary finding—that violent insurgencies have succeeded in over 75 percent of cases since 1976—is based on data in which nearly 48 percent of the cases were stalemates. Thus only 29.5 percent of their insurgencies since 1976 actually succeeded in defeating their state adversaries, a statistic that is much closer to our own. Lyall and Wilson also exclude ongoing campaigns from their findings, whereas we code such cases as failures through 2006.[23]

The difference in measurement is one way that our findings diverge from Lyall and Wilson's. But perhaps the most important difference is that they do not compare the relative effectiveness of violent insurgency with nonviolent campaigns. If we analyze the success rates of nonviolent campaigns since 1976, we see a much higher rate of nonviolent campaign success (57 percent).

Thus our study represents a departure from techniques used by those arguing that violent insurgency is effective. As Baldwin argues, "Only comparative analysis of the prospective success of alternative instruments provides policy-relevant knowledge" (2000, 176). Our approach involves the relative comparison of nonviolent and violent campaigns, which sheds more light on how unsuccessful violent campaigns really are.[24]

WIDER IMPLICATIONS

Beyond scholarly contributions, this research possesses a number of important implications for public policy. Research regarding the successes and failures of nonviolent campaigns can provide insight into the most effective ways for external actors—governmental and nongovernmental—to aid such movements. From the perspective of an outside state, providing support to nonviolent campaigns can sometimes aid the movements but also introduces a new set of dilemmas, including the free-rider problem and the potential loss of local legitimacy. This study strongly supports the view that sanctions and state support for nonviolent campaigns work best when they are coordinated with the support of local opposition groups; but they are never substitutes.

For instance, although there is no evidence that external actors can successfully initiate or sustain mass nonviolent mobilization, targeted forms of external support have been useful in some cases, like the international boycotts targeting the apartheid regime in South Africa. The existence of organized solidarity groups that maintained steady pressure on governments allied with the target regimes proved to be very helpful, suggesting that "extending the battlefield" is sometimes necessary for opposition groups to enhance their leverage over the target. Lending diplomatic support to human rights activists, independent civil society groups, and democratic opposition leaders while penalizing regimes (or threatening penalties) that target unarmed activists with violent repression may be another way that governments can improve the probability of nonviolent campaign success. Coordinated multinational efforts that used a combination of positive and negative sanctions to isolate egregious rights violators supported successful civil resistance movements in South Africa and Eastern Europe.

PLAN OF THE BOOK

The remainder of the study examines the specific mechanisms by which nonviolent campaigns succeed and fail. It does so by interchanging quantitative and qualitative analyses of nonviolent and violent campaigns in the Middle East (Iran and the Palestinian Territories) and Southeast Asia (the Philippines and Burma). Each of the four cases features periods of both violent and civil resistance against repressive regimes, but with varying degrees of success. This allows us to more closely examine the conditions under which nonviolent and violent campaigns succeed and fail, both within and across the cases.

The book proceeds as follows. First, in chapter 2, we introduce the general argument of the study and explore how this argument converges and diverges with the findings of other scholars. We argue that civil resistance campaigns are more successful than violent campaigns at overcoming barriers to participation, an important prerequisite of success.

In chapter 3, we explore the major alternative arguments—that regime features may independently affect the outcomes of the nonviolent or violent conflicts, or that the origins and outcomes of resistance campaigns are endogenous. First, we test whether opponent regime type (i.e., democracy or nondemocracy), capabilities, or use of violent repression against the challenge group reduces the likelihood of success for nonviolent resistance. We also test the effects of time, region, and campaign goal on the probability of success. We find that even when taking into account structural features, nonviolent resistance is still a more effective strategy than violent resistance.

Chapter 3 also addresses the issue of endogeneity head-on, that is, whether violent campaigns fail because they emerge in conditions in which failure is extremely likely, thus explaining their poor success rates relative to nonviolent campaigns. We find that nonviolent and violent insurgencies are likely to emerge in very similar circumstances, such that their outcomes cannot be explained exclusively on the basis of endogeneity.

In part 2, we compare nonviolent and violent resistance campaigns and their outcomes in Iran, the Palestinian Territories, the Philippines, and Burma. We explain the case selection in detail before the substantive chapters begin. Chapter 4 discusses the Iranian Revolution (1977–1979). In this case, violent campaigns failed to dislodge the Shah, whereas the nonviolent campaign succeeded. Chapter 5 explains why violent Palestinian campaigns orchestrated by an exiled leadership achieved little or no success before the First Intifada (1987–1992), whereas the mass popular uprising that originated inside the occupied territories achieved partial success through some important Israeli concessions.

Chapter 6 deals with the successful case of the People Power movement in the Philippines (1983–1986), which ousted Ferdinand Marcos from power. This mass uprising achieved what the Maoist and Muslim-led insurgencies in that country had been unable to achieve. Chapter 7 identifies a case of failed nonviolent resistance: the Burmese prodemocracy uprising of 1988. Both nonviolent and violent campaigns failed in this case, which provides a useful deviating outcome for comparison.

Part 3 explores the implications of this research across multiple dimensions. First, in chapter 8, we discuss the consequences of violent insurgency, particularly violent insurgent success. Our statistical evidence suggests that countries in which violent insurgencies exist are more likely to backslide into authoritarianism or civil war than countries where nonviolent campaigns exist, which often become more stable, democratic regimes.

Finally, the concluding chapter summarizes the key findings, highlighting how these findings make a contribution to the literature. This chapter also argues for the incorporation of nonviolent conflict into security studies inquiry and suggests ways to improve and expand upon our study. The last section identifies the policy implications derived from this research.

Although not the final word in any sense, we hope that this book challenges the conventional wisdom concerning the effectiveness of nonviolent struggle and encourages scholars and policy makers to take seriously the role that civilians play in actively prosecuting conflict without resorting to violence.

CHAPTER TWO **THE PRIMACY OF PARTICIPATION IN NONVIOLENT RESISTANCE**

What is a rebel? A man who says no.
ALBERT CAMUS

WHAT EXPLAINS THE SUCCESS of nonviolent resistance campaigns relative to violent campaigns? We argue that a critical source of the success of nonviolent resistance is mass participation, which can erode or remove a regime's main sources of power when the participants represent diverse sectors of society. All resistance campaigns—violent and nonviolent—seek to build the personnel bases of their campaigns. Personnel are recruited for their special skills, knowledge, material resources, and their willingness to fight and support the resistance. The quantity and quality of campaign participation is a critical factor in determining the outcome of resistance struggles (DeNardo 1985; Lichbach 1994; Weinstein 2007; Wickham-Crowley 1992).

This chapter has two aims. First, we establish that nonviolent campaigns are more likely to attract higher levels of participation than violent campaigns because the barriers to participation are lower. Second, we argue that high levels of participation in resistance campaigns can activate numerous mechanisms that improve the odds of success. Such mobilization is not always manifested in the form of mass rallies and street demonstrations but rather can manifest in numerous forms of social, political, and economic noncooperation. The tactical and strategic advantages of high levels of diverse participation explain—in large part—the historical success of nonviolent campaigns.

PARTICIPATION DEFINED

We define participation in a resistance campaign as the active and observable engagement of individuals in collective action. As such, when measuring campaign participation, we use estimated counts of observed individuals.[1] Instead of constructing cumulative counts, which would be nearly impossible, we count the maximum number of estimated participants that participated in peak events in the campaign. For example, if a resistance campaign holds mass protests in, say, September with 12,000 people, November with 24,000 people, and December with 20,000 people, we use the November figure for our estimate. That is, we code that particular campaign as having 24,000 participants. We use estimates of armed participants to generate figures about the level of participation in violent insurgencies.[2] Of the 323 resistance campaigns analyzed in this book, we were able to collect reliable membership data for 259 campaigns—80 nonviolent and 179 violent—by referencing multiple sources that estimated the maximum number of participants in each campaign.[3]

This is a rather strict conceptualization of participation, and we recognize that many forms of participation are impossible to observe, such as providing sanctuary, food, and supplies to guerrillas, raising funds, communicating messages, acting as informants, or refusing to cooperate with government attempts to apprehend insurgents. For instance, for some individuals, simply refusing to report the presence of guerrillas in one's village to state police may be a form of participation in a resistance campaign, albeit one that is more passive and impossible for us to quantify. Recent studies have identified multiple and complex levels of such participation. As Roger Peterson writes, "there are collaborators, neutrals, locally based rebels, mobile fighters, and gradations in between" (2001, 8).

We do not dispute that our definition likely misses many unobserved participants, but we find the definition both necessary and justified for two reasons. First, in our definition of nonviolent resistance participation, civilians are the active and primary prosecutors of the conflict, executing nonviolent methods against the adversary with varying degrees of risk. This is quite different from the typical conception of civilians as serving a supportive role to combatants.

Second, we assume that some types of unobservable participation occur in approximately equal measure in both nonviolent and violent resistance campaigns. Out of necessity, we focus exclusively on the participants that make themselves visible to observers and opponents as a rough measure of campaign mobilization. The risks of visibility should be similar for both nonviolent and violent resistance campaigns, which in our study often involve illegal and at times high-risk actions against powerful and repressive adversaries.

We do wish to avoid the misconception, however, that civil resistance always assumes the form of mass protests in the streets. Nonviolent resistance is just as likely to take the form of stay-aways, sit-ins, occupations, economic boycotts, and so forth, in which the numbers of participants are extremely difficult to estimate. When such estimations are possible because of reliable recording of such events, we include them in our figures.

HOW TO MOBILIZE?

Mass mobilization occurs for many different reasons, which multiple scholars have analyzed in great depth (see, for instance, Kalyvas 2006; Peterson 2001). In this chapter, we do not seek to explain why mobilization occurs. Rather, we argue that once mobilization begins, a nonviolent resistance campaign has wider appeal than a violent one, thereby enlarging the personnel base of the former and bringing more assets and resources to the fight against a state opponent.

Skeptics may disagree. It is often argued, for instance, that violent insurgencies provide immediate results—such as loot, prestige, score settling, or territorial gains—that give them more appeal than nonviolent resistance. Beyond the prospect of achieving political objectives, the potential to obtain material payoffs from resistance leaders, to seize territory and weapons, to gain control over lucrative extractive industries, trade, and trafficking routes, to inflict casualties, or to exact revenge are factors that may attract some recruits to violent resistance.

The psychosocial dimensions of participation in armed conflict have similarly attracted a great deal of attention. Frantz Fanon famously advocated armed resistance on the grounds that it bestows feelings of communal solidarity through actively fighting against injustice while being willing to die for a cause greater than self (Boserup and Mack 1974; Fanon 1961).[4] Violence may have its own attraction, especially for young people, for whom the allure may be further perpetuated by cultural references and religious defenses of martyrdom (Breckenridge 1998).[5]

Despite its supposed appeal, however, the resort to violence is rare at both individual and group levels and therefore may not have the allure that some theorists ascribe to it (Collins 2008, 20). On the whole, physical, informational, commitment, and moral considerations tend to give nonviolent campaigns an advantage when it comes to mobilizing participants, which reinforces the strategic benefits to participation.

We have found strong evidence suggesting that nonviolent campaigns have been, on average, more likely to have a larger number of participants than violent campaigns. The average nonviolent campaign has over 200,000

TABLE 2.1 TWENTY-FIVE LARGEST RESISTANCE CAMPAIGNS, 1900–2006

PEAK MEMBERSHIP	YEARS	LOCATION	TARGET	TYPE	OUTCOME
4,500,000	1937-45	CHINA	JAPANESE OCCUPATION	VIOLENT	FAILURE
2,000,000	1978-9	IRAN	PAHLAVI REGIME	NONVIOLENT	SUCCESS
2,000,000	1983-6	PHILIPPINES	MARCOS REGIME	NONVIOLENT	SUCCESS
1,000,000	1988	BURMA	MILITARY JUNTA	NONVIOLENT	FAILURE
1,000,000	2006	MEXICO	CALDERON REGIME	NONVIOLENT	FAILURE
1000000	2005	LEBANON	SYRIAN INFLUENCE	NONVIOLENT	SUCCESS
1000000	1993-9	NIGERIA	MILITARY REGIME	NONVIOLENT	SUCCESS
1000000	1989	CHINA	COMMUNIST REGIME	NONVIOLENT	FAILURE
1000000	1984-5	BRAZIL	MILITARY RULE	NONVIOLENT	SUCCESS
1000000	1967-8	CHINA	ANTI-MAOISTS	NONVIOLENT	SUCCESS
1000000	1922-49	CHINA	NATIONALIST REGIME	VIOLENT	SUCCESS
700000	1990-1	RUSSIA	ANTI-COMMUNIST	NONVIOLENT	SUCCESS
700000	1983-9	CHILE	PINOCHET REGIME	NONVIOLENT	SUCCESS
550000	1956-7	CHINA	COMMUNIST REGIME	NONVIOLENT	FAILURE
500000	2002-3	MADAGASCAR	RADSIRAKA REGIME	NONVIOLENT	SUCCESS
500000	1989	UKRAINE	KUCHMA REGIME	NONVIOLENT	SUCCESS
500000	2001	PHILIPPINES	ESTRADA REGIME	NONVIOLENT	SUCCESS
500000	1989	CZECHOSLOVAKIA	COMMUNIST REGIME	NONVIOLENT	SUCCESS
500000	1963	GREECE	KARAMANLIS REGIME	NONVIOLENT	SUCCESS
400000	1991-3	MADAGASCAR	RADSIRAKA REGIME	NONVIOLENT	SUCCESS
400000	1953	EAST GERMANY	COMMUNIST REGIME	NONVIOLENT	FAILURE
400000	1941-45	SOVIET UNION	NAZI OCCUPATION	VIOLENT	FAILURE
340000	1958-75	VIETNAM	U.S. OCCUPATION	VIOLENT	SUCCESS
300000	1990-5	NIGERIA	NIGERIAN REGIME	NONVIOLENT	FAILURE
300000	1944	POLAND	NAZI OCCUPATION	VIOLENT	FAILURE

members—about 150,000 more active participants than the average violent campaign. A look at the twenty-five largest campaigns yields several immediate impressions. First, twenty of the largest campaigns have been nonviolent, whereas five have been violent. Second, of the nonviolent campaigns, fourteen have been outright successes (70 percent), whereas among the five violent campaigns, only two have been successful (40 percent). In other words, among these massive campaigns, nonviolent campaigns have been much more likely to succeed than violent campaigns.[6]

The Iranian Revolution of 1977–1979 is illustrative. Although violent insurgencies such as those of the fedayeen and mujahideen had resisted the Shah since the 1960s, they were able to attract only several thousand followers. Pahlavi's regime crushed the armed groups before they produced meaningful change in the regime. The nonviolent revolution that emerged between 1977 and 1978, however, attracted several million participants and included nationwide protests and boycotts involving all sectors of society that paralyzed the economy and eroded the Shah's most important pillars of support.

These trends are further borne out in the data set. Nonviolent campaigns are persistently associated with higher levels of membership, even when controlling for the population size of the entire country. Consider table 2.2, which shows the effects of a nonviolent resistance type on the number of participants, controlling for population size.[7] Thus nonviolent resistance campaigns have been associated with higher levels of participation. In this section, we argue that the physical, informational, and moral barriers to participation are lower in nonviolent campaigns than in violent campaigns.

Physical Barriers

Active participation in a resistance campaign requires variable levels of physical ability. The physical risks and costs of participation in a violent resistance campaign may be prohibitively high for many potential members.

TABLE 2.2 **THE EFFECT OF NONVIOLENT RESISTANCE ON NUMBER OF PARTICIPANTS**

	NUMBER OF PARTICIPANTS, LOGGED
RESISTANCE IS PRIMARILY NONVIOLENT	2.26*** (.29)
POPULATION, LOGGED	.23* (.13)
CONSTANT	6.70*** (1.17)
N	163
PROB > F	.0000
R²	.3543

SIGNIFICANCE LEVELS: *** $p < .01$, ** $p < .05$, * $p < .1$; ORDINARY-LEAST-SQUARES REGRESSION WITH ROBUST STANDARD ERRORS CLUSTERED AROUND TARGET COUNTRY.

Actively joining a violent campaign may require physical skills such as agility and endurance, willingness to train, ability to handle and use weapons, and often isolation from society at large. While certain of these qualities, including endurance, willingness to sacrifice, and training are also applicable to participation in nonviolent resistance, the typical guerrilla regimen may appeal only to a small portion of any given population.

Physical barriers to participation may be lower for nonviolent resistance since the menu of tactics and activities available to nonviolent activists is broad and includes a wide spectrum, ranging from high-risk confrontational tactics to low-risk discreet tactics.[8] Generally, participation in labor strikes, consumer boycotts, lockdowns, and sit-ins does not require strength, agility, or youth. Participation in a nonviolent campaign is open to female and elderly populations, whereas participation in a violent resistance campaign is often, though not always, physically prohibitive. Although female operatives—such as female suicide bombers and guerrillas—have sometimes been active in violent campaigns in Sri Lanka, Iraq, Pakistan, Palestine, El Salvador, and East Timor, they are nevertheless exceptions in most cases.

Informational Difficulties

Scholars have found that individuals are more likely to engage in protest activity when they expect large numbers of people to participate (Goldstone 1994; Granovetter 1978; Kuran 1989; Kurzman 1996, 2004; Lichbach 1994; Marwell and Oliver 1993; Oberschall 1994; Olson 1965; Rasler 1996; Schelling 1978; Tullock 1971). To successfully recruit members, campaigns must publicize their activities to demonstrate their goals, abilities, and existing numbers to potential recruits. Because of the high risks associated with violent activity, however, movement activists may be limited in how much information they can provide. They may need to remain underground, thereby exacerbating informational problems. Although violent acts, including assassinations, ambushes, bombings, and kidnappings, are public and often attract significant media attention providing signals of the campaign's abilities, the majority of the campaign's operational realities—including information about the numbers of active members—often remain unseen and unknown.[9] The absence of visible signs of opposition strength is, therefore, problematic from the perspective of recruitment. Thus violent resistance may be at a disadvantage in this regard, since the actual number of activists may not be explicit. The counterargument, of course, is that dramatic acts of violence achieve a bigger bang for the buck. Whereas nonviolent organization requires communication and coordination involving larger numbers of people, a single suicide bomber can wreak great damage while attracting significant media attention at relatively little cost. Violent campaigns often rely on propaganda materials that try to exaggerate their size and strength to attract recruits. In the propaganda realm, violent campaigns may have a tactical advantage over many nonviolent campaigns.

On the other hand, nonviolent, public tactics have important demonstration effects, which help address the informational problem. Nonviolent campaigns sometimes include clandestine activities (e.g., the use of samizdat underground publications during the Polish Solidarity struggle, or the actual planning of nonviolent campaigns by the leadership), particularly during the early stages when the resistance is most vulnerable to regime repression and decapitation. Typically, however, nonviolent campaigns rely less on underground activities than do armed struggles.[10] When communities observe open, mass support and collective acts of defiance, their perceptions of risk may decline, reducing constraints on participation. This contention is supported by critical-mass theories of collective action, which contend that protestors base their perceptions of protest opportunities on existing patterns of opposition activity (Kurzman 1996, 154). Courage breeds courage, particularly when those engaged in protest activities are ordinary people who would be conformist, law-abiding citizens under typical circumstances. Media coverage amplifies the demonstration effects of their acts of defiance.

Another factor that enhances participation in nonviolent campaigns is the festival-like atmosphere that often accompanies nonviolent rallies and demonstrations—as exemplified by the recent nonviolent campaigns in Serbia, Ukraine, Lebanon, and Egypt—where concerts, singing, and street theater attracted large numbers of people (particularly young people) interested in having fun while fighting for a political cause. Humor and satire, which have featured prominently in nonviolent campaigns (less so in armed campaigns), have helped break down barriers of fear and promote solidarity among victims of state-sponsored oppression (Kishtainy 2010).

Moral Barriers

Moral barriers may constrain potential recruits to resistance campaigns, but such constraints may inhibit participation in nonviolent resistance far less than participation in violent activities. Although an individual's decision to resist the status quo may follow a certain amount of moral introspection, taking up weapons and killing adds a new moral dimension. Unwillingness to commit violent acts or to support armed groups necessarily disqualifies segments of the population that sympathize with the resistance but are reluctant to translate that sympathy into violence.[11] For violent resistance campaigns, the leadership may need to rely on the proportion of the population that is willing to use violence against the adversary and its supporters, while settling for sympathy and passive support from the rest of the population.

Nonviolent resistance campaigns, however, can potentially mobilize the entire aggrieved population without the need to face moral barriers. Although the moral quandaries associated with nonviolent resistance might involve putting at risk one's freedom, family well-being, life and livelihood, joining such a campaign "requires less soul-searching than joining a violent one. Violent methods raise troublesome questions about whether the ends justify the means, and generally force the people who use them to take substantial risks" (DeNardo 1985, 58).

Commitment Problems

Beyond physical, informational, and moral barriers, nonviolent resistance campaigns may offer an opportunity to participate to people with varying levels of commitment and risk tolerance. Campaigns that rely primarily on violent resistance must depend on participants who have high levels of both commitment and risk tolerance for four principal reasons.

First, the new recruit to a violent campaign may require more training than a recruit to a nonviolent campaign, creating a lag between volunteering and participation. This lag—and the strenuous requirements for participation in a violent campaign—may reduce the number of people who join a violent campaign on a whim.[12]

Second, violent campaigns typically enforce higher levels of commitment at the outset. Screening potential participants is much more intense in violent movements. Often new recruits to violent movements must undertake a violent act to demonstrate their commitment. This is a further inhibition to participation in armed struggles, because potential recruits may wish to eschew drastic screening processes or movement leaders may find it hard to trust new recruits.

Third, during the prosecution of a conflict, participants in nonviolent campaigns can often return to their jobs, daily lives, and families with lower risk than a participant in a violent campaign.[13] Compared with those in armed struggle, participants in civil resistance can more easily retain anonymity, which means that they can often commit acts of resistance without making major life sacrifices. This is particularly true when a campaign uses nonviolent methods of dispersion (a concept we elaborate on later), such as stay-at-home strikes or a consumer boycott, in which cooperation is withdrawn without providing the state with a tangible target for repression (Burrowes 1996, 224–25; Schock 2005, 52). The commitment required by people who join violent campaigns often prevents them from resuming their lives during or after the conflict, and they are more likely to go underground to evade state security.

Fourth, nonviolent resistance offers a greater repertoire of lower-risk actions. Although nonviolent struggle is rarely casualty-free, as the nonviolent struggle in Egypt recently demonstrated, the price of participating (and being caught) in armed struggle is often death. The possibility of accidental death during training exercises or through friendly fire is omnipresent as well. Thus the likelihood of being killed while carrying out one's duties as an armed insurgent is high, whereas many lower-risk tactics are available to participants in a nonviolent resistance campaign. The wearing of opposition insignia, the coordinated banging of pots and pans and honking of horns, the creation of underground schools, participation in candlelight vigils, and the refusal to obey regime orders are a few examples of less-risky nonviolent tactics that have been used by groups around the world (Sharp 1973).

Mobilization during the Iranian Revolution demonstrates the latter point. Notwithstanding the Shah's deep unpopularity among large numbers of Iranians, many Iranian citizens were unwilling to participate in protest activity until the revolution had attracted mass support, which occurred only after nonviolent popular struggle replaced guerrilla violence as the primary mode of resistance (Kurzman 1996). A similar dynamic could be seen in the 1988 popular ouster of General Augusto Pinochet in Chile, and the 1986 People Power revolution against Ferdinand Marcos in the Philippines, where armed challenges to the dictatorships invited harsh regime reprisals without attracting mass support or threatening the regime's grip on power, whereas nonviolent actions opened up space for broad-based, multisectoral participation (Ackerman and DuVall 2000; Boudreau 2004; Schock 2005).

The dynamics of participation discussed thus far point in one direction. They suggest that nonviolent campaigns will be more successful at generating large bases of participants. When large numbers of people in key sectors of society stop obeying and engage in prolonged acts of social, political, and economic disruption, they may fundamentally alter the relationship between ruler and ruled. If mass participation is associated with campaign success, then nonviolent campaigns have an advantage over violent ones.

PARTICIPATION AND SUCCESS GO TOGETHER

We have established how and why nonviolent resistance campaigns are able to attract a larger number of active participants than violent struggles. But is mass participation truly important? After all, many regimes specialize in controlling large populations. Some might suspect that a smaller number of well-armed comrades competing against an unsuspecting military and government could have better odds than a million unarmed protestors engaging a repressive opponent (see, e.g., DeNardo 1985). This expectation is certainly corroborated by several empirical examples: the Cuban Revolution shows the success of small, armed bands, whereas the massacre at Tiananmen Square demonstrates the failure of a large-scale nonviolent campaign.

The data, however, reveal a different pattern. Over space and time, large campaigns are much more likely to succeed than small campaigns. A single unit increase of active participants makes a campaign over 10 percent more likely to achieve its ultimate outcome.[14] Consider figure 2.1, which shows the effects of number of participants per capita on the predicted probability of campaign success. The trend is clear that as membership increases, the probability of success also increases.[15]

We recognize, however, that numbers alone do not guarantee victory in resistance campaigns. As some cases demonstrate, a high number of participants does not automatically translate into success. Some enormous campaigns—like the anticommunist campaigns in East Germany in the 1950s (boasting about four hundred thousand participants) and the anti-Japanese insurgency in China during the 1930s and 1940s (with over 4 million participants)—failed utterly.

Thus, numbers may matter, but they are insufficient to guarantee success. This is because the quality of participation—including the diversity of the resistance participants, strategic and tactical choices made by the opposition, and its ability to adapt and innovate—may be as important as the quantity of participants. As proposed in the preceding, lower barriers to participation enjoyed by nonviolent campaigns will increase not only the size of the campaign but also the diversity of the campaign. The more diverse the participation in the resistance—in terms of gender, age, religion, ethnicity, ideology, profession, and socioeconomic status—the more difficult it is for the adversary to isolate the participants and adopt a repressive strategy short of maximal and indiscriminate repression. Of course, this does not mean that nonviolent campaigns are immune from regime repression—typically they are not—but it does make the opponent's use of violence more likely to backfire, a point we return to later.

Moreover, thick social networks among members of the resistance and regime actors, including members of the security forces, may produce bonds that can become very important over the course of the resistance. Diverse participation also increases the likelihood of tactical diversity, since different groups and associations are familiar with different forms of resistance and bring unique skills and capacities to the fight, which makes outmaneuvering the opponent and increasing pressure points more plausible.

As with any campaign, strategic factors like achieving unity around shared goals and methods, establishing realistic goals, assessing opponent

FIGURE 2.1 **THE EFFECT OF PARTICIPATION ON THE PROBABILITY OF CAMPAIGN SUCCESS**

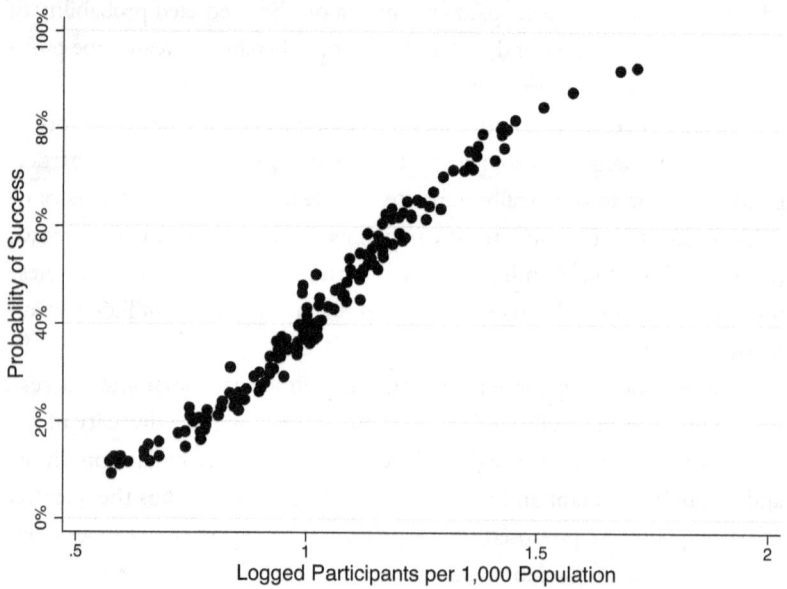

vulnerabilities and sources of leverage, sequencing tactics, and navigating structural constraints (including regime repression) are also likely to be crucial determinants of campaign outcomes. These strategic factors are independent of the mechanisms we develop in the following but can affect whether the mechanisms actually translate into effectiveness. We emphasize these features more prominently in our case studies. In the meantime, however, we suggest that the execution of any resistance strategy—violent or nonviolent—and the ability to stay in the contest with the adversary depend on the availability of willing recruits.

As such, large-scale and diverse participation may afford a resistance campaign a strategic advantage, which, in turn, increases the pressure points and enhances the leverage that the resistance achieves vis-à-vis its state adversary. The ability of nonviolent campaigns to more easily exploit these advantages of broad-based mobilization, and the high costs of prolonged disobedience and noncooperation by large numbers of dissenters, explain in part why civil resistance has been so much more effective than violent resistance.

PARTICIPATION AND MECHANISMS OF LEVERAGE

In this section, we discuss the mechanisms through which broad-based mobilization and the systematic application of nonviolent sanctions by large numbers of people allow nonviolent campaigns to maximize leverage over their adversaries, even when their adversaries appear to have an advantage in terms of military prowess, resources, and other forms of power. Leverage, writes Kurt Schock, is "the ability . . . to mobilize the withdrawal of support from opponents or invoke pressure against them through the networks upon which opponents depend for power" (Schock 2005, 142). Thus leverage is not necessarily dependent on the number of weapons available to a resistance movement but on the ability of the campaign to impose costs on the adversary for maintaining the status quo, or for retaliating against the resistance.

The disruptive effects of violent and nonviolent resistance may raise the political, economic, and military costs for an adversary (DeNardo 1985). The results of sustained disruption include the failure of the government to perform basic functions, a decline in GDP, investment, and tax revenues, loss of power by government elites, and the breakdown of the normal order of society (Wood 2000, 15). The sum total of the domestic and international costs of sustained disruption may cause members of the target regime to accommodate resistance campaigns—or force them to give up power completely.

Coercion

Violent campaigns physically coerce their adversaries, which may significantly disrupt the status quo.[16] Destroying or damaging infrastructure, killing or threatening government and military elites and local populations, and disrupting the flow of goods and commerce may raise perceptions of ungovernability and continued instability while loosening the regime's grip on power. The more the regime is perceived as illegitimate by the local populace, the more likely it is that the latter will sympathize with the armed insurgents, as the revolutions in Cuba and Vietnam, the Sunni insurgency in Iraq, and the ongoing Pashtun-led armed resistance in Afghanistan and Pakistan demonstrate. But sympathy is not the same as active participation in the resistance.

Beyond attempting to coerce the opponent, a sustained violent resistance campaign may serve an important communicative role. For example, the Palestine Liberation Organization's (PLO) use of terrorism and guerrilla violence from the mid-1960s to the late 1980s is often credited with keeping the Palestinian issue alive internationally. The armed wing of the East Timorese independence movement, the Falintil, similarly used armed attacks against Indonesian military targets to attract media attention and to demonstrate that there was opposition to the Indonesian occupation. The Iranian guerrilla movement similarly justified its use of armed attacks against the Shah's regime as a way of demonstrating that the reality was not as the Shah presented it, and that there was opposition to the monarchy (Behrooz 2004). The Maoist guerrillas in Nepal launched armed attacks against the monarchical regime for years, signaling their opposition and resulting in hundreds of fatalities and prolonged instability in the country.[17] The Taliban continue to use suicide bombings, improvised explosive device (IED) attacks, and assassinations targeting International Security Assistance Forces (ISAF) and Afghan government officials and security forces to demonstrate their rejection of the internationally backed regime of President Hamid Karzai.

In the aforementioned cases, however, there is scant evidence of a causal relationship between political violence and political victories, suggesting that disruption should not be confused with victory. Although the armed resistance may have had a symbolic function, many of the major changes that have ultimately occurred in these cited cases—except in Afghanistan, where the insurgency continues—were precipitated by mass, nonviolent campaigns. In the case of Nepal, for instance, what directly preceded the restoration of democratic rule in Nepal was not armed resistance but a brief mass civil resistance campaign, where even the Maoists chose to put down their guns so that they could participate alongside large numbers of unarmed civilians.

The coercive capacity of nonviolent resistance is not based on violent disruption to the social order. Rather, it is based on the removal of the adversary's key sources of power through sustained acts of protest and noncooperation. Some may argue that nonviolent resistance is powerful only because regimes fear that they will become violent, thereby posing even greater threats. Social movement scholars refer to this dynamic as a "positive radical flank effect." This concept posits that violence may sometimes increase the leverage of challengers, which occurs when states offer selective rewards and opportunities to moderate competitor groups to isolate or thwart the more radical organizations. In other words, the presence of a radical element in the opposition may make the moderate oppositionists in the nonviolent campaign seem more palatable to the regime, thereby contributing to the success of the nonviolent campaign. In this way, some argue that violent and nonviolent campaigns can be symbiotic, in that the presence of both types improves their relative positions.[18]

But opposition violence is just as likely—if not more likely—to have the opposite result. A "negative radical flank effect," or spoiler effect, occurs when another party's violence decreases the leverage of a challenge group. In this case, the presence of an armed challenge group causes the regime's supporters to unify against the threat without making a distinction between violent and nonviolent challenges, which are lumped together as the same threat deserving the same (violent) response.

There is no consensus among social scientists about the conditions under which radical flanks either harm or help a social movement.[19] In our estimation, however, many successful nonviolent campaigns have succeeded because they systematically eroded or removed entirely the regime's sources of power, including the support of the economic and military elites, which may have hesitated to support the opposition if they had suspected that the campaign would turn violent. The more a regime's supporters believe a campaign may become violent, or that their interests will be gutted if the status quo is changed, the more likely that those supporters and potential participants may perceive the conflict to be a zero-sum game (Stephan and Chenoweth 2008, 9–13). As a response, regime supporters are likely to unite to counter the perceived threat, while potential participants may eschew participation for the reasons just identified. A unified adversary is much harder to defeat for any resistance campaign. In conflicts perceived as zero-sum, furthermore, it is difficult for erstwhile regime supporters to modify and adapt their ideologies and interests according to shifts in power. Instead, they will fight tooth and nail to keep their grip on power, relying on brutal force if necessary. There is less room for negotiation, compromise, and power sharing when regime members fear that even small losses of power will translate into rolling heads. On the other hand, our central point is that campaigns that divide the adversary from its key pillars of support are in a better position to succeed. Nonviolent campaigns have a strategic advantage in this regard.[20]

To summarize, rather than effectiveness resulting from a supposed threat of violence, nonviolent campaigns achieve success through sustained pressure derived from mass mobilization that withdraws the regime's economic, political, social, and even military support from domestic populations and third parties. Leverage is achieved when the adversary's most important supporting organizations and institutions are systematically pulled away through mass noncooperation.

For example, sustained economic pressure targeting state-owned and private businesses and enterprises has been an important element in many successful popular movements (Ackerman and DuVall 2000; Ackerman and Kruegler 1994; Schock 2005; Sharp 1973; Zunes, Kurtz, and Asher 1999). As the antiapartheid struggle in South Africa demonstrated, massive collective actions such as strikes and boycotts can impose significant economic costs on those benefiting from the status quo.[21]

As in South Africa, the cumulative costs of continuous nonviolent resistance may limit the possible or desirable courses of action available to economic and political elites, often forcing them to negotiate on terms favorable to the nonviolent campaign. Sustained pressure through civic mobilization, combined with the belief that the opposition represents a burgeoning and viable governing alternative, can influence key regime adherents, causing them to reconsider their preferences and alternatives to the status quo (Wood 2000, 21). This dynamic has marked a number of democratic transitions, including those in Chile, the Philippines, and Eastern Europe (see, e.g., Ackerman and Karatnycky 2005; Bernhard 1993; Brownlee 2007; Collier 1999; Eckstein 2001; McFaul 2007; Schock 2005; Sharp 1973).

In cases where there is an inverse economic dependency relationship (meaning the opposition is more dependent on the state than vice versa) it may be difficult for a civil resistance campaign to achieve significant leverage without working through parties with closer political and economic ties to the state. Examples of nonviolent campaigns in this circumstance are the Palestinians in the Occupied Palestinian Territories, the Tibetans in China-controlled Tibet, and the West Papuans in Indonesian-controlled West Papua, all of whom are more economically dependent on the state than vice versa. Although consumer boycotts and labor stoppages launched by populations living under foreign occupation can impose certain degrees of economic costs on the occupying power (as occurred when Palestinians boycotted Israeli products and withheld labor during the First Intifada), the impact is much smaller than when the regime is more economically dependent on the resisting population, as is the case with many nonviolent campaigns challenging regimes (Dajani 1994; King 2007; Stephan 2005, 2006). This may be especially true when a state is subsidized from the outside such that it can survive internal economic disruption.[22] These so-called rentier states, which rely on external sources, including export sales in natural resources, tourism, and economic aid for a sizable portion of net income, have proven to be especially resistant to domestic pressure (Carothers 1999; Carothers and Ottoway 2005; Diamond 2008; Ibrahim 2008).

An inverse dependency relationship between a state and a nonviolent campaign does not doom the nonviolent campaign to failure, however. In a number of antiauthoritarian struggles, economic crises combined with organized mass nonviolent pressure have led to the ouster of regimes reliant on external rents believed to be immune to such pressure (e.g., Iran, Indonesia). In certain cases of foreign occupation, working with or through third parties has helped nonviolent campaigns to "extend the nonviolent battlefield" and gain increased leverage over its adversary.[23]

Violent campaigns, we suggest, are more likely to reinforce the adversary's main pillars of support and increase their loyalty and obedience to the regime, as opposed to pulling apart and reducing their loyalties to the regime. A "rally around the flag" effect is more likely to occur when the adversary is confronted with violent resistance than with a disciplined nonviolent campaign that makes its commitment to nonviolent means known.

Although small armed groups may be perceived as threatening to a regime's survivability, states may be more susceptible to internal fissures in the face of massive nonviolent action than to limited, violent opposition. In short, campaigns of nonviolent resistance tend to enjoy mass, broad-based support and, in some cases, mass defections by erstwhile regime supporters, who see a future in supporting a growing opposition movement as opposed to supporting the regime or a relatively small group of armed oppositionists.

Loyalty Shifts

When a resistance campaign is able to influence the loyalties and interests of people working in society's dominant institutions, it increases its chances of success (Greene 1974, 57; McAdam, McCarthy, and Zald 1996, 306). Campaigns can shift power relations vis-à-vis the adversary by accessing sympathizers or defectors within the elite or among ordinary people who work below the elite. Regimes often grant concessions when acts of protest or noncooperation lead to shifts in people's loyalties and interests—or perceptions thereof. Thus measuring the impact of different forms of resistance on the loyalties and interests of a regime's key pillars of political and military support may help to predict campaign success and failure.

Evidence of defections within the ranks of the military, for instance, would suggest that the regime no longer commands the cooperation and obedience of its most important pillar of support. We generated a dichotomous variable that identifies defections among a regime's security forces. This measure does not include routine individual defections but rather large-scale, systematic breakdowns in the execution of a regime's orders.[24] We consider security defections a strict measure of loyalty shifts within the regime, not capturing civil servant or bureaucrat loyalty shifts. This strict measure includes defections occurring up to the end of the campaign.

The ability to produce divisions among elites may be augmented when the resistance has widespread participation. With a large number of participants, the chances for kinship ties or other social networks linking members of the elite to the larger civilian population increase. The importance of even loose ties between regime elites and the resistance is illustrated by Srdja Popovic, a member of the student group Otpor in Serbia. Popovic made the following observations regarding the relationship between Milosevic's police and the mass, nonviolent resistance movement that was pressuring the regime to stand down following stolen elections in 2000:

We were producing the [*sic*] sympathy in the wider audience . . . It was quite normal to produce in people who are parents because they can recognize their own children in Otpor activists. But as for the police, we tried three times to approach them and third time it was useful [*sic*]. First time, we developed a message . . . Our message was "there is no war between police and us." Somebody else is misusing the police against students. It's abnormal. There is no reason for the police to fight against the future of this country—and we were repeating that and repeating that in our public actions. (Popovic 2009)

Popovic's mention of members of the regime as "parents" of some of the Otpor activists underscores the importance of wide networks that link members of society to members of the regime itself. As other scholars have shown, the larger the resistance, the more likely such networks exist, with meaningful links between the regime and the resistance (Binnendijk 2008; Binnendijk and Marovic 2006; Jaafar and Stephan 2010). This is another reason why the actions and proclivities of a state's security forces—the military and the police—are barometers of the strength of the opposition movement. We illuminate this point in the case study section of the book.

While their demands strain state budgets, nonviolent campaigns may also lead soldiers, policemen, and (often later) their commanding officers to question the viability, risks, and potential costs of military actions against the nonviolent campaign (Hathaway 2001). This occurred within the ranks of the Iranian armed forces during the anti-Shah resistance, to Filipino armed forces during the anti-Marcos uprising, within the Israeli military during the First Intifada, and over the course of the Indonesian military campaign in East Timor, to take but a few examples. Fighting an armed actor is likewise costly but is less likely to create as much introspection among the commanding officers, who might instead feel physically threatened by the violence and view the violent insurgents as minorities within the population resorting to violence out of desperation or a desire to inflict punishment. Regime functionaries are therefore less likely to see violent protestors as potential bargaining partners than with nonviolent groups.

Among economic elites within the regime, perception of costly continued conflict may convince them to pressure the regime to adopt conciliatory policies toward the resistance. Wood argues that the accumulating costs of the insurgencies in South Africa and El Salvador and their attendant repression ultimately convinced economic elites to press the regimes to negotiate, changing the balance of power within the regimes between those willing to consider compromise and those resolutely opposed (2000, 6).

If our theory is correct, nonviolent campaigns should be more successful at inducing loyalty shifts within the regime than violent campaigns, especially nonviolent campaigns with mass participation. We tested this hypothesis by measuring whether there were significant shifts in loyalty among state security forces during the course of a campaign.[25]

The results in Model 1(a) in table 2.3 suggest that large campaigns with a commitment to nonviolent resistance are more likely than violent insurgencies to produce defections within security forces. In fact, the largest nonviolent campaigns have about a 60 percent chance of producing security-force defections, an increase of over 50 percent from the smallest nonviolent campaigns. The substantive effects of nonviolent campaigns on security-force defections are visible in figure 2.2. For nonviolent campaigns, the probability of security-force defections steadily increases as membership in the resistance campaign grows. On the other hand, the odds of successfully converting military forces to the insurgent side remain between 10 percent and 40 percent for violent insurgents, with only a modest increase in probability as participation increases. Faced with a violent insurgency, security forces are likeliest to unify behind the regime, as the fight becomes a contest of brute force rather than strategic interaction. Under such conditions, security

TABLE 2.3 **THE EFFECT OF NONVIOLENT RESISTANCE ON MECHANISMS**

MODEL 1(A)	PROBABILITY OF SECURITY FORCE DEFECTIONS	MARGINAL EFFECTS
NUMBER OF PARTICIPANTS, LOGGED	.25** (.11)	+5%
POPULATION, LOGGED		
NONVIOLENT* PARTICIPANTS	-.18 (.14)	--
CONSTANT	-1.77 (1.56)	26%
N	163	
CHI²	5.52	
PROB > CHI²	.0632	
PSEUDO R²	.0413	

MODEL 2(A)	PROBABILITY OF INTERNATIONAL SANCTIONS AGAINST THE REGIME	MARGINAL EFFECTS
NONVIOLENT CAMPAIGN	3.50** (3.35)	+62%
NUMBER OF PARTICIPANTS, LOGGED	.64*** (.22)	+10%
POPULATION, LOGGED	-.01 (.12)	--
NONVIOLENT* PARTICIPANTS	-.42** (.32)	--
CONSTANT	-7.16*** (2.46)	20%
N	163	
CHI²	10.59	
PROB > CHI²	.0315	
PSEUDO R²	.0842	
MODEL 3(A)	PROBABILITY OF STATE SPONSORSHIP	MARGINAL EFFECTS
NONVIOLENT CAMPAIGN	-2.72*** (.77)	-44%
NUMBER OF PARTICIPANTS, LOGGED	.29** (.15)	+6%
POPULATION, LOGGED	-.25** (.12)	-5%
CONSTANT	-.37 (1.82)	26%
N	163	
CHI²	17.55	
PROB > CHI²	.0005	
PSEUDO R²	.1569	

SIGNIFICANCE LEVELS: *** $P < .01$, ** $P < .05$, * $P < .1$; LOGISTIC REGRESSION WITH ROBUST STANDARD ERRORS CLUSTERED AROUND TARGET COUNTRY CODE.

forces may become even more loyal to the regime, or the regime may purge ambivalent troops from its ranks.

But security-force defections are only the most extreme form of loyalty shifts in an opponent regime. We cannot quantify the noncooperation of civilian bureaucrats, economic elites, and other members of society whose withdrawal of consent from the regime may be critical to the outcome of a resistance campaign. But such groups may be even more threatened by violent insurgency than the military, which can provide its personnel with nominal physical protection. One might expect civilian bureaucrats to be even more inclined toward regime loyalty when faced with a violent insurgency. They may be more introspective, though, faced with a mass, nonviolent campaign.

FIGURE 2.2 **THE EFFECT OF PARTICIPATION ON SECURITY-FORCE DEFECTIONS**

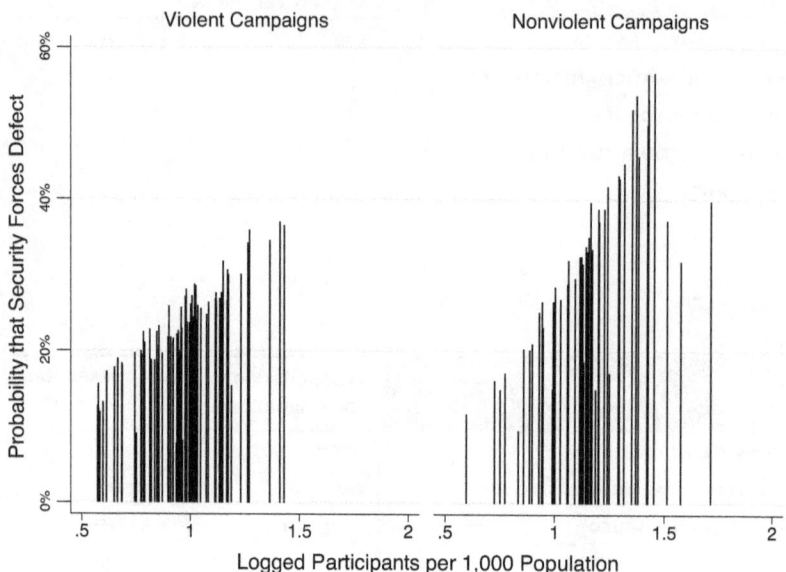

Backfiring

Loyalty shifts may occur directly in response to opposition activities, or in response to regime actions that are perceived as unjust or excessive. One common scenario leading to loyalty shifts is when the regime violently cracks down on a popular nonviolent campaign with mass civilian participation. In this case, the regime's actions may backfire, a process that occurs when an action is counterproductive for the perpetrator (Martin 2007, 3). Backfiring creates a situation in which the resistance leverages the miscalculations of the regime to its own advantage, as domestic and international actors that support the regime shift their support to the opposition because of specific actions taken by the regime (Binnendijk and Marovic 2006, 416).[26]

Repressing nonviolent campaigns may backfire if the campaigns have widespread sympathy among the civilian population by turning erstwhile passive supporters into active participants in the resistance (DeNardo 1985, 217). Alternatively, repressing nonviolent activists may lead to loyalty shifts by increasing the internal solidarity of the resistance, increasing foreign support for it, or increasing dissent within the enemy ranks—provided violent counterreprisals by the resistance do not occur. This effect may be catalyzed further if the repression is communicated to domestic and international audiences that are prepared to act (Boserup and Mack 1974, 84; Martin 2007; Stephan and Chenoweth 2008).[27]

Resistance of any kind against a regime is often met with repression. In fact, in our data set, 88 percent of all campaigns met with violent resistance from their adversaries. However, it is easier for states to justify violent crackdowns and draconian measures (like the imposition of martial law or states of emergency) to domestic and international audiences when they are challenged by an armed insurgency (Martin 2007, 163).[28] On the other hand, converting, co-opting, or successfully appealing to the interests of those targeted with violence is more difficult, because, as mentioned, regime members and security forces are more likely to think defensively in the face of a violent threat (Abrahms 2006). This explanation is counterintuitive, because it is often assumed that violent repression always *weakens* nonviolent campaigns relative to violent campaigns (Schock 2003, 706).

If we are correct, then a nonviolent strategy should be more likely to succeed against a repressive opponent than a violent strategy. We test this hypothesis in Model 1(b) in table 2.4. The results suggest that when regimes crack down violently, reliance on a nonviolent strategy increases the probability of campaign success by about 22 percent. Among the campaigns we explore here, backfiring may be an important mechanism through which nonviolent campaigns achieve success.

TABLE 2.4 **THE EFFECTS OF MECHANISMS ON THE PROBABILITY OF SUCCESS**

MODEL 1(B)	PROBABILITY OF SUCCESS, WHEN REGIME CRACKS DOWN	MARGINAL EFFECTS
NONVIOLENT CAMPAIGN	.92*** (.36)	+22%
POPULATION, LOGGED	-.20* (.12)	-5%
CONSTANT	1.21 (1.08)	41%
N	181	
CHI²	8.27	
PROB > CHI²	.0160	
PSEUDO R²	.0453	

TABLE 2.4 (CONTINUED)

MODEL 2(B)	PROBABILITY OF NONVIOLENT CAMPAIGN SUCCESS	MARGINAL EFFECTS
NUMBER OF PARTICIPANTS, LOGGED	.49** (.17)	+9%
VIOLENT REGIME REPRESSION	-.76 (.80)	--
SECURITY FORCE DEFECTIONS	3.18*** (.74)	+58%
STATE SPONSORSHIP	.97 (1.43)	--
INTERNATIONAL SANCTIONS	-.99 (1.23)	--
CONSTANT	-4.20** (1.97)	57%
N	80	
CHI²	24.33	
PROB > CHI²	.0002	
PSEUDO R²	.2953	

MODEL 3(B)	PROBABILITY OF VIOLENT CAMPAIGN SUCCESS	MARGINAL EFFECTS
NUMBER OF PARTICIPANTS, LOGGED	-.11 (.13)	--
VIOLENT REGIME REPRESSION	-.98 (.64)	--
SECURITY FORCE DEFECTIONS	.18 (.40)	--
STATE SPONSORSHIP	.86** (.48)	+15%
INTERNATIONAL SANCTIONS	.82 (.62)	--
CONSTANT	.00 (1.37)	21%
N	178	
CHI²	11.10	
PROB > CHI²	.0494	
PSEUDO R²	.0614	

SIGNIFICANCE LEVELS: *** P < .01, ** P < .05, *P < .1; LOGISTIC REGRESSION WITH ROBUST STANDARD ERRORS CLUSTERED AROUND TARGET COUNTRY CODE.

International Sanctions and External Support

A resistance campaign may also achieve leverage over its adversary through diplomatic pressure or international sanctions against the adversary. International sanctions are certainly controversial; common arguments against them include the point that they often harm the civilian population more than the targeted regimes (Cortright 2001; Seekins 2005).[29] They may be effective, however, in many cases (Marinov 2005). Such sanctions had discernible effects in supporting successful opposition campaigns in South Africa and East Timor, to take just two examples (Martin 2007, 13, 15, 23). The ANC leadership had demanded sanctions for decades, but they came about only after mass nonviolent resistance had spread.[30] Some argue that the international sanctions against the apartheid regime in South Africa were critical in creating a bargaining space for the resistance campaigns to finally come to the negotiating table.[31]

Conversely, lack of sanctions or diplomatic pressure has often been cited as contributing to the failure of some opposition groups. Some have suggested, for example, that the application of sanctions by China or Russia would hasten the Burmese junta's downfall, or that pressure by South Africa would hasten the demise of the Robert Mugabe regime in Zimbabwe (Seekins 2005; U.S. State Department 2004). Absent economic and diplomatic backing from China, the Kim Jong Il regime in North Korea would be on weak footing. Arab regimes in places like Saudi Arabia and Egypt benefit tremendously from Western (notably U.S.) political, economic, and military support.

International sanctions may be more easily generated when outside actors see large numbers of resistance participants as a sign of the movement's legitimacy and viability. The international repercussions of a violent crackdown against civilians who have made their commitment to nonviolent action known may be more severe than against those that could be credibly labeled as terrorists. We believe that the international community is more likely to contribute diplomatic support to nonviolent campaigns than to violent ones.

To test our thinking, we drew upon international sanctions data collected by Hufbauer, Schott, and Elliott (1992).[32] In Model 2(a) in table 2.3, we measure the effects of nonviolent resistance and campaign membership on the likelihood that international sanctions will be applied against the opponent of the resistance movement.

The data show that large, nonviolent campaigns are likelier than small, armed campaigns to successfully receive international diplomatic support. Once again, it is not only the quantity of participants in terms of their numbers but also the reliance on civil resistance that leads to diplomatic support through sanctions. A nonviolent campaign is 70 percent likelier to receive diplomatic support through sanctions than a violent campaign.

State sponsors may also give direct assistance to resistance campaigns, depending on the political context and domestic conditions. Specifically, outside states may choose to contribute arms or financial assistance to an insurgency when they have mutual interests with the insurgents. Pakistan and the United States, for example, supported the anti-Soviet insurgency in Afghanistan during the 1980s because both countries wished to see the end of the Soviet occupation of Afghanistan. Nonviolent campaigns also sometimes receive direct support from foreign governments, international organizations, nongovernmental organizations (NGOs), and global civil society. The aid often comes in the form of government financial assistance, sanctions targeting the adversary, diplomatic recognition or other forms of support for leading opposition activists, or NGO funding or training.[33] The Serbian resistance movement Otpor, for example, received millions of dollars from funding agencies linked to the United States and European governments prior to the toppling of the Milosevic regime.

We find, however, that foreign governments are likelier to lend direct material support to violent resistance campaigns—which the states may see as their proxies—than to nonviolent campaigns.[34] Whereas 35 percent of the violent insurgencies received material support from a foreign state, less than 10 percent of nonviolent campaigns did so.

As Model 3(a) in table 2.3 identifies, holding other potential confounding variables constant, violent resistance campaigns are over 40 percent likelier to receive material support from a foreign state sponsor than nonviolent campaigns.

The aid of an external donor may help violent insurgents to wage successful campaigns against more powerful adversaries (Record 2006).[35] Many would argue, for example, that Franco's revolutionary fascists would have been defeated by the Spanish Republicans without the support of Nazi Germany and fascist Italy.

Ironically, however, external state support may also undermine insurgents' odds of success. State support is unreliable, inconsistently applied to opposition groups around the world, and sometimes ineffective in helping campaigns. States are fickle, as the PLO learned when Jordan expelled it in 1970. States are also known to attach many conditions to their aid, greatly complicating the strategic maneuverability of different actors (Byman 2005). Even when state sponsorship could be helpful to a campaign, as Clifford Bob notes, the decision to support resistance movements depends on a variety of internal considerations, including the donor's mission, sponsors, and the political atmosphere (2005).

State support may also create a free-rider problem, in which local populations perceive that participation in the campaign is unnecessary because of foreign patronage. In fact, external support can at times delegitimize a movement in the eyes of the domestic population by leading to accusations of corruption within the movement. Alternatively, foreign support may drive away potential recruits who may be reluctant to act on behalf of a foreign state or to be associated with a foreign state's political designs.

State support may also undermine insurgent incentives to treat civilian populations with restraint, because civilians are viewed as dispensable rather than as the main sources of support. As Weinstein argues, for instance, insurgencies that must rely on local populations to finance the insurgency are much likelier to treat such populations with restraint and respect (2007). Insurgencies that obtain resources from elsewhere—such as from natural resource deposits or foreign donors—are much more likely to abuse the local population, thus undermining the ultimate goals of the insurgency.

Thus state support may be a double-edged sword, rife with trade-offs for insurgent groups. While it may provide violent insurgencies with more war matériel with which to wage the struggle, it may also undermine the relationship between the insurgency and the civilian population, a population whose support may be critical to the outcome of the campaign. Civil resistance movements, which by definition rely on civilian support for mobilization, do not face this conundrum, since over 90 percent of them execute their campaigns without the direct financial assistance of a foreign regime.

Tactical Diversity and Innovation
Strategic innovation occurs with some regularity in both nonviolent and violent campaigns. However, we suggest that the greater the number of participants from different societal sectors involved in the campaign, the more likely the campaign is to produce tactical innovations. Charles Tilly, Sidney Tarrow, and Kurt Schock have argued that tactical innovation occurs "on the margins of existing repertoires," and as such, "the more expansive the margins, the greater the likelihood of permutation and innovation" (Schock 2005, 144). We have already pointed out that nonviolent campaigns attract a larger number of more diverse participants than violent campaigns because the physical, moral, and informational barriers to mobilization are lower. The diversity of these campaigns therefore offer them advantages with regard to tactical innovation (Schock 2005, 144).

A specific type of tactical diversity is shifting between methods of concentration and methods of dispersion. In methods of concentration, nonviolent campaigns gather large numbers of people in public spaces to engage in civil resistance (Schock 2005, 51). Well-known applications of this method include the Gandhi-led Salt March in India, the student protests in Tiananmen Square, and the occupation of Red Square during the Russian Revolution. More recent examples of concentration methods include the mass sit-ins in Maidan Square in Kiev during the Orange Revolution, the creation of a tent city in downtown Beirut during the Lebanese Independence Intifada (also known as the Cedar Revolution), and the massive gatherings of Egyptians in Tahrir Square during the 2011 revolution. Methods of dispersion involve acts that spread out over a wider area, such as consumer boycotts, stay-aways, and go-slow actions at the workplace. Dispersion methods, like the consumer boycotts in South Africa, intentional obstructionism at the workplace by Germans during the French occupation of the Ruhr, labor strikes by oil workers during the Iranian revolution, and the banging of pots and pans by Chileans during the anti-Pinochet movement, force an adversary to spread out its repressive apparatus over a wider area, afford greater protection and anonymity to participants, and allow participants to engage in less-risky actions.

In violent campaigns, tactical diversity could include alternating between concentrated attacks and ambushes in urban areas and more dispersed hit-and-run attacks, bombings, and assassinations in smaller towns and villages. The Taliban's shift from direct engagements to reliance on IEDs targeting Afghan and international coalition forces is an example of tactical innovation in armed resistance. For both violent and nonviolent campaigns, adopting diverse tactics reduces the effectiveness of the adversary's repression and helps the campaign maintain the initiative (Schock 2005, 144). Tactical innovation enhances the campaign's adaptability and its room for maneuvering when the state focuses its repression on a particular set of tactics. This is especially crucial when the repression makes some tactics, like street protests, highly risky and dangerous (Schock 2005, 144).

Because tactical innovation occurs on the fringes of a movement, campaigns with larger numbers of participants, and consequently wider margins, are more likely to produce tactical innovations. The relatively larger number of active participants expands the repertoire of sanctions available to nonviolent campaigns, allowing them to shift between methods of concentration and dispersion while maintaining pressure on the adversary.[36] Tactical diversity and innovation enhance the ability of nonviolent resistance to strategically outmaneuver the adversary compared with armed insurgencies.

Tactical innovation in turn affects the resilience of campaigns over time, an issue we take up in the next section.

Evasion and Resilience
Another significant challenge of resistance is opposition resilience, which "refers to the capacity of contentious actors to continue to mobilize collective action despite the actions of opponents aimed at constraining or inhibiting their activities" (Schock 2005, 142). Researchers can observe levels of resilience by determining a campaign's ability to maintain a significant number of participants, recruit new members, and continue to confront the adversary in the face of repression.

Many scholars consider resilience a crucial factor for campaign success, since it may determine the ability of the campaign to maintain its strategic advantage despite adversary oppression or attempts at co-optation (Bob and Nepstad 2007; Francisco 2004; Khawaja 1993; Koopmans 1993; Lichbach 1994; Moore 1998; Schock 2005; Weinstein 2007, 45). Continual regime counterattacks against a resistance campaign can remove key members of the campaign and raise the costs of continued participation among remaining members. States often use decapitation to undermine a campaign's organizational coherence over time.

A common assumption in security studies is that the ability to wage a successful war of attrition against a regime is a necessary determinant of resilience (Weinstein 2007, 37). Seizing territory or enjoying sanctuary from a neighboring state may allow violent insurgencies to meet two key challenges for resilience, maintaining their membership and recruitment operations in the face of state repression. Though their numbers may be smaller than mass nonviolent campaigns, violent insurgencies may be able to survive for decades, like the Karen insurgency in Burma, which has endured since 1949, and the FARC, which has waged guerrilla warfare against the Colombian state since 1964, and, for four decades (until their defeat in 2009), the Tamil Tigers (LTTE) waged a violent insurgency against the Sri Lankan central government. Although durable violent campaigns boast impressive stubbornness in the face of repressive and powerful adversaries, longevity does not necessarily translate into strategic success. Isolation in the countryside, in the mountains, or in neighboring safe havens does not necessarily afford violent insurgencies leverage over their state adversaries. The only reason why some violent insurgencies have been able to survive is that they operate in remote areas not penetrated by the state, as with Taliban affiliates who maintain sanctuary in Pakistan's North-West Frontier.[37]

Persistence may be necessary to campaign success, but it is insufficient. To achieve success, a campaign must go beyond persistence and achieve a shift in power between the opposition and the adversary. Resilience involves increasing mobilization and action, maintaining key assets and resources, and bringing a diverse constellation of assets and tactics to bear against the adversary, regardless of whether the adversary is materially more powerful. Successful campaigns endure despite regime repression while making tangible progress toward stated goals, even if those goals change over time. Because of the tendency of nonviolent campaigns to involve mass numbers of diverse participants, they should be better suited than violent campaigns to maintain resilience and continue their operations regardless of the adversary's actions. Regime crackdowns arguably debilitate armed campaigns more than similar crackdowns against unarmed campaigns, because of the greater number of potential assets and "weapons" available to nonviolent resistance campaigns. This argument, which we illustrate in the case studies, clearly challenges the conventional wisdom.

WHICH FACTORS MATTER MOST? EXPLAINING THE SUCCESS OF CIVIL RESISTANCE

We have demonstrated that civil resistance campaigns have routinely outperformed violent insurgencies. We have also theorized that the participation advantages that nonviolent resistance campaigns enjoy activate a series of mechanisms—sometimes in conjunction with one another and sometimes independently—that lead to success. Nonviolent resistance campaigns are more likely to pull apart the opponent's pillars of support rather than push them together; to divide rather than unify the opponent; and to raise the political, social, and economic costs to the regime rather than to the regime's opposition. We now demonstrate which of these factors seem most influential in determining failure and success.

Interestingly, as table 2.4 shows, there are different determinants of success based on the primary resistance type. Nonviolent campaigns (Model 2[b]) have been most successful when they have produced security-force defections.[38] In fact, such defections increase the likelihood of success by nearly 60 percent. The number of participants is also important for nonviolent campaigns. An increase of a single unit improves the odds of success by nearly 10 percent. Notably, however, neither foreign state support, nor international sanctions, nor regime crackdowns seem to positively or negatively affect the outcomes of nonviolent campaigns.

What these results suggest is that domestic mechanisms are the most critical components of the success of nonviolent campaigns. Regime crackdowns often backfire and are therefore not necessarily determinants of campaign failure. While foreign support or international sanctions may have been critical in some cases, there is no general pattern indicating that they are necessary for successful campaign outcomes.

The results are especially striking when compared with the determinants of violent insurgent success (Model 3[b]). Security-force defections and the number of participants are much less important in predicting the success of violent insurgencies. Instead, the presence of a foreign state sponsor is the main determinant of success. For violent insurgencies, neither international sanctions nor violent crackdowns have systematic effects in determining success or failure, though they may matter in individual cases. The presence of a foreign state sponsor increases the likelihood of success by about 15 percent, controlling for other factors.

WHEN VIOLENT CAMPAIGNS SUCCEED: SOME KEY OUTLIERS

It is worth noting that there are some important deviations from our assumption that violent campaigns attract only limited numbers of participants. The Russian Revolution (1917), Chinese Revolution (1946–1950), Algerian Revolution (1954–1962), Cuban Revolution (1953–1959), and Vietnamese Revolution (1959–1975) come to mind as major examples of violent conflicts that did generate mass support sufficient to bring about revolutionary change. Such cases are key outliers to the argument that nonviolent campaigns are likelier than violent campaigns to galvanize mass participation.

Upon examining the revolutions, however, it is clear that many of the features common to successful nonviolent campaigns occurred in these revolutions, especially diverse, mass mobilization, which led to loyalty shifts within the ruling regimes' economic and military elites. They also often had direct material support from foreign states. These and other successful armed campaigns typically succeeded both in achieving the direct support of foreign sponsors and in building a strong base of popular support while creating parallel administrative, political, social, and economic structures.[39]

The importance placed on mass mobilization and civilian noncooperation by scholars and theorists of revolutionary warfare suggests that the nonviolent components of successful armed campaigns are as significant—or possibly even more significant—than the military component.

We do not dispute, therefore, that violent insurgencies succeed. In fact, about 25 percent of the cases in our data set have succeeded. But violent insurgencies succeed at much lower rates than civil resistance campaigns, and one must consider the consequences of such victories, as we do in chapter 8. Although violent insurgencies captured power in some cases, the human costs were very high, with millions of casualties. Moreover, the conditions in these countries after the conflict ended have been overwhelmingly more repressive than in transitions driven by nonviolent civic pressure. In all five cases, the new regimes featuring the victorious insurgents were harsh toward civilian populations after the dust had settled, with retaliatory violence targeting supporters of the former regime and lack of respect for human rights and minority rights being the norm. None of these countries could be classified today as democratic.

Such trends are not limited to these five cases. In a recent study of sixty-seven regime transitions between 1973 and 2000, Ackerman and Karatnycky find that among the twenty cases where opposition or state violence occurred, only four (20 percent) qualified as "free" (according to 2005 Freedom House criteria) at the time of the study (2005, 19). On the other hand, among forty cases where the major forces pushing the transition were nonviolent civic coalitions, thirty-two (80 percent) were classified as "free" at the time of the study (2005, 19).

There are some clear theoretical reasons why successful nonviolent resistance leads to fewer civilian casualties and higher levels of democracy after the conflict than does successful violent resistance. Victorious violent insurgents often feel compelled to reestablish the monopoly on the use of force and therefore seek to purge any remaining elements of the state. Although they may seek to establish a democratic order, doing so will be difficult under circumstances of constant violent threat from regime holdovers. Even if the violent insurgency enjoyed mass support, the new state led by the former insurgents will quickly attempt to consolidate its power and remove the ability of the masses to rise up against it. Because the insurgents used violent methods to succeed in gaining power, there will be fewer inhibitions against the use of violent methods to maintain power. Indeed, the capacity to do so may only increase. Therefore, although violent insurgency sometimes works, the long-term consequences leave much to be desired.

As for nonviolent campaigns that succeed, it is likely that these successes will become reference points for those particular societies, and nonviolent resistance will be regarded as an effective method of transforming conflicts. This does not suggest that such states will become pacifist states or that serious human rights violations will never occur, but rather that the shift from noninstitutional to institutional types of nonviolent means of dealing with dissent will be easier, even when normal channels for resolving conflicts are blocked, ineffective, or in the hands of a hostile party.[40] At the same time, the way in which nonviolent resistance tends to decentralize power in society leads to a greater ability of the population to hold elites accountable.[41] Scholars have long noted the positive impacts that a vibrant civil society can have on the quality of democracy (Putnam 1993). Opposition leaders that come to power via nonviolent resistance may feel the need to deliver public goods to the masses given that failure to respond to public demands may result in yet another ouster. In these ways, mass participation and mobilization through nonviolent action may contribute to a greater sense of trust and accountability when the conflict is over.

CONCLUSION

The primary aims of this chapter have been twofold. First, we argue that nonviolent resistance campaigns have been more successful at achieving higher and more diverse participation than violent insurgencies. Domestic mobilization is a more reliable source of power than foreign sponsorship, which most violent insurgencies must seek to pursue their ends. Second, we argue that large-scale participation often translates into tactical and strategic advantages, as the mass withdrawal of cooperation forces the regime to capitulate to the campaign's demands. The ability of nonviolent campaigns to mobilize a higher number of participants with a more diverse array of skills, abilities, and perspectives explains why they have been so successful at activating local mechanisms of change in their societies, including shifts in loyalty from the regime to the resistance and the ability to make regime repression backfire. The historic tendency of nonviolent movements to effectively compel regime loyalists to their side underscores the primacy of participation in generating the mechanisms that determine campaign victory or defeat.

CHAPTER THREE EXPLORING ALTERNATIVE EXPLANATIONS FOR THE SUCCESS OF CIVIL RESISTANCE

Nothing succeeds like success.
ALEXANDRE DUMAS

Circumstances are beyond human control, but our conduct is in our own power.
BENJAMIN DISRAELI

IN THE PREVIOUS CHAPTER, we argued that nonviolent resistance is consistently more effective than violent resistance because of lower barriers to active participation and the ability of nonviolent campaigns to maneuver more effective mechanisms of leverage against the regime opponent. The empirical record raises multiple related questions: First, are there other explanations, such as features of the political environment or the regime opponent, for why these campaigns are succeeding? Second, are there types of opponents against which campaigns are likelier to succeed, and, if so, are nonviolent campaigns more successful because they systematically target such opponents? Third, do violent campaigns emerge where success is highly unlikely, thus explaining their higher rates of failure?

This chapter responds to two potential critiques of our argument. The first is that structural conditions, like the relative power of the opponent or whether the opponent is a democracy or authoritarian regime, dictate the outcomes of campaigns irrespective of the type of resistance used. Our study accounts for this possibility by exploring whether regime features (regime type and government capacity), the regime's use of violent repression, or factors unique to a region or time may explain the outcomes of violent or nonviolent conflicts. The evidence suggests that civil resistance is often successful regardless of environmental conditions that many people associate with the failure of nonviolent campaigns.

The second critique is that the relationship between civil resistance and success is endogenous. Endogeneity occurs when the conditions that determine the main independent variable also determine the outcome of interest. A concrete example is the apparent relationship between nuclear weapons and international conflict. Some scholars hypothesize that states with nuclear weapons tend to engage in more wars than states without nuclear weapons (Jervis 1984; Sagan 1989). Pakistan and India, for instance, came close to major war during the 1999 Kargil conflict even after both countries had tested nuclear weapons in 1998. On the surface, one might conclude that nuclear weapons cause conflict, because of the potential for accidents, overconfidence, and belligerence among members of the nuclear club. Recent scholarship, however, shows the relationship to be endogenous: most states that seek nuclear weapons do so because they already feel threatened by their environments and seek nuclear weapons because they feel that war is likely (Gartzke and Jo 2009). So the nuclear weapons are not the causes of conflict, they are symptoms of a threat environment already predisposed to war. This certainly makes sense in the Pakistan-India relationship, where territorial disputes erupted into major war in 1947, 1965, and 1971, before India and Pakistan had tested their first nuclear bombs.

Our findings would be endogenous if nonviolent resistance proved to be the *symptom* of a high probability of campaign success rather than the *cause* of success, or that the conditions that motivate the choice to use violent resistance are the same conditions that predict campaign failure. Responding to the endogeneity problem is necessarily tricky, because we need to untangle whether violent resistance is actually causing failure, or whether it is just correlated to failure because of external conditions that have made civil resistance impossible and success unlikely. We walk through some illustrative examples that indicate that nonviolent resistance does not necessarily emerge where success is already likely, and that major violent and nonviolent campaigns emerge in analogous circumstances. We then use an instrumental variable approach with several estimation procedures to test for endogeneity. The results make us optimistic that our findings about the relative failure of violent campaigns are not driven by endogeneity.

TESTING STRUCTURAL EXPLANATIONS FOR SUCCESS

In chapter 2 we described the processes under which nonviolent campaigns succeed—through mass mobilization and disruptive activities that raise the costs of the status quo and divide the opponent from its most crucial pillars of support, notably its security forces. We found that domestic factors, such as mobilization and regime loyalty shifts, are crucial to the success of nonviolent campaigns, whereas international factors, such as sponsorship by a foreign regime, improve the chances of success for violent resistance campaigns.[1] But these relationships could emerge for a number of different reasons, and multivariate analysis is required to tease them out.

We are not the first to attempt such an investigation. One recent study has found that contrary to what one might assume, factors such as regime type, level of economic development, literacy rate, or fractionalization of society along ethnic, linguistic, and religious lines have not had a statistically significant impact on the ability of a civic movement to achieve success through civil resistance campaigns (Marchant et al. 2008). The major implication of these findings is that seemingly hopeless conditions can change as a result of skillful resistance, though conditions may shape strategic choices, as the relationship between state and opposition is iterative. By this we mean that they engage in a tit-for-tat interaction, so each side is responding to the actions of the other.

Within the social movement, contentious politics, and conflict literatures, widespread consensus exists that political actors' choices are constrained by their environments. That is, certain structural factors make success more or less likely. These same factors can also make certain types of political activity more or less difficult, thus reducing or increasing mobilization or causing political actors to substitute one type of activity (violent resistance) for the other (nonviolent resistance) when those conditions change. We return to the latter problem later in this chapter, but first we examine the structural conditions that could affect conflict outcomes.

Political-opportunity approaches argue that movements will succeed and fail based on the opening and closing of opportunities created by the political structure. Two categories of structural conditions are salient: features of the political system that make success more or less likely and regime responses to the resistance. First, regime type (democracy or nondemocracy) is often cited as a critical variable in determining whether a challenge group will succeed or fail. Some argue, for instance, that democratic polities are prone to violent challengers since they have historically conceded to insurgents rather than engage in unpopular counterinsurgency operations (Downes 2009; Merom 2003). Because democracies are more sensitive to domestic and international public opinion and more observant of international norms, they may be easier to coerce than nondemocracies (Merom 2003; Pape 2005). We also examine the material capabilities available to the regime, as the most powerful states in the system may be more immune from defeat.

Second, we must address the question of regime repression in more detail. Regime repression is not as much a structural condition as a choice. But skeptics may argue that violent repression can easily thwart civil resistance given the vulnerability of unarmed protestors, whereas violent resistance may be more resilient against repression. Without question, this has sometimes been the case. Furthermore, the anticipation of extreme repression has likely convinced some insurgents to choose violence before even attempting civil resistance.

Regime counterresponses need not determine the outcomes of resistance campaigns, however. While economically and militarily superior opponents are often presumed to have an upper hand against opponents with inferior weapons, scholars of asymmetrical warfare, insurgency, and counterinsurgency have sought to explain how and the conditions under which weaker parties sometimes achieve victory over stronger opponents. Ivan Arreguín-Toft argues that the interaction of the strategies employed by the different sides engaged in asymmetrical conflict—as opposed to the relative power between the two sides—is the decisive variable in determining outcome (2001, 2005). Whereas states with extensive security forces and a large population "excel at defeating weak ones in conventional, direct fights, they fare less well in guerilla, indirect fights . . . By contrast, Mao's victory in China made 'revolutionary warfare' seem the ideal style of warfare for small powers" (2007, 2). Arreguín-Toft cites the French attempt to reestablish control of Indochina, the U.S war against the Vietcong, and the Soviet experience in Afghanistan as examples of how insurgents succeeded using unconventional, indirect strategies (2007).

Although Arreguín-Toft's empirical findings are limited to wars between states and armed challengers, he acknowledges that his strategic interaction theory may remain valid when used to explain outcomes of asymmetrical conflicts pitting states against unarmed, nonviolent challenge groups (2005). Like successful armed insurgencies, successful nonviolent insurgencies are able to challenge their more advanced adversaries with indirect strategies, using unconventional means (boycotts, strikes, protests, noncooperation, and so forth) to target and erode their adversaries' critical pillars of political, social, economic, and military support.

In sum, the structure of the political environment necessarily shapes and constrains the perceptions of resistance leaders; at the same time, the actions of resistance movements will often have distinguishable and independent effects on the structure of the system. This approach follows from a number of recent works in security studies and the social movement literature (Arreguín-Toft 2005; Schock 2005; Weinstein 2007; Wood 2000, 2003). While the applicability of the strategic interaction thesis to asymmetrical contests pitting states against unarmed populations makes intuitive sense, it is nevertheless important to contend with the structural perspective. As such, this chapter probes whether the aforementioned structural conditions have systematic effects on the outcomes of these campaigns.

While we do not dispute that structural conditions affect the range of options available to resistance campaigns, including whether traditional political and economic institutions are accessible to opposition groups, we make the case that voluntaristic features of campaigns, notably those related to the mechanisms put into effect by the resistors, are better predictors of success than structural determinants.

DIFFICULT OPPONENTS?

The literature on contentious politics identifies several structures that should make successful mobilization difficult: an authoritarian opponent, an extremely powerful opponent with abundant resources, and a repressive opponent. We explore how these three structural conditions could affect the likelihood of success.[2]

Authoritarian Opponents

Opponents with few constraints on their actions should be more likely to defeat insurgencies. Authoritarian regimes are thought to be less constrained by domestic electoral incentives, international commitments to respect human rights, or domestic institutional barriers that commonly exist in democracies. Conversely, scholars assume that democracies are more constrained by institutional, electoral, and normative barriers to harsh counterinsurgency methods (Merom 2003), although this assumption is sometimes contested (Downes 2008). Thus, one might expect nonviolent campaigns to emerge where they are most likely to succeed—in democratic regimes that are open to different forms of contestation and whose executives are obligated against using severe forms of repression.

In figure 3.1, however, it is clear that most nonviolent campaigns have emerged in precisely the opposite conditions. The vast majority of nonviolent campaigns have emerged in authoritarian regimes (where the polity score is -10 through 0), where even peaceful opposition against the government may have fatal consequences.

We find, moreover, that even when we control for the target regime type, nonviolent resistance remains significant in improving the odds of success (Model 1). The number of campaign participants, which we've identified as a key driver of success, also remains significant, increasing the likelihood of success by about 10 percent, controlling for other factors. Therefore, whether

FIGURE 3.1 **PERCENTAGE OF CAMPAIGNS BY LOCATION'S POLITY SCORE**

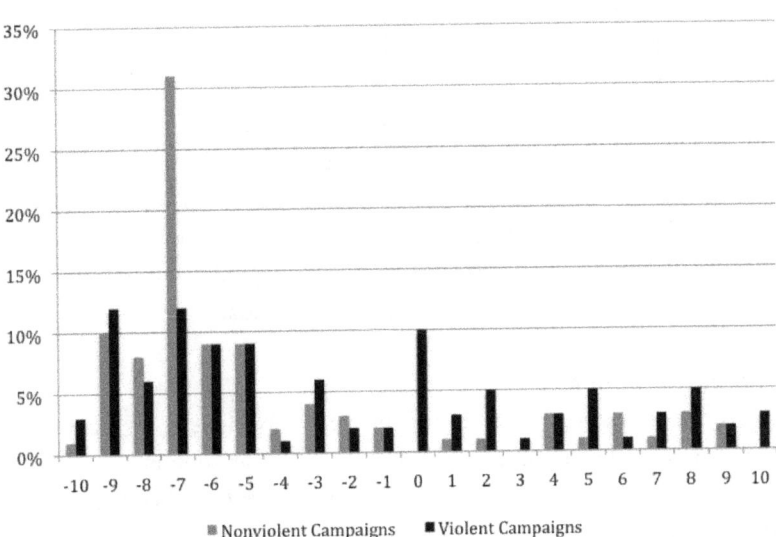

the opponent is democratic or nondemocratic seems to matter little with regard to the success of nonviolent campaigns.

Powerful Opponents

As Arreguín-Toft notes, a core tenet of international relations theory is that power implies victory in conflict (2001, 96). Following this logic, powerful states should be more impervious to challenge—particularly from unarmed opponents—than weak states. We consider two possibilities, that nonviolent campaigns are more likely to emerge in weaker states and that states with access to a large number of resources are more likely to defeat nonviolent or violent campaigns.

We measure a country's capabilities using an oft-used measure of power in international relations scholarship, the Correlates of War's Composite Index of National Capabilities (CINC), which contains annual values for total population, urban population, iron and steel production, energy consumption, military personnel, and military expenditure.[3]

We find, that the power of the state in question does not determine whether a campaign that emerges is nonviolent or violent. Most notably, nonviolent campaigns emerge in some of the most objectively powerful states in the world. Consider figure 3.2, which clearly shows that nonviolent campaigns are equally likely to emerge in the most powerful countries as in the weakest states. Moreover, they emerge in roughly equal probability to violent campaigns, regardless of the objective power available to the country in which they emerge.

Interestingly, we also find no relationship between the target's capabilities and the probability of success, although the effects of civil resistance remain robust (Model 2), with nonviolent campaigns over 12 percent likelier to succeed than violent campaigns, holding other variables at their means. Nonviolent resistance continues to be effective regardless of how powerful the opponent state is according to the CINC criteria.[4]

Repressive Opponents

Many scholars have found that regime crackdowns lead to increases in mobilization, whereas other scholars have found variation in the effects of repression on mobilization (Bob and Nepstad 2007; Francisco 2004; Koopmans 1993; Rasler 1996). But they have not explored the possibility that the broader population's tolerance of government crackdowns may depend on whether the resistance campaign is nonviolent or violent, as repressing nonviolent campaigns may backfire. Backfiring occurs when an unjust act—often violent repression—recoils against its originators, leading to power shifts by increasing the internal solidarity of the resistance campaign, creating dissent and conflicts among the opponent's supporters, increasing external support for the resistance campaign, and decreasing external support for the opponent (Martin 2007). For these reasons, the internal and external costs of repressing nonviolent campaigns may be higher than the costs of repressing violent campaigns, where regimes can offer self-defense and public security considerations to justify the crackdowns. Thus, we argue that an opponent's violence is more likely to backfire when a campaign remains nonviolent despite repression, and when a campaign's commitment to nonviolent means is communicated to internal and external audiences.

In Model 3, we do find that violent regime repression reduces the likelihood of campaign success by nearly 35 percent. But we also show that even controlling for violent repression, nonviolent resistance is still considerably more effective than violent resistance, further reinforcing the evidence that repression is more likely to backfire when used against nonviolent campaigns. So even though a high level of repression can be a formidable obstacle to the success of violent and nonviolent resistance campaigns, we contend that repression does not in and of itself determine the outcome of the campaign.

In sum, the evidence presented in this section suggests that civil resistance can be more effective than violent resistance, regardless of circumstances commonly thought to condition the probability of success. In the following section, we consider how campaign goals might affect the outcomes of nonviolent campaigns.

DIFFICULT GOALS?

Some types of campaign goals may be less conducive to campaign success than others. In particular, campaigns with goals that are perceived as maximalist (fundamentally altering the political order) may be less likely to succeed than goals perceived as more limited in nature (e.g., finite political rights).

In this book, we deliberately choose campaigns with goals commonly perceived to be maximalist in nature: regime change, antioccupation, and secession.[5] In all three categories, regime opponents must make concessions that fundamentally alter the political order or the nature of the state concerned.

Among these three categories, secession campaigns should be the most difficult for insurgents to win. Multiple scholars have identified that secessionist conflicts are unique compared with other types of conflicts (Bartkus 1999; Coggins 2004; Englebert and Hummel 2005; Fuhrmann and Tir 2009; Heraclides 1990; Horowitz 1981; Seymour, 2006). The stakes for governments are high because of the military, political, and reputational costs of losing large sections of their territories. The stakes for insurgents are also high because such conflicts typically involve issues of ethnic identity (Toft 2003) and control over resources. With regard to their success, Donald Horowitz has hypothesized that the outcomes of secession campaigns are "determined largely by international politics, by the balance of interests and forces that extend beyond the state"—factors largely out of the campaigns' control (2000, 230).

Distinguishing antioccupation and secession campaigns was difficult and required us to make several judgment calls. We ultimately decided that antioccupation campaigns meet several important criteria: either the opponent is a foreign power that is not proximate to the territory where the self-determination claim is made (e.g., anticolonial campaigns in Africa), the opponent is annexing the territory (e.g., the Indian annexation of Hyderabad),

TABLE 3.1 THE EFFECTS OF STRUCTURAL FACTORS ON CAMPAIGN OUTCOMES

	MODEL 1	MODEL 2[a]	MODEL 3[a]	MODEL 4	MODEL 5	MODEL 6	MODEL 7	MODEL 8[a]
NONVIOLENT CAMPAIGN	.90* (.48)	.52*** (.43)	.43*** (.43)	1.08*** (.25)	1.26*** (.26)	1.08*** (.28)	.96* (.53)	.43*** (.68)
TARGET POLITY SCORE	.05 (.03)						.00 (.03)	.03 (.04)
NUMBER OF PARTICIPANTS, LOGGED	.38*** (.13)	-.41*** (.12)	.44*** (.13)				.39*** (.12)	.52*** (.17)
POPULATION, LOGGED	-.44** (.17)	-.44*** (.15)	-.42** (.18)				-.46*** (.18)	-.44** (.21)
TARGET CAPABILITIES		3.45 (5.10)					1.63 (5.64)	3.88 (7.52)
VIOLENT REGIME REPRESSION			-1.44** (.64)				-1.78*** (.62)	-2.77*** (.98)
SECESSIONIST CAMPAIGN				-1.03 (.64)			.39 (1.34)	-.34 (1.35)
ANTI-OCCUPATION CAMPAIGN				.59 (.54)			2.69* (1.41)	2.26* (1.23)
REGIME CHANGE CAMPAIGN				.57 (.44)			1.19 (1.01)	.30 (.98)
AMERICAS					.04 (.32)			.40 (.66)
ASIA					-.76** (.35)			-1.04* (.59)
FORMER SOVIET UNION					-.26 (.41)			-.88 (1.05)
EUROPE					-.56 (.39)			.44 (.85)
MIDDLE EAST					-1.02* (.53)			-2.58*** (.74)
AFRICA					(REFERENCE)			(REFERENCE)
1900-1909						-1.56 (1.15)		--
1910-1919						-.40 (.97)		--
1920-1929						-.75 (.58)		--

	(1)	(2)	(3)	(4)	(5)	(6)	(7)
1930-1939						-.48 (.65)	--
1940-1949						.14 (.66)	--
1950-1959						.04 (.63)	-1.30 (1.10)
1960-1969						-.24 (.61)	-1.62* (.89)
1970-1979						.46 (.51)	.80 (.70)
1980-1989						.18 (.39)	.73 (.78)
1990-1999						(REFERENCE)	(REFERENCE)
2000-2006						.08 (.39)	.77 (1.32)
CONSTANT	-.11 (1.54)	-.47 (1.50)	.57 (1.61)	-1.43*** (.42)	-.71*** (.24)	-1.00*** (.31)	.75 (2.20)
N	141	153	163	323	323	323	134
CHI²	23.05	25.87	26.21	30.31	34.60	38.99	56.56
PROB > CHI²	.0001	.0000	.0000	.0000	.0000	.0001	.0000
PSEUDO R²	.1627	.1438	.1682	.0900	.0832	.0790	.3376

SIGNIFICANCE LEVELS: ***p<.01; **p<.05; *p<.1; LOGISTIC REGRESSIONS WITH ROBUST STANDARD ERRORS CLUSTERED AROUND TARGET COUNTRY CODE.
§ NONVIOLENT RESISTANCE AND LOGGED PARTICIPANTS ARE JOINTLY SIGNIFICANT AT P = .000.

FIGURE 3.2 **PERCENTAGE OF CAMPAIGNS BY LOCATION'S RELATIVE POWER**

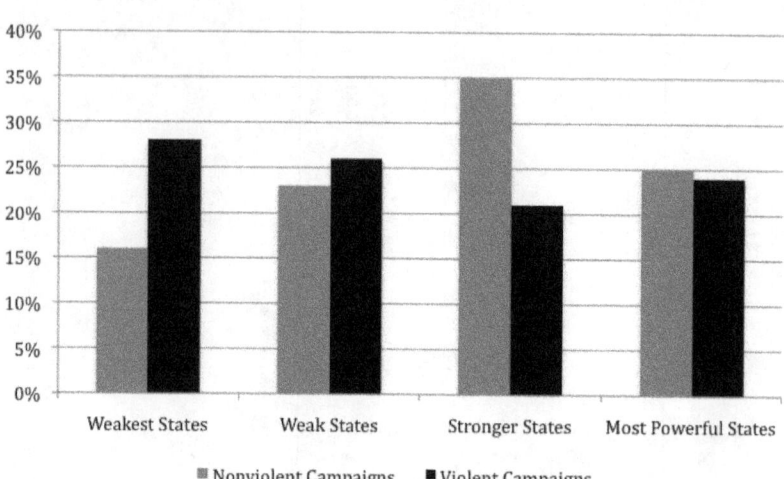

or the territory in question is internationally recognized as independent of the target state (e.g., the Palestinian Territories).

Secession campaigns are those self-determination campaigns where a portion of the contiguous state is seeking separation. The territory is internationally recognized as part of the target state. Thus the Chechen struggle against Russia, the Tigrean Liberation movement against Ethiopia, and the Tamil independence movement against Sri Lanka all fall under the category of local self-determination campaigns, called secession campaigns here for simplicity.

If campaigns' objectives account for their success, we should expect to see the effects of nonviolent resistance become insignificant when we control for the campaign objective. Instead, in Model 4, the effects of nonviolent resistance remain positive and significant, while none of the variables for campaign objective are significant. Thus, the campaign goal does not significantly influence the effectiveness of a nonviolent campaign.

When we create separate samples based on each campaign objective, however, the results begin to change. Table 3.2 demonstrates how nonviolent resistance affects the probability of partial[6] and full success by campaign objective. Indeed, as table 3.2 reports, among 312 campaigns, nonviolent re-

TABLE 3.2 **DISTRIBUTION OF VIOLENT AND NONVIOLENT CAMPAIGN OUTCOMES BY CAMPAIGN OBJECTIVE**

	REGIME CHANGE		ANTI-OCCUPATION		SECESSION	
	VIOLENT	NONVIOLENT	VIOLENT	NONVIOLENT	VIOLENT	NONVIOLENT
FAILURE	61%	17%	54%	24%	68%	100%
LIMITED SUCCESS	12%	24%	10%	41%	22%	0%
SUCCESS	27%	59%	36%	35%	10%	0%
N	111	81	59	17	41	4
PEARSON CHI²	37.06***		9.73***		1.78	

SIGNIFICANCE LEVELS: ***P<.01; **P<.05; *P<.1.

sistance methods have been more than twice as effective in achieving limited and full success among antiregime campaigns.[7] Nonviolent and violent resistance campaigns have the same rates of full success in antioccupation campaigns, but the use of nonviolent resistance makes partial success (i.e., autonomy or power sharing) more likely. In the case of antiregime or antioccupation resistance campaigns, we can see that the use of a nonviolent strategy enhances the likelihood of success.

With secessionist campaigns, however, nonviolent resistance appears to have a negative effect on the likelihood of success, with all four campaigns failing. When we look closer at the data, however, we can see that violent secessionist campaigns are also extremely likely to fail. Whereas no nonviolent secession campaigns were successful, only four of the forty-one violent secession campaigns succeeded.

The implication of these findings is that campaigns that seek secession are highly unlikely to succeed regardless of whether they employ nonviolent or violent tactics. Thus we find the pattern of failure among secessionist campaigns no major obstacle to our argument that nonviolent campaigns are, in general, more effective than violent campaigns in contexts where either type of resistance has the potential to succeed.

DIFFICULT TIMES AND PLACES?

We consider two other conditions that may affect the outcomes of campaigns: region of the world and time.

First, one might suspect that nonviolent campaigns would be more successful in Europe, the former Soviet Union, and the Americas, where societies are perceived to be more tolerant of nonviolent forms of contention (Tarrow and Petrova 2007). We compare the rates of success of violent and nonviolent campaigns in Africa, the Americas, Asia, Europe, the former Soviet Union, and the Middle East (fig. 3.3).

Nonviolent campaigns tend to succeed more often than violent campaigns in all regions of the world. They have been the most successful in the former Soviet Union and the Americas, and they have been the least successful in the Middle East and Asia. Violent campaigns, on the other hand, have had the most success in Africa and have been more likely to fail in the former Soviet Union and the Middle East. They are about equally likely to succeed in the Americas, Asia, and Europe.

When we control for regional effects on the outcomes of campaigns (Model 5 in table 3.1), the effect of nonviolent resistance remains robust. Overall, resistance campaigns are less likely to succeed in Asia and the Middle East relative to the other world regions, although events since 2006 may suggest a shift in this finding. These results suggest that even when controlling for regional effects, nonviolent campaigns are more effective than violent campaigns.

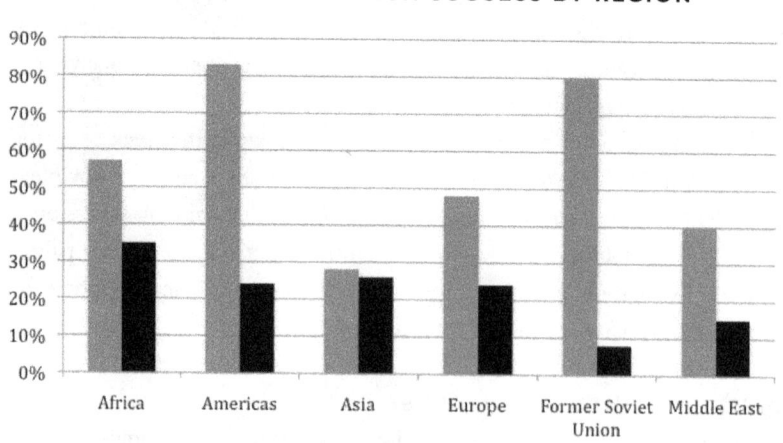

FIGURE 3.3 **RATES OF CAMPAIGN SUCCESS BY REGION**

Finally, one might expect that nonviolent campaigns would be most likely to succeed during certain times, such as the end of the Cold War. The collapse of the Soviet Union and democratic revolutions that took place around the world could be associated with a higher incidence of success because of an overrepresentation of successful nonviolent campaigns during this period.

When we look at variations in campaign success across decades, however, we find little support for this expectation (Model 6 in table 3.1). In fact, both nonviolent and violent campaigns have had an equal probability of success throughout each decade of the twentieth century relative to the 1990s. Although there is a slight increase in success rates over time, the effect is not statistically significant. In general, therefore, global changes occurring during specific times have not significantly altered the outcomes of the campaigns in a systematic way.[8]

The final results in table 3.1 present unified models, one that includes all the variables that deal with difficult opponents and difficult goals (Model 7) and another that includes all these variables plus the regional and time dummies (Model 8). We find that nonviolent resistance and participation are always positively correlated with success, even when controlling for a variety of factors. We also find that violent regime repression consistently reduces the probability of success although nonviolent campaigns fare better than violent campaigns under repressive conditions, and that campaigns in Asia and the Middle East are less likely to succeed through 2006 than campaigns in other regions.

Taken together, the evidence presented here is suggestive of a fairly robust relationship between nonviolent resistance and campaign success, even when controlling for structural or environmental factors that might condition the outcomes of the campaign. We can remain fairly confident that the results presented in chapter 2 are robust regardless of whether the regime is democratic or authoritarian, powerful or weak, or violently repressive toward the campaign. Moreover, the results do not significantly change when we examine the relationship between nonviolent campaigns and outcomes over time and space; while some world regions demonstrate higher propensities for failure through 2006, the effect of civil resistance remains robust.

On the surface, therefore, it appears that nonviolent campaigns can succeed under even the direst of circumstances. Next we consider whether these results hold even when we take into account other factors that might make groups choose nonviolent resistance in the first place.

DO NONVIOLENT CAMPAIGNS EMERGE ONLY WHERE VICTORY IS LIKELY?

We next consider the possibility that the outcomes of nonviolent campaigns are endogenous to the conditions under which they emerge. Regarding our study, concerns about endogeneity may take several forms. First is the possibility that nonviolent campaigns succeed so often because they emerge when the regime has shown its vulnerability or is in the midst of a transition that signals to the opposition that the time is right to go on the offensive. If this were true, nonviolent campaigns do not cause change. Rather, a high probability of success makes groups choose nonviolent resistance.

The second related concern is the possibility that violent campaigns are unsuccessful because they emerge under the most difficult circumstances where success is highly unlikely. Thus the choice of resistance method is determined by the situation under which the resistance emerges: if success is judged to be unlikely or other methods have failed, then violent resistance is a choice of last resort—and is by extension a last-gasp effort in an already fruitless situation.

A third and similar concern is that violent campaigns are simply failed nonviolent campaigns, that violent campaigns emerge only after nonviolent resistance has been tried and failed. If this is true, then our data set is not really comparing violent and nonviolent campaigns; it is really comparing successful nonviolent campaigns to unsuccessful nonviolent campaigns, many of which have turned violent *because* they have failed.

Testing for these possibilities is not easy and requires multiple strategies. We have already tested the effects of different environmental factors on the outcomes of success, and we found these factors to be generally insignificant. In the sections that follow, we bolster this evidence first by discussing some illustrative examples to demonstrate why we suspect that, in general, endogeneity is not driving our primary results. Next, we employ several statistical methods that test whether the factors that motivate the choice to use violence are also associated with campaign failure. We find strong evidence to the effect that the factors that determine the choice to use violent resistance are not conditioning our primary findings.

Some Qualitative Evidence: A Few Illustrative Examples

Although evidence is often scarce, we think the concern that endogeneity drives our findings is probably misplaced. First, violent resistance does not always emerge only after major nonviolent resistance has failed. Observers often point to a few key examples, such as the Northern Irish conflict, where extreme government repression "forced" erstwhile peaceful movements to adopt violence (White 1989). Although they may be justified in some cases, in general such claims are dubious. As Walzer writes,

> It is not so easy to reach the last resort. To get there, one must indeed try everything (which is a lot of things)—and not just once, as if a political party or movement might organize a single demonstration, fail to win immediate victory, and claim that it is now justified in moving on to murder. Politics is an art of repetition. Activists learn by doing the same thing over and over again. It is by no means clear when they run out of options . . . What exactly did they try when they were trying everything? (2001, 16)

Besides, almost all major civil resistance campaigns face violent repression. Of those that march on, many maintain their commitments to nonviolent resistance and ultimately succeed. Take, for example, the Serbian student movement Otpor. The Milosevic regime confronted this campaign with considerable repression and intimidation, but the campaign maintained its commitment to nonviolent methods and, ultimately, succeeded.

Contrast this case with the First Intifada, during which Palestinian society mobilized against Israeli occupation. Despite extensive Israeli repression, the campaign maintained its nonviolent character for about eighteen months (see table 5.1). Indeed, the campaign was making substantial progress. It was only when internal fissures overwhelmed the campaign and it spiraled into violence that the campaign lost its effectiveness. The return to violence was unnecessary. And, in this case, the move undermined a succeeding nonviolent campaign that was fighting for the same outcome.

Our second point, though, is that many violent campaigns do not even attempt nonviolent resistance in the early stages of the conflict, opting to use violence from the outset (Abrahms 2008, 84–85). The Sunni insurgency in Iraq, for instance, seemed to select violence immediately, without even considering a mass civil resistance campaign to expel the Coalition occupation or reestablish Sunni hegemony in government.

In fact, even when violent methods have failed to produce meaningful results and opportunities arise to negotiate or pursue political change peacefully, insurgents often continue to toil along in futility (Abrahms 2008, 85–86). For example, although many Palestinians question the ingenuity of the offer, several Palestinian groups responded to Israeli prime minister Ehud Barak's offer of independence for the Gaza Strip and most of the West Bank, which was accompanied by settlement expansion and other provocative Israeli actions, with an unprecedented wave of violence (Abrahms 2008, 86–87). Thus, violence is not always a last resort, nor do insurgents readily discard it when it has proved fruitless.

Third, nonviolent and violent campaigns often coexist, suggesting that in nearly identical situations, distinct groups evaluate the strategic value of resistance methods differently. Consider the Philippines, where the nonviolent People Power campaign emerged while two violent insurgencies were targeting the Marcos regime. Even though these groups faced the same repressive opponent in the same general conditions, one campaign opted for a violent resistance method while the other chose civil resistance. Thus it is variation within the groups—not the opponents they face—that determines whether they choose a nonviolent or violent strategy.

Fourth, nonviolent campaigns may be just as likely to emerge from failed violent campaigns. Consider the East Timorese civil resistance campaign against Indonesian occupation. Early resistance took the form of guerrilla warfare, perpetrated mainly by the armed wing of the Revolutionary Front for an Independent East Timor (Fretilin), which was called the Armed Forces for the National Liberation of East Timor (Falintil). An outgrowth of the Fretilin student movement, called the Clandestine Front, formed during the 1970s. This movement planned and led a series of nonviolent campaigns inside East Timor, in Indonesia, and in foreign capitals starting in 1988. Although Indonesia's counterinsurgency campaign against Falintil was largely successful, the Clandestine Front eventually morphed into a widespread civil resistance campaign. With branches inside East Timor and Indonesia, the Clandestine Front developed a large decentralized network of activists who relied on various nonviolent tactics to expose Indonesian brutality and win supporters inside Indonesia and internationally (Stephan and Chenoweth 2008, 27). The nonviolent campaign was ultimately successful in achieving independence from Indonesia after decades of futile violent insurgency.

Finally, one might argue that we may have simply overlooked many nonviolent campaigns because they were unreported or overshadowed by subsequent violent phases. Perhaps insurgents did attempt to use nonviolent methods, but these attempts were crushed by the regime and were never recorded. There are situations such as this in our data set, like the Defiance Campaign in South Africa, a nonviolent antiapartheid campaign in the 1950s and 1960s. After brutal suppression, this campaign abandoned nonviolent methods (and is thus coded as a failure in our data set) and became what many observers would call a terrorist group. But what if we missed many similar cases because of underreporting?

Especially for the latter half of the twentieth century, we find it unlikely that we missed many major nonviolent campaigns, but for a moment we will imagine that half of the violent campaigns in our data set (146) are really failed (albeit unobserved) nonviolent campaigns. Even if we recode these 146 cases as failed nonviolent campaigns, the success rates of nonviolent resistance remain striking (about 25 percent), equal to or higher than the success rates of violent campaigns. There is no credible claim that violent resistance is necessary if nonviolent campaigns succeed in equal measure even under the most skeptical interpretation of the data.

Testing for Endogeneity: A Large-N Assessment

The problem with these illustrative examples is just that—they are only a few illustrative examples. To determine whether endogeneity is driving our results requires an analysis of the entire data set using a statistical method that can test for endogeneity. To do this, we construct an instrument for the choice of a violent resistance method. We then use the instrument as a substitute for our main explanatory variable in two separate models: a two-stage simultaneous equations model and a simple model that performs the endogeneity test automatically.[9] Combined with the evidence presented in the preceding and in the case studies, these tests may help to satisfy concerns about endogeneity.

Instrumental variables are difficult to design because the covariates selected to produce the instrument must be uncorrelated with the outcome (success), uncorrelated with the error term, and strongly correlated with the main explanatory variable. To produce an instrument, we first create a model of the determinants of violent resistance. Based on the literature, we articulate a model of several factors that should condition the choice of violent resistance but are uncorrelated with failure.

When observers perceive resistance to have a low probability of success, because of a powerful opponent or because the campaign's demands are too extreme, skeptics might expect resistance to be violent rather than nonviolent. Thus, when the opponent is very powerful, many scholars would expect a campaign to use violent rather than nonviolent resistance because violent resistance is commonly assumed to be the only way to face such an opponent (Goodwin 2001). Furthermore, where the issue at stake is difficult to achieve, such as secession, one would expect a campaign to resort to violence.[10]

We also include several factors thought to influence the onset of violent civil conflict, including mountainous terrain, ethnic fractionalization, and the presence of simultaneous violent movements or ongoing internal wars. Mountainous terrain is thought to make the onset of a violent insurgency likelier, because of the perception that potential insurgents will be able to evade counterinsurgency operations (Fearon and Laitin 2003). Ethnic fractionalization supposedly increases the probability of violent conflict because of ethnic tensions among groups competing for power in society (Fearon and Laitin 2003; Horowitz 2000). The presence of simultaneous violent movements or ongoing internal conflicts may also increase the perceived necessity of using violence (Bloom 2005; Chenoweth 2006; Collier 2009). Many scholars have also found a strong correlation between poverty and the outbreak of violent internal conflict (Collier 2009), so we include the per capita GDP of the campaign's location in the model.

Where violent resistance is perceived to have a high likelihood of success, one would expect the resort to arms to be likely. Many scholars have argued, for instance, that democracies are more susceptible to successful, violent, nonstate challenges than authoritarian regimes (Merom 2003; Pape 2005). Thus, target-regime type may be an important determinant of the resort to violence. Moreover, where a state is engaged in an interstate war, potential insurgents may view the diversion of troops to a foreign campaign as an opportunity to strike the opponent at home. Therefore, we take into account the potential diversionary effects of war. All these variables are lagged one year behind the onset of the campaign. The online appendix includes more details on how we develop the instrumental variable and conduct the tests.

	EXOGENOUS MODEL	ENDOGENOUS MODEL 1	ENDOGENOUS MODEL 2	ENDOGENOUS MODEL 3
VIOLENT RESISTANCE	-.68*** (.20)	-.81** (.41)	-.77* (.44)	-1.85** (.79)
VIOLENT REGIME REPRESSION	-.58* (.31)	-.52 (.35)	-.14 (.09)	-.30 (.37)
POPULATION, LOGGED	-.17** (.07)	-.10 (.10)	-.46 (.39)	-.19*** (.07)
CONSTANT	2.36*** (.75)	1.64* (.97)	1.89* (1.02)	3.02 (.89)***
N	205	127	127	205
WALD CHI²	17.95	8.14	9.78	17.89
PROB > CHI²	.0004	.0431	.0206	.0005
PSEUDO R²	.0866	.0508	.0580	.0635

SIGNIFICANCE LEVELS: *** P < .01, ** P < .05, * P < .1; LOGISTIC REGRESSION WITH ROBUST STANDARD ERRORS CLUSTERED AROUND TARGET COUNTRY CODE. THE REFERENCE CATEGORY IS AFRICA.

TABLE 3.3 **THE EFFECT OF VIOLENT RESISTANCE ON CAMPAIGN SUCCESS**

If the significance of our main explanatory variable in the exogenous model changes in the endogenous models, we know that the results are most likely due to endogeneity. But the results in table 3.3 tell us that our initial findings hold up to these tests. Model 2 contains the endogeneity model using the two-stage method. Models 3 and 4 report the endogeneity models using the automated test. Model 3 uses the most robust instrument with a smaller number of observations, and Model 4 uses a less-robust instrument with a higher number of observations.[11]

The coefficients change slightly because of different numbers of observations, but violent resistance has a consistently negative and statistically significant effect on success. This tells us that success occurs because of nonviolent resistance itself, not because of other factors that make groups choose nonviolent resistance. Correspondingly, there is no systematic relationship between the places where nonviolent campaigns are most likely to emerge and the places they are most likely to succeed.[12]

Although these results reassure us that endogeneity is not driving our core findings, social science research has yet to develop foolproof techniques to overcome this problem. We combine the results in this chapter with the case studies in part 2 to increase confidence in our findings, but we also recognize that our conclusions require further testing.

CONCLUSION

This chapter has identified and responded to two groups of critiques that could challenge the results presented in chapter 2: first, that campaign outcomes are functions of structural circumstances rather than the strategic advantages of nonviolent resistance, and second, that the relationship between resistance type and outcome is endogenous to factors that predict *both* resistance type *and* campaign outcome. We have provided evidence to the effect that structural factors and endogeneity do not systematically condition our findings, although further investigation is required. Rather, the findings presented in chapter 2 are robust even under the most difficult of circumstances, during difficult times, in difficult places.

We do acknowledge that extreme regime brutality, regime economic domination, and sophisticated population control through harassment and intimidation are formidable obstacles to mobilization. Under these conditions subtle acts of defiance and clandestine activities are more prevalent—and, by definition, less observable. But our main point is that regimes (like opposition movements) are not monolithic actors; rather, they are propped up by pillars made up of individuals whose loyalties are malleable and shifting. Whichever side (regime or opposition) is able to divide the opponent from its main pillars of support will ultimately succeed. And nonviolent campaigns have historically had an advantage over violent campaigns in this regard.

In support of this conclusion, we have suggested that the strategies employed by the challenge group, and the strategic interaction between the regime and the campaign (violent and nonviolent), are more decisive determinants of asymmetrical conflict outcomes than structural factors. Meanwhile, we have identified key variables contributing to the relative strategic effectiveness of civil resistance compared to armed struggle in this and the previous chapters. These include lower barriers to active participation in nonviolent resistance, the disruptive effects of mass nonviolent noncooperation, and the increased likelihood of backfiring and loyalty shifts during nonviolent campaigns. Next, we turn to in-depth studies of four countries that have experienced nonviolent and violent campaigns to explore how these dynamics unfolded in these cases.

PART TWO
Case Studies

INTRODUCTION TO THE CASE STUDIES

In part 2, we compare the dynamics and outcomes of civil resistance campaigns in the Middle East (Iran and the Palestinian Territories) and Southeast Asia (the Philippines and Burma). Our main focus in this part is to consider why nonviolent campaigns succeed and fail, although we also briefly compare nonviolent and violent campaigns in each case.

We chose these cases for four major reasons. First, these cases contain variation on the dependent variable, which is campaign success. Among the four cases, we have two successes (Iran and the Philippines), one partial success (Palestinian Territories), and one failure (Burma) of civil resistance. This allows us to compare the conditions under which nonviolent campaigns succeed across cases, which further allows us to form some generalizations that are broader than a single case. Moreover, the cases where nonviolent campaigns were unsuccessful can be treated as opportunities to identify whether mischaracterized or omitted variables can help to explain why the outcome is different than expected (Lieberman 2005).

Second, the cases provide considerable variation in the independent variables. In particular, in chapter 2, we found that nonviolent campaigns are more likely to attract larger numbers of participants, increase the diversity of tactics brought to bear against the opponent while raising the costs of

TABLE II.A **CASE SELECTION**

	CHAPTER 4 IRANIAN REVOLUTION	CHAPTER 5 FIRST PALESTINIAN INTIFADA	CHAPTER 6 PHILIPPINE PEOPLE POWER REVOLUTION	CHAPTER 7 BURMESE REVOLUTION
NONVIOLENT CAMPAIGN	SUCCESS	PARTIAL SUCCESS	SUCCESS	FAILURE
VIOLENT CAMPAIGN	FAILURE	FAILURE	FAILURE	FAILURE

the status quo, create divisions within the regime, and lead to backfiring when the regime cracks down, but these mechanisms vary across cases. We determine whether these mechanisms are in place by using process tracing, and we rely primarily on secondary sources to glean this evidence (George and Bennett 2005). Some of the information is based on interviews with campaign activists conducted by Maria Stephan, which allow us to get a better sense of the dynamics at play.

Third, each case features asymmetrical conflicts pitting nonstate actors against militarily superior opponents. All cases feature periods of both violent and nonviolent resistance against repressive regimes and foreign occupations but with varying degrees of success. Selecting cases that contain both nonviolent and violent campaigns allows us to employ within-case comparison, thus reducing the confounding effects of other factors that may influence the outcome (Brady and Collier 2004). For example, instead of trying to compare a nonviolent resistance campaign in Serbia with a violent campaign in the Philippines, we compare both types of campaigns in a single country. In this way we avoid trying to compare violent and nonviolent campaigns that occurred in different circumstances that might have affected the outcomes.

Fourth, the cases are intrinsically interesting. Each features nonviolent campaigns that emerged in highly repressive environments, in regions of the world with long histories of authoritarianism and political violence. The Middle East, the least-democratic region of the world, has witnessed a disproportionate amount of wars, insurgencies, terrorism, and foreign interventionism. At the same time, the region has featured some remarkable, albeit understudied, cases of popular nonviolent struggles (Stephan 2010). Southeast Asia is also very important in geopolitics, as it has featured prominently in the current wave of democratization and economic development. Like the Middle East, however, it has often been characterized by undemocratic and repressive regimes, frequently challenged by armed groups within their borders. Also like the Middle East, Southeast Asia contains important examples of civil resistance.

CASE STUDY PROCEDURE

The case studies allow us to develop the argument in several ways. First, they allow for further theory testing. One virtue of case studies is that we can look below the surface of the data to see whether the relationships identified in the statistical section are spurious. The case studies allow us to look at the timing of the different conflict dynamics and the sequencing of the interactions over time. When researching the cases, we ask the following questions:

- Was the nonviolent campaign relatively more successful than the violent campaign?
- Did the nonviolent campaign have greater visible participation than the violent campaign?
- Is there evidence that the nonviolent campaign had lower physical, moral, informational, and commitment barriers to participation than the violent campaign?
- Did defections occur among the security forces? Which campaign (nonviolent or violent) helped to create these defections?
- How did government repression affect the campaign? Did the repression backfire, or did it suppress the campaign?
- Did the campaign receive outside sponsorship from another state? What about nonstate actors like international solidarity groups and diasporas?
- Did any foreign allies of the target regime withdraw their support in solidarity with the resistance?

Second, the case studies allow us to identify additional, omitted variables that we overlooked when constructing the data set. These omitted variables may include complexities in the cases that are difficult to quantify. Throughout the theory section, for instance, we have argued that the quality of campaign membership is as important as the quantity, and that strategic factors can be critically important in determining the outcome of the campaign. Thus we ask the following questions:

- Was the campaign's membership diverse? Did it include a range of people across age, gender, and racial or ethnic groups? Did it include different ideologies, or was it ideologically exclusive? Did the campaign's membership cut across class cleavages and the urban/rural divide?
- Did the campaign's organization (i.e., centralized vs. decentralized, single leader dominated or dispersed leadership) affect the outcome of the campaign or the long-term consequences of the campaign?

- Did the campaign shift between methods of dispersion and methods of concentration, or did it rely on a single method of conflict prosecution?
- If there was no evidence of overt state support for the campaign, were there other types of support that seemed critical in determining the outcome?

These questions, informed by the theory, allow us to explore the strategic interactions of the campaign and the opponent to better capture how the conflict unfolded, a goal that is not possible using statistical analysis with the data in its current form.

Finally, the case studies permit us to consider potential alternative arguments. We deal with some of these arguments with the case selection itself. For example, the within-case study design, which identifies cases where both nonviolent and violent campaigns exist, allows us to dismiss the idea that violent campaigns emerge where nonviolent campaigns cannot (and are thus unlikely to succeed). We consider one question in particular, which is whether the presence of a violent campaign actually helped the nonviolent campaign succeed.

CASE STUDY PLAN

Part 2 proceeds as follows. Chapter 4 discusses the Iranian Revolution (1977–1979) that ousted the Shah. In this case, violent guerrilla challenges to the Shah's undemocratic regime achieved no success, whereas the popular, broad-based nonviolent campaign succeeded. Chapter 5 explains that the First Intifada (1987–1992) achieved unprecedented progress toward Palestinian self-determination through some important Israeli concessions but ultimately failed, in part because of internal strife within the movement and its inability to remain resilient in the face of Israeli repression.

Chapter 6 deals with the successful case of the People Power movement in the Philippines (1983–1986), which forced Ferdinand Marcos from power after violent challengers had failed to do so. Chapter 7, however, identifies a case of failed nonviolent resistance: the Burmese prodemocracy uprising of 1988. Both nonviolent and violent campaigns failed in this case, which provides a useful opportunity for comparison.

In each of these studies, we aim to demonstrate how the lower physical, moral, informational, and commitment barriers of the nonviolent campaigns attracted participants who were reluctant to participate in simultaneous violent campaigns. These cases also illustrate, however, that mass participation can be an insufficient factor for success when unaccompanied by persistent efforts to divide the regime from its main sources of power, maintain unity in the face of regime responses (repression or accommodation), and employ a mix of different tactics in response to regime repression. Thus, the quality of participation matters as much as the quantity of participants.

CHAPTER FOUR **THE IRANIAN REVOLUTION, 1977-1979**[1]

THE 1979 IRANIAN REVOLUTION (also known as the Islamic Revolution) ousted an unpopular monarchy and led to the installation of an Islamic republic following an intense period of mass mobilization and collective civil disobedience.[2] Earlier attempts to depose Shah Reza Pahlavi's regime through assassinations and guerrilla warfare were unable to achieve what mass-based protests, strikes, stay-aways, and noncooperation achieved in less than one year. Whereas the Shah's security apparatus infiltrated and decimated main guerrilla groups in the 1970s, the civil resistance that began in earnest in late 1977 exerted significant pressure on the monarchy and became impossible to contain or suppress. The sustained pressure exerted by Iranian workers, students, professionals, clerics, and other segments of Iranian society, even in the midst of harsh regime repression, divided the regime from its most important pillars of support. The popular uprising neutralized the Shah's security apparatus. On February 11, 1979, when the Iranian Armed Forces Joint Staff declared that the Iranian military would "remain neutral" in disputes between the Shah's regime and the nation, the final page had been turned on the monarchy.

THE LEAD-UP TO A REVOLUTION
The Iranian Revolution was as much a surprise to many around the world as the rapid demise of the Eastern European communist regimes a decade later. Scholars have long puzzled over the question of how a seemingly stable neopatrimonial dictatorship, whose regime was a central pillar in a superpower's Cold War foreign policy, could lose power so quickly (Rasler 1996, 132; Smith 2007). Previous scholars have made the case that the structural weaknesses of the Iranian state alone did not precipitate the Islamic Revolution. Standard political, economic, organizational, cultural, or security explanations cannot account for the rapid, and ultimately successful, mobilization of anti-Shah resistance (Burns 1996; Kurzman 2004; Rasler 1996). Instead, one must analyze the opposition movement in order to understand

how political opportunities existed despite high levels of regime repression, the factors that made mass mobilization possible, and how the nonviolent resistance ultimately stripped away the monarchy's key sources of power (Kurzman 2004). Although others have argued that the regime was inherently vulnerable to challenges from below because of its inability to compel loyalty from the masses (Smith 2007), we argue that domestic opposition consistently failed to exploit these vulnerabilities until the primary method of resistance was nonviolent. Once the nonviolent campaign began to attract mass participation, the regime's inability to maintain loyalty among economic elites and security forces became central to the campaign's success.

Shah Mohammad Reza Pahlavi came to power in 1941 after his father, Reza Shah, was deposed following an invasion of allied British and Soviet forces. The Shah ruled until 1953, when he was temporarily forced to flee the country following a power struggle with Prime Minister Mohammad Mossadegh, a democratically elected leader who had nationalized the country's oil fields and attempted to usurp control over the armed forces. Following a military coup supported covertly by the CIA and MI6, Dr. Mossadegh was arrested and the Shah was returned to power.

Like his father, who looked to Kemal Atatürk's Turkey as a model, Shah Pahlavi sought to modernize and "Westernize" Iran while marginalizing the role of the ulema (clergy). Reforms enacted through the Shah's so-called White Revolution in 1963 included land redistribution to the peasantry, a campaign against rural illiteracy, and female political emancipation. These reforms could not, however, mask the repressive authoritarianism, rampant corruption, and extravagance that characterized the Shah's rule (Harney 1998, 37–167; Mackey 1998, 236, 260). The Shah ruled Iran with an iron fist, imprisoning political activists, intellectuals, and members of the ulema who opposed him, shutting down independent newspapers and using an extensive security apparatus and secret police (SAVAK) to suppress dissent. By the late 1960s his regime had officially banned all opposition parties, unions, and formal and informal associations. In 1975, the Shah established a single party, Rastakhiz (Resurrection), to which the entire adult population was required to belong and pay dues.

The Shah's domestic legitimacy was further weakened by the widely held belief that he was a puppet of the non-Muslim West, notably the United States, which supported the Shah's rise to power and anticommunist position. Iran's clerical establishment was especially infuriated by what it considered to be the Shah's un-Islamist policies, like eliminating the Islamic *hijri* calendar in 1976, hosting lavish parties, and actively promoting Western art and culture. The Shah's economic policies were similarly unpopular. Although the Shah promised economic rewards from the oil boom of 1974, instead there was high inflation, food shortages, and a growing disparity in wealth between the rich and poor and between urban and rural areas (Graham 1980, 94). The Shah's economic austerity plans, including an anti-profiteering campaign that resulted in the arrests of hundreds of businessmen, alienated major sectors of society, including middle-class government workers, merchants from the bazaar sector, and oil workers, "who would not normally have been rebellious" (Burns 1996, 359; Zones 1983).

Early Opposition: 1960s
Following a typical revolutionary pattern, it was the Iranian middle class and liberal intellectuals, long-standing targets of the Shah's repression, who initiated organized dissent, demanding political reforms and liberal freedoms (Abrahamian 1989, 29–30; Bakhash 1984, 14; Burns 1996, 359). The Second National Front, a group founded in July 1960 by some former colleagues of the ousted Mossadegh, headed early opposition to the Shah. University students, professional unions such as the teachers' union, and some Islamist and Marxist activists, joined the front, calling for free elections and other political reforms. Like the Communist (Tudeh) Party before it, the Shah's regime effectively suppressed the National Front in 1963. The other main opposition groups during this time were the Liberation Movement of Iran, which was made up of religious figures associated with the front (prominent among them Mehdi Bazargan and Ayatollah Mahmud Taleqani), along with an opposition political group formed around Khalil Maleki known as the Third Force. These oppositionists supported constitutional means to bring about political reforms inside Iran, and many supported the return to a constitutional monarchy.

Islamist Challenge
The other major challenge to the Shah came from the grand ayatollahs representing the top Shia religious leadership in Iran, led by the charismatic figure Ayatollah Ruhollah Khomeini. Khomeini, who was regarded as the descendant of the beloved Shia Imam Husayn ibn Ali, boasted great moral authority stemming from his long-standing opposition to the Shah's regime (Burns 1996, 366). These clerics rejected the reforms proposed by the Shah

under the 1963 White Revolution and the regime's anticlerical bent. Khomeini accused the Shah of "[embarking] on the destruction of Islam in Iran," and he condemned the Shah's close cooperation with Israel and his decision to grant diplomatic immunity to U.S. military personnel (Moin 2000, 75).

Khomeini's arrest in June 1963 led to the first massive outbreak of riots throughout Iran since the 1953 coup. The regime's brutal suppression of the 1963 protests, resulting in the deaths of hundreds of protestors, led many Iranians inside and outside the country to conclude that armed struggle was the only viable option to challenge the Shah's dictatorship (Behrooz 2000; Kurzman 2004; Sazegara and Stephan 2010). Shortly after the protest, in 1964, Khomeini was sent into exile—first to Turkey then to the Iraqi holy city of Najaf, where he spent fifteen years before moving to Paris in 1978.

While in exile, Khomeini developed the concept of an Islamic republic, according to which the Islamic government was to be ruled by the leading Islamic jurist (*wilayat al-faqih*). His lectures were transcribed and published as the book *Islamic Government*, which was widely circulated and read by religious scholars in and outside Iran. Khomeini broke from traditional Shia scholarship by insisting on the deposition of the Iranian monarchy and the concentration of ultimate Islamic authority (and political power) in a single individual (Kurzman 2004, 65–66). Khomeini's concept of government ruled by clerics was revolutionary, though it was not readily discussed by nonclerical anti-Shah forces before and during the revolution. To avoid creating divisions within the ranks of the opposition during the revolution, Khomeini never explicated the practicalities of the Islamist government during discussions or interviews. Indeed, as Gene Burns has argued, the "ambiguous ideology" that characterized the Iranian revolution helped unite a disparate Iranian population around an anti-Shah, anti-imperial platform. Although this ideological ambiguity encouraged broad, cross-cutting mobilization, it also set the stage for a struggle over the meaning of the revolution after the fall of the monarchy (1996, 375).

Guerrilla Resistance
Inspired by Marxist-Leninist writings and influenced by the anticolonial struggles in Algeria, Cuba, Angola, and other parts of the world, a guerrilla movement inside Iran took root in the mid-1960s. After the violently suppressed 1963 uprising, even those who advocated reform from within the system became outspoken advocates of armed struggle. Although there

were some smaller armed groups inside Iran,[3] the most significant guerrilla factions were the Organization of People's Feda'i Guerrillas (henceforth fedayeen), the Mujahedin e Khalq Organization (henceforth the Mujahedin or MKO), and the Marxist-Leninist MKO, an offshoot of the latter group established in 1975.

The fedayeen, a Marxist-Leninist group formed in 1971, conducted mostly urban attacks from 1971 to 1979 (Behrooz 2000, 2004). The Mujahedin, established in 1965, was a revolutionary Muslim guerrilla group that "represented a genuine attempt by young Moslem revolutionaries to reinterpret traditional Shia Islam and infuse it with modern political thinking in order to turn it into a viable revolutionary ideology" (Behrooz 2004, 191).[4] The Marxist-Leninist Mujahedin formed out of a split within the MKO in 1975, a split that was followed by internecine violence as Muslims clashed with Marxists.[5] In 1978 the Marxists left the MKO and established their own organization, Sazmane Peykar dar Rahe Azadieh Tabaqe Kargar (Organization Struggling for the Freedom of the Working Class).

One of the founding members of the fedayeen, Amir Parviz Pouyan, wrote in a short pamphlet entitled *The Necessity of Armed Struggle and a Refutation of the Theory of Survival* that armed struggle was the path to overcoming the state of apathy and organizing the opposition. Pouyan wrote that the apathy was compounded by the general perception that the Shah's regime was invincible and all-powerful. Bizhan Jazani, another leading thinker of the guerrilla movement, wrote in 1963, "There is no doubt that once the government decided to respond to the opposition (be it university students, or bazaaris and others) with armed military force, it came to us that what can bring victory to the nation is resorting to violent means of struggle" (Behrooz 2004, 189). A founding member of the Mujahedin, Mohsen Nejat-hoseini, captured the essence of guerrilla thinking at the time when he wrote in his memoirs, "In a situation where the shah's regime was suppressing the nationalist and freedom-seeking forces by relying on its armed mercenaries, talk of political [manner of] struggle was adventuresome. Combating the shah's regime empty-handedly was a type of suicide" (Behrooz, n.d.).

These Iranian intellectuals developed a conception of armed struggle whereby a small armed vanguard would use its minimal resources to launch armed attacks against the Shah's regime, thereby igniting a revolutionary movement. Although there were disagreements within Iranian revolutionary circles about whether the "objective conditions for revolution" existed, and about the relative importance of military versus political dimensions of the revolution, these thinkers were united in their belief that only armed struggle would have a chance against a regime that had shown a willingness to use violent force against unarmed protestors. The key challenge for the armed vanguard, writes Behrooz, was organizing the movement from scratch and developing a mass base among the working class and the masses under relentless regime repression (2000, 2004).

In fact, the membership of the armed movement never exceeded fifty thousand. From 1965 to 1966, the fedayeen formed small underground cells, with a larger network dedicated to political action and a smaller subgroup prepared for armed insurrection. Members of the subgroup succeeded in collecting some small arms and made plans to attack state-run banks in order to secure funds for future military activity. The first guerrilla attack took place on February 8, 1971, a few months before the Shah hosted a lavish ceremony in Persepolis-Shiraz to celebrate 2,500 years of the Persian Empire. A group of nine fedayeen guerrillas attacked a gendarmerie post in the small village of Siahkal, in the northern province of Gilan. The attack proved disastrous: the guerrillas' contact in the village had already been captured by SAVAK, and the local farmers turned against the guerrilla fighters. The Shah's government sent in thousands of troops and several helicopters to sweep the countryside until all the guerrillas were killed or captured.

Despite the military defeat endured by the fedayeen, the attack was a propaganda coup for the guerrillas, as it demonstrated hitherto unseen resistance to the Shah. The regime's massive response to the attack, scholars have suggested, imbued the guerrillas with a popular mystique (Behrooz 2000; Zia-Zarifi 2004, 188–90). The Siahkal attack was the unofficial start of eight years of armed activity against the Shah's regime.

After the Siahkal attack, the fedayeen launched a series of assassinations targeting senior government officials they accused of being implicated in the detention and torture of anti-Shah activists. The government, in response, captured and killed nearly a dozen top guerrilla leaders in retaliation for the assassinations. In 1976, the Shah launched a major counterinsurgency campaign that devastated the guerrilla movement. The remaining guerrilla forces continued to launch sporadic armed attacks in the late 1970s, though they were overshadowed by a different, far more effective form of resistance.

A NEW FORM OF PROTEST

In 1976, Jimmy Carter campaigned for the presidency of the United States on a platform that emphasized the promotion of human rights. His focus on human rights deeply worried the Shah, a strong Cold War ally to the United States who publicly insisted that Iranians were not ready for rights but instead needed strong tutelage for the foreseeable future while the country developed socially, economically, and politically (Kurzman 2004, 12–13). But Iranian liberal oppositionists regarded Carter's outspokenness on human rights issues as a political opening.

Intellectuals and other members of the liberal opposition, who were few in number in the early 1970s, began to publish open letters critical of the Shah and calling for constitutionalism and the respect for human rights. In the summer of 1977, they began to organize semipublic protest activities, which were treated with relative leniency by the Shah's security forces. Ten consecutive nights of poetry readings with sharp political overtones attracted thousands of Iranians to the Iran-Germany Association in Tehran in October. That same month, a group of liberal oppositionists formed the Iranian Committee for the Defense of Human Rights.

The Shah showed signs of leniency by issuing new laws and royal edicts that were supposed to strengthen habeas corpus and enhance prisoner rights. Yet Kurzman writes that these reforms were "limited in scope and not always applied in practice" (2004, 19). Peaceful protests continued to be violently suppressed, including those led by shanty dwellers, relatives of political prisoners, and students. In mid-1977, twenty-five religious scholars were arrested, including Ayatollah Mahmud Taleqani, a senior religious leader and longtime opponent of the monarchy, who was sentenced to ten years in prison. Reports of torture in the prisons continued to emerge, and most Iranians still feared the repercussions of participating in any form of protest activity (19).

"The Shah Must Go"

At the end of 1977, Khomeini's supporters began to mobilize, reactivating the Society of Qom Seminary Instructors and the Society of Struggling Religious Scholars, which began to issue pronouncements and to organize neighborhood committees. After Khomeini's eldest son, Mostafa, died suddenly on October 23, thousands of devout Muslims partook in mourning ceremonies in cities throughout Iran, which took the form of mass street demonstrations. After that, the exiled leader spoke of an "awakening" inside Iran. Further taboos were broken in the aftermath of Mostafa's death, when mourners in Shiraz and Tabriz marched out of mosques and began shouting "Death to the Shah"—the first time the slogan was raised (Kurzman 2004, 27). A week later, merchants at the Tehran bazaar commemorated the death of Khomeini's son by organizing a general strike.

The Shah's security forces launched a massive crackdown on the protestors a couple of weeks after the mourning ceremonies began. Yet this crackdown failed to deter the Islamists, who began to mobilize seminary students in Qom for even larger mourning ceremonies scheduled for the fortieth day after Mostafa's death (per Shia tradition).[6] The fortieth day was marked with merchants' strikes and overtly political speeches by religious leaders, who presented a "fourteen point resolution" calling for, among other things, the return of Khomeini from exile, the release of political prisoners, the reopening of religious and university institutions, free speech, the banning of pornography, protecting the right of women to wear the *hejab*, an end to relations with Israel, and support for the poor (Kurzman 2004, 28). As Kurzman notes, "these resolutions fell far short of demands for the replacement of the monarchy by an Islamic republic, but they represented the Islamists' first concerted entry into the political field in more than a decade" (29; see also Abrahamian 1989, 6).

Three weeks later, December 20–21, the Islamists turned the annual religious processions of Tasu'a and 'Ashura into occasions for mass political demonstrations. Thousands of protestors carrying signs with anti-Shah slogans marched through the bazaars in Tehran and were attacked and arrested by the Shah's riot police. By the end of 1977, Islamists had begun to believe that their consciousness-raising activities and parallel institution building of the 1960s and early 1970s, when they founded independent schools, publishing houses, and disseminated journals and pamphlets, had finally born fruit. As Khomeini himself acknowledged in a speech on November 12, demonstrations indicated that "hate towards the tyrannical regime [of the Shah] and an actual referendum on the vote of no confidence towards the treacherous regime . . . The nation—from the clergy and academics to the laborers and farmers, men and women—all are awakened" (Kurzman 2004, 31, citing "Ayatollah Khomeini's Letter," 1977, 106–8). But the real awakening would not occur until late summer 1978, when masses of Iranians began to participate in revolutionary protests.

The Ulema-Bazaari Network and 1978 Mass Mobilization

The high number of urban centers in Iran, where the clerics, bazaaris, students, workers, professionals, and urban poor who opposed the Shah were concentrated, facilitated the rapid mass mobilization that began in earnest in 1978 (Farhi 1990, 65–73; Gugler 1982). Equally important was the powerful mosque network inside Iran. There were more than nine thousand mosques Iran in the early 1970s, which were linked together by religious leaders in every town and village in the country. The mosques "constituted a massive institutional network, perhaps the largest civil organization in the country" (Kurzman 2004, 38). The mosque network provided crucial infrastructure and sanctuary for the revolutionaries and was the main distributor of audio cassette tapes featuring recorded speeches and specific instructions from Khomeini and his close advisers, which were smuggled into Iran from Najaf (later Paris). An official with the Ministry of National Guidance, Abolhassan Sadegh, noted at the time that tape cassettes were "stronger than fighter planes" (Zunes 2009a).

The Iranian opposition's hopes that the Carter administration would apply significant pressure on its regional ally to improve its human rights record were short-lived. When the Shah visited Washington in November 1977, human rights issues in Iran were discussed only in private, and mostly in positive terms. Instead, Carter famously offered the Shah a toast: "Iran, because of the great leadership of the Shah, is an island of stability in one of the more troubled areas of the world. This is a great tribute to you, Your Majesty, and to your leadership and to the respect and the admiration and love which your people give you" (Jimmy Carter, cited in Kurzman 2004, 14).

After the Shah's meeting with Carter in November, the level of repression inside Iran worsened. Security forces began to break up poetry readings and student protests with force. As liberal opposition leader Mehdi Bazargan told U.S. diplomats several months later, "Following the shah's visit to Washington, repression again seemed the order of the day" (Kurzman 2004, 20). An internal State Department memo noted in December 1977 that the Shah's government was "substantially increasing its use of force in dealing with political opposition" (20). In response to the increased repression, the liberal opposition seriously curtailed its activities.

But during this same period of intensified repression, the Islamist opposition began to increase its protest activities. Radical Islamists and students applied significant pressure on the moderate clerical leaders to support the revolutionary cause. On January 7, 1978, after an article was published in a Tehran newspaper mocking Khomeini and insinuating that his opposition to the Shah's modernization polices was bought with British oil interests, a group of radical seminary students and scholars from Qom won the backing of leading ayatollahs to organize a daylong strike. The strike, on January 9, closed down the bazaar. Students were joined by thousands of protestors as they marched door-to-door to pressure religious leaders to offer them public support. By this time, specific instructions had been given to the protestors to avoid antagonizing the security forces (Kurzman 2004, 36). Rather than shouting angry slogans, the protestors marched in silence.

As long as the protests remained fairly small, they were vulnerable to security-force repression. A bloody crackdown on protestors in Qom on January 9 was another turning point in the revolution. When a group of demonstrators approached a police barricade, someone (either a protestor or an agent provocateur) threw a brick through a bank window. The security forces, having a justification to respond with force, began to fire live rounds on the crowd of protestors. While perhaps less than a dozen people were killed during the protest, rumors spread that hundreds of protestors had been killed and their bodies taken away by government trucks. The Qom massacre triggered a wave of demonstrations that touched all parts of the country.

Those killed at Qom were commemorated on the fortieth day of mourning, generating protests in other cities. Protesters killed by the Shah's security forces in Tabriz, Yazd, and other cities were similarly commemorated forty days later, triggering a cycle of mobilization that some called "doing the forty-forty" (Kurzman 2004, 50). While mourning the death of the deceased on the fortieth day is a traditional practice in Shia Islam, the ceremony is normally a small event attended by close family and friends. Islamists transformed this religious custom into a political event as a means to promote mass mobilization (55).

On June 17, 1978, the campaign leadership told the Iranian people to halt the public protests and mourning ceremonies and instead to stay in their homes as part of a national stay-away strike. Pragmatism drove the shift away from concentrated street demonstrations to dispersed, nonconfrontational tactics. As one liberal opposition activist noted, "the people were well aware of the police's destructive strategy of provocation. They gave the dictatorial regime's agents no excuse to intervene" (Kurzman 2004, 50). One of Khomeini's most prominent militant lieutenants insisted at the time, "We have received the request of our Muslim brothers that no excuse be handed to the enemy" (52). Although some radical Islamists opposed the pause in public protests, calling it a form of appeasement to the dictatorship, they respected Khomeini's call for calm, which was supported by moderate and militant oppositionists alike.

The Shah Offers Concessions

During the summer of 1978 there were sporadic protests and random acts of sabotage (e.g., Islamist radicals burned theaters they accused of showing immoral films and bombed restaurants frequented by foreigners), but nothing that rose to the level of a national uprising. During this time, true to the carrot-and-stick approach that would characterize his response to the opposition movement, the Shah made overtures to the opposition. In July he announced that free elections would be held the following year and declared his support for political liberties.

The Shah's conciliatory overtures threatened to split the opposition. Whereas the exiled Khomeini declared the Shah's announcement "a trick," leaders of the liberal opposition were more enthusiastic about the possibilities afforded by the Shah's concessions. Mehdi Bazargan, the leading liberal oppositionist from the National Front and close adviser to Khomeini (who would later be named prime minister of the interim Islamic government after the revolution), expressed cautious support for the Shah's proposals and called for a "step-by-step" approach to dealing with the monarchy.

The gradualist approach favored by Bazargan and others, however, was quickly rejected by the Islamists, who began to revive street protests and demonstrations in cities throughout the country. "The response [to the Shah's liberalizing overtures] was larger crowds of demonstrators chanting for an Islamic Republic" (Rasler 1996, 144). Notably, the birthday of the Hidden Imam on July 21, a normally joyous occasion in the Shia calendar, was transformed into a day of mourning and contemplation of the evils of the Shah's regime. Ramadan that year, similarly, was changed from a month of religious purity and piety to four weeks of political protests.

The Abadan Fire and Black Friday

Expanding beyond the Islamists' core group of supporters and building a truly mass movement remained a central challenge for the Islamist leadership. Although a few demonstrations had attracted fifty thousand protestors, this was still a relatively small number for a population of more than 15 million. The remainder of the summer of 1978 was marked by a number of protests sparked by local events, many of which were met with massive bloodshed.

The protest movement expanded considerably after a fire at a movie theater in Abadan on August 19, 1978 that killed four hundred people. When it was discovered that the doors to the theater had been locked from the outside, and when the fire department was late to arrive, many Iranians blamed the government for the deadly arson. "Burn the Shah!" was shouted during mourning protests, which multiplied in number and intensity after the theater massacre. Eleven cities had been placed under martial law by the end of August. The Shah then offered a series of measures designed to appease the Islamists—like appointing a new reform-minded prime minister (Jafar Sharif-Emami) on August 27 and returning to the Muslim solar calendar. Casinos were shut down and new press freedoms were allowed. Religious demonstrations were permitted for Eid al Fitr, the day marking the end of Ramadan.

This official permission, notes Kurzman, suggested two things for the opposition: "First, it meant violent repression was less certain than for previous protests, so that supporters beyond the hard core might consider it safe enough to protest. Second, if the soft core was expected to protest, the event might get big enough to generate safety in numbers, attracting even further participants" (2004, 62). A large-scale demonstration on Eid al Fitr expanded the base of protestors well beyond the core Islamists. Bazaaris, liberal oppositionists, and leftists joined the Islamists for a massive demonstration, prompting Khomeini to refer to that year's celebration as an "Eid of epic movement" (64).

Martial Law and General Strike
On September 8, one day after a mass demonstration, the Shah declared martial law in Tehran and other cities. Several thousand protestors nevertheless gathered in Zhaleh Square in Tehran. Security forces fired tear gas and shot live rounds at the crowd. Casualty counts on that day, which came to be known as Black Friday, ranged from less than a hundred to many thousands. No matter the actual number of slain protestors, Black Friday, like the Abadan fire before it, further solidified the ranks of the anti-Shah movement. Meanwhile, U.S. president Jimmy Carter, who at the time was

helping to broker a peace deal between Israel and Egypt, called the Shah and reiterated his support for the regime.

After Black Friday, the opposition once again halted outdoor protests and demonstrations and shifted to less-confrontational strikes. In the weeks following the massacre, wildcat strikes spread throughout the country, starting with workers from the oil refineries on September 9. By the first week of November, almost every sector of Iranian society had stopped working, including journalists, the national airline and railroad workers, customs officials, power-plant workers, and banks. "The stranglehold on international trade was so complete that for awhile the central bank was forced to stop issuing Treasury bills to raise money for the Government because the ink for certification was held up on the quayside" (Kurzman 2004, 78).

The oil workers' strike had the most profound impact on the Iranian economy, as the oil fields supplied the regime with its most important source of revenue. When oil workers went on strike in October, Iranian oil exports dropped from more than 5 million barrels a day to less than 2 million barrels in two weeks' time. According to Asef Bayat, whereas workers had struck numerous other times in Iranian history, their demands had tended to focus on purely economic issues like increased pay and subsidized housing. This time, however, included in the list of demands announced by the oil workers' strike committee was ending martial law, support for striking teachers, release of political prisoners, and the Iranianization of the oil industry (Kurzman 2004, 78).

Khomeini did not at first intend for the national strike to go on for an extended period. "Nobody will die of hunger from several days of striking shops and businesses, in submission to God," he said (Kurzman 2004, 78–79). It was not until a month later that Khomeini expressed support for an indefinite national strike until the regime collapsed. In early November 1978, with strikes being launched throughout the country, students from Tehran University organized a march that turned violent when the students clashed with security forces outside the gates of the university. A number were killed, triggering a student-led riot the next day. Buildings throughout Tehran were torched, including the British embassy compound.

At this point, the Shah launched a major crackdown. He fired his civilian prime minister and appointed a military government. Martial law was declared, and tanks and armored vehicles were ordered to enter cities and towns throughout the country in order to prevent further demonstrations.

The army took over the National Iranian Radio and Television and clamped down on the print media—only the ruling party newspaper was allowed to go to press. Leading opposition figures were arrested. The army forced oil workers to go back to work, and strike committee leaders were threatened to increase oil production or risk death.

Meanwhile, in his announcement to the nation about the new military government, the Shah insisted that he was sympathetic to some aspects of the revolution and promised to crack down on lawlessness and corruption and to restore a national unity government to oversee free elections. He condemned the wave of strikes that had paralyzed the country, notably in the oil sector, and demanded that the strikes end and that order be restored. Some scholars contend that the Shah's sickness at the time (he was, unbeknownst to the rest of the population, dying of cancer) helps to explain his vacillating, inconsistent response to the revolutionary movement at the time. Because the state had been constructed to rely on the Shah, his incapacity paralyzed the state. That the Shah told his close associates and foreign emissaries that he was unwilling to order a large-scale massacre in order to stay in power is also cited as an explanation for the success of the revolution (Kurzman 2004, 107).

Yet as Kurzman notes, "the refusal to authorize slaughter does not necessarily indicate lack of will or state paralysis" (2004, 108). Indeed, throughout the fall 1978, security forces routinely used live fire against protestors, and protestor fatalities increased during the final few months of the Shah's rule. Rather, one must appreciate that the massive nature of the protests, along with specific tactics used by the protestors against the security forces, helped to neutralize them. As Kurzman and other scholars have pointed out, there was no optimal strategy that the Shah could have used to suppress the revolutionary movement. Even if the Shah's response to the movement had been more brutal than it was, "the problem for the Shah was that Iranians had stopped obeying" (111; Smith 2007, 162). No matter how deep the Shah's reservoir of coercive capacity ran, no state can repress all the people all the time.

Not only were there too many protestors for the Shah's police to arrest in the fall of 1978, but also the security forces simply did not have the resources or manpower to enforce martial law. There were not enough hands to enforce bans, and not enough prison space to accommodate those arrested. Transcripts of a security meeting held in January 1979 reveal that Iran's military chiefs discussed plans to arrest a hundred thousand opposition activists, but an assessment of the jails showed that only five thousand additional detainees could be added (Kurzman 2004, 112). Prisoners were released to make room for new ones.

Even more problematic from the regime's perspective, the Shah's soldiers and police were incapable of running the organizations and institutions that they had taken over. When the military attempted to force state television to run pro-Shah programs, the television officials warned that their workers would see the programs and not show up for work. Workers at Iran's electrical facilities began cutting off power for two hours each night in order to disrupt the state-run evening news and to offer the cover of darkness to protestors who were violating the 8:00 p.m. curfew. In order for the Shah's security forces to take over the facilities and stop the blackouts, they would have needed to assume control over all the stations at the same time, and they simply lacked the personnel to do that.

Taking over the oil refineries similarly proved to be impossible. The Shah sent in hundreds of navy technicians to operate the pumping stations, but they didn't have a clue how the system functioned. Instead, they tried to force oil workers to return to the oil fields, sometimes by invading their homes and dragging them back to work. The oil workers decided to go back to the oil fields, where they would work for a short time and then launch another massive walkout. A recognizable pattern developed in all Iran's major industries, including the national airline (Iran Air), telecommunications, banking, and even customs officials: "Industries would strike, return to work when forced to, then go back on strike as soon as possible" (Kurzman 2004, 113). The interconnectedness of these different industries only intensified the impact of the national strike. In an apparent recognition of his regime's inability to control the Iranian people by force, the Shah said in an October 1978 interview, "You can't crack down on one place and make the people on the next block behave" (Kurzman 2004, 115). Beyond crackdowns, the regime lacked the capacity to quell mobilization with means other than raw force, a crucial weakness that proved to undermine its ability to survive the crisis (Smith 2007, 159).

Neutralizing the Security Forces
The Iranian opposition undermined the seemingly stable and loyal security apparatus, the Shah's most important pillar of support. Opposition lead-

ers, secular and Islamist, met with security officials and entreated them to join the opposition, or at least not to obey with orders to crack down on the protestors. Khomeini himself pleaded with the security forces, "Proud soldiers who are ready to sacrifice yourself for your country and homeland, arise! Suffer slavery and humiliation no longer! Renew your bonds with the beloved people and refuse to go on slaughtering your children and brothers for the sake of the whims of this family of bandits!" (cited in Kurzman 2004, 114).

Fraternization was an important part of the opposition's strategy. During demonstrations, protestors handed flowers to the soldiers and chanted slogans, "Brother soldier, why do you kill your brothers?" and "The army is part of the nation." A Tehran-based religious scholar ran an operation to assist deserters, whereby foot soldiers were given civilian clothes to change into, and higher-ranking officers were sent back to the barracks to collect intelligence (Kurzman 2004, 115). While the effectiveness of these forms of pressure is unclear (and the number of actual desertions remained relatively low until the Shah left Iran), what is clear is that the opposition's efforts lowered morale in the army and police. The number of authorized leaves increased dramatically, the number of small-scale mutinies began to rise, and there is much evidence of decreasing loyalty among junior personnel (115). In early January 1979, Chief of Staff Abbas Gharabaghi estimated during a meeting with fellow officers that the military was running at about 55 percent capacity (115).

Fearing a disintegration of the military, security officials loyal to the Shah drew up plans to restrict contact between soldiers and protestors. "We should round up the units and send them someplace where [the demonstrators] won't have contact with the soldiers. Because yesterday they came and put a flower in the end of a rifle barrel, and another on the [military] car . . . The soldiers' morale just disappears" (Kurzman 2004, 115). Dissident officers, on the other hand, intentionally deployed soldiers to places where they would be exposed to fraternization. Loyal officers closed prayer rooms on military bases to prevent soldiers from listening to recordings of Khomeini's speeches.

By late 1978, the Shah's security forces had simply been outnumbered and outmaneuvered by the protestors. As Kurzman points out, "The shah's military-security complex was not so much weakened as overwhelmed. No system of repression is intended to deal with wholesale popular disobedience like that which emerged in Iran in late 1978" (2004, 165). The opposition began to produce hoax cassettes, supposedly containing a voice that sounded like the Shah's giving the generals orders to shoot demonstrators in the streets. While most Iranians did not participate in direct confrontations with the Shah's security forces (preferring to stay at home, where they would shout anti-Shah slogans from their rooftops), casualties seemed only to intensify the mass mobilization.

Meanwhile, as the Islamist movement gained rapid momentum in 1978, internal divisions plagued the armed guerrilla factions. The Mujahedin was in the middle of an internal debate about whether to continue the armed struggle and engaged in few armed actions in 1978. One fedayeen leader said that the guerrilla movement, which "disintegrated and disappeared after the blows of 1976," had "set itself principally to protecting itself" and engaged in only "scattered actions" to show that it still existed.[7] However, the number of leftist guerrilla attacks picked up slightly in late 1978 (claiming credit for a half dozen actions) and in early 1979 (a dozen actions) (Kurzman 2004, 146).

The Shah Flees; Khomeini Returns

At the end of 1978, the Shah offered the prime ministerial post to key members of the liberal opposition. While these reform-minded individuals almost assuredly would have accepted the Shah's offer only weeks earlier, by late 1978 accepting such an offer would have been a form of political suicide. With the country engaged in mass rebellion and under the pretext of seeking medical attention in the United States, Shah Pahlavi fled Iran on January 16, 1979.

The Shah's newly appointed prime minister, Shapour Bakhtiar (who was himself a nationalist leader opposed to the Shah), tried to assume control over the situation and buy time for the protests and strikes to die down. But time was not on the side of the caretaker government. Khomeini called on the civil servants who worked in government ministries not to allow Bakhtiar's cabinet ministers to enter the ministries and to refuse any form of cooperation with them.

Bakhtiar's government, whose grip on power was being eroded on all fronts, lasted only thirty-seven days. On February 1, 1979, Ayatollah Khomeini returned from exile. His safe arrival on an Air France flight had been ensured through negotiations between liberal opposition members and the Bakhtiar government. Khomeini was mobbed by enthusiastic supporters. Absent any mechanism for ensuring a peaceful transition, and with Bakhtiar still in office, Khomeini took matters into his own hands and appointed his own prime minister, Mehdi Bazargan, at a press conference on February 4. For two weeks, Iran had two governments.

On February 9 in the evening, fighting broke out on a Tehran air force base between prorevolution military technicians and the Shah's Imperial Guards. The guards fired on pro-Khomeini officers and members of the crowd outside, killing at least two. When word of the incident spread, masses of civilians rushed to the base to defend mutineers (a scene that would be replayed during the People Power revolution in the Philippines six years later). Ayatollahs urged calm and called on the protestors to avoid confrontations. Khomeini issued a proclamation warning of holy war but refrained from calling for it:

> Although I have not given the order for sacred jihad, and I still wish matters to be settled peacefully, in accordance with the will of the people and legal criteria, I cannot tolerate these barbarous actions [of loyalist forces] and I issue a solemn warning that if the Imperial Guard does not desist from this fratricidal slaughter and return to its barracks, and if the military authorities fail to prevent these attacks, I will take my final decision, placing my trust in God. (Kurzman 2004, 160)

Yet "Khomeini never needed to declare a holy war. Iranians were already fighting one" (160). On February 10, soldiers from the Imperial Guard returned to the air base but were unable to subdue insurgents, who were surrounded by masses of civilians. At this point, leftist guerrillas assumed a prominent role in supporting the mutiny at the Tehran air force base.[8] Opposition violence intensified after weapons taken from armories and fallen soldiers were given to young men. Crowds of Iranians formed barriers around the tanks, and a few tanks, targets of Molotov cocktails, caught fire. Around the country, crowds of people surrounded garrisons and prevented military reinforcements from reaching Tehran. Imperial Guard tanks made their way through hostile (and now highly armed) crowds, fighting with insurgents and killing hundreds of protestors in the final two days.

On February 11, after tanks failed to reinforce besieged guards of the Tehran munitions factory, chiefs of staff met and declared that the military would remain neutral in the political disputes between the nation and the state and that its personnel would be returning to their garrisons. At this point, Iran's Islamic Revolution had effectively triumphed (Sazegara and Stephan 2010).

Iran After the Revolution

After assuming power, Khomeini appointed liberal opposition leader Bazargan as the provisional prime minister and filled his cabinet with a number of other liberal oppositionists. But hopes that an acceptable power-sharing arrangement would pave the way to a peaceful transition in postrevolution Iran were short-lived. Within a few months, Khomeini had withdrawn his delegation of authority and the liberals were frozen out of the cabinet. After resigning, the liberal opposition was forced out of postrevolutionary electoral politics.

Violent clashes between Islamists and leftists, which had begun before the Shah was overthrown, intensified in the period after the revolution. Khomeini had warned during the revolutionary period against "those who deviate and oppose Islam" and had long condemned leftist groups. Competition over control of the oil industry in southern Iran furthered the hostility between these groups. Soon, leftist groups resorted to terrorist bombings, and Islamists resorted to arrest, torture, and executions. By 1982, the organized left in Iran had been virtually eliminated (Kurzman 2004, 147). Liberals, leftists, nationalists, and ethnic minorities were all targeted by the radical clerics who controlled the new theocracy. Nearly 20,000 people were killed in the postrevolutionary period (the Islamic Republic accepts a figure of 12,000), thousands were jailed, and, a decade later, 4,448 of these political prisoners were executed in Iranian jails on the orders of Ayatollah Khomeini.

ANALYSIS

In assessing the impact of different forms of resistance used by Iranian opposition groups against the monarchy, it is evident that the greatest amount of pressure generated against the regime came from mass protests, the national strike, and organized noncooperation. Nonviolent resistance made the country ungovernable while systematically stripping away the Shah's (and later Bakhtiar's) key sources of social, political, economic, and military power. It did this by enlisting the active support of clerics, workers, bazaaris, youth, women, and other groups whose obedience and resources the regime depended on for its power; by avoiding a demonization of the Shah's armed defenders; and by denying the regime justification for indefinite repression.

From 1971 to 1979 the guerrillas launched sporadic attacks, though their impact was minimal. Not only were the guerrilla ranks depleted following a successful counterinsurgency strategy launched by the regime in the mid-1970s, but also they failed to develop a mass base of support. Internecine violence between different armed factions (particularly when the Mujahedin broke into two factions in 1975, followed by revenge killings) further weakened the guerrilla movement. The guerrillas did play a more prominent role during the final days of the Bakhtiar caretaker government. This period of struggle, incidentally, corresponds to the most casualty-intensive period of the revolution.

Analyses that credit the guerrilla movement for raising morale within the anti-Shah coalition during the 1970s nevertheless acknowledge that the guerrillas were not at the forefront of the successful revolution:

> [The guerrilla movement] clearly had a romantic and heroic aspect, which at points even gave birth to myths. The significance of the movement is not in its professed revolutionary alternative (be it the Marxist or Islamist versions) or in its inability to reach its ultimate goal of securing state power. In both of the above cases they clearly failed. The guerrillas were not able to organize the khalq [people] under the banner of a revolutionary movement, they failed to lead the revolution, and their revolutionary alternative seems irrelevant today (Behrooz n.d.)

Whereas only a tiny percentage of the Iranian population fought as guerrillas—mostly young men from urban areas—the masses became the vanguard in the nonviolent resistance. This form of resistance, which began in late 1977 and rapidly accelerated after the summer of 1978, was characterized by mass participation from nearly every segment of Iranian society. A decentralized ulema-bazaari network facilitated the mass mobilization, which began with mourning ceremonies that took the form of street demonstrations that spread throughout the country and later included a national strike that paralyzed the country. Rather than attacking the regime's security forces, the main target for violent revolutionaries, the civilian-led opposition fraternized with the Shah's soldiers and police. Although the regime responded to the street protests with violence and later attempted to force the striking population to restore normalcy, no amount of violent coercion could suppress an entire population that was refusing to cooperate. Whereas the guerrilla attacks caused the occasional disruption, the mass nonviolent resistance was responsible for systematically removing the monarchy's sources of political, economic, and military power.

A less-rigid ideology and lower barriers to participation gave nonviolent resistance an advantage over armed struggle in the area of recruitment. The main armed factions inside Iran, the fedayeen and the Mujahedin, were unable to obtain or sustain broad-based membership or popular support and were plagued by internal divisions. Whereas a Marxist litmus test was applied to the guerrilla movement, there was nothing monolithic or ideologically rigid about the mass-based anti-Shah coalition. As Kurzman notes, the intellectuals sought intellectual freedom, while Iranian merchants were concerned primarily with freedom of commerce. Leftists sought social justice, and workers sought raises and other benefits. Even a drug counterculture got involved, with the creation of the Hippi-Abad (Hippie Town) in a northern Tehran park. For these groups, "Khomeini's authority stemmed not so much from religious scholarship or aspirations as from his position as leader of a viable movement" (Kurzman 2004, 142–43).

Participants in the resistance demonstrated a higher willingness to participate in nonviolent resistance because of its lower physical, moral, informational, and commitment barriers. Indeed, recruits to the resistance cited its nonviolent character when explaining their participation in the campaign. As one participant claimed during the uprising, "'we have had enough of violence and casualties'" (anonymous street peddler in Qom, interviewed by Nicholas B. Tatro, AP Wire Services, June 17, 1978, cited in Kurzman 2004, 52). Participants also expressed a reluctance to participate in violent actions, often citing concerns about risk, personal commitment, and efficacy (72).

The clerics assigned leaders to manage the rallies, with the explicit goal of preventing participants from shouting inflammatory slogans like "Death to the Shah!" Instead, participants were encouraged to yell more hopeful slogans so as to attract even more participants (Kurzman 2004, 120). Though they may have been motivated by pure pragmatism, Khomeini's clerical and liberal advisers seemed to grasp that less opposition violence would translate into greater support for the opposition and less support for the regime, as the regime's use of violence would be increasingly regarded as unjust and illegitimate. The single most common shared characteristic among participants in Iran was some experience with government repression that hit close to home. Most participants were not attracted to high-risk activities like militias but rather to lower-risk actions available through nonviolent resistance (Sazegara and Stephan 2010, 200–202).

Indeed, the campaign's ability to adapt to the Shah's repression and rely on tactics of dispersion, including stay-aways, allowed the campaign to increase its participation despite government repression. Thus, engaging in nonviolent civil resistance created lower barriers—in this case remaining in one's home—so that anyone could participate in the resistance.

While the relationship between repression and mobilization is neither simple nor straightforward, empirical studies of the Iranian Revolution suggest that regime repression decreased the amount of protest activity in the short term but in the long run led to greater mass mobilization (Francisco 2004; Koopmans 1993; Martin 2007). Explaining why this was the case, Rasler argues that mass mobilization in Iran was facilitated by the presence of informal associations and networks that supported anti-Shah protest activity (1996, 143). Though opposition to the Shah began in the 1960s with protests by writers, intellectuals, lawyers, judges, students, and other liberal oppositionists, their protests were restricted mostly to Tehran. Years of intense regime repression targeting these secular groups helped contain their activities. Thus by 1977 the mosques had become the sole viable institutions that existed to mobilize opposition on a national scale (141).

The activation of the mosque network, backed by the powerful bazaari community, was the most significant component of revolutionary recruitment. This activation did not occur automatically, however. Many moderate and conservative religious leaders were suspicious of the aims and objectives of Ayatollah Khomeini and the radical clerics and were loath to become actively involved in revolutionary activities. It took pressure by local leaders, including radical clerics and their allies among bazaaris, students, and moderate politicians, to transform the mosque network into a tool of mass mobilization. The fact that many Iranians were linked to the mosques through neighborhood religious associations (*hay'at i madhabi*), many of which were run by the bazaari, enhanced the recruitment opportunities (Rasler 1996, 141). The *hay'ats*, as Rasler notes, were where "interpersonal, political, and social networks forged the national alliance between radical clerics (*ulema*), bazaaris, and the intelligentsia" (141). There were twelve thousand *hay'ats* in Tehran alone. The bazaari-ulema networks mobilized most of the demonstrations reported during the revolutionary period (Ashraf and Banuazizi

1985, 559; Rasler 1996, 141). The decentralized mosque network provided an effective communication channel (facilitating the mass dissemination of cassettes containing Khomeini's speeches and instructions), resources, and a platform for mass mobilization.

As critical mass theory would predict, recruitment to the opposition accelerated once participation in the resistance looked safe and seemed likely to succeed (Kurzman 2004, 132). Interview and events data indicate that as more Iranians saw their compatriots engaged in protest activity, they were more likely to join in, "because they [had] greater safety in numbers and [had] a chance to make history by doing what they [believed] to be right (132). The perception that the anti-Shah movement had a chance at success, coupled with the relative ease with which ordinary people could participate in nonviolent acts of resistance and defiance through informal networks, made recruitment to nonviolent resistance easier.

When the regime's armed defenders refused to obey orders to repress the campaign, the Shah was unable to remain in power. However, the refusal to obey was contingent upon the campaign's remaining nonviolent. As troops whispered to protestors during the summer of 1978, "'We belong to the people, but we are in the service, do not commit any violence, we do not want to shoot'" (cited in Kurzman 2004, 63). Had the campaign turned violent, the troops would have adhered to their government service responsibilities.

Student networks at the universities also enhanced opposition resilience by providing a steady reservoir of young recruits with relatively fewer inhibitions about engaging in protest activity that targeted both the Shah's regime along with more moderate oppositionists.[9] Women too were encouraged by Khomeini to join in demonstrations, but in modest garb deemed sacred by Islamists.[10] Some secular women wore the *hejab* as a symbol of opposition to the monarchy. Though the Shah turned to coercion in an attempt to force oil workers, transport workers, bankers, members of the media, and others back to work in late 1978, it was ineffective in the face of mass noncooperation. The Shah's regime did not have the capacity or the resources to arrest and detain hundreds of thousands of opposition activists, nor could it effectively manage the takeover of industries and institutions after imposing martial law.

The opposition employed a diverse repertoire of nonviolent sanctions, which also enhanced its resilience. The forty-day period of mourning followed by a memorial observance, which took the form of street demonstrations, expanded the geographic scope of the protest activity. The transformation of recognizable cultural referents to serve revolutionary purposes, Moaddel wrote, assisted the recruitment and micromobilization process:

> Shi'a metaphors, symbols and ceremonies transformed the general social discontent into a revolutionary crisis by providing not only an effective channel of communication between participants in the revolution and their leaders but also a mechanism for the political mobilization of the masses against the state. (Moaddel 1993, 163, cited in Rasler 1996, 143)

At the same time, the fortieth-day mourning ceremonies exposed the civilian population—the recruitment base for nonviolent resistance—to regime repression. The decision to halt the street protests in June 1978 and replace them with tactics of dispersion allowed the opposition to readjust and avoid excessive casualties. The stay-aways, boycotts, and turn to symbolic activities (like shouting from rooftops) permitted mass participation while shielding the population from the regime's use of force. After martial law was declared in November 1978, the power of dispersed acts of noncooperation was revealed when the entire country went on strike, paralyzing the state and economy. At that point, it did not matter that the Shah continued to receive the backing of the U.S. government or that its security forces were deployed to coerce the population back to normalcy; the power of mass disobedience had neutralized the state's repressive capacity.

The conscious refraining from the use of armed struggle during the revolutionary period further contributed to opposition resilience. Khomeini and followers refrained from mobilizing paramilitary groups, even after the Qom massacre in 1978 and even though some Islamists had received military training from the Palestine Liberation Organization before the revolution and underground cells had been created in Qom and elsewhere. In fact, when activists called for more militant confrontation with the regime in 1979, shouting slogans like "Khomeini, Khomeini give us arms" and "Machine guns, machine guns, the answer to all," Khomeini continued to hold them back. He sent an envoy to the Mujahedin, who gave little encouragement and few resources to these groups (Kurzman 2004, 156). Ayatollah

Asadollah Madani, a militant religious leader of Hamadan, flatly rejected a proposal for an armed uprising in November 1979, according to a SAVAK report, while a number of religious leaders signed a proclamation in January 1979 calling on people to remain calm and not provoke the security forces.

The diverse application of nonviolent tactics, the mixing of methods of concentration and dispersion, and the conscious nonviolent discipline helped keep the Shah's forces off balance while avoiding an overescalation that could have dampened protest activity. The decentralized nature of the bazaari-ulema network and the tactical innovation employed by the opposition allowed it to weather the storm of regime repression while facilitating mass mobilization.

CONCLUSION

Contrary to common perception, the Iranian Revolution is an example of a successful nonviolent campaign. The ability of the civil resistance campaign to attract millions of participants who did not directly threaten regime security forces with violence gave the campaign an advantage compared with the violent Mujahedin and fedayeen movements, which remained small, ineffectual, and easily suppressed.

We summarize the mechanisms and outcomes comparing the nonviolent and violent campaigns in table 4.1. However, the revolution points to an interesting theoretical puzzle, which is that the successful nonviolent mass movement resulted in a repressive theocracy rather than a democracy. This outcome challenges widely held suppositions about the relationship between civil resistance and democratic transitions. Nonviolent civil resistance has driven a sizable majority of recent transitions from authoritarianism (fifty out of sixty-seven in the past three decades), and civil resistance tends to be associated with fewer deaths during and after the transition to democracy (Ackerman and Karatnycky 2005).

Iran's 1979 revolution clearly falls off that trend line. The coalition of political and religious forces that united around the goal of ending the Shah's rule collapsed violently about a year after the monarchy fell. While religious moderates and secular nationalists believed that the Islamists would be sidelined after the revolution, this is not what occurred. Instead, a group of radical clerics came to power, exhibiting little tolerance for dissenting views and rejecting democratic principles of governance.

One could explain this outcome as follows. The prevailing ideology of the nonviolent campaign emphasized the consolidation of power into a single

	NONVIOLENT CAMPAIGN	VIOLENT CAMPAIGN
ESTIMATED PARTICIPATION	APPROX. 2,000,000	MAXIMUM OF 50,000
PRIMARY PARTICIPANTS	MIDDLE CLASS	URBAN MALE YOUTH
	LIBERAL INTELLECTUALS	MARXISTS
	SHIA ISLAMISTS	
	CLERICS	
	STUDENTS	
	WOMEN	
	UNIONS	
	OIL WORKERS	
	PROFESSIONAL GROUPS	
	MARXISTS	
SECURITY LOYALTY SHIFTS	YES	NO
TACTICAL DIVERSITY	CLEAR	UNCLEAR
EXTERNAL STATE SPONSOR	NO	NO
INTERNATIONAL SANCTIONS	NO	NO
EFFECTS OF REGIME REPRESSION	BACKFIRE	SUPPRESSION
OUTCOME	SUCCESS	FAILURE

TABLE 4.1 **THE NONVIOLENT AND VIOLENT IRANIAN CAMPAIGNS COMPARED**

individual, Khomeini. The opposition coalesced around a strong anti-Shah sentiment but failed to unify around a shared vision of post-Shah governance in Iran. Furthermore, the presence of a violent leftist movement gave the new regime a pretext for purging the society of its secular voices of dissent. Exiled leadership played a large role in the uprising, which revolved around Khomeini's charisma rather than a durable commitment from different parts of the opposition to build a democratic state after the Shah. As such, the revolution itself possessed very little discussion of a post-Shah vision. The moderate Islamist and secular opposition were unable to organize a broad-based movement to support Bazargan, whom the more radical clerics quickly ousted. The Iran-Iraq War, which commenced in 1980 and continued until 1989, further consolidated the power of the ayatollahs.

These features of the campaign underscore how the ideology of a resistance campaign can shape the political and social milieu after victory and highlight the problematic nature of violent fringe groups in consolidating posttransition democracy. The Iranian case also illuminates the complexities of nonviolent resistance, challenging the perspective that civil resistance always results in democratic consolidation. Sometimes nonviolent revolutions can empower groups or individuals who do not represent the interests of the entire mass movement.

In chapter 8 we see, however, that the authoritarian regime emerging after the Iranian Revolution is an anomaly, as democratic governments follow most nonviolent campaigns, even if the campaigns fail. The nondemocratic ideology and organization of the anti-Shah resistance can help explain the bloody aftermath and consolidation of a theocratic dictatorship. These features may help us to explain other cases of successful civil resistance that are succeeded by authoritarian regimes.

CHAPTER FIVE **THE FIRST PALESTINIAN INTIFADA, 1987–1992**

THE FIRST INTIFADA, which began in December 1987, was a popular Palestinian uprising against the Israeli occupation of the West Bank, Gaza Strip, and East Jerusalem.[1] The intifada (literally, "shaking off") began as a spontaneous eruption in a Gaza refugee camp and quickly spread throughout the occupied territories. Its diverse, mass participation, scope, intensity, and relatively nonviolent character made the First Intifada an exceptional event that altered Palestinian society and transformed its relationship with Israel. While the first eighteen months of the intifada were highly successful, the popular uprising eventually succumbed to factional divisions and violence and failed to obtain all its objectives.

Some may be skeptical that the First Intifada—at least during its early and most robust phase—was primarily nonviolent. Given the bloody conflicts before and since, critics may argue that this campaign was also violent. Many remember the iconic stone throwing by Palestinian youth during the First Intifada, as well as violent confrontations between Israeli troops and Palestinian protestors.

But this image of the intifada obscures the fact that over 97 percent of campaign activities reported by the Israeli Defense Force were nonviolent, including mass demonstrations, strikes, boycotts, and other acts of defiance and civil disobedience (King 2007; Pearlman 2009, 14). Thus, while Palestinians committed isolated acts of violence against Israelis (and against fellow Palestinians) during the intifada, particularly after 1990, the idea that the bulk of the resistance during the First Intifada consisted of stone throwing is incorrect, though that activity captured the most Israeli and international media attention. Furthermore, the Palestinian leadership failed to explain why such violent, angry tactics were counterproductive. But there was something fundamentally different about the First Intifada, certainly compared with the forms of Palestine Liberation Organization (PLO) resistance that preceded it, that ultimately made it a more potent, effective form of resis-

	UNARMED PROTEST INCIDENTS	SHOOTING INCIDENTS	PERCENTAGE OF ALL INCIDENTS INVOLVING FIREARMS
1988	23053	38	0.16%
1989	42608	102	0.24%
1990	65944	158	0.24%
1991	30948	262	0.84%
1992	24882	344	1.36%

SOURCE: PEARLMAN (2009:14), CITING ISRAEL DEFENSE FORCES SPOKESMAN'S UNIT, INCIDENTS IN JUDEA, SAMARIA AND THE GAZA DISTRICT SINCE THE BEGINNING OF THE UPRISING (JERUSALEM, DECEMBER 1992):6-7.

TABLE 5.1 **PALESTINIAN DISTURBANCES IN THE WEST BANK AND GAZA STRIP, 1988-1992**

tance that Israel found difficult to suppress and that allowed Palestinians, at least temporarily, to win the moral and strategic high ground.

Although many blame Israel's heavy-handed response to the popular uprising, including the sidelining of moderate Palestinian leaders, for the intifada's eventual descent into violent chaos, there were profound weaknesses within the intifada itself, including the inability of the leadership to convince youths to stop throwing rocks, divisions between secular and Islamist strands, internecine violence, and PLO fecklessness. These weaknesses should be highlighted because they are instructive in terms of why the intifada ultimately failed. But the mass, popular participation that characterized the first year and a half of the intifada (including Israeli participation) was the result of the Palestinian population's overwhelming reliance on nonviolent tactics, and this different form of resistance was, at least for eighteen months, effective at forcing Israeli and U.S. concessions.

THE ORIGINS OF RESISTANCE TO ISRAELI OCCUPATION (1967-1987)

During the Six-Day War of 1967, Israeli forces captured the West Bank and Gaza Strip, territories that had been under the control of Jordan and Egypt, respectively, since 1948. The Israeli occupation of the West Bank, Gaza Strip, and East Jerusalem was total. More than fourteen hundred military orders were enforced in the occupied territories that controlled nearly every aspect of Palestinians' lives.[2] According to Israeli law at the time, "terrorist activities" included everything from painting slogans and graffiti to singing national songs to making the victory sign, displaying the Palestinian flag, throwing stones, burning tires, demonstrating, and forming political gatherings. Authorities arrested or detained close to half a million Palestinians for these reasons prior to and during the First Intifada (Benvenisti 1987). The occupied territories were made entirely dependent, economically, on Israel. Palestinian products were denied entry into Israel, and nearly 90 percent of all goods imported into the territories came from Israel.

In 1977 the right-wing Likud Party in Israel led by Yitzhak Shamir, an ideological adherent of the notion of greater Israel, came to power and launched a major expansion of settlements. Gush Emunim, an ultraorthodox Israeli Jewish settler organization, was allowed to initiate a "long march" of colonization that crossed most of the West Bank. These policies convinced most Palestinians that the occupation was not something temporary and that their very existence as a nation with its own land was under threat (Saleh 2002).

Palestinians inside the occupied territories launched a number of early campaigns of nonviolent direct action. When Israeli authorities tried to impose an Israeli curriculum on West Bank schools, Palestinian parents and teachers went on strike. Three months later, following negotiated compromise with Israeli authorities, the schools were reopened and the former curriculum reintroduced (Grant 1990). Meanwhile, during this time Palestinians organized student and professional associations, social and cultural associations, and other grassroots structures. These institutions consolidated Palestinian nationalism and support for the outside Palestinian leadership, the PLO, as the sole representative of Palestinian national aspirations (Rigby 1991, 6).

PLO Armed Struggle

The Palestinian leadership in exile, on the other hand, was committed to armed struggle against the occupying power. The PLO was a nationalist political and paramilitary umbrella organization created in 1964 and consisting of four main political factions: Fatah, the Democratic Front for the Liberation of Palestine (DFLP), the Popular Front for the Liberation of Palestine (PFLP), and the Palestinian Communist Party (PCP). A core group of Palestinian Fatah members, including Yasser Arafat and Khalil al-Wazir (Abu Jihad), dominated the PLO. Although the four factions coalesced into a single PLO, major ideological divisions existed between the different PLO factions, along with differences in perspective over the ultimate goals and strategies of the liberation movement (Dajani 1994, 32–37).

Before the intifada the PLO-led government in exile looked to other anticolonial struggles, notably in Algeria, as models for the Palestinian liberation struggle. In the early years, "armed struggle was to become the overarching tenet guiding the movement" (Dajani 1994, 32). Article 9 of the Palestinian National Charter (Al-Mithaq al-Watani al-Filastini), drafted in 1968 by the Palestine National Council, says that Palestinian liberation would be achieved through armed struggle alone.[3] Referring to Arafat and Abu Jihad, Schiff and Ya'ari write,

> Ever since 1967 they had operated on the assumption that the inhabitants of the territories, loath to endanger themselves in any serious confrontation with the Israeli authorities, were unlikely to spearhead the Palestinian national struggle. It took time for them to absorb the enormity of their mistake. (1989, 49)

During the 1970s and early 1980s, the PLO sought to fight Israeli occupation of Palestine, using mainly multilayered guerrilla raids and terrorist attacks from bases in Lebanon, Jordan, and Syria, as well as within the West Bank and Gaza Strip. Although the PLO achieved some substantial victories, such as recognition by the United Nations and membership in the Arab League in 1974, its violence against Israelis—and its involvement in armed struggles in neighboring countries—only widened the conflict and provoked further Israeli retaliation.

After being kicked out of Jordan following the Black September events of 1970, the PLO established headquarters in Lebanon, where it fought in that country's civil war. The PLO was deemed a terrorist organization by Israel and the United States until the Madrid Conference in 1991. The reversal in diplomatic recognition occurred only after a different form of popular struggle led by Palestinians living inside the occupied territories forced the PLO to moderate its position or risk irrelevance.

The First Intifada

The PLO suffered crushing multiple military defeats in Lebanon, where it had fought first against Lebanese Maronite Christian militias, then against

Israel (whose six-month offensive in 1982 forced thousands of PLO fighters to flee). In 1982, the PLO was forced to relocate to Tunis. Remaining PLO affiliates in refugee camps within Lebanon would continue to fight against the Syrian-backed Amal militia in the so-called War of the Camps, which lasted until 1988.

Palestinians living in the occupied territories recognized that neither Arab armies nor the PLO would liberate them from Israeli occupation. At the November 1987 Arab Summit held in Amman, Jordan, Arab leaders snubbed the PLO and dropped the Palestinian issue from its priority list. Meanwhile, by 1988, more than 140 Jewish settlements comprising more than one hundred forty thousand people were inside the occupied territories.

The trigger event that sparked the uprising occurred on December 7, 1987, near the Jebaliya refugee camp in the Gaza Strip. Four Palestinians were killed and eight others seriously injured after an Israeli military vehicle struck a car carrying Palestinian day laborers in Israel. The incident sparked mass demonstrations that began in the refugee camps in Gaza and the West Bank. As part of the spontaneous uprising, Palestinians raised flags, burned tires, and confronted the soldiers en masse. The uprising spread quickly to other parts of the West Bank and Gaza. The speed with which the mobilization took place made it practically impossible for the Israeli army to know who was inciting the mass protests and when and where they would take place. A week after the intifada broke out, senior Israeli army officers held meetings with Israeli-appointed Palestinian mayors and other leaders, who insisted that the revolt was beyond their control and in the hands of the masses (Rigby 1991).

Israel and the PLO Caught by Surprise

The uprising caught the Israeli government and military completely by surprise. As Israeli military historians Schiff and Ya'ari write,

> By their rebellion, the Palestinians opened a third front . . . a new kind of warfare for which Israel had no effective response. Since the standard tools of military might are not designed to handle defiance of this sort, the IDF was wholly unprepared for the uprising in terms of its deployment, its combat doctrine, and even its store of the most

basic equipment. The result was that overnight Israel was exposed in all its weakness, which was perhaps the real import of the surprise. (1989, 31)

The PLO was also taken by surprise by the strength and intensity of the popular uprising. After the PLO leadership in Tunis grasped the significance of the intifada, it was quick to establish control over the popular uprising. By January 1988, Abu Jihad, Arafat's deputy and the coordinator of Fatah's activities in the territories, acknowledged that the battlefield had shifted. He spent the weeks following the outburst of protest activity rallying Fatah followers in the territories to join the uprising and expand its scope and reach. Israeli commandos then assassinated Abu Jihad, by far the most popular Palestinian leader and the bridge between the outside and inside, a few months into the intifada.

The intifada transformed quickly into a mass-based, organized resistance, facilitated by the political organizing that had taken place over the previous two decades (King 2007). A new and distinctive Palestinian leadership—university educated, nationalistic, and more democratic minded than the older generation—shifted the locus of power.

> With the rise of this new elite, authority had spread downward in society and become much more diffused within it than before. This was of critical importance. Earlier attempts to confront the occupation had largely failed because authority in Palestinian society was concentrated in a small stratum at the top of society. Israel could cut off the metaphorical head of the beast, and the nascent rebellion would collapse. In the Intifada, when one group of leaders was arrested another would immediately spring up. (Robinson 1997, x–xi)

Soon after the launch of the intifada, an entire network of popular committees (*lijan shabiya*) formed on an ad hoc basis "to establish an alternative organizational infrastructure to meet people's needs and provide some of the services previously administered by Israel and its appointees" (Rigby 1991, 21). The popular committees, which were created at the neighborhood, village, regional, and national levels, included education committees, medical-relief committees, social-reform committees (including community-based conflict-resolution services), agricultural committees, merchants' committees, and guard committees, which provided advance warning of attacks from soldiers and settlers and filled the law and order gap left by the resignation of the police (21).

By the spring of 1988, popular committees were found in every Palestinian city, village, and camp. They formed along factional lines, with each committee loosely tied to one of the four main PLO factions. Released Palestinian political prisoners, who had become effective organizers inside Israeli prisons, had great influence over most of them. The Israeli government, in response, banned the popular committees and made the penalty for participating in them ten years in prison. The illegal parallel structures nevertheless continued to thrive in the face of repression.

The United National Leadership of the Uprising

Within a month after the launch of the intifada the clandestine branches of the PLO's four main factions inside the occupied territories came together and formed the United National Leadership of the Uprising (UNLU, Al-Qiyada al-Wataniya al-Muwahhada).[4] The UNLU was both the local hub of the organized resistance and the middleman between the local popular committee leaders and the PLO on the outside. The UNLU's central command consisted of four individuals representing the main PLO factions. Contact and coordination with the PLO took place through factional channels of communication (Jarbawi 1990, 304). The leadership rotated, and UNLU leaders frequently changed location inside the territories to avoid being arrested, deported, or assassinated.[5]

The UNLU maintained a visible presence by distributing regular communiqués (*nida'at*) to Palestinians inside the occupied territories. These numbered leaflets, which appeared on street corners throughout the West Bank and Gaza approximately every two weeks, coordinated the campaigns of the resistance and indicated the specific actions. These included economic strikes, the boycott of Israeli products, resigning from the Israeli civilian administration, protesting the treatment of Palestinian political prisoners, and promoting agricultural self-sufficiency (Bennis 1990, 22). During the early months of the intifada, said one Palestinian, "the leaflets were followed word for word by everyone in the West Bank and Gaza—they were like a sacred text."[6]

The UNLU made explicit its direct relationship with the PLO in Tunis in the third leaflet, which appeared on January 18, 1988. All future leaflets read, "Issued by the PLO/UNL of the Uprising."[7] Although the four PLO faction leaders met to discuss and decide on the contents of the leaflets, each faction and its leadership was responsible for writing and distributing their own communiqués. Factional differences led to tactical differences and the occasional issuing of altogether different leaflets. The PLO in Tunis and local Palestinian leaders did not always see eye to eye; one area of disagreement involved the use of violence. Although the PLO distributed a leaflet calling for the death of one Israeli for each Palestinian killed, the grassroots did not respond. Intifada participants later told interviewers that they considered nonviolent means to have led to their greatest successes, and they expressed unwillingness to abandon nonviolent methods as the directive recommended (Grant 1990).

The PCP was unique in that its leaders emphasized the need for nonviolent discipline when confronting Israeli forces. Politically, the PCP insisted from the very beginning on recognizing the state of Israel within its 1967 borders—the only PLO faction to do so. The PCP advocated a progressive escalation of the intifada, distanced itself from terrorism, and emphasized the importance of local development and mass mobilization. As the only Palestinian political faction whose central leadership was located inside the occupied territories, the PCP came up with the model for popular committees during the 1970s in the form of voluntary work committees. According to Husain Barghouti, "The simplicity, efficiency, flexibility, democracy, and diffused leadership of the VWCs have been sources of inspiration in the formation of the popular committees of the uprising" (Barghouti 1990, 108). Israeli analysts appeared to concur:

> More than any other organization in the territories, the Communist party was deployed for swift action. Orders were carried out efficiently. Activists were encouraged to demonstrate (without masks) but not to draw attention to themselves or overstep the line between demonstrations and violence. Above all they were told to help establish local committees to guide the population through the turmoil. (Schiff and Ya'ari 1989, 200)

The PCP was not, however, one of the historical diaspora resistance organizations and did not join the PLO until 1974. Its communist ideology alienated many Palestinians, notably devout Muslims.

Israeli authorities imposed curfews and systematically arrested influential UNLU and popular committee leaders, outlawed research centers, banned Arab-language newspapers, and closed charitable organizations. The Israel Civil Authority destroyed most of the projects and infrastructure created by the popular committees and made above-ground organization almost impossible (Rigby 1991, 32).

Palestinian Citizens of Israel React

Arab citizens of Israel, a marginalized population of Palestinians who became citizens of Israel after the 1948 war, sympathized with Palestinians inside the occupied territories but feared the repercussions of active involvement in the uprising.[8] After the intifada broke out, Arab-Israelis organized support groups to send food and medicine to the territories. Gradually they held protest rallies, including a massive "peace day" march in December 1987 to express solidarity with the intifada. Other demonstrations involving tens of thousands of Arab-Israelis were held in Haifa and Nazareth. They collected funds, donated blood, and organized campaigns designed to publicize the plight of Palestinians living in the besieged camps and villages (Schiff and Ya'ari 1989, 171). Leaflets were secretly printed in shops inside East Jerusalem and some Palestinian citizens of Israel opened their bank accounts to the PLO.

The Israeli government worried about a spillover of the intifada into Israel proper, including coordination between Palestinians inside the occupied territories and Palestinian citizens of Israel. The thwarted Ship of Return (Al-Awda) incident reflected this Israeli fear. In February 1988, the PLO commissioned a ship, the *Sol Phryne*, to transport 130 Palestinians who had been deported since 1948 from Cyprus to Haifa. The campaign was meant to raise international awareness about the plight of Palestinian deportees, particularly after the UN Security Council passed a resolution in January 1988 calling on Israel to rescind its decision to deport Palestinians, which the United States supported (Kagian 1988).

The Palestinians aboard the ship, including prominent Palestinian mayors, university presidents, and other local leaders, were joined in the campaign by three hundred media personnel and two hundred prominent guests, including members of the American Jewish community, a member of the U.S. Congress, and Jewish and Arab-Israeli peace activists. Mohammed Milhem, a member of the PLO Executive Council and former West Bank mayor who had been deported in 1980, announced to the media, "We have chosen to go back with no guns, no explosives, and not even any stones."[9]

Israeli prime minister Yitzhak Shamir declared the voyage a "declaration of war" and announced that the boat was "loaded with killers, terrorists, and those who want to kill every one of us," and he vowed to prevent it from reaching the Haifa port.[10] A day before the *Sol Phryne* was supposed to leave Cyprus a mine blew a hole in the bottom of the ship, preventing it from leaving port.[11] The Israeli Mossad was responsible. Schiff and Ya'ari write, "In one of its few clear-cut victories during the *Intifada*, Israel not only foiled the PLO's plot to cause it embarrassment but averted what could well have been a violent clash between its Arab citizens and the army or police" (1989, 172).[12] The PLO never again made an attempt to coordinate a major nonviolent campaign involving the active participation of Palestinian citizens of Israel.

The Islamist Challenge

Although Palestinian nationalist factions were strongest at the beginning of the intifada, the Islamic movement gained strength over the course of the uprising. The largest of the Islamist groups inside the West Bank and Gaza, the Muslim Brotherhood, called for an Islamic reorientation of social life, actively opposed the secular state policies adopted in many Arab countries, and were outspoken in rejecting Western colonialism and Zionism.[13]

The Muslim Brotherhood and its offshoots, Islamic Jihad and the Islamic Resistance Movement (Harakat al-Muqawama al-Islamiyya, or Hamas) shared the goal of an Islamic Palestine governed by Islamic law (sharia) with strong ties to the larger Islamic world. Central to the ideology and teachings of the Islamic movement is that Palestine is Islamic land, held in trust for all Muslims until Judgment Day. Because of this, no leader, Palestinian or otherwise, had the right to divide it, and none of it could be ceded to Israel (or to any other non-Muslim entity).[14]

Islamic groups began to issue their own set of leaflets shortly after the outbreak of the intifada. The first Hamas leaflet, dated February 11, 1988, was uniquely different from those of the PLO-UNLU. It referred to the intifada as "al-Intifada al-Islamiya al-mubaraka"—a blessed Islamic uprising—as opposed to a national one. Prior to December 1987, Islamic Jihad had called for armed struggle against Israeli occupation forces (Hunter 1991, 67). Once the intifada began, however, Islamic Jihad, like the PLO factions, "foreswore the use of guns, grenades, and explosive devices and limited its activity to the consensual tactic of confronting Israeli soldiers in the streets with stones and petrol bombs" (67).

Neither Hamas nor Islamic Jihad was officially represented in the UNLU, although there was cooperation between nationalist and Islamic leaders at the local level. The relationship between secular nationalist and Islamic groups remained uneasy, a tension exploited by Israel. The Israeli military provided Islamist activists with weapons and supported Islamic groups as an alternative to the PLO during the 1980s.[15]

"Force, Power, and Blows" Policy Backfires

Within the first eighteen months of the uprising, Israeli troops and settlers killed about six hundred fifty Palestinians. On December 22, 1987, the UN Security Council passed a resolution denouncing Israel's disproportionate use of force against Palestinian civilians. (The United States did not exercise its veto.) In early 1988, Israeli defense minister Yitzhak Rabin introduced a policy of "force, power, and blows." The policy authorized scaling up the use of violent force against Palestinian resistors and implementing various forms of collective punishment. Israeli army chief of staff Dan Shomron explained the policy: "'They will not go to work, they will not earn a living, and they will not receive permits and business licenses until they realize that peace is as vital for them as it is for us'" (Hunter 1991, 91).

Israel's use of disproportionate violence against Palestinians, captured by the media, eventually backfired. In February 1988, CBS news footage showing Israeli soldiers breaking the limbs of four Palestinian youths with rocks and clubs caused outrage around the world (Rigby 1991, 58–59). Other incidents that attracted significant media coverage included a "live burial" of Palestinian youths.[16] Prominent members of the American Jewish community, fearful of the impact of these events on Israel's international image and on U.S. support for Israel, condemned the Israeli government's actions (Hunter 1991, 82–85). Schiff and Ya'ari write that the "shock of being caught off guard was further aggravated by Israel's failure in addressing world public opinion; it was simply incapable of making a case for its position while its army was shooting down unarmed women and children" (1989, 31).

Israeli authorities quickly responded to the public relations disaster by adopting measures designed to limit media coverage of the situation inside the occupied territories. These included extreme forms of censorship, banning Palestinian newspapers and magazines, revoking the visas of foreign journalists or suspending their press credentials, declaring military closures, and arbitrarily denying access to the occupied territories.[17]

Nonetheless, the intifada polarized Israeli society between those who supported reaching accommodation with Palestinians and those who advocated increasing the repression (Grant 1990, 68). The popular uprising had the immediate effect of reinvigorating the peace movement inside Israel. After the launch of the intifada, Israeli peace activists and members of the Knesset began to defy the Prevention of Terror Act, an Israeli law that forbade any Israeli citizen, Israeli official, or Palestinian resident to meet a PLO member in any capacity or context.[18] By mid-February 1988 there were more than thirty different organizations active in Israel to protest Israel's violent repression of the uprising (Kaminer 1996, 47–48). Peace Now, the largest of these, mobilized thousands of Israelis for rallies demanding a negotiated settlement to the Israeli-Arab conflict. Other groups, including the Dai La'kibush (End the Occupation), The Twenty-first Year, and Yesh Gvul (a military refuser group that grew out of the war in Lebanon) demanded Israeli withdrawal from the occupied territories.[19]

The spread of civil disobedience within the Israeli military was a crucial development. By early June 1988, more than five hundred reservists had signed a petition refusing to serve in the occupied territories.[20] In a country where military service is considered a sacred duty, refusing military service is highly controversial. Refusers argued that the type of military activities authorized and carried out in the occupied territories were immoral, did not promote Israel's security, and were undermining Israeli democracy and world standing. Prominent military officials became the leading advocates of "land for peace."[21]

Meanwhile, a handful of organizations united Israeli and Palestinian nonviolent activists across the Green Line. The Birzeit Solidarity Committee (BSC), a group formed in 1981 to protest Israel's closure of Birzeit University in the West Bank, was the first Israeli peace group to physically move its activities to the occupied territories.

> We wanted to show the Palestinians that some Israelis are willing to risk beating and tear-gassing. The army would not kill us because we are Jews . . . But our presence on the West Bank stirred a lot of enthusiasm among the local population. We went to Ramallah, Hebron, Dheisha refugee camp—wherever repression took place—and

put a spotlight on many dark corners of the occupation which the Israeli public would have preferred to pretend did not exist.[22]

In the mid-1980s the BSC spawned another committee, the Committee Confronting the Iron Fist (CCIF). Rigby notes, "whilst the Israeli and Palestinian members [of the committee] failed to agree on a common political platform, both sides were prepared to work together to protest against the occupation, as an exercise to further dialogue and mutual understanding" (1991, 173).

Mubarak Awad, the leading Palestinian advocate of nonviolent struggle and a resident of East Jerusalem, had spent the late 1980s calling for the creation of an "unarmed fedayeen" to conduct total resistance to the occupation. At the start of the intifada Mubarak Awad and his followers traveled to over three hundred villages under curfew to encourage popular defiance. They invited Israeli soldiers to follow them. "The more widespread the movement, the more time and money it cost the Israelis to deal with us . . . We wanted Israel to react to us rather than us react to them. This was very important."[23]

The Israeli Ministry of the Interior announced that it would not renew Awad's visa and that he would be deported. When his appeal to the Israeli High Court of Justice and intervention by U.S. diplomats on his behalf failed, Awad was deported to the United States. UNLU leaflets were nevertheless filled with calls for popular nonviolent defiance that Awad had advocated for years.

Political Victory: Jordan Cuts Ties to the West Bank

Less than eighteen months into the intifada, the popular uprising achieved a significant, albeit unexpected, victory. On July 31, 1988, Jordan's King Hussein went on television to announce his decision to sever Jordan's administrative and judicial ties with the West Bank. King Hussein declared in his public announcement that "Jordan is not Palestine" and said, "Jordan does not have any sovereignty over the West Bank. The West Bank belongs to the Palestinians" (Gause 1991, 201). King Hussein said that Jordan would not participate in a joint Palestinian-Jordanian delegation to any peace conference, as the PLO was the official representative of the Palestinian people. He called for the creation of an independent Palestinian state (201).

King Hussein's abrupt decision came as a surprise to both the United States and Israel. It forced both to recognize that there was no way around dealing with the PLO. The so-called Jordanian option, whereby Jordan would maintain sovereignty over part of the West Bank while negotiating with Israel on the behalf of Palestinians (an option that was almost universally rejected by the local leaders of the intifada), was off the table.

King Hussein's decision paved the way to the PLO's declaration of independence. On the same night that Hussein made his declaration, the Israeli police arrested Feisal al-Husseini, the senior Fatah person in the West Bank, and confiscated a document entitled "Plan for Making a Declaration of Independence" from his office. The plan, which became known as the Husseini document, envisioned the declaration of an independent Palestinian state within the borders laid down in the original 1947 partition plan. The uniqueness of the plan was not only its determination to declare Palestinian independence but also its emphasis on local leadership assuming a focal role in the new government (Schiff and Ya'ari 1989, 279).[24]

Declaration of Independence and International Response

In November 1988 at the Palestine National Council (PNC) special session convened in Algiers, PLO chairman Arafat read a Palestinian declaration of independence. Within three weeks more than fifty countries had recognized Palestinian independence. Although the declaration of independence received the unanimous support of the PNC delegates, the Palestinians remained divided about how to achieve independence in practice. Rival Palestinian leaders and political factions were "unable to formulate a coherent, unified political program to take full advantage of the vacuum King Hussein had created. Some were still determined to pursue the armed struggle, while others were in favor of negotiations" (O'Ballance 1998, 51).

On December 14, 1988, during a special UN General Assembly session in Geneva, Arafat recognized Israel's right to exist, endorsed Resolution 242 and a two-state solution, and rejected terrorism in all its forms (Schiff and Ya'ari 1989, 294–326).[25] The long-held aim of the PLO to liberate all of historic Palestine had been modified by the intifada. Arafat called for a three-point peace initiative advocating the establishment of an international peace conference under UN auspices, a UN peacekeeping force to assist Israeli withdrawal from the occupied territories, and a comprehensive peace settlement based on UN resolutions 242 and 338.

Arafat's announcement, denounced by Palestinian members of the "rejectionist front," nevertheless led to a significant change in U.S. foreign policy. President Ronald Reagan's secretary of state, George Shultz, declared that a thirteen-year U.S. ban on direct contact with the PLO was ended and that official dialogue with the PLO would begin. The announcement stunned Prime Minister Shamir's government, making Israel feel vulnerable (Pollock 1991).

After Arafat's announcement, the United States applied significant pressure on the Israeli government to develop a peace plan.[26] The first concrete U.S. diplomatic initiative, known as the Shultz Plan, envisioned elections inside the occupied territories to select leaders to negotiate with Israel, the convening of an international conference, and initial agreement on transitional arrangements followed by negotiations on a final settlement. Shamir remained adamant that there would be no Palestinian state, no talks with the PLO, and no international conference (Hunter 1991, 178). Infuriating the U.S. administration, Shamir announced in January 1990 that "a big *aliya* [Jewish immigration] requires a big Israel" (Pollock 1991, 126).

Reagan's successor, President George H. W. Bush, was "viscerally opposed to new Israeli settlements in the territories" (Gruen 1991, 257). Newly installed U.S. secretary of state James Baker, in a critical speech given before the American Israel Public Affairs Committee, called on Israel to stop dreaming of "Greater Israel," to stop building settlements, and to reach out to Palestinians (O'Ballance 1998, 69).[27] In January 1990, Senator Robert Dole called for a cut in U.S. foreign aid to Israel, which he insisted had turned into an "entitlement program."[28] One analyst noted that a majority of American Jewish leaders shared President Bush's sentiments (Gruen 1991).[29]

Continued Civil Resistance and Increasing Violence

As politicians began to consider different peace plans, Palestinian civil resistance inside the occupied territories continued. In 1989, the village of Beit Sahour, a small, mostly Christian Palestinian village located near Bethlehem on the West Bank, launched six weeks of total civil disobedience to the occupation. The entire village of Beit Sahour burned their identity cards and refused to pay taxes to Israeli authorities.[30] The Israeli military's response to Beit Sahour's self-declared "no taxation without representation" campaign was expectedly swift and harsh. Israeli troops besieged the city, declared a curfew, ransacked homes and shops, and prevented anyone from entering or leaving the village.

Beit Sahour's civil resistance attracted significant media attention. Well-known international personalities including Archbishop Desmond Tutu of South Africa expressed solidarity with the people of Beit Sahour (Saleh 2002, 11). Israeli and international solidarity activists slipped through checkpoints to join the village in their resistance and refused to leave when ordered by the Israeli military. Although the United States vetoed a UN resolution condemning the Israeli crackdown on Beit Sahour, the siege was lifted after six weeks.

At the same time, by 1990 the intifada had begun to lose momentum. Diplomacy stalled, economic conditions inside the occupied territories worsened, and the intifada no longer captured international headlines. It had also become increasingly violent and, thus, less participatory. In May 1990 the Palestine Liberation Front (PLF) launched a dramatic seaborne raid on the Tel Aviv beach. Israel immediately accused Arafat of reneging on his Geneva promise to abandon terrorism.[31] When Arafat refused President Bush's demand that he condemn the failed raid and expel the PLF from the PLO, Bush ordered a suspension of talks with the PLO.

Intra-Palestinian violence took a toll also on the resistance. Despite attempts to broker an accord between Fatah and Hamas, the level of violent clashes between these groups intensified. "It seemed as though the tempo of the *Intifada* was slowing down as the Palestinians in the Occupied Territories were becoming more involved in internecine struggles than civil resistance against Israel" (O'Ballance 1998, 131). For example, by the spring of 1990, more Palestinians were being killed by fellow Palestinians than by Israeli soldiers (Rigby 1991, 45).

The 1990–1991 Gulf War and Madrid Conference

One Palestinian activist called the 1990–1991 Gulf War "the start of the end of the intifada."[32] Yasser Arafat's support for Saddam Hussein, who linked Iraq's withdrawal from Kuwait to Israel's withdrawal from the occupied Palestinian Territories, had disastrous consequences for Palestinians. Images of Palestinians "cheering" in the streets helped malign the Palestinian national cause, led to feelings of betrayal in the Israeli peace movement, and caused a financial crisis for the PLO, whose funding from Arab countries was seriously reduced. The Gulf War encouraged Palestinian leaders to abandon the local struggle and to look to the outside for solutions to the conflict.

[The Gulf War] took the focus away from the local struggle and made people think that the answer would come from the outside. The Palestinian leadership came to the conclusion that the balance of power had shifted and that the interests of the United States would dictate the solution. They believed the U.S. would force Israel to pull out of the occupied territories because the occupation was becoming too much of a burden and was against its interests in the region. This proved to be very shortsighted.[33]

With its prestige and regional position strengthened following victory in the Gulf War, the Bush administration pressed forward with a regional peace initiative. The Madrid Conference, launched in October 1991, was the official start of the peace process. Israeli and Palestinian delegations met for bilateral talks for the first time. The PLO, however, was not allowed to participate in the Madrid talks. Instead, the Palestinian delegation was led by Haider Abdel Shafi, Feisal al-Husseini, and Hanan Ashwari, local leaders from inside the occupied territories who had ties to the PLO in Tunis.[34] The Israeli delegation was led by Prime Minister Shamir and Benjamin Netanyahu, a Likud member and deputy foreign minister.

After more than eight months of Madrid talks, participants had made little progress on resolving key issues involved in the Israeli-Palestinian conflict. The issue of Jewish settlements inside the occupied territories was one that led to a stalemate in the Madrid talks (later, this issue was bypassed altogether in the Oslo Accords).

1992 Election of Yitzhak Rabin

In the June 1992 elections, Israeli Labour leader Yitzhak Rabin defeated the incumbent Shamir, ending fifteen years of Likud rule. Rabin ran on a platform that supported participating in the U.S.-sponsored Middle East peace process (he criticized Shamir's stalling tactics), improving Israeli relations with the United States, and halting the construction of "political" housing developments in the occupied territories.[35] Rabin announced that he would work to achieve Palestinian autonomy within a year, followed by a five-year interim administration and then final status talks.

A preelection poll of retired Israeli generals and senior intelligence officials conducted by the newspaper *Maariv* revealed that some 75 percent backed Rabin and over 90 percent thought that Israel should negotiate with the PLO. "Shamir lost the elections because of the widespread belief among Israelis that we had to do something about the Palestinian problem. The *Intifada* shattered the status quo. That was its greatest achievement" (O'Ballance 1998, 127).

The 1993 Oslo Accords

In 1993, a secret negotiating track between Israeli and exiled PLO officials began in Oslo. These talks, which excluded Palestinians from inside the occupied territories, culminated in the signing of the Declaration of Principles (DOP) by Yitzhak Rabin and Yasser Arafat in September 1993 on the White House lawn. The DOP paved the way for a series of agreements known collectively as the Oslo Accords.[36]

Oslo established a new, complex political reality in the West Bank and Gaza.[37] The Oslo Accords created the Palestinian Authority (PA), which was dominated by PLO leadership from Tunis. The PA assumed limited control over parts of Gaza and the West Bank. In this interim phase of limited Palestinian autonomy, 75 percent of Palestinians continued to live under Israeli rule. Israel retained de facto control over the land, water, and air access to the occupied territories. Glenn Robinson writes that the irony of the Oslo Accords was that they brought to power an outside leadership that had not stepped foot inside the territories for almost three decades, and which promised to end the popular struggle against the occupation rather than lead it:

> Oslo revived a fiscally bankrupt and politically dying PLO in Tunis and put in power in Gaza and the West Bank a political elite quite removed from the realities of modern Palestine . . . The elite that actually took power in Palestine after Oslo was not the same as the political elite which produced the Intifada. Put bluntly, the PLO in Tunis successfully captured political power in Gaza and the West Bank not because it led the revolution but because it promised to end it. The PA had to construct its own political base, which would diminish the possibility of a new elite inside the West Bank and Gaza while consolidating its own power. (1997, 175–77)

In the post-Oslo period, Jewish-only bypass roads and illegal Israeli settlements expanded, carving up the future Palestinian state into noncontiguous enclaves. The number of Jewish settlements doubled during this time.[38] Continued occupation policies like military closures and further restrictions on the freedom of movement (like denying Palestinians access to Jerusalem), combined with the PA's own economic mismanagement, incompetent governance, and divide-and-rule tactics, increased the level of poverty and political repression inside the occupied territories during the Oslo peace period (Roy 2001).

The Oslo Accords brought the PA into the occupied territories to confront Hamas and the more radical Palestinian groups that posed a threat to Israeli security. Arafat created more than fifteen different security forces to achieve this end, and as part of his own strategy of divide and rule. In the post-Oslo period, Palestinian women were largely excluded from the political decision-making process. Palestinian women, who had been leaders in popular committees (and even in the UNLU) and in the forefront of nonviolent campaigns during the intifada, were marginalized after the PA was installed inside the occupied territories.[39]

During this time there was very little contact between Palestinian and Israeli civilians, with restrictions imposed by both sides on freedom of movement, such as an Israeli law that prohibited Israeli citizens from entering some Palestinian areas. During the post-Oslo period, Palestinian and Jewish extremists led violent attacks on civilians from the other side, intensifying the level of distrust and animosity between the two sides. A combination of Palestinian frustration with the PA and a lack of progress in the peace process led to the outbreak of violence following Ariel Sharon's visit to the Haram al-Sharif/Temple Mount in September 2000 and the start of the second, Al-Aqsa Intifada.[40]

Some analysts have considered the suicide bombing campaign during the Al-Aqsa Intifada successful because of Israel's partial withdrawal from the West Bank and Gaza Strip (Pape 2003, 2005). It would be very difficult, however, to argue that the suicide terrorism campaign has actually moved the Palestinian population closer to the goal of independent statehood. On the contrary, the campaigns led to the cessation of negotiations, repeated elections of hawkish Israeli governments, and a 2009 war in the Gaza Strip between Israel and Hamas. Thus the temporary withdrawal of Israeli military forces during the Al-Aqsa Intifada must be seen in the context of the wider conflict between the two sides, which has not subsided. The Al-Aqsa Intifada represented an intensification of violent resistance that has resulted in few strategic gains for either side.

ANALYSIS

The First Intifada achieved a number of important intermediate political goals and transformed Palestinian society. This stands in stark contrast to the decades of PLO-led armed struggle that preceded it. However, Palestinian-led civilian-based resistance was eventually overshadowed by violence and was not part of the PA's political strategy for ending the Israeli occupation. In our data set, we categorize the First Intifada as a partial success, but it was far more successful than its violent counterparts.

Participation in Civilian-Based Resistance

According to Palestinian activist Ghassan Andoni, "with the 1987 intifada, especially in the first two years, Palestinians set a great example of how civilian-based resistance could actually beat an occupation army."[41] Every sector of Palestinian society was actively involved in acts of resistance, including sewing Palestinian flags, growing backyard gardens, defying curfews, painting graffiti, creating "illegal" classrooms, destroying identity cards, refusing to pay taxes or to work for the occupying authorities, and boycotting Israeli products. Palestinians built autonomous structures and institutions and activated a vast network of popular committees that allowed the uprising to sustain itself. Broad-based participation in the committees helped Palestinian society overcome social fragmentation while providing the mechanism for mass mobilization.

The UNLU, a unique feature of the First Intifada, brought the different PLO factions together in an unprecedented manner and injected the uprising with leadership, discipline, and direction. As a leader from a Palestinian women's association said at the time, the "reason people follow the UNLU has to do with the fact that the leadership is not just coming down from above. It's not just giving orders to the people that some might choose to follow and some choose not to. The leadership really comes from inside the people themselves, reflecting the people's own aspirations" (Bennis 1990, 24).

Although little data exist concerning Palestinian attitudes toward violent and nonviolent action during the First Intifada, some data do exist. In a 1994 poll at the end of the First Intifada, only 33 percent expressed support for armed attacks against Israeli targets in the occupied territories (CPRS Survey Research Unit 1994).[42] More recently, a 2002 study demonstrates that Palestinians are much more supportive of and willing to participate in nonviolent mass actions than in violent action (Kull et al. 2002).

The use of nonviolent methods appealed to different participants for not only moral reasons but also the lower barriers to participation. Of women's involvement in the intifada, Rana Nashashibi, a Palestinian activist, remarked that "'it has not been easy for women to defy their traditional roles and go out in public to participate actively in the national struggle.'"[43] The UNLU's commitment to nonviolent methods of struggle provided a lower barrier for women to mobilize, whereas requiring violent acts may have dissuaded large numbers of women from participating.

Even Palestinian children expressed a reluctance to engage in violence. A 1990 study of Palestinian children indicated that only 2 percent aspired to participate in armed struggle, whereas others expressed a desire to develop a trade or become teachers, nurses, or doctors.[44]

Thus lower physical, moral, and informational barriers made participation in the nonviolent campaign easier than participation in the violent campaigns.

Impact on Israeli Society and the Region

The intifada shifted the battlefield to Israel's doorstep and shattered the popular myth that Israel could annex the West Bank and Gaza Strip without significant resistance. The intifada was a different form of resistance, and one that Israel was not well equipped to deal with. As one Israeli general described it, "The mass-based nature of the intifada and its relatively nonviolent character convinced many Israelis that there was a partner on the other side. We knew we could do business with them."[45] The intifada prompted Israelis to challenge their government in unprecedented ways.

> Frustration [inside Israel] also stems from the fact that many Israelis, of all political persuasions, have come to feel that where the conflict with the Palestinians is concerned, their country is living a lie. They now believe that their leaders deceived them in pronouncing that the Palestinian people did not exist; that the Arabs in the territories did not want their leaders; that the PLO forced itself on the Palestinians by violence and intimidation; that the status quo of occupation could be maintained indefinitely. (Schiff and Ya'ari 1989, 289)

Groups like the BSC and the CCIF brought together Israelis and Palestinians who did not always agree on political objectives but were nevertheless united in their opposition to the occupation. Mainstream groups like Peace

Now brought the masses out to the streets to challenge occupation policies, notably the building of settlements. Because of Israel's heavy-handed response to the uprising, "the *Intifada* had created cracks in American Jewry's monolithic support for Israel; more than any time in the past, Israel's policy vis-à-vis the Palestinians was being criticized by Jewish circles in the United States" (Schiff and Ya'ari 1989, 303).

Further afield, the popular uprising shattered the idea that Jordanians could negotiate on behalf of Palestinians and forced the PLO to moderate its political position, thereby paving the way to direct negotiations between the PLO and Israel. The ending of the Jordanian occupation of the West Bank and the mutual recognition between the Israeli government and the PLO were major political successes of the intifada. As one noted Israeli scholar concludes, "It is impossible to understand Yitzhak Shamir's acceptance of the 'Madrid framework' or the Labour Party's victory in the 1992 elections without understanding the effect of this change" (Rabinovich 2004, 34).

Weaknesses of Palestinian Civilian-Based Resistance

The popular uprising nevertheless failed to transform the power relationship between Palestinians and the Israeli government sufficiently to bring about Israeli troop withdrawal or the ending of settlement construction inside the occupied territories. The creation of the PA ended up being an additional barrier to, rather than an extension of, the popular resistance movement. External factors, notably U.S. foreign policy and American domestic politics, clearly influenced the trajectory and outcome of the First Intifada. At the same time, organizational and strategic shortcomings of the Palestinian resistance, particularly its inability to exploit Israel's dependency relationships, weakened the popular uprising.

As Radwan Abu Ayyash, a UNLU leader during the intifada, reflected, "What was lacking was a clear strategic vision. We Palestinians have virtue but no strategy."[46] Whereas most UNLU and popular committee leaders regarded the intifada itself as the vehicle for the achievement of Palestinian goals and emphasized the need to upgrade the struggle (which they argued should not be compromised by premature negotiations), the public figures "believed that diplomatic maneuvers should receive priority, and hence urged compromise, restraint, and moderation" (Hunter 1991, 74). At the same time, continued calls by the Palestinian leadership for strikes and work stoppages at a time when Palestinians were barely able to make ends meet caused only further frustration and disillusionment.⁴⁷ In the post-Oslo period, noted Ghassan Andoni, "People were demoralized and convinced that they had no role to play. There was no trusted leadership. In civilian-based resistance, if there is no trusted leadership, you cannot mobilize the people."⁴⁸

Failure to Achieve Unity

The Palestinian leadership during the First Intifada failed to achieve unity around a shared political vision and strategy. Fundamental divisions persisted related to strategy and tactics between the different PLO factions, between outside and inside leadership, and between Islamists and secular nationalists.

> The variety of official and unofficial organizations to which Palestinians belong, as well as the factionalism and rivalry between groups and organizations claiming to represent them, remained a constant problem. These conditions have compromised the ability of Palestinians to arrive at a strategic consensus on how to proceed with their resistance. (Dajani 1994, 56)

The inability of the Palestinian leadership to create an inclusive, nonpartisan resistance organization left the Intifada vulnerable to Israeli divide-and-rule tactics. Meanwhile, the PLO was dominated by one political faction (Fatah), which weakened its claim to represent the entire Palestinian people. With the exception of the PCP, the PLO factions followed different external chains of command. The UNLU as a body did not have a direct relationship with the PLO leadership in Tunis.

The persistence of PLO splinter groups and a "rejectionist front" undermined its ability to achieve centralized command and control. The leading Islamic factions, Islamic Jihad and Hamas, never joined the PLO's centralized command structure and never bought into the PLO's negotiating strategy. The local leadership of the uprising, including UNLU and popular committee leaders, deferred to the outside PLO leadership on issues of policy and strategy.

Undisciplined Violence

Intra-Palestinian violence (referred to as the intra-fada by some) significantly weakened the Palestinian struggle. At the beginning of the intifada a number of Palestinian collaborators turned over their Israeli-issued weapons in mosques and declared their allegiance to the Palestinian nationalist cause.[49] Over the course of the intifada, however, nonviolent forms of intra-Palestinian conflict resolution were replaced by threats and executions. Israel's policy of deporting, arresting, and assassinating local Palestinian leaders only exacerbated this problem of disunity and significantly weakened the defensive base of the Palestinian resistance.

The mixing of violent and nonviolent sanctions also weakened the popular uprising by encouraging disunity and discouraging popular participation. At the beginning of the intifada, the UNLU and Hamas both explicitly banned the use of firearms. Radwan Abu Ayyash explained why this gave Palestinians a strategic advantage over Israel: "We knew that we could not neutralize Israel's power with weapons. We won the media game at that time by showing Israelis attacking unarmed Palestinians. Israel was defeated politically."[50] Schiff and Ya'ari (1989) describe the strategic advantage of the early Palestinian ban on weapons:

> Despite animosity and rage, the Palestinians did not resort to arms—giving them a distinct advantage in the contest for sympathetic public opinion. There was a modest collection of arms within the territories, and even these few weapons could have wreaked havoc among unsuspecting Israelis, especially civilians. But the Palestinians appreciated almost instinctively that restraint was in their own self-interest; resort to arms would only justify the IDF's sweeping use of its far superior firepower and cause the Palestinians punishing losses. (32)

At the same time, there was no Palestinian consensus about the role of violence in their struggle. Splinter groups like Fatah-RC, PFLP-GC, and Islamic groups like Hamas never accepted the strategic rationale behind nonviolent struggle. An undisciplined form of violence eventually overtook the intifada. Paramilitary groups inside the occupied territories held parades, brandished axes and clubs, and attended camps that provided training in throwing Molotov cocktails and engaging in hand-to-hand combat with knives. Particularly in the villages, local militias became prominent fixtures (Schiff and Ya'ari 1989, 287). As many respected local leaders were imprisoned or deported over the course of the intifada, it became difficult to control the youth. Rocks, petrol bombs, and knives, which obviously did not compare in lethality to Israeli weaponry, nevertheless occasionally killed Israeli soldiers and civilians and alienated potential supporters inside Israel.

Failure to Extend the Nonviolent Battlefield

The Israeli government did not rely entirely on Palestinians inside the occupied territories to maintain the occupation. It could compensate for Palestinian-led strikes by bringing in cheap labor from outside. Additionally, Israel received significant amounts of military and economic aid from the United States. Still,

> one way for the Palestinians to increase their direct leverage against Israel is to promote political divisions within Israel and cultivate the support of Israeli citizens for the Palestinian cause. Another way of doing this is to mobilize pressure from abroad, particularly from the United States, which has the leverage to vitally affect the options open to Israel. However, the Intifada failed to mobilize the support of third parties, such as Israeli citizens or the U.S. government. (Schock 2005, 160–61)

Despite the significant impact the intifada had on the Israeli public, the Palestinian outreach strategy was deficient. "For most Palestinians the Israeli public and government constituted a secondary strategic target. No explicit strategy was formulated to affect these specifically, except insofar as they would be influenced indirectly by the pressure of the *Intifada*" (Dajani 1994, 83).

Adam Keller, an Israeli peace activist, said that the Palestinian struggle was weakened because Israelis never perceived what was happening inside the occupied territories as nonviolent. Most of the campaigns of Palestinian civil resistance were carried out in cities and villages inside the occupied territories. These campaigns were largely out of sight for most Israelis. Keller added, "Most Israelis do not consider stone throwing to be nonviolent, and this is mostly all they ever saw."[51]

Mubarak Awad argues that the PLO could have encouraged Palestinian citizens of Israel to launch a nonviolent movement for equal citizen rights inside Israel in order to support the Palestinian struggle for self-determination inside the occupied territories:

> I supported extending the *Intifada* to Israel where Palestinians on the inside fight for civil rights and human rights and equality inside Israel. But the PLO said "no way." I was upset with the PLO because if we had an *Intifada* there and here and in different places we could place so much pressure on Israel. But the PLO said "no". . . . This was a huge strategic mistake. It showed the shortsightedness of the PLO, who believed in non-interference in the internal affairs of Israel.[52]

Azmi Bishara, a Palestinian and former member of the Israeli Knesset, said that during the First Intifada there was no strategic cooperation between the UNLU and leaders of the Arab-Israeli community.[53] The one major nonviolent campaign involving coordination between the PLO and Arab-Israeli leaders, the thwarted Ship of Return episode, demonstrated the potential power of a functional alliance between the two populations of Palestinians.

The United States as a Main Center of Gravity

At the beginning of the intifada, images of Palestinian children confronting Israeli tanks galvanized international support for the Palestinian cause, including inside the United States. The United States voted twice against Israel for its disproportionate use of violence and for its policy of deportations at the beginning of the uprising. Dr. Mark Lance, who was active in the U.S.-based organization Stop US Tax-Funded Aid to Israel Now (SUSTAIN), said that the intifada had a profound impact on American civil society groups:

> The intifada was very successful in that for the first time inside the U.S. Palestinians were viewed as victims of aggression. The intifada was presented by the U.S. media as a positive shift away from terrorism and towards nonviolent resistance. Progressive American peace groups, including those who had opposed the war in Vietnam, began to discuss the Israeli occupation in the context of their larger peace work. This was the first time that this had ever happened. The media images helped build a grassroots movement inside the U.S. For example, a coalition of Arab-Muslim groups, small Jewish groups, and peace and justice groups began to build a coalition around a two-state solution.[54]

A source of great frustration for many solidarity activists inside the United States, nevertheless, was that Arafat and the PLO leadership never made the creation of a global grassroots movement in support of Palestinian rights a strategic priority. As Lance put it succinctly, "The PLO was no ANC."[55]

After the signing of the Oslo Accords, said Ghassan Andoni, "The PLO came back and the Palestinian people did not pay attention to the details like settlements and Jerusalem. As land confiscation continued, the PLO convinced people that these were only temporary 'growing pains' from the negotiations."[56] With gross power asymmetries remaining between Palestinians inside the occupied territories and the Israeli government, Palestinian-led civilian resistance was ended prematurely and replaced by a less-participatory form of resistance.

TABLE 5.2 **THE NONVIOLENT AND VIOLENT PALESTINIAN CAMPAIGNS COMPARED, 1987-1992**

	NONVIOLENT CAMPAIGN	VIOLENT CAMPAIGN
ESTIMATED PARTICIPATION	HUNDREDS OF THOUSANDS	TENS OF THOUSANDS
PRIMARY PARTICIPANTS	MIDDLE CLASS	MALE YOUTH
	STUDENTS AND INTELLECTUALS	PLO AND ISLAMIC
	TRADE UNIONS	EXTREMIST GROUPS
	BUSINESSES	
	POOR	
	WOMEN'S GROUPS	
	ISLAMIC GROUPS	
	MARXISTS	
	PALESTINIAN DIASPORA	
SECURITY LOYALTY SHIFTS	YES	NO
TACTICAL DIVERSITY	CLEAR	UNCLEAR
EXTERNAL STATE SPONSOR	NO	YES
INTERNATIONAL SANCTIONS	YES	YES
EFFECTS OF REGIME REPRESSION	BACKFIRE	SUPPRESSION
OUTCOME	PARTIAL SUCCESS	FAILURE

CONCLUSION

The First Intifada demonstrates how diverse and numerous participants can activate different mechanisms that translate into leverage over the opponent.

Because of the active participation of hundreds of thousands of diverse participants, the nonviolent campaign was able to generate significant political and economic pressure on Israel and win over sympathetic audiences within Israel and abroad. This stands in contrast to the violent elements of the campaign, which were relatively homogeneous and disconnected from potential levers of change within Israel and abroad. Repression against nonviolent activists generated outrage at home and abroad, whereas the same audiences perceived repression against violent elements as legitimate.

The intifada also highlights some instructive dynamics that help to explain its inability to succeed completely. In particular, the presence of simultaneous violent campaigns and the inability to achieve internal unity undermined its success. This finding reinforces our earlier proposition that maintaining discipline in nonviolent action may be a prerequisite for success. The failure was probably not due entirely to the effectiveness of the Israeli response or to any preconditions that doomed the campaign to end. Rather, the mismanagement of the resistance campaign may provide an equal or better explanation of the outcome.

CHAPTER SIX **THE PHILIPPINE PEOPLE POWER MOVEMENT, 1983-1986**

IN FEBRUARY 1986, less than two years after the start of a mass popular uprising, the Philippine dictator, Ferdinand Marcos, was ousted from power.[1] At the time scholars predicted that the Marcos regime would be overthrown by a communist insurgency or a military coup (Snyder 1992, 1998; Thompson 1991, 1996). Instead, a popular uprising that involved nearly every segment of society, including Marcos's armed defenders, ultimately toppled the regime. The mass civil resistance that followed a political assassination and stolen election undermined the dictator's most important sources of domestic and international power and led to a relatively peaceful democratic transition. While that transition has not been without problems since 1986, the Philippines People Power movement stands as an impressive example of effective nonviolent resistance.

THE RULE AND DEMISE OF FERDINAND MARCOS

Ferdinand Marcos rose to power in a postcolonial, postindependence Philippines at a time when bureaucrats were eclipsing landed elites as the dominant economic and political powers inside the country (Anderson 1988). After he was first elected president in 1965, Marcos consolidated his power by centralizing state institutions, restructuring the military, and institutionalizing cronyism. He initially took over the national defense portfolio and reined in a dispersed military structure by creating Regional Unified Commands that replaced soldiers' loyalties to provincial landowners with ties to him and the state. Police forces and the constabulary were brought under the Armed Forces of the Philippines (AFP) in 1967, and Marcos created an antiriot squad that expanded the Presidential Security Force, placing them under the command of his cousin, Fabian Ver, who was later put in charge of the entire AFP.

Using a combination of promotions, salary raises, and other perks, Marcos created a loyal security force "with broad powers and substantial autonomy from Philippine society" (Boudreau 2004, 71; McCoy 1999, 124–30).

With the backing of the United States, Marcos consolidated executive power while amassing great wealth through centralization, state monopolies, patronage, external aid, and loans from international financial institutions.

Early Protest Activity

Resistance to the Marcos regime began in the late 1960s, when students, workers, and farmers launched mostly symbolic, ad-hoc protests targeting various government policies. Student activism was aided by the proliferation of "university belt" campuses that brought youths from the provinces into the cities and encouraged ties between young people and expanding urban labor communities. The youth wing of the Communist Party of the Philippines (CPP), a Maoist offshoot of the Partido Komunista ng Pilipinas (PKP) created in 1968, was very active in using protests to expose regime largesse, and the CPP became the leading force behind the creation of underground resistance to the Marcos regime (Boudreau 2004, 74; De Dios 1988). At the same time, Church-supported groups like the Federation of Free Farmers and the Federation of Free Workers organized protests and sit-ins to challenge the regime's agrarian policy (Boudreau 2004, 72; Wurfel 1988).

Other forms of resistance in the early 1970s challenged Marcos's moves to centralize power. In 1971, demonstrations calling for a fair Constitutional Commission turned into broad denunciations of the Marcos regime. Clashes between students and police outside the Malacanang Palace in January 1971 left six protestors dead. By February, protests were raging on all the university campuses, and public plazas had become the site of teach-ins by new activist organizations. In March, transport workers went on strike; this was followed by a joint student-worker People's March that ended in violence. This "First Quarter Storm" was "the Philippines' first urban movement to make national, integrated demands" (Boudreau 2004, 73).

Until the time that Marcos declared martial law in September 1972, the judiciary remained independent and had even passed decisions curtailing U.S. influence over the Philippine economy. In 1972, the Constitutional Convention delegates showed signs of support for a new parliamentary system in which Marcos and his wife were barred from holding executive power. Media reports accused Marcos of bribing and pressuring delegates to influence the draft. That same year, Marcos's Nacionalista Party was defeated in the legislative elections by the Liberal Party. With his opponents poised to take power, Marcos turned to the "globally accessible language and methods of anti-communist authoritarianism" and portrayed himself as being in a life-and-death struggle with leftist insurgents (Boudreau 2004, 74). His regime even organized fake attacks against officials and set off explosions around Manila in order to shore up domestic and international support for his declaration of martial law later that year (74; van der Kroef 1974, 40).[2]

Armed Challenges to the Regime

A leftist armed insurgency concentrated in the north and a Muslim-led insurgency concentrated on the southern Philippine island of Mindanao posed armed challenges to the Marcos regime. On the left, the New People's Army (NPA) was created in early 1969 as the armed wing of the CPP, which was founded in December 1968.[3] The CPP was based on Marxist-Leninist-Maoist thought, and the NPA was guided by Maoist guerrilla principles (Schock 2005, 70). Although the CPP and the NPA were relatively weak in the early 1970s, their influence expanded after Marcos declared martial law in 1972, and legal avenues of dissent were shut down. As in Burma, hundreds of educated Filipino youth were driven into the rural areas, where they joined the armed guerrilla movement. Still, in the early part of the decade the NPA had bases in only one province (Isabella) and adopted Yenan-style fixed bases that "over-estimated rebels' military power" (Boudreau 2004, 138). The Marcos regime's counterinsurgency efforts, which concentrated nearly 7,000 troops in the northern provinces, had reduced the number of NPA forces from 2,500 (500 armed guerrillas and 2,000 civilian supporters) in 1972 to approximately 500 combined fighters and supporters by 1974 (Boudreau 2004, 138).

The Marcos regime simultaneously faced a Muslim insurgency from 1971, concentrated on the southern island of Mindanao. Unlike the CCP and the NPA, the Mindanao independence movement (the precursor to the Moro National Liberation Movement) received some support from Libya and Malaysia, and strong support from the village level (Boudreau 2004, 139; Byman et al. 2001, 14). Although the Islamic separatist movement was stronger than the communist insurgency, it waged provincial battles "that distracted, but did not disrupt state-building projects" (Boudreau 2004, 139). Differences between the Muslim insurgents and anti-Marcos Catholics prevented a close alliance between these groups, though in the 1980s there was some agreement reached between them. While there is little evidence that the Muslim insurgency succeeded in extracting political concessions from the Marcos regime, Boudreau notes that the armed attacks in the south did force a greater concentration of AFP troops there, sapping the counterinsurgency efforts against the northern communists, which "unarguably helped the NPA to survive" (139; Overholt 1986).

Martial Law

Soon after his reelection in 1969, Marcos systematically removed constitutional restraints on his power until he finally declared martial law on September 21, 1972. Marcos cited an intensifying threat posed by armed insurgencies and the need to eliminate corruption and implement land reform to defend martial law. In July of that year the government had intercepted a shipment of arms from North Korea intended for the NPA. Meanwhile, the number of bomb explosions in Manila increased that summer, and an alleged assassination attempt on Defense Minister Juan Ponce Enrile's life proved to be the final act used by Marcos to justify martial law (Goodno 1991, 65; Wurfel 1977, 7). More realistically, note scholars, "martial law was declared to prevent a presidential election, in which Marcos would most likely have been replaced by Benigno Aquino, and to facilitate Marcos's concentration of wealth" (Schock 2005, 68).

Under martial law, Marcos ruled via unilateral presidential decree. He suspended the Supreme Court and legislature, closed down the Constitutional Commission and shut down important media outlets. Soldiers were deployed throughout the country to arrest activists and prevent demonstrations. The regime imprisoned parliamentary rivals, student activists, labor-union leaders, and opposition political leaders, including opposition senator Benigno Aquino, who remained in prison until 1980 (Boudreau 2004, 7).

Martial law, according to Wurfel, did not eliminate opposition activists but disbursed them (Thompson 1995, 57–63; Wurfel 1988, 114–53). Similarly, the regime's crackdown on the NPA caused a dispersion of the armed leftist movement until it encompassed all regions of the country by the 1980s (Schock 2005, 70–71; Wurfel 1988, 223–27). The CPP responded to the regime's counterinsurgency drive by focusing more on political activities.

Reformist and Underground Opposition

Although Marcos encountered some resistance from his political rivals in the early 1970s, during this time the mainstream opposition leaders were largely silenced or co-opted, and opposition political parties were in disarray (Mendoza 2009). For the first six years of martial law, Schock notes, "the reformist opposition was impotent, as most opposition leaders were in prison, in exile, or collaborating with the regime" (2005, 70). Marcos largely tolerated his reformist political opponents as long as they did not unify or mobilize mass support (Wurfel 1988, 204–6).

The CPP, whose armed presence expanded geographically in the countryside, began to develop an urban base as well. In 1974, the CPP announced the creation of its National Democratic Front (NDF). The NDF, designed to promote a more broad-based movement, contained civil associations that passed under martial law. The NDF brought together groups representing the urban poor, peasants, and university students. Although a portion of NDF activities included nonviolent protests, including a demonstration of four thousand students, workers, and slum dwellers in November 1975 to denounce Marcos's presidential decree banning labor strikes, the CPP viewed the underground networks "primarily as an operational and recruitment ground for armed struggle" (Boudreau 2004, 140). Unlike the reformist opposition, the CPP and the revolutionary opposition "had an explicit and agreed-upon strategy for gaining power—armed insurrection" (Schock 2005, 71). Although the CPP began organizing associations of women, peasants, and urban poor, "nevertheless, party strategy still emphasized armed struggle, and held neither hope nor affection for a reforming process. Rather, by supporting these organizations, CPP leaders hoped to radicalize and recruit among political moderates when the state resorted to violence" (Boudreau 2004, 146).

By the mid-1970s both the urban protest movement and the rural insurgency had rebounded and remained active, sometimes operating in tandem, often separately (Boudreau 2004, 8; Thompson 1995; Wurfel 1988). The NPA expanded into new Visayan base areas and began to examine the formation of alliances with the Muslim insurgency in Mindanao (Molloy 1985). The strategic hamlet program used by the Marcos regime as a counterinsurgency technique came under attack from international human rights groups, and U.S. State Department reports made under the new Carter administration contained criticisms of the Marcos regime's human rights record (Boudreau 2004, 141; Daroy 1988, 76–78). Marcos nevertheless continued to close down newspapers, harass student and labor organizers, and imprison political opponents.

The Catholic Church and Grassroots Organizing

The Catholic Church, which would play a crucial role in the People Power campaign, was the last remaining national institution that maintained independence and legitimacy during Marcos's rule. The Church, whose policy toward the Marcos regime at the beginning of martial law had been one of "critical collaboration," became an important channel of political opposition (Schock 2005, 71; Wurfel 1988). Parts of the Church had opposed the dictatorship from the start and were involved in the reformist, revolutionary, or progressive opposition (Wurfel 1988). Inside the Church hierarchy, the most important figure was Archbishop Cardinal Jaime Sin. Cardinal Sin became an outspoken opponent of martial law as early as 1974, when he led a prayer vigil and denounced the regime's military raid on a seminary and arrest of dozens of people. More than five thousand people attended the vigil, which was the largest protest against martial law at the time. Sin continued to denounce the regime's use of torture and other human rights abuses into the 1980s, while at the same time rejecting the use of violence to challenge the regime. Worried about the growing radicalization of certain elements of the Catholic Church and the rise of the NPA, Cardinal Sin focused on bringing together various strands of the opposition, which eventually led to their convergence in the 1980s (Schock 2005, 71; Wurfel 1988, 220–22). This was an important step that helped prevent a violent radical flank from undermining nonviolent discipline during the popular uprising.

Between the revolutionary opposition and the elite-dominated political parties, a grassroots movement with a progressive orientation expanded its roots under martial law. Activists from grassroots organizations and the Catholic Church focused on mobilizing marginalized segments of the population, which led to the creation of a network of sectoral organizations concerned with issues related to workers, peasants, women, students, and the urban poor (Schock 2005, 72; Zunes 1999). Some more progressive and radical elements of the Catholic Church organized Basic Christian Communities in the rural areas to focus on raising political consciousness and addressing local grievances. The alliances forged between activist clergy and peasants strengthened Church-based mobilization while drawing away potential recruits from the guerrilla resistance (Schock 2005, 72). The noncommunist left was further strengthened when a group of labor federations split away from the government-controlled Trade Union Congress of the Philippines and founded the Kilusang Mayo Uno (KMU, First of May Movement) in 1980. The formation of an independent federation of trade unions would play an important role in the mass mobilization process that began in earnest in the mid-1980s.

1978 Elections

In response to domestic and international pressure by the Carter administration, Marcos agreed to moderate reforms in the late 1970s, announcing elections for an Interim Batasang Pambansa (IBP, Interim National Legislature) scheduled for 1978. The opposition was divided about whether to participate in the IBP elections. Aware that violence and fraud would inevitably accompany the elections, certain opposition elements nevertheless used the democratic facade to mobilize and organize. Benigno Aquino campaigned for the elections from his prison cell under the newly formed LABAN Party (Lakas ng Bayan, Strength of the Nation), with Senator Tanada as the LABAN chairman. LABAN was supported by other prominent oppositionists and political parties, including the Jesuit-backed Philippine Social Democratic Party. Not all opposition groups participated in the elections. The CPP, joined by the Liberals, led a boycott of the election.

Not surprisingly, the Marcos-led Kilusang Bagong Lipunan (KBL, New Society Movement) declared victory in an election marked by vote stealing and intimidation, which led to organized protest activity. On election night, upset voters banged on pots and pans, honked horns, and exploded firecrackers for three hours in response to reports of ballot theft (Boudreau 2004, 143; Lande 1978). Demonstrations continued over the next several days, leading to a regime crackdown: 561 demonstrators were arrested on April 9 and a seminary office was raided (Boudreau 2004, 143). Despite martial law restrictions, broader student protests, including short "lightning" rallies and longer marches and demonstrations, occurred regularly after that. The moderates that Marcos had hoped to co-opt with the elections were "radicalized by the fraud" and began to think beyond political parties to the organization of a broad-based movement (143).

Moderates Turn to Violence

At the same time that the huge voter turnout for the 1978 parliamentary elections encouraged some members of the opposition to organize and participate in future elections, other, frustrated oppositionists turned increasingly to armed struggle starting in late 1978. Several armed and clandestine organizations with Social Democratic (SD) bases were formed; in July 1979, soldiers arrested a hundred armed insurgents, erstwhile moderates, undergoing military training in northern Cotabato.[4]

The clearest examples of moderates turning to violence was the creation of two linked terrorist movements, the Light a Fire Movement (LAFM) of 1979 and the April 6 Liberation Movement (A6LM) in 1977 (Boudreau 2004, 144). As early as 1977, a small group aligned with Aquino had begun to discuss a strategy of insurrection, and members of the parliamentary opposition considered allying with CPP cadres to engage in extra-electoral activity (Neher 1981; Thompson 1995; Toye 1980). Meanwhile, SD activists "called for combining movement politics, electoral campaigns, and—in proportion to their limited capacities—armed struggle" (Boudreau 2004, 144).

The LAFM remained a small and conspiratorial group and preferred acts of arson and sabotage (including the torching of several Manila buildings in 1979) rather than mass demonstrations. The group collapsed when customs officials caught one of the LAFM's leaders, Ben Lim, smuggling explosives into the country; while in custody Lim revealed the names of many members of the group, dealing it a harsh blow (Boudreau 2004, 144; Psinakis 1981). The A6LM, which consisted of some LAFM members, U.S.-based individuals, and a group organized by the SD (the Kapulungan ng mga Sandigan ng Pilipinas, Organization of Defenders of the Philippines), engaged in arson and sabotage, including an attack on a meeting of the American Society of Travel Agents in October 1979.[5]

Economic Crisis and Elite Divisions

The Marcos regime was racked by a major economic downturn in the early 1980s. An economic crisis brought on by the 1979 oil shock saw a 40 percent decline in the Philippines' terms of trade, causing serious economic hardship (Manning 1984/1985, 396). The Philippine economy further tanked after the International Monetary Fund (IMF) withheld important import credits. At this point, the Philippine business community began to adopt an aggressive antiregime stance. Business groups, including the Makati Business Club, formed in 1981 and made up of noncrony capitalists, began to openly denounce state corruption, notably the accumulation of public debt resulting from payouts to cronies. The economic crisis focused popular discontent on the endemic corruption and largesse of the Marcos regime, which spent lavishly on projects like the Cultural Center, an ill-fated nuclear power plant, and an $8 million bust of Marcos in northern Luzon (Diokno 1982; Rafael 1990). The Catholic Church, along with grassroots groups and trade unions, became even more outspoken critics of the regime.

Faced with mounting pressure from the United States and international economic institutions like the IMF and increased opposition by domestic groups, Marcos announced plans for further "normalization" when he lifted martial law on January 17, 1981. Although the level of open repression dropped and the number of arrests decreased after martial law was lifted, the number of secret, extra-judicial killings increased. The regime's counter-insurgency strategy in the countryside forced half a million village residents into strategic hamlets. New restrictions were put into place banning strikes, and Marcos continued to rule by presidential decree (Boudreau 2004, 145).

Before martial law was lifted, a broad coalition of reformist elements created the United Democratic Opposition (later, the United Nationalist Democratic Organization, or UNIDO), when former allies of Marcos's, Jose and Salvador Laurel, defected to the opposition.[6] The reformist elements of UNIDO decided to boycott the plebiscite scheduled for April 7, 1981, and the presidential elections set for June. Following the elections Marcos "won" an additional six years in office. Although there was increased cooperation between reformist elements during this time, the reformist opposition "lacked mass support or the active support of the economic elite" (Schock 2005, 70; Wurfel 1988).

By 1983, Marcos's "normalization" policies were showing few results. As Schock has written, "efforts at co-opting the reformist opposition had failed, segments of the reformist opposition were beginning to cooperate with the Left, elite divisions were becoming increasingly more pronounced, and the Catholic Church was becoming increasingly critical of Marcos" (2005, 73).

Benigno's Assassination

With Marcos's health deteriorating and questions being raised about presidential succession, opposition leader Benigno Aquino, who was living in the United States following his exile in 1980, decided to make a return to his country in 1983. Aquino had spent his years in exile lobbying the U.S. government to withdraw support from Marcos, while remaining in contact with the opposition inside the Philippines (Schock 2005, 69). For many, notes Boudreau, "[Aquino] combined a flamboyant oppositional style with essentially moderate political perspectives, and represented the greatest hope for change" (2004, 178). Aquino, whose return coincided with the "politically auspicious" combination of a weakened president and frustrated economic elite, may have hoped to negotiate a transfer of power with Marcos. This was not to be. On August 21, moments after Aquino had arrived at Manila International Airport, he was assassinated by a military escort.

The opposition leader's killing sparked domestic and international outrage. After Marcos banned television coverage of Aquino's funeral, over 2 million Filipinos from all socioeconomic strata showed up for his funeral procession, which turned into an eleven-hour demonstration against the dictator. Following the initial shock and outrage over Aquino's assassination, anti-Marcos forces stepped up their mobilization efforts. Various strands of the opposition converged (Schock 2005, 74).

Aquino's assassination was the catalyst that moved the Philippine middle and business classes and more mainstream elements of the Catholic Church from passive acceptance to active resistance (Schock 2005, 74). On September 14, 1983, the powerful Makati business community organized the first of what would become weekly anti-Marcos demonstrations in the Makati business district of Manila. Nearly one hundred thousand office workers marched down the streets as protestors threw down yellow pieces of shredded telephone directories from the surrounding skyscrapers. These weekly "confetti demonstrations" became one of the most visible signs of growing anti-Marcos ferment (Diokno 1988, 136–37; Lindsey 1984, 1201–4; Macaranza 1988, 39; Tiglao 1988). While no activist organization early on was coordinating these protests, they were sustained by resources from the business community, which closed offices, provided financial resources, and recruited workforces to participate in the demonstrations (Boudreau 2004, 179). In February 1984, middle-class protestors organized a seventy-five-mile "Tarlac to Tarmac" run from Aquino's home to the Manila airport, in which an estimated half million people participated (Schock 2005, 74; Thompson 1995, 115–20).

The symbolism of Aquino's death had a powerful resonance for the country's devoutly Catholic population (Schock 2005, 74). Cardinal Sin condemned the Aquino murder in the strongest terms and declared the slain leader a national martyr. Meanwhile, a number of Filipino military officers expressed their condolences to Aquino's widow, Corazon (Cory) Aquino, and Defense Minister Juan Ponce Enrile visited with mourners. Between October 1983 and February 1985, over 165 rallies, marches, and other demonstrations took place (Thompson 1995, 116). Protests were coordinated by a broad-based coalition of opposition currents, which brought together Social Democrats with progressive left-leaning groups like Justice for Aquino, Justice for All, and later the National Movement for Freedom Justice and

TABLE 6.1 **THE NONVIOLENT AND VIOLENT PHILIPPINE CAMPAIGNS COMPARED**

	NONVIOLENT CAMPAIGN	VIOLENT CAMPAIGN
ESTIMATED PARTICIPATION	2,000,000	SEVERAL THOUSAND
PRIMARY PARTICIPANTS	LEFTISTS	RURAL COMMUNISTS
	CATHOLIC CHURCH	MALE YOUTH
	STUDENTS	
	WORKERS AND UNIONS	
	SOME ISLAMIST GROUPS	
	WOMEN'S GROUPS	
	BUSINESS COMMUNITY	
	PEASANTS ASSOCIATIONS	
	URBAN POOR	
	NGOS; GRASSROOTS GROUPS	
SECURITY LOYALTY SHIFTS	YES	NO
TACTICAL DIVERSITY	CLEAR	UNCLEAR
EXTERNAL STATE SPONSOR	NO	YES
INTERNATIONAL SANCTIONS	NO	NO
EFFECTS OF REGIME REPRESSION	BACKFIRE	SUPPRESSION
OUTCOME	SUCCESS	FAILURE

Democracy (Boudreau 2004, 178; Diokno 1988, 133–35; Lane 1990, 4; Thompson 1995, 116).

The Marcos regime, in response to the protests, stepped up the level of repression. Security forces fired on Manila demonstrators on September 21, 1983, and eleven activists were killed and dozens injured in January 1984 after a constitutional referendum. By mid-1984, the regime's security forces were using truncheons, tear gas, and bullets to break up demonstrations. The increasingly mainstream participation in protest activities made the periodic state crackdowns more shocking (Boudreau 2004, 180).

1984 Elections

The May 1984 Batasang Pambansa elections provided another mobilization opportunity for the opposition. As is often the case in nondemocracies, the opposition remained divided about whether to participate in the elections:

UNIDO, the democratic front led by Salvador Laurel and Benigno Aquino's wife, Corazon Aquino, the Philippine Democratic Party in coalition with the LABAN, and a faction of the former Liberal Party participated in the election. Opposition groups boycotting the elections, including the other main faction of the Liberal Party and the CPP, formed an antielection coalition, the Coalition of Organizations for the Restoration of Democracy (CORD), and launched boycott demonstrations.

Corazon Aquino proved to be an effective campaigner and opposition candidates won 60 of 183 contested legislative seats and 15 of 21 in Manila, despite violence, widespread government cheating, and limited media access (Mendoza 2009; Thompson 1995, 124). A newly created autonomous election-monitoring body, the National Movement for Free Elections (NAMFREL), helped rein in fraud in the urban areas where it operated, though the opposition clearly would have won the majority of the seats if the elections had been free and fair. At the same time, the extraordinarily high turnout for the elections—90 percent of the electorate voted—convinced most parts of the political opposition to participate in future elections. Only the CPP continued to insist on the boycott of elections and was isolated in its strict adherence to armed struggle (Thompson 1995, 131–32).

While the opposition's center and left showed increased political viability, the civil resistance inside the country was expanding, intensifying, and diversifying. Independent labor groups, peasants' organizations, student and teacher associations, women's groups, human rights groups, and groups of urban poor joined forces for sit-ins and demonstrations. After boycotting the 1984 elections, CORD shifted its focus to organize other forms of noncooperation, notably the *welgang bayan* (people's strikes). During *welgang bayans* there was a general workers' strike, shops were closed, public transportation was stopped, and private vehicles were stopped (Schock 2005, 75; Scipes 1992, 91). The first *welgang bayan* in Davao City quickly spread to other cities. By the end of 1984, transportation strikes had paralyzed parts of Manila and central Luzon and in southern cities such as Davao, Butuan, Cagayan de Oro, Bacolod, and Cebu. In December 1984 a strike in Bataan shut down 80 percent of transportation in the province; in other places strikes were up to 95 percent effective (Schock 2005, 75–76; Timberman 1991, 132; Zunes 1999, 134–35).

In May 1985, a large antidictatorship front that grew out of CORD, BAYAN (Bagong Alyansang Makabayan, New Nationalist Alliance), was created as an umbrella organization to unite progressive groups, including the

Peasant Movement of the Philippines (Kilusang Magbubukid ng Pilipinas, KMP) and the KMU independent labor organization, to engage in noncooperation against the Marcos regime. BAYAN helped organize a massive *weglan bayan* throughout Mindanao in early May, followed by a strike that attracted 10,000 people at the nuclear power plant in Bataan Province in June. Disagreements within BAYAN led to the creation of an alternative anti-Marcos front, the BANDILLA (Bansang Nagkaisa sa Diwa at Layunin, The Nation, Unified in Spirit and Purpose). However, these two opposition fronts committed their organizations and resources to sustained protests in 1985, including a one-day general strike in February involving 140,000 workers from 187 labor unions after the killing of a labor leader (Boudreau 2001; Villegas 1985, 130–31). That same month, close to 7,500 farmers from central Luzon marched to Manila and staged a nine-day sit-in in front of the Agricultural Ministry (Zunes 1999, 134–37).

By 1986, BAYAN boasted a national membership of 2 million, including 600,000 KMU members and 100,000 KMP members, and alliances with over five hundred grassroots organizations (Schock 2005, 76; Timberman 1991, 133; Zunes 1999, 134). Religious groups stepped up their protest activity. After the killing of an Italian priest by the regime's security forces in April, over 300 nuns and priests demonstrated outside Camp Crane in Metro Manila. Other incidents of regime crackdowns resulting in protestor deaths in September and October "triggered some of the largest anti-regime protests, and deepened elite support for the anti-dictatorship movement" (Boudreau 2004, 183).

Snap Elections

Although we argue that external support is often not the critical factor for success in nonviolent campaigns, the *decline* of U.S. support for the Marcos regime may have constrained his options. U.S. support, which had been based in part on Marcos's staunch anticommunism, continued to wane in the aftermath of the Aquino assassination. At the end of 1985, with U.S. support wavering and Marcos's domestic legitimacy severely shaken, the Philippine dictator called for snap elections. Confident that the elections scheduled for February 1986 would once again divide the opposition, or believing that they could be successfully rigged like previous elections, Marcos announced the elections on American television.

While the CPP and BAYAN insisted on a boycott of the 1986 elections, the reformist opposition was united under the banner of UNIDO with Cory Aquino as the presidential candidate and Salvador Laurel as the vice presidential candidate. In the period leading up to the elections, Aquino urged nonviolent discipline, making it clear that violent attacks against opponents would not be tolerated (Schock 2005, 76; Zunes 1999 142). Church leaders, similarly, insisted on nonviolent discipline. Aquino enjoyed the support of NAMFREL, the Catholic Church, and the Philippine business community, along with members of the Reform the Armed Forces Movement (RAM), who were opposed to the politicization of the military under Marcos.

Although Marcos controlled the media, the Church-owned Radio Veritas and *Veritas* newspaper provided crucial coverage of the UNIDO campaign. Archbishop Sin, who had played a vital role in forging the Aquino-Laurel ticket and bringing together members of the reformist opposition, issued a pastoral letter calling on the population to vote for candidates who were "honest and respected human rights"—it was a thinly veiled repudiation of Marcos. The Catholic Bishops' Conference of the Philippines called on the population to use nonviolent resistance in the event of stolen elections. NAMFREL, which was closely tied to the Catholic Church, mobilized and trained five hundred thousand volunteers to monitor elections in approximately 90 percent of the country's precincts (Schock 2005, 77). The presence of community-based mobilizing structures—like the Catholic Church in the Philippines and the extensive mosque network in Iran—may be another factor that increases the chances of success.

The 1986 election was marked by widespread fraud, with regime thugs attacking election workers and scrambling voter rolls. NAMFREL exposed serious discrepancies in the vote returns as reported by the government-controlled Commission on Elections (COMELEC). Protests began almost immediately after the polls closed. As the count discrepancy between NAMFREL and COMELEC widened, poll counters from NAMFREL locked themselves inside COMELEC headquarters. On February 9, thirty COMELEC workers responsible for the vote tabulations walked off their jobs in protest of the fraud being committed.[7] On February 15, the KBL-controlled Batasang Pambansa formally approved the COMELEC-reported election results and declared Marcos the winner.

The 1986 electoral cheating in the Philippines was not entirely different from earlier fraud, but the mass mobilization and expansion of movement organizations positioned activists to seize upon those events in even greater ways (Boudreau 2004, 242). On February 16, Cory Aquino spoke to a crowd of nearly 2 million people at a rally in Manila and proclaimed victory for herself and "the people." Condemning Marcos, Aquino announced a seven-part "triumph of the people" program of nonviolent civil disobedience, including a general strike to be launched on February 26 (a day after Marcos's planned inauguration), a mass withdrawal of funds from crony-controlled banks, a boycott of state-controlled media and crony businesses, including the San Miguel Corporation, nightly noise barrages, and other forms of nonviolent action (Schock 2005, 77–78). Aquino declared during the rally, "If Goliath refuses to yield, we shall keep dipping into our arsenal of nonviolence and escalate our nonviolent struggle."

People Power Triumphs

Before the "triumph of the people" campaign was implemented, a different, four-day EDSA (Epifanio de los Santos Avenue) Revolution took the country by storm and led to Marcos's ouster. The EDSA Revolution began with a military mutiny when Defense Minister Juan Ponce Enrile and Deputy Chief of Staff Fidel Ramos, along with a group of officers from RAM, planned an attack on the Malacanang Palace. After the defectors' plans were discovered by General Ver, Enrile gathered nearly four hundred mutinying soldiers on February 22 and barricaded themselves in Camps Crane and Aguinaldo, two major military camps outside Manila. General Ramos declared his support for the rebellion and called on the armed forces to join the defectors. Ramos and Enrile called a press conference to announce their break from the Marcos regime, highlighting evidence of massive cheating during the election. The officers declared that Cory Aquino was the rightful president of the republic. General Enrile then called the U.S. ambassador Stephen Bosworth and Cardinal Sin to ask for their support.

That night during a televised press conference, Marcos ordered the rebel faction to surrender, claiming to have uncovered an assassination plot against him by the reform movement. Two hours earlier, Cardinal Sin had made an appeal over Radio Veritas, asking the people to support "our two good friends." Starting at around midnight and lasting into the morning of the twenty-third, tens of thousands of ordinary citizens responded to the cardinal's appeal and amassed outside the rebel camps along the EDSA highway, bringing food and supplies for the soldiers. The protestors, including groups of nuns, priests, and clergy in their white cassocks, formed a human barricade outside the camp gates in an attempt to block any armed attack. The independent media ignored Marcos's insistence on censorship, and Filipinos disobeyed a government-declared curfew and orders to evacuate the area surrounding the military bases. In response to the mass defiance, a group of AFP soldiers destroyed Radio Veritas's transmission tower, blocking news of the rebellion in Manila from the provinces.

On February 23, Enrile and Ramos met with a group of businessmen, officers, and politicians who declared their support for the defectors. Marcos, responding to accusations that his ill health was enfeebling him as president, declared, "I intend to stay as President and if necessary I will defend this position with all the force at my disposal." The military mutineers, meanwhile, prepared for an assault by loyalist forces. Facing his supporters gathered alongside outside Camp Crane, Ramos called for a "revolution of the people," while Enrile appealed over Radio Veritas for a greater civilian presence. He declared that up to 90 percent of provincial military commanders supported the defectors and would support the people against the Marcos regime.[8]

For the next three days men, women, and children filled the streets of the EDSA and surrounded the Defense Ministry in support of the military defectors. Despite rumors that loyalist soldiers were coming in from the north to suppress the massive gathering with bullets, the opposition held its ground. Protestors blockaded the streets, cut down trees, and parked buses in intersections to impede the progression of tanks. Whole families camped out on the streets of Manila, and a carnival-like atmosphere prevailed with masses of protestors singing, dancing, and holding prayer vigils.

Marcos deployed a large marine contingent composed of tanks and armed personnel carriers to attack Camp Crane. A mile from the gate, however, the loyalist forces were stopped by a wall of tens of thousands of people (Schock 2005, 78). Although a commanding general threatened to open fire on the crowd if they did not disperse, the protestors, a number of whom had been trained in nonviolent action, did not budge (Elwood 1986; Zunes 1999, 146–52). Instead, the civilian protestors sat down in front of the tanks and greeted AFP soldiers with flowers, chocolates, prayers, and other peaceful symbols and called on the soldiers to defect and join the opposition. The tanks withdrew without a single shot being fired.

Government troops ultimately retreated and a nationwide mutiny of soldiers and officers followed the internationally televised standoff. Jet fighter pilots ordered to attack the military bases where the mutineers were barricaded refused to carry out orders, since they knew that doing so would result in countless civilian casualties (Schock 2005, 78). As more members of the military began to side with the anti-Marcos protestors, "intoxicating mass celebrations broke out" (Boudreau 2004, 185). Ramos pledged to put the "new armed forces" at the service of the "newly constituted authorities"— Aquino and Laurel. Marcos, meanwhile, refused to resign and lashed out at the defectors: "If they think I am sick, I may even want to lead the troops to wipe out this Enrile and Ramos. I am just like an old war horse, smelling powder and getting stronger" (quoted in the *Los Angeles Times*, "Marcos Declares Emergency, Pledges to 'Wipe Out' Rebels: Cites Panic, Takes Over Radio and TV," February 24, 1986).

On February 24, a day before his planned inauguration, Marcos announced a state of emergency. That night, after loyalist General Fabian Ver announced that his forces were "ready to destroy" the defectors, rebel troops attacked and seized the government-controlled television station Channel 4 in Manila, cutting off a transmission of a live Marcos broadcast. The former government station began to broadcast opposition programming. Firefights between loyalist and rebel forces ensued and tens of thousands of civilians surrounded Channel 4 to counter a possible attack by loyalist forces. When several platoons of loyalist soldiers attempted to take back Channel 4, they were immediately surrounded by civilians. The people shook the loyalist soldiers' hands and offered the troops hamburgers, donuts, and orange soda—after a short while the commanding officer agreed to withdraw his troops (People Power in the Philippines 1997).

On the afternoon of the twenty-fourth, Corazon Aquino visited the barricades near the rebel camp with her family, declaring victory and singing "Ave Maria" with the crowd. That evening, the Reagan administration, a major pillar of support for the Marcos regime, issued a formal statement declaring that Marcos should resign in order to prevent bloodshed. Marcos, in response, announced that he refused to resign and would fight "to the last drop of blood." As the crowds on the EDSA grew to the hundreds of thousands, Aquino announced plans to formalize her government the next morning.

The next morning, Aquino and Salvador Laurel were sworn in as president and vice president by a Supreme Court justice, thereby forming a parallel government (similar to the parallel government formed by Ayatollah Khomeini in Iran). Enrile was named defense minister and Ramos was appointed chief of staff of the armed forces. Two hours later, Marcos took his oath of office at the Malacanang Palace. Afterward, the remaining government-controlled television stations were taken over by opposition soldiers. Without a mouthpiece, without U.S. government support, and with troops defecting in increasing numbers, Marcos had lost his final grip on power. When his power-sharing offer to Enrile was rejected, the dictator then appealed to the general for safe passage for himself and his family.

Following negotiations between Marcos, Aquino, and U.S. ambassador Bosworth, U.S. military helicopters transported Marcos and thirty members of his family and entourage to a nearby U.S. air base, where they boarded jets that took them to Hawaii. After news of the dictator's departure reached the people, crowds of Filipinos gathered at the Malacanang Palace. Fireworks, street dancing, and prayer vigils marked what Filipinos referred to as their day of liberation. Though some fighting broke out between Aquino supporters and Marcos loyalists when the palace gates were thrown open, there was only minimal looting and no casualties before the capital became calm later that night.

Reflecting on the nature of the Philippine revolution, one commentator wrote, "After violent revolutions there are always scores to settle, grudges to satisfy, revenge to extract, and the cycle of violence continues. But because the Filipino people created major political change largely without violence, national reconciliation was that much easier" (People Power in the Philippines 1997).

ANALYSIS

The nonviolent campaign in the Philippines succeeded in attracting enough participants to activate a series of mechanisms that forced the Marcos regime from power. The campaign contained two hundred thousand active participants, with as many as 2 million engaging in rallies and other functions over the course of the campaign. The nature of the participation in the campaign reveals that barriers to participation in nonviolent action were quite low. As Cristina Jayme Montiel writes,

> Not all those who participate in People's Power possess idealistic motives and beliefs. The Filipino respondents interviewed gave different reasons behind their participation in the mass actions. Some came with a clear objective in mind—to fight for democracy and to topple the dictatorship in a peaceful way. Others joined out of curiosity, or were prodded by friends, coworkers, and family members to join the street movement, even if they were not clear on its objectives. (Montiel 2006, 186)

This type of participation, based on informal and temporary commitments to action, speaks to the low barriers required to participate in nonviolent action. This stands in contrast to the violent insurgencies that were ongoing in the Philippines, where martial values precluded informal participation.

The mass participation in the nonviolent resistance allowed the anti-Marcos opposition to shed the "radical" label while stripping away Marcos's sources of power. Reflecting on the nature of the popular uprising, Teodoro Benigno, bureau chief of Agence France Presse, noted at the time,

> For the first time, the middle class came out. It struck me as being significant and crucial. You had husbands, mothers, children, teen-agers, and people from all professions—lawyers, doctors, and engineers. And finally you had the Makati [business] people joining in. That was the most unprecedented. They were the most conservative people in the Philippines; they couldn't care less about demonstrations. (EDSA Revolution Web site, http://library.thinkquest.org/15816/thebeginning.html)

Similar to the 1979 Iranian Revolution and the partially successful First Intifada, the ability of the Philippine resistance to expand beyond its radical base to include more moderate, centrist elements was critical to its success. As Boudreau explains, "Philippine authorities depended so heavily on portraying dissidents as communist that they rapidly lost support when ordinary people (businessmen, housewives and clergy) moved to the opposition's fore. By easing the political polarization that Marcos required, moderate resistance became far more subversive than radical insurgency" (2004, 241).

The diverse membership of the nonviolent campaign led to several major points of leverage, which made it more effective than the violent insurgencies persisting in the countryside. First, the campaign succeeded in creating security-force loyalty shifts, which we have seen are so critical to the success of a campaign. The popular nature of the opposition resistance legitimized defection among erstwhile regime supporters, including members of the security forces. As more centrist, moderate leaders joined the opposition and its protest activity demonstrated both organization and a high degree of nonviolent discipline, disaffected elites considered switching sides. This was easier when erstwhile regime supporters could have some assurances that they would neither be hanged nor dispossessed following a change in regime.

> Moderate movement leaders were credible and familiar to regime members concerned about the economic crisis, corruption, political polarization and presidential succession. The movement's strong elite base and established institutional support, moreover, helped assure potential regime defectors and undecided elites that the democratic process would keep the genie of social redistribution in the bottle. Because democratic protests were organized, the movement could present itself as an alternative to the regime rather than appealing, for instance, to a faction of the AFP. (Boudreau 2004, 246)

The loyalty shifts that occurred in the business and economic communities were followed by a dramatic schism in the Philippine military. The military defection movement that began with Generals Enrile and Ramos spread rapidly once it gained the backing of Cardinal Sin and had access to Radio Veritas. Once tens of thousands of civilians, including nuns and clergymen, had formed a human shield around the barracks where the defectors had sought refuge and knelt in prayer before approaching tanks, the dynamics of the contest between loyalist forces and defectors were transformed.

Instead of hurling rocks or Molotov cocktails at the loyalist troops, supporters of Corazon Aquino offered them food and appealed to their sense of nationalism as encouragement to join the prodemocracy movement. This nonviolent discipline was demanded from the highest ranks of the opposition movement, including the defecting generals. It is difficult to imagine that a mass defection of military forces would have occurred in the absence of the nonviolent discipline shown by the opposition movement. As a counterpoint, loyalist forces showed no qualms about confronting armed insurgents with massive firepower, and there is no evidence of splits in the ranks during counterinsurgency operations.

Guerrilla warfare aimed at toppling the Marcos regime, conversely, was largely unsuccessful at winning broad support or compelling security-force defections. Without the guarantee of physical safety, security forces were unlikely to sympathize with violent movements such as the NPA or the Islamic insurgents in Mindanao. (It is hardly surprising that Marcos was successful at commanding the security forces to crack down on such movements, resulting in human rights violations among guerrillas and civilians in nearby villages.) Although the military-coup plotters, including Generals Enrile and Ramos, had not initially supported an Aquino presidency, with nearly a million people in the streets demanding that Aquino be sworn in and giving praise to the military defectors for contributing to the effort, "the would-be generalissimos swallowed the pill, announced their support for Aquino's presidency, and accepted positions in the new government" (Boudreau 2004, 185).

Second, when the regime attempted to repress the People Power movement, that repression backfired to produce even more mobilization. The communist and Islamic insurgencies bore the brunt of regime repression in the 1970s and early 1980s without generating mass support or bringing sizable pressure to bear on the regime. Instead, Marcos used the threats posed by these groups as a justification for martial law and the repression of any opposition activities. Although some scholars have suggested that the armed and nonviolent resistances were complementary in the struggle against Marcos (Boudreau 2004, 152–75), the anti-Marcos opposition did not pose a significant challenge to the regime until it was backed by a broad coalition of groups, including moderate and centrist elements of Philippine society.[9] The two armed insurgencies were incapable of offering themselves as an alternative to the Marcos regime with broad-based popular appeal. Although the NPA had supporters within the Church (notably among lower-ranking priests) and did have a significant following among the population while forming occasional alliances with the reformist political opposition, its political front, the CPP, was eventually marginalized because of its reliance on armed struggle, ideological rigidity, insistence on party rule, and its decision to boycott elections (Schock 2005, 71; Wurfel 1988, 227–31).

Remarkably, the mass protests against the Marcos regime almost never deteriorated into looting or rioting, nor did protestors target regime functionaries or secondary targets (like Chinese merchants) with violence. The nonviolent discipline shown by the opposition was a function of effective leadership, strong movement networks, and the cementing of internal class alliances in the democracy movement (Boudreau 2004; Schock 2005). The strong insistence on nonviolent discipline by Church leaders, notably Cardinal Sin, and by opposition political leaders, like Cory Aquino and Salvador Laurel, strengthened the movement's nonviolent character, which played a significant role in winning over erstwhile regime supporters. "By demonstrating an explicitly nonviolent and democratic alternative," notes Boudreau, "the movement triggered defections from the state and diverted international alliances in ways that critically weakened Marcos" (2004, 247).

Ultimately the Reagan administration, Marcos's primary ally, refused to continue to support the regime. This backfiring represented a departure from previous outcomes of repression against the guerrilla groups. Although the Marcos regime undoubtedly committed many human rights violations during the repression of the insurgents, the repression served only to isolate the violent groups. But the violent groups were unable to translate the repression into disruption of the regime's domestic and international pillars of support.

Third, other scholars have noted how the diversity of the campaign membership led to tactical innovations, which allowed the campaign to maneuver away from the regime's repressive apparatus (Schock 2005). As Boudreau notes, the organizational and tactical networks across different sectors of society "prevented authorities from eliminating the civil space that claim makers required, encouraged quite conservative opposition groups to adopt more radical forms, and provided broad institutional support for antidictatorship struggle" (2004, 156).

Fourth, while no states formally sanctioned the Marcos regime, Marcos agreed to leave power only after the U.S. government made it clear that it would no longer provide the massive amounts of military and economic aid that kept his regime in power—making this a primary example of how a nonviolent uprising could prompt effective sanctions from external actors, even if such sanctions were not codified in an official issue of sanctions in the United Nations or another international body. Though the late reversal of U.S. support for the Marcos regime may have been an important factor in ensuring that the dictator left without massive bloodshed, the actual power shift that occurred in Philippine society preceded this shift in the U.S. position. This was most apparent in the wake of the 1986 stolen elections. A summary of these dynamics is found in table 6.1.

Did the Presence of the Violent Insurgency Help or Hurt the Nonviolent Campaign?

Although we have made the case that the nonviolent campaign was necessary and successful in removing Marcos from power, others have been critical of this interpretation. In particular, some analysts argue that the combined presence of the nonviolent and violent campaigns triggered the demise of

Marcos's regime, that the nonviolent campaign would never have been effective without the presence of an armed collaborator. This suggests a "positive radical flank effect," in which an armed wing of a broader social movement adds to the nonviolent movement's power. Social movement scholars have identified possible radical flank effects in cases such as the South African antiapartheid movement, the civil rights movement in the United States, and El Salvador.[10]

In the case of the Philippines, Boudreau argues that the violent and nonviolent resistance strategies were complementary in the anti-Marcos struggle (2004, 147). Despite such claims, however, the causal influence of the violent radical flank remains unclear. Just because violent insurgents are active in the society during the time of the regime transition does not automatically suggest that they were the primary (or even secondary) drivers of the ultimate outcome. In the case of the Philippines, the presence and growth of the nonviolent campaign and Marcos's missteps best explain the mechanisms of change that occurred, particularly with regard to the loyalty shifts of regime forces. Had the primary opposition been violent, there is no reason to believe that Marcos's soldiers would have disobeyed his orders in the final throes of conflict. Instead, as Boudreau concedes, "the regime itself was so isolated that soldiers refused to follow orders to fire upon the EDSA demonstrators," although the soldiers may have had no objections to following orders if the demonstrators had been threatening them with violence (249).

Furthermore, it is clear from the history and evolution of the conflict in the Philippines that only *after* the emergence of the nonviolent mass movement did change occur. Leftist and Islamist violence only emboldened the regime and encouraged it to tighten its grip on power. When the nonviolent campaign emerged, however, the regime's pillars of support began to crumble. In this case, therefore, one can say with confidence that the nonviolent campaign was necessary and had a distinct effect on eroding the regime's pillars of support. It is not as easy to contend that the simultaneous violent insurgency had a discernible impact on the outcome.

CONCLUSION

Notwithstanding the posttransition in the Philippines, the fact that the transition from dictatorship to democratic rule in the Philippines was achieved with minimal casualties can be explained by the type of movement that brought the democratically elected leader to power. As Boudreau notes,

With its formidable organizational apparatus, the Philippine movement could step itself into power, and was credible enough to attract support away from the old regime . . . The movement itself supported the new regime long enough, and with sufficient enthusiasm, to allow the Aquino government to consolidate. While consolidation took the new government far from its movement origins, and the movement fragmented after 1986, the activists' initial power, both relative to defecting regime members and to Philippine society, seems to have stabilized the transition, if not to have democratized its social outcomes. (2004. 249)

Although the Philippine military played a central role in the events leading up to Marcos's ouster, the dictator did not suffer a military defeat. Schock argues that "the success of the people power movement was not a function of the military revolt. More accurately the opposite was true—the success of the military revolt was a function of the people power movement" (2005, 79; Zunes 1994). The military defector movement was preceded by months of intense mass mobilization and nonviolent resistance that grew to involve nearly every segment of Philippine society, including moderate reformers, businesspeople, religious leaders, and erstwhile regime supporters.

The successful EDSA Revolution highlights certain strategic advantages of nonviolent resistance compared with armed struggle in campaigns against authoritarian regimes. By involving the active participation of a large and diverse cross-section of Philippine society, and by multiplying points of pressure and leverage over the regime, the nonviolent resistance was able to effectively strip away Marcos's most important pillars of domestic and (later) international support and power. At the same time, the opposition achieved sufficient organization and popular backing to be able to advance itself as a viable alternative to the existing regime, which facilitated the bloodless transition: "Without moderate protest that engaged participatory opportunities (i.e. elections) and movement organizations that were powerful and credible to disaffected state actors, the regime's decay might well have polarized society between authorities and the armed left, and officials almost certainly would have closed ranks against the movement" (Boudreau 2004, 188–89).

For years, the Marcos regime had relied on a polarized Philippine society and the threat posed by armed groups to maintain his grip on power. The regime's divide-and-rule strategy ultimately backfired, a process accelerated by Benigno Aquino's assassination, when an organized opposition coalition coalesced around a viable political alternative, represented by UNIDO and Corazon Aquino, while making the country ungovernable under Marcos. The massive withdrawal of consent and cooperation by Filipinos in key social, political, economic, religious, and even military organizations was most acutely responsible for Marcos's ouster.

CHAPTER SEVEN **WHY CIVIL RESISTANCE SOMETIMES FAILS: THE BURMESE UPRISING, 1988-1990**

IN 1988 A POPULAR UPRISING in Burma posed an unprecedented challenge to that country's military dictatorship. Spontaneous student-led protests against police violence in Rangoon quickly grew into a nationwide campaign to dismantle the junta involving large numbers of Burma's ethnically and linguistically diverse population. Despite some opposition gains, including the temporary replacement of military with civilian rule and the holding of multiparty elections in 1990 won by the opposition National League for Democracy (NLD), the 1988 campaign is best characterized as a failure. A new military dictatorship came to power that ignored the election results and maintained power without any significant concessions to the democratic opposition (Fink 2001).[1]

FROM FLEDGLING DEMOCRACY TO DICTATORSHIP

Burma, a country inhabited by multiple ethnic groupings, including the Burman (ethnic majority group), Mon, Shan, Rakhaing (Arkanese), Karen, Karenni, Chin, Kachin, Palaung, Pa-O, Kayang, Wa, and Lu, was ruled by a series of dynasties before becoming part of the British Empire in 1885.[2] Resistance to foreign occupation and domination has historically brought Burma's various ethnic groups together, even if only temporarily. A Burmese nationalist movement led by Ba Maw and General Aung San challenged British colonial rule after 1885. After the Japanese invasion and occupation of Burma during the World War II, Burma was granted nominal independence under Japan's fascist administration.

From the very beginning, deep ethnolinguistic cleavages, unresolved self-determination claims, and the presence of multiple ethnic militant factions have challenged Burmese national development. Burma's minority groups, suspicious of the majority Burman's intentions, began to assert their national rights even before independence. In February 1947, General Aung

San, a prominent anticolonial resistance leader (and an ethnic Burman) met with Shan, Kachin, and Chin leaders at Panglong to sign what came to be known as the Panglong Agreement. The agreement acknowledged the frontier peoples' right of autonomy in a federal union and assured them of democratic rights and nondiscrimination in the allocation of federal resources. The ethnic minority leaders recommended that equality and the right of self-determination should be granted to all Burma's ethnic groups, and that the right of secession be recognized in Burma's new 1947 constitution.

The leading Burmese pro-independence coalition, the Anti-Fascist People's Freedom League (AFPLF), initially brought together Socialists, the Burmese Communist Party (BCP, formed in 1939), the Communist Party of Burma ("red flag" communists), and the People's Volunteer Organization. The coalition collapsed after its central unifier, Aung San, was assassinated in July 1947. After Aung San's assassination the BCP broke away from the AFPLF and a number of different military groups defected. The AFPLF, which assumed power after the British left Burma in January 1948, was left divided and confronted with multiple domestic challengers.

The new government and its armed forces, the Tatmadaw, faced both communist and ethnic-based insurgencies after independence. Communist, Karen, and Kachin troop rebellions in 1948 seriously weakened the Burmese military. By 1949, large swaths of the Irrawaddy Delta and suburbs of Rangoon had fallen to BCP or Karen forces. Within the AFPLF, the Socialist Party consolidated greater control while offering local militant leaders guns and promises of greater local autonomy. However, the new Burmese government mostly ignored the Panglong principles and treated the ethnonational claims with indifference, instead creating a sham federal union that concentrated power in Rangoon.

Armed struggle by the new country's ethnic minority groups ensued. The Karen National Union (KNU), created in 1948, was one of the largest ethnic insurgent groups that sought autonomy from the Burmese government. The KNU, which numbered several thousand fighters, launched mostly hit-and-run attacks against government forces.[3] The other main ethnic insurgent groups formed after independence were the Shan State Army (SSA) and the Karenni National Progressive Party (KNPP).

By the mid-1950s the Tatmadaw had emerged as Burma's first centralized but national institution and began to challenge the enfeebled civilian leadership (Boudreau 2004, 48). When the socialist government led by U Nu split apart in 1958, U Nu temporarily stepped down as prime minister and turned power over to a military caretaker government led by General Ne Win. Ne Win and the military elite in the Tatmadaw were angered by the concessions of autonomy that U Nu had extended to Burma's ethnic minority groups; they instead emphasized nonsectarian policies and anti-insurgency operations.

Although little data exist regarding the membership of each ethnic insurgent group during the 1948–1989 period, the seventeen major groups yielded a combined membership of less than forty thousand members in 2006.[4] Precise data on when each armed group was created does not exist, and distinguishing between the political and armed factions of the different ethnic-based groups is difficult.

Military Coup and Martial Law

Incensed by the sectarian policies of the civilian leadership and the latter's incompetence and corruption, the Tatmadaw plotted a governmental takeover. On March 2, 1962, General Ne Win spearheaded a military coup and formed the Revolutionary Council to wield power in the new military government. He declared martial law and set about centralizing politics and expanding the role of the military in the government, bureaucratic administration, and the economy (Schock 2005, 92). The junta nationalized banks, industries, and large commercial enterprises as military personnel took over the administration of businesses and the civil service (93).

Ne Win's Burma Socialist Program Party (BSPP), formed in 1962, banned independent trade unions and political parties. Universities were taken over by the regime and media outlets were shut down. At the same time that it led a crackdown against BCP supporters, the BSPP attempted to win over popular support by creating BSPP-associated student organizations, along with National United Front groups and Village Organizing Councils. Many leftist activists were at first exuberant about being part of a grassroots socialist transformation (Boudreau 2004, 84).

Popular support for the socialist regime declined several months after the successful coup. On July 7, 1962, members of the Tatmadaw surrounded the University of Rangoon, where students, mostly BCP supporters, were protesting military rule. After students shouted insults at the soldiers, the troops opened fire on the protestors. Soldiers then dynamited a student union building where students had taken shelter, killing thousands of young people.

The student union massacre sent shock waves throughout Burmese society (Boudreau 2004, 50–51). Although the Ne Win regime continued with its counterinsurgency efforts, the prospect of an organized urban protest movement posed a greater threat. Regime authorities "reached periodic accommodations with insurgent forces that would never have been conceived as a strategy against urban protest" (90). Urban protest groups were atomized and there were no ties between urban oppositionists and the guerrilla movement in the rural areas.

As BSPP repression and surveillance on university campuses intensified, students began an exodus to the countryside to join the leftist guerrillas. However, "campus activism did not prepare students for jungle warfare, and they dragged the insurgent forces" (Boudreau 2004, 87). In our formulation, the students perceived the costs of participation in the violent insurgency less severe than nonparticipation. Later, their choices would not seem so limited, as joining a mass, nonviolent resistance became an option.

The 1960s brought only limited protests. In 1965, around two thousand monks protested state interference in the Buddhist sangha (monastic organization). The regime responded by arresting more than a hundred monks and imposing controls on the sangha. A severe rice shortage prompted riots led by workers and peasants. Security forces responded with mass arrests and killings, including the killing of two hundred seventy people during a food riot in Arakan (Boudreau 2004, 90; Smith 1999, 225).

Meanwhile, Burmese armed insurgents began receiving significant outside support during the late 1960s. Following violence in Burma targeting Chinese merchants, teachers, schools, and the Chinese embassy during the food riots, China funneled more money and weapons to the BCP while providing Burmese communist guerrillas access to and sanctuary in Chinese territory along the Burma-China border. The new resources from China "encouraged the BCP to adopt a more exclusively insurgent line against the state" (Boudreau 2004, 91). External support to the leftist insurgents had mixed results:

> Although Chinese arms and logistical support helped the BCP gain vast territory over the next five years, Burmese communism never re-

covered its authority in urban politics, and its organizational separation from the cities, emphasized by the move to distant basing areas, was virtually complete. (Boudreau 2004, 91; see also Lintner 1994, 203)

The communist insurgency failed to attract and mobilize cross-sectoral support and fell victim to internecine violence. As the Cultural Revolution raged inside China, purges were similarly launched within the BCP in 1967, killing most student recruits and some of the party's most dynamic organizers and leaders (Boudreau 2004, 91).[5] The internecine violence involving the left in Burma seriously weakened it vis-à-vis the highly organized junta.

Economic grievances drove a wave of protests in Burma during the 1970s. In May 1974, an industrial strike and factory sit-in launched by oil workers began in Chauk and spread to Rangoon. The workers, who carefully avoided criticizing the Ne Win government, instead demanded better wages and working conditions. In June government soldiers surrounded the mill where workers were striking and fired on the workers, killing between twenty-eight and one hundred (Smith 1999, 269). The Tatmadaw invaded university campuses and arrested students presumed to be sympathizers, further decimating the ranks of student activist leaders.

The next opportunity for mass mobilization came later that year after the death of former UN Secretary-General U Thant. When Thant, a highly respected Burmese statesman, was denied a burial with honors in his homeland thousands of angry students and monks seized U Thant's body and marched it through the downtown area. The students eventually buried U Thant's corpse near the spot where the student union building once stood on the Rangoon University campus. After U Thant's burial, tanks rammed through the university gates, and troops dug up the former secretary-general's body and took it to a different cemetery for burial. Riots broke out across the capital after at least sixteen students were killed by soldiers while trying to prevent U Thant's coffin from being taken. Around forty-five hundred were arrested (Boudreau 2004, 94–95). As Robert Taylor notes, the Tatmadaw consistently responded to protests with "minimal manpower and maximum firepower to demonstrate, as rapidly as possible, its determination to keep the unrest from spreading and to serve as a deterrent" (1987, 336).

The U Thant demonstrations nevertheless revealed greater organization than any earlier protests and produced a new core of activist leaders. Antiregime activism at the universities accelerated in 1974–1975, and a general strike committee organized a march on Insein Prison to demand the release of political prisoners. The BCP, for its part, seemed to ignore the developments in the cities, continuing to concentrate on its rural insurgency war with the government (Boudreau 2004, 98).

THE NATIONAL DEMOCRATIC FRONT
In May 1976, an alliance of non-Burman ethnic armed opposition groups created the National Democratic Front (NDF) to press for a federal union in which ethnic equality and the national right to self-determination were recognized (Oo 2007). NDF members included the KNU, the Shan State Army–South (SSA-South), the KNPP, the Arakan Liberation Party, the Kachin Independence Party, the Lahu National Unity Party, the Union Pa-O National Organization, the Palaung State Liberation Organization, and the Kayan New Land Party. Military cooperation between these groups proved to be elusive, however, because of the distance between the armed groups and the state's military dominance over their territories (Oo 2007).

While some insurgent groups joined forces under the NDF, nonviolent protests continued in the urban areas. On March 23, over two thousand students marched from Rangoon University to the tomb of a famous Burmese poet, Thakin Kodaw Hmine, to protest the regime's commemoration of Hmine's death. Afterward, military agents arrested the key student leaders and executed one well-known leader, Tin Maung Oo, and sent his family to prison. The extreme brutality of the military regime, coupled with Burma's relative isolation from the outside world and the simultaneous self-determination conflicts involving its ethnic minorities may explain why the emergence of a broad-based antijunta nonviolent movement was extremely difficult. Yet, a popular uprising involving multiple ethnic groups did occur in the late 1980s; we argue that regime brutality alone cannot fully explain its ultimate failure.

1987 Triggers
By 1987, Burma was facing a severe financial crisis following decades of socialist isolationism. Exacerbating an already desperate economic situation, Ne Win introduced demonetization policies in September, wiping out the savings of many Burmese families.[6] The regime's economic policies, combined with anger over continued regime repression, prompted massive protests, starting on the university campuses, that endured until the following year.

On March 13, 1988, students protesting outside the Rangoon Institute of Technology (RIT) clashed with the Tatmadaw and an engineering student was shot dead. Phoe Maw's killing, which went unpunished, prompted large student protests and greater regime repression. Students from the RIT and Rangoon University joined forces and launched daily protests that were explicitly antigovernment and prodemocracy (Schock 2005, 94). On March 18 riot police shot at students who were marching from Rangoon University to the RIT near Inya Lake, killing scores and arresting more than a thousand activists. Burmese officials later admitted that forty-one students died in that incident, while other reports suggest that over two hundred students were killed (Boudreau 2004, 194).

After this so-called Bloody Friday massacre, government forces invaded and occupied the Rangoon University campus, arresting around a thousand more university students and sending other activists fleeing. The fleeing students were joined by individuals from working-class neighborhoods as demonstrations spread throughout Rangoon, and major landmarks like the Shwedagon and Sule pagodas became resistance rallying points. Clashes between security forces and high school students wielding rocks and firebombs resulted in scores of activist casualties.

The Ne Win government then shut down the schools and universities, sending students to their provincial hometowns, where they recounted the atrocities in the cities. Underground Burmese cells, which were responsible for coordinating the protests, were not in any significant way connected to party structures or movement organizations. However, after the regime shut down the schools in March 1988, the interaction between activists and underground cells intensified (Boudreau 2004, 197). Some leaders of the noncommunist demonstrations in 1975–1976 gave workshops on protest strategies and tactics, including the use of media and how to organize lower-risk lightning demonstrations (Boudreau 2004, 197, citing an interview with Htun Aung Kyaw in 1997).

After the universities were reopened in late May student-led protests resumed. The students demanded the release of arrested students, the reinstatement of hundreds who had been expelled, and the right to organize independent student unions (Schock 2005, 94). This time there was a new youth leadership in charge of the protests who emphasized meetings, organization, and focused on explicit political demands (Boudreau 2004, 192). The student movement demonstrated unprecedented organization and politicization, and new networks were tapped by activists who had spent time in prison together. Student leaders disseminated leaflets and organized lightning strikes while intensifying efforts to unite the different campuses. By June 16, protests were taking place at all Rangoon universities.

On June 21, after the government announced its decision to close Rangoon University, massive protests broke out across Rangoon. Thousands of students were joined by Buddhist monks and workers from nearby factories, along with disaffected members of the urban poor and unemployed. By the time the protest march reached downtown Rangoon, there were tens of thousands of protestors (Schock 2005, 94). The unarmed protestors were again met with violence from the riot police, and between eighty and a hundred protestors were killed. The regime imposed a new curfew and the universities were again closed. Meanwhile, antiregime protests erupted in cities and towns outside Rangoon, in places like Pegu, Prome, Mulmein, and Mandalay (Lintner 1990; Moksha 1989; Schock 2005, 95; Smith 1999; Taylor 1991).

The June protests were not entirely nonviolent. Some antiregime activists used "jingles" (sharpened, poisoned bicycle spokes fired through a slingshot) to kill members of the riot police. Over a hundred people (including approximately twenty members of the security forces) died during the June 1988 clashes. Police rounded up hundreds of activists and sent them to Insein Prison, where oppositionists formed even tighter bonds and bridged factional divides.

In response to the growing protest activities, the regime announced that it would hold a special BSPP congress the following month. At the congress, held July 23, Ne Win announced the release of detained students, took personal responsibility for the March and June shootings, and reasserted his reservations about the "Burmese Way to Socialism." Ne Win then resigned as leader of the party and suggested during the congress that a national referendum on multiparty democracy could help defuse the national crisis (Boudreau 2004; Burma Watcher 1989). However, the BSPP congress rejected the proposed referendum. Ne Win announced that his successor would be General Sein Lwin, the despised commander most responsible for the June killings. The dictator also issued a warning to protestors, declaring that "when the army shoots, it shoots to hit" (Boudreau 2004, 200). Full democracy and the ouster of Sein Lwin would be central rallying cries in the massive popular uprising that began the following month.

8-8-88

Campaign leaders planned a nationwide general strike for the astrologically auspicious date of August 8, 1988 (8-8-88). Burmese opposition groups, whose organizational capacity had grown considerably over the past year, launched nationwide protests in the days leading up to the general strike. Posters and pamphlets announcing the protests began to appear in Rangoon, bearing the fighting-peacock insignia of the underground All-Burma Students' Union (Boudreau 2004, 202). The creation of strike committees throughout the country helped mobilize the opposition and coordinate the protests.

During this time there were protests in almost all Burmese cities and towns, coordinated by strike committees and characterized by synchronized marches, speeches, the unfurling of fighting-peacock banners, and the circulation of opposition publications. Student activists denounced the government and called for further demonstrations in support of democracy. Monks, who carried their alms bowls upside down as a sign that they would not accept donations from the military, joined students. Strike committee members barricaded villages and channeled protestors from outlying areas to central demonstrations and collected donations to support the rallies.

The protests culminated on 8-8-88, when interviews broadcast over the BBC and VOA called on the Burmese people to converge on Rangoon—a reminder of the critical importance of media and communications in nonviolent mass mobilization. Hundreds of thousands of students, monks, workers, civil servants, unemployed people, professionals, and members of various ethnic groups marched carrying signs and banners demanding democracy. There were marches every day until September 19. Students and activists from the cities returned to their villages and formed strike committees to lead the mass mobilization efforts and to coordinate the protest activities. There were huge demonstrations in Sagaing, Mandalay, Taunggyi, Prome, Pyinmanar, Moulmein, Tavoy, and Bassein (Maung 1992, 59; Schock 2005, 95; Smith 1999, 5).

The campaign did not endorse a strategy of creating loyalty shifts, but student marchers made appeals to members of the security forces and encircled soldiers and police in an attempt to protect them from possible protestor attacks. Still, on the night of 8-8-88, soldiers fired on crowds of unarmed protestors with automatic weapons and opened fire inside the Rangoon General Hospital, killing scores of nurses and doctors. By August

12, at least two thousand protestors had been killed (Schock 2005, 95; Sharp 2005, 246–47). The violence was not completely one-sided, as some protestors fought back with jingles, rocks, and firebombs.

As the protests intensified, Sein Lwin announced his resignation, on August 12—a direct result of the unarmed insurrection (Schock 2005, 95). One week later, on August 19, Dr. Maung Maung, a more moderate BSPP insider and a civilian, became the new Burmese president. The next day, tens of thousands of protestors denounced Maung Maung's nomination and called for an end to one-party rule. The opposition announced a national strike for August 22 and set up strike centers throughout the country. Many workers refused to return to their jobs until an interim government was formed.

In what appeared to be a concession to the opposition, Dr. Maung Maung announced the lifting of martial law on August 24. He ordered government forces to stand down, and in some parts of the country the troops disappeared altogether. With fear lowered, over a million people participated in protest demonstrations in Rangoon and hundreds of thousands joined in protests in other cities (Burma Watcher 1989). The next three weeks have been referred to as the apogee of the Burmese democracy movement. Throughout the country, people resigned from their membership in the BSPP and burned their BSPP membership cards (Fink 2001, 58–60; Schock 2005, 95). Burmese citizens from all walks of life, including government workers, monks, a small number of Tatmadaw members, customs officials, teachers, and hospital staff participated in the protests.

The Rise of Aung San Suu Kyi

During this peak period of nonviolent resistance, Aung San Suu Kyi, the daughter of a Burmese independence hero, became the public face of the democracy movement. On August 26 Aung San Suu Kyi, who had recently returned to Burma to care for her sick mother, addressed a crowd estimated to number at least half a million assembled at Shwedagon Pagoda. Aung San Suu Kyi, who called for multiparty democracy, national unity, nonviolent action, and nonviolent discipline, developed a strong domestic following and became the most recognized face of the Burmese opposition internationally (Aung San Suu Kyi 1995; Schock 2005, 96).

Still, the most prominent opposition politicians, including Aung San Suu Kyi, along with Tin Oo, Aung Gyi, and U Nu, operated mainly on their own, reluctant to form alliances with the students or other grassroots opposition groups. Attempts made by students to unite the opposition leaders in a single leadership council during the national strike largely failed. Not only were ties between the elite leadership and the masses weak, but also the leadership was itself internally divided. The divisions were exacerbated on August 26 when U Nu announced that he was the legitimate prime minister and named a shadow government. This incident eliminated the tenuous cohesion among the resistance leadership and confused activists within the movement (Boudreau 2004, 210; Burma Watcher 1989).

The August general strike nevertheless severely weakened the regime and many thought that the government would topple (Schock 2005, 96). But by mid-September the opposition protests had turned increasingly violent and unruly, with clashes between soldiers and protestors more prevalent. Agents provocateurs and saboteurs from the military, along with criminals the government released from prison, engaged in arson, looting, violence, and other destabilizing activities (96). Angry Burmese murdered a number of Military Intelligence Service agents believed to be provocateurs or saboteurs.

The protests and general strike effectively paralyzed the country. President Maung Maung attempted to offer concessions to the opposition, but he was rebuffed by the opposition (mostly by the students), who insisted that the regime be immediately replaced with an interim transition government.[7] The opposition elites were too divided to approach the regime with a common strategy.

September 18 SLORC Coup

Amid the chaos and as opposition elites fought among themselves, a group of generals organized by Ne Win and led by Generals Saw Maung, Khin Nyunt, and Than Shwe staged a coup on September 18, establishing the State Law and Order Restoration Council (SLORC). SLORC's stated purpose was to restore law and order and to prepare the country for democratic elections. SLORC immediately dissolved the government and reimposed martial law, banning gatherings of more than five people and enforcing a strict curfew. It became illegal to criticize SLORC or the military. At least three thousand Burmese protestors, mostly monks and students, were gunned down that day by SLORC forces in Rangoon and other towns and villages (BBC News 2007).

SLORC crushed strike committees throughout the country and became a ubiquitous presence on streets and in villages throughout the country. The general strike collapsed when Burmese workers, without food and money, returned to work. As SLORC ramped up the violence, thousands of students fled to the border areas controlled by ethnic rebels and took up weapons against the dictatorship (Sharp 2005, 248).[8]

Reminiscent of Marcos's tactic in the Philippines, SLORC scheduled elections for 1990 in order to defuse domestic and international pressure, achieve legitimacy, and win foreign aid. Key opposition groups, including the All Burma Federation of Student Unions (ABFSU), the Democratic Alliance of Burma (DAB), and the NLD (which registered as a political party) mobilized for the elections. After being named NLD general secretary, Aung San Suu Kyi toured the country from November 1988 through July 1989, distributed literature critical of the regime, and called for a "Revolution of the Spirit," a campaign of nonviolent resistance to promote democracy (Schock 2005, 97). Despite SLORC's draconian restrictions on campaigning, the NLD leader drew huge crowds.

By mid-1989, SLORC had stepped up its intimidation campaign against Aung San Suu Kyi and the NLD. Leaders from the ABFSU were arrested and imprisoned, including the vice chair (Aung Din) in April 1989. On July 20, 1989, the regime placed Aung San Suu Kyi under house arrest and imprisoned most members of the NLD executive committee. By November 1989, over six thousand political prisoners were languishing in Burmese prisons (Aung San Suu Kyi 1995; Kreager 1991).

Starting in May 1989 SLORC signed cease-fire agreements with most of the insurgent groups operating in the border regions.[9] These deals, which were later extended to most of Burma's ethnic insurgent groups, gave the rebels autonomy within their own regions "while the junta secured peace in the borderlands giving it breathing room to better deal with the democracy movement in the Myanmar heartland."[10] A number of armed groups allied with the Tatmadaw fought against other ethnic insurgencies that had not signed cease-fires. Armed groups, including the United Wa State Army, whose fighters were mostly ex-BCP members (the BCP became essentially defunct in 1988), and the Myanmar National Democratic Alliance Army, became powerful drug-trafficking armies that were largely tolerated by the regime.[11] SLORC later used the Wa insurgents as a proxy force against other guerrilla rivals, such as the Mong Tai Army along the Thai border.

On May 27, 1990, multiparty elections took place for the Pyithu Hluttaw (National Assembly). Although the regime expected to win the elections given the severe restrictions on campaigning and the arrests of thousands of opposition leaders, the outcome came as a surprise. Of 485 parliamentary seats, the NLD won 392 seats and the United Nationalities League for Democracy (UNLD) won 65 seats. The SLORC-backed National Unity Party won only 10 seats. SLORC was stunned by the election results, which saw the NLD win 80 percent of the seats, and refused to honor its pledge to turn power over to the winning party.

Instead, the regime arrested and imprisoned leaders from the NLD and UNLD. NLD chairman Aung San Suu Kyi was arrested and placed under house arrest in July 1990, and many young NLD activists were killed or arrested. The guerrilla resistance in the border areas was meanwhile gaining no traction. Instead, the armed zones once held by ethnic guerrilla armies were largely reduced in size, and most ethnic insurgencies had demobilized after having signed cease-fire agreements with SLORC (Beer 1999; Sharp 2005, 249).

However, unlike in the Philippines, the opposition was largely demobilized and not in a position to resist the stolen elections through campaigns of noncooperation or other forms of mass defiance (Schock 2005, 97–98). As one Burmese leader of the 1988 uprising later recounted, the opposition had "no endgame" and was too divided to be able to seize on the opportunity afforded by the stolen elections (Fogarty 2008). As a result, after more than two years of resistance, during which time the opposition succeeded in ousting Sein Lwin from power and forcing the government to hold multiparty elections, the opposition was ultimately unsuccessful in toppling the military regime (Schock 2005, 98).

ANALYSIS

In this book, we argue that nonviolent campaigns should have the advantage compared with violent campaigns in attracting more members and activating different mechanisms that remove a regime's main sources of power. However, in the Burmese case, the nonviolent campaign was not able to obtain the support it needed or create the needed shifts within the regime to succeed.

We explain the failure of the Burmese uprising as the result of two major strategic shortcomings, as well as contextual factors that led to campaign failure. First, the campaign did not create or maintain strong, cohesive, and decentralized networks with diverse membership. Internal disunity and the

	NONVIOLENT CAMPAIGN	VIOLENT CAMPAIGNS
ESTIMATED PARTICIPATION	1,000,000	SEVERAL THOUSAND
PRIMARY PARTICIPANTS	STUDENTS	RURAL COMMUNISTS
	LIBERAL INTELLECTUALS	MALE YOUTH
	BUDDHIST MONKS	VARIOUS ETHNIC GROUPS
	UNIONS	
	LAWYERS	
SECURITY LOYALTY SHIFTS	NO	NO
TACTICAL DIVERSITY	UNCLEAR	UNCLEAR
EXTERNAL STATE SPONSOR	NO	YES*
INTERNATIONAL SANCTIONS	NO	NO
EFFECTS OF REGIME REPRESSION	SUPPRESSION	SUPPRESSION
OUTCOME	FAILURE	FAILURE

*THE BCP RECEIVED EXTERNAL SUPPORT FROM CHINA, BUT THE BCP IS NOT INCLUDED AS A SEPARATE INSURGENCY IN THE NAVCO DATA SET.

TABLE 7.1 **THE NONVIOLENT AND VIOLENT BURMESE CAMPAIGNS COMPARED**

presence of multiple armed factions weakened the opposition resistance, particularly after the stolen elections in 1990. Second, the subsequent struggle against the regime was unable to create loyalty shifts within the regime and therefore separate the regime from its sources of power.

Third, international actors did not significantly pressure the Burmese regime to capitulate to the demands of the prodemocracy movement. A country's extreme isolation may make successful antiregime resistance (violent and nonviolent) very difficult. Diplomatic support for the resistance—and the withdrawal of erstwhile material support for the regime—is probably much more important in these situations, particularly for nonviolent campaigns. Moreover, when nondemocratic regimes provide significant political, economic, or military support to other nondemocratic regimes (as China does for Burma), it may be more difficult for indigenous civil resistance campaigns to successfully erode the regime's external pillars of support. This is equally true for the violent campaigns, however, which were probably even more dependent on external aid to wage their attrition campaigns against the government.

Campaign Participation and Disorganization

Missing in the Burmese 1988 uprising were strong decentralized networks and a unified front of political opposition groups and grassroots organizations that could pose a sustained challenge to the regime. Before late July 1988, the Ne Win regime had effectively prevented antistate mobilization in lowland Burma. Furthermore, routine political processes that could spur participation, like elections, were absent in Burma until 1990. Extreme regime repression drove activists to the insurgent countryside or into fragmented and isolated underground cells (Boudreau 2004).

Critics may argue that strong decentralized networks were not even possible in Burma because of the regime's extremely repressive techniques. This may be true, but starting late July 1988, Burmese activists engaged in prodigious planning and coordination efforts, including the rapid proliferation of strike committees, strike newspapers, and national protests in the lead-up to 8-8-88. Although efforts were under way to unify the opposition, notably absent in Burma were autonomous institutions that could have provided support for the movement and helped it withstand SLORC's crackdown. The flight of students and other activists to the countryside to join the insurgency made regime repression easier.

> Because the authorities held power by holding the cities, they withstood the movement's assault by murdering students, and chasing survivors into the countryside. Authorities had good reason to prefer this kind of fight to protest in the streets, for they had stable, almost routine ways of dealing with insurgency, and surely could accommodate an influx of inexperienced fighters into enemy camps. (Boudreau 2004, 242)

One of Burma's most extensive and decentralized organizations, the Buddhist sangha, was brought under the control of the junta. Sangha leaders, particularly older monks, largely did not protest the regime's repression. A group of younger, dissident monks did form the All Burma Young Monks' Union to challenge the regime. However, monks who organized a religious boycott against the regime were disrobed, arrested, and tortured. The Young Monks' Union called for the transfer of power to a democratically elected national assembly following the 1990 elections, but SLORC arrested hundreds of its members and the union collapsed. The sangha, therefore, was unable to function as an autonomous mass-mobilization mechanism for the Burmese people power movement as the Catholic Church did in the Philippines, the ulema-bazaari network did in Iran, and the popular committees did in Palestine during the First Intifada.

Although the junta's use of violence against the unarmed opposition initially backfired during the "Rangoon Spring" from June to September 1988, resulting in an increase in mass mobilization, after SLORC assumed power in mid-September an intensified state-sponsored repression led to the demobilization and suppression of the movement. Regime censorship and the elimination of independent media posed serious obstacles to opposition. The alternative print media that sprung up during the Rangoon Spring period was, according to Schock, crucial in transforming the student-centered protests into a mass movement. During this period state-run newspapers were taken over by the workers, who published news of the demonstrations and pressed for movement demands. However, when SLORC assumed power in September 1988 it shut down independent media. When the public no longer had access to alternative sources of information, it became increasingly difficult to sustain the movement (Schock 2005, 116).

Finally, the political elites and the grassroots opposition did not create a unified alternative to the military government. Ties between movement leaders and mass society, if extensive, were quite weak (Boudreau 2004, 244). The failure to form a national umbrella organization to aggregate and coordinate the resistance seriously weakened the opposition vis-à-vis the organized and efficient SLORC (Schock 2005). There were attempts to form a national umbrella organization to coordinate resistance. For example, in November 1988 the All Burma Students' Democratic Front and the DAB were created in the Karenni-controlled region near the Thai border. However, the DAB had little contact with activists in central Burma and therefore did not coordinate resistance against SLORC or mobilize the population after the regime rejected the 1990 election results.

The National Coalition Government of the Union of Burma (NCGUB), formed by Dr. Sein Win in December 1990 to bring together MPs-elect who were forced to flee Burma after the SLORC crackdown, was an important step in bringing together the fractured opposition. However, by then the population had largely been demobilized and could not be rallied to challenge the regime. Operating in exile, the NCGUB focused on mobilizing support from the international community rather than acting as a parallel government within Burma (Schock 2005).

Not only was the opposition unable to form a parallel government inside Burma or create a situation of multiple sovereignty (crucial to success of nonviolent movements in the Philippines and Iran), but also the nonviolent tactics it employed were insufficiently disruptive. For example, after SLORC took control in September 1988, the opposition focused on participating in state-controlled channels of political participation (elections) and was unable to shift strategies after the elections were stolen in 1990. As Schock notes, "When the regime refused to honor the elections, the inability of the challengers to disrupt the regime through campaigns of non-cooperation ensured that it would not be able to contribute to political change (2005, 109).

Lack of Loyalty Shifts

Resistance failure can be explained by the fact that the Burmese opposition failed to separate the regime from its main sources of social, political, economic, and military power. The dramatic exercise of opposition capacity during the Rangoon Spring never diminished the state's ability to respond, nor did it create sufficient disunity within the regime: "Despite unprecedented social mobilization and the truly surprising degree of organization among its various centers, the protest movement never split the state or applied significant drag on its repressive apparatus" (Boudreau 2004, 214). In fact, the nonviolent resistance did not spend much time or many resources attempting to disrupt or convert members of the regime, so there were few opportunities to provoke loyalty shifts within the regime (245). The large social and political distance between the regime and opposition movement discouraged "democratizing defections" from erstwhile regime supporters. The gap between potential state defectors and movement leaders was never bridged in Burma. The BSPP did not have a large middle stratum or deep roots in society, which meant that it was not as vulnerable to social pressure as was true in other places where the ruling party (or elites) had closer ties to society.

The possibility of regime defections was furthermore discouraged by the lack of organizational linkages between the regime elites and the opposition movement:

> [No] opposition parties, newspapers, or even consultative state offices existed to provide dissident intellectuals or elites with some stake

in an incremental transformation or standing among regime elites to allow cooperation in that transition. (Boudreau 2004, 211)

Mass military defections or noticeable loyalty shifts did not occur in Burma (213; Callahan 1998, 1). In fact, Aung San Suu Kyi explicitly discouraged members of the resistance from attempting to sow divisions within the military. In a speech she delivered at the Shwedagon Pagoda on August 26, 1988, she asked campaign participants to continue to support the military: "I feel strong attachment to the armed forces. Not only were they built up by my father, as a child I was cared for by his soldiers . . . I would therefore not wish to see any splits and struggles between the army which my father built up and the people who love my father so much" (Suu Kyi 1995, 195). In an interview with Karan Thapar later that month, Aung San Suu Kyi repeated this position, asserting that "I am not looking for any assistance from the army . . . I strongly believe that the army should keep away from politics to preserve its own integrity, as well as for the good of the people" (200).

Thus, the Burmese military remained far more cohesive than its counterpart in the Philippines and Iran; individual officers defected, but they were not backed by military factions and were often purged (e.g., Aung Gyi, Tin Oo). To further increase the social distance between soldiers and the population, Sein Lwin brought combat troops from insurgent areas to deal with protestors. Some violent ethnic insurgencies benefited from defections from the Burmese military, including the notable defection of Colonel Sai Yee, a Shan State National Army commander, in 2005 (Maung Than 2007). Such rare but notable defections, however, did not influence the outcomes of the violent insurgencies either, since their operations against the Burmese regime were largely futile.

The few soldiers who joined the democracy protests came mainly from lower ranks of the air force, which was less politically powerful than the army. Major internal divisions in the ranks of the Burmese military did not occur, and most rank-and-file troops carried out regime orders to fire on unarmed demonstrators.

No External Support

As we saw in chapter 2, external support is generally more useful for violent insurgencies than for nonviolent campaigns. In the case of the Philippines, however, the Reagan administration's withdrawal of support from the Marcos regime indicates that a well-timed diplomatic or economic gesture can make a difference, in combination with other factors, most notably the size and strength of the opposition.

The insularity of the Burmese economy and its reliance on illicit trade and trafficking may also be major explanatory variables for opposition failure. At the same time, it suggests that effective nonviolent resistance in these cases must target and sever these external sources of power, which is arguably more difficult than when the regime is reliant mostly on domestic pillars, and even more difficult when the major external backers are authoritarians (as is the case with China's backing of the junta).

The United States and other Western powers denounced the junta's brutality and offered rhetorical support to the opposition. However, unlike the situation in the Philippines, the Burmese regime had fewer ties to or dependencies on the outside world than the Marcos regime, and "many closer states soon resumed relations with the new government" (Boudreau 2004, 214; see also Yawnghwe 1995). There was little Western powers could do—or were willing to do—to impose sanctions and cut off aid to Burma. Burma's proximity to China made Western intervention less palatable. Japan refused to join the West in an economic boycott of Burma because of powerful economic interests inside the country. SLORC has close business ties with Thailand, Singapore, and China. The regime has joint ventures involving Thai logging interests and benefits from foreign investment and joint ventures with corporations in fishing, oil exploration, gemstones, tourism, and other industries. These sources of income allowed the military government to purchase arms from Pakistan, Singapore, and China, which it used against its own population (Schock 2005, 113).

Aung San Suu Kyi's campaign for human rights and democracy has won the opposition movement international sympathy, but this has not translated into significant pressure against the military government. Severe travel restrictions into Burma have further weakened the amount of outside pressure targeting the regime. As a result, "Burma remained cut off from transnational social movements except for a brief period during the 'Rangoon Spring' of 1988" (Schock 2005, 111).

CONCLUSION

The 1988 Burmese uprising, which was unprecedented in size and scale, forced a regime leader to resign and paved the way to 1990 multiparty elections, but it ultimately failed to oust the military dictatorship. The Burmese opposition faced considerable obstacles in its struggle against the junta, notably the inability to unify the opposition in a sustained organized campaign, the country's ethnolinguistic diversity and concurrent self-determination conflicts, and the regime's profound insularity and repressiveness—all of which made opposition mobilization and sustained pressure difficult.

Moreover, from the onset of military rule in 1962 until the popular uprising in 1988, the Burmese regime was faced with communist and ethnic-based violent insurgencies. None of these armed groups, whose recruitment occurred mainly along ideological and ethnic lines, posed a significant challenge to the junta. Although there were attempts to unite the different ethnic insurgent groups (notably the creation of the NDF in 1976), military cooperation between these groups was limited and difficult to implement in practice. Since 1989, SLORC has used other armed groups as proxy forces against insurgencies that refused to sign cease-fires with the government. Thus the insurgent groups never united in a military sense and were unable to separate the regime from its most important pillars of support.

In fact, the most intense period of Burmese opposition resistance, when the greatest amount of pressure was applied on the junta, corresponds to its most nonviolent phase. In August 1988, hundreds of thousands of Burmese from all classes, genders, walks of life, and ethnicities participated in marches, rallies, demonstrations, and nationwide strikes. While students and monks were often in the front lines of the nonviolent resistance, professionals—notably lawyers—provided resources and mobilization networks to the nonviolent mass mobilization. But the failures of the campaign to maintain unity and cohesion of purpose, to develop and exploit ties within the regime, and to attract sufficient support from potential external allies caused the campaign to expire before achieving its ultimate aims.

CASE STUDY SUMMARY

THE CASE STUDIES illuminate several important patterns. We first consider the comparison between the outcomes of nonviolent and those of violent campaigns, and then summarize the comparison between successful and unsuccessful nonviolent campaigns.

NONVIOLENT AND VIOLENT CAMPAIGNS COMPARED

Our argument is that nonviolent campaigns are successful because they are better at achieving large numbers of diverse participants that allow for multiple points of leverage against which the opponent has little defense. Violent campaigns are less successful because they cannot gain large numbers of diverse participants and must therefore rely on foreign sources of support, which they use to confront the adversary using methods in which the opponent often (but not always) has a decided advantage. All the statistical findings identified in part 1 are probabilistic, and the case studies reflect this fact.

Nonviolent campaigns in Iran, the Palestinian Territories, and the Philippines were indeed more successful than their violent counterparts. The nonviolent campaign in Burma was unsuccessful, but violent campaigns in Burma have also failed.

In all cases, nonviolent campaigns have succeeded in generating mass mobilization, whereas violent campaigns have relied on smaller numbers. People who sympathize with violent opposition movements often express reluctance to participate because of fear of regime reprisals. Although participating in a nonviolent campaign is frequently quite dangerous, ordinary citizens perceive it to be safer than participating in a violent campaign.

The diversity of participants has been as important as the numbers of participants. Some violent campaigns, like the Philippine insurgency, mobilized tens of thousands of members. However, most of these participants were young men who rallied around the Marxist ideology, thus excluding those who found that ideology unattractive. Perhaps more important from a strategic perspective, the reliance on a single opposition ideology cut the

Marxist insurgents off from the opponent regime. More diverse campaigns, which include multiple age groups, classes, occupations, ideologies, and genders, are likelier to have links to members of the regime, such that opportunities to create divisions within the regime become more ubiquitous.

Third, in the first three cases, the nonviolent campaigns applied sufficient pressure to begin dividing the regime from its main pillars of support. One of the most visible outcomes of this strategy was loyalty shifts among security forces, an outcome that would be difficult to imagine if the campaigns had been violent. Once security forces refused to obey the regime, the state was forced to capitulate to the campaign's demands. However, violent campaigns actually emboldened opponent regimes against the campaigns in all four cases. Although there were significant defections in Israel during the First Intifada, for instance, violent factions that emerged before and during the popular uprising largely reversed the Israeli divisions and unified the Israeli government, making subsequent loyalty shifts within the regime less likely.

Next, resistance campaigns are most effective and resilient when they are able to shift between methods of concentration and methods of dispersion, which can be equally as effective in exerting pressure on the regime when participation in the campaign is large and diverse. Nonviolent campaigns that prosecute the conflict using a mixture of concentrated methods (e.g., protests, sit-ins, and so on) and dispersed methods (e.g., stay-aways, boycotts, strikes, leaflets, and so forth) are better able to evade regime repression and force the regime to extend its forces beyond its capacity (Schock 2005). In particular, both methods are more likely to exert pressure when campaign participation is large and diverse. A stay-away is much less effective with several thousand participants than it is with hundreds of thousands of participants.

As predicted in chapter 2, the nonviolent campaigns in these case studies were better able to attract widespread, diverse support. Key advantages—loyalty shifts, the removal of support for the regime by international actors, tactical diversity, and resilience—flowed directly from the ability of the campaign to mobilize large numbers of diverse participants.

SUCCESSFUL AND FAILED NONVIOLENT CAMPAIGNS COMPARED

In our case studies, we further pursue the question of why nonviolent campaigns sometimes fail. What explains why the nonviolent campaigns succeeded in Iran and the Philippines, obtained only partial success in the Palestinian Territories, and ultimately failed in Burma?

We did not find any structural factors that predetermined the outcomes of these campaigns. For instance, we saw campaigns emerge, mobilize, and succeed even under repressive circumstances, as in the Philippines and Iran, whereas repression is clearly an insufficient explanation for the failure of the Burmese and Palestinian campaigns.

What is clear, however, is that mobilization is a necessary but insufficient condition for success. Instead, multiple points of leverage are necessary, leverage that can be achieved only through strategic maneuvering against the adversary. While mass mobilization makes it more likely that a campaign will be able to outmaneuver the opponent, as the campaign is better able to draw on the diverse skills and experience of a wider pool of participants, nothing substitutes for strategic creativity and innovation in determining whether the opposition will carry the day.

Consider table II.b, which identifies summary variables examined in each case study. The comparison allows us to ask what was different in the Palestinian and Burmese cases that caused the nonviolent campaigns to fail there. In Palestine and Burma, the nonviolent campaigns attracted a larger

TABLE II.B **CASE STUDY SUMMARY OF NONVIOLENT CAMPAIGNS**

	CHAPTER 4 IRANIAN REVOLUTION	CHAPTER 5 FIRST PALESTINIAN INTIFADA	CHAPTER 6 FILIPINO PEOPLE POWER REVOLUTION	CHAPTER 7 BURMESE REVOLUTION
PARTICIPATION	MILLIONS	HUNDREDS OF THOUSANDS	MILLIONS	ONE MILLION
MEMBERSHIP DIVERSITY	DIVERSE	DIVERSE	DIVERSE	DIVERSE
LOYALTY SHIFTS	YES	YES	YES	NO
TACTICAL DIVERSITY	CLEAR	CLEAR	CLEAR	UNCLEAR
EXTERNAL STATE SPONSOR	NO	NO	U.S. REMOVAL OF SUPPORT FOR MARCOS	NO
INTERNATIONAL SANCTIONS	NO	YES	NO	NO
EFFECTS OF REPRESSION	BACKFIRE	BACKFIRE	BACKFIRE	SUPPRESSED
OUTCOME	SUCCESS	PARTIAL SUCCESS	SUCCESS	FAILURE

number of participants than their violent counterparts, but this membership did not trigger the desired mechanisms for change.

To fully understand why membership sometimes activates these mechanisms (as in Iran and the Philippines) and other times does not (Israel and Burma), we must consider the strategic choices that the campaign leadership made. For instance, resistance campaigns may be construed as competitions over who succeeds at dividing and ruling the opponent. While opposition movements are notorious for having divided elite leaderships, one of the most important roles a nonviolent mass movement can play is forcing the opposition leaders to unite, even if only temporarily. That way, the opposition has a chance against even brutal regime opponents. Civil resistance campaigns succeeded in uniting the opposition in the Philippines and Iran, united the PLO factions (but not secular-Islamist leaders) in the Palestinian Territories, and failed to unify the leaders in Burma. The presence of community-based mobilizing structures—like the Catholic Church in the Philippines and the extensive mosque network in Iran—may have helped them to organize the resistance, maintain unity throughout the conflict, and attract broader bases of support.

In turn, broad-based participation increased the likelihood that these campaigns could achieve meaningful links within the regime that they used as leverage during the conflict (Galtung 1989, 13–33). Resistance leaders in Iran and the Philippines deliberately focused on producing loyalty shifts, galvanizing international attention, and shifting methods of resistance to maintain resilience in the face of repression. Resistance leaders in the Palestinian Territories failed to achieve unity, despite the creation of the United National Leadership of the Uprising, and lost control of their own campaign throughout and after the Oslo process, reducing their leverage over the Israeli opponent. Part of the failure of the First Intifada can be attributed to the campaign's inability to establish consequential links to potential Israeli and U.S. government elites. The failure to extend the nonviolent battlefield to potential allies in Israel and abroad was costly in this case.

The secretive negotiations at Oslo, which Yasser Arafat and other exiled PLO leaders conducted, left the campaign leadership with little leverage. The subsequent struggle for power over the Palestinian Authority divided the Palestinian movement, creating infighting and ending the UNLU's nonviolent struggle when it could have mattered the most.

Burmese resistance leaders similarly failed to unite the disparate ethnic groups and were unable to achieve loyalty shifts in the military. In Burma, the campaign has explicitly avoided dividing the military, a strategy that follows from Aung San Suu Kyi's personal loyalty to the military. Her reluctance to sow divisions in the army reflects the fact that her legitimacy as a leader is dependent largely upon her father's legacy of being the creator of the independent Burmese army.

Backfiring occurred in all four cases but did not occur continually in Burma as it did in the other cases. The role of the media (including the alternative media) in communicating opposition activities was critical to producing backfiring for the Philippines campaign. If a tree falls in the forest and nobody hears it, then it doesn't make a sound. In Burma, the nonviolent campaign's prospects of producing continual backfiring may have improved if media coverage had been more sustained (Martin 2007).

Although no states provided direct material support to nonviolent campaigns in any of the four cases, the removal of support for the regime at key moments in the Philippines created opportunities for the campaign to claim the illegitimacy of their opponents. Ronald Reagan's withdrawal of U.S. aid to the Marcos regime was the last straw for his regime.

Israel largely maintained U.S. support during the First Intifada, although the United States did withhold its veto power in the UN Security Council when a resolution was passed condemning Israel's deportation policy. Furthermore, Secretary of State James Baker put significant pressure on Israeli Prime Minister Shamir to engage in meaningful negotiations with the PLO. In the case of Burma, SLORC maintained support from regional powers, including Japan and China, whose withdrawal of support might have weakened the regime. But withdrawal of support is not necessary for a campaign to succeed, as we saw in the Iranian case, where the United States maintained support for the Shah until he fled the country.

Although all the nonviolent campaigns did use some mix of methods of concentration and dispersion, the Burmese campaign was perhaps the least clear. The campaign did employ methods of dispersion, such as general strikes, but they were short-lived. Substituting methods of concentration, such as election rallies and protests, resulted in repression by the regime. But when the regime cracked down against the campaign and put movement leader Aung San Suu Kyi under house arrest, the resistance leadership did not revert to methods of dispersion. Instead, student organizers simply fled to the Thai, Chinese, Indian, and Bangladeshi borders to join armed insurgents there (Schock 2005, 104).

Thus, the Palestinian and Burmese cases contain several lessons. First, overreliance on a single personality for leadership in a movement is likely to constrain the campaign in key ways. In the Burmese case, Aung San Suu Kyi's lineage prevented her from activating a key point of leverage—the division of the military—which seems necessary for the success of a nonviolent campaign. In the Palestinian case, the overreliance on Arafat undermined the unity of the UNLU campaign, creating divisions among the Palestinians rather than exacerbating divisions in Israel.

Second, although directly aiding nonviolent campaigns may actually harm them, the persistence of support for the opponent regime by key patron states removes one potential source of leverage for campaigns. Although campaigns may be able to succeed even though the opponent maintains its international alliances, the withdrawal of support may create opportunities for a campaign to pressure regime elites to choose sides. And persistent media coverage may be a necessary element in drawing attention to and galvanizing support for a campaign.

Third, just because a campaign is nonviolent does not guarantee its success. Just as on a battlefield, poorly managed campaigns are likely to fail. Campaigns that constantly update their information, adapt to conditions, and outmaneuver the adversary are more likely to succeed than campaigns that expect to succeed merely by virtue of their causes and methods.

PART THREE
The Implications of Civil Resistance

CHAPTER EIGHT **AFTER THE CAMPAIGN: THE CONSEQUENCES OF NONVIOLENT AND VIOLENT RESISTANCE**

When the sword of rebellion is drawn, the sheath should be thrown away.
ENGLISH PROVERB

It is never easy to convince those who have acquired power forcibly of the wisdom of peaceful change.
AUNG SAN SUU KYI

SO FAR, THIS BOOK HAS argued that nonviolent campaigns are more effective than violent campaigns in achieving strategic objectives. Two major questions emerge from our analysis. First, the Iran case in the previous section highlights the question of whether civil resistance actually leads to desirable long-term social outcomes, such as civil peace and democratic governance.

Second, we know that in our sample, about one in four violent campaigns have succeeded. We do not dispute this point, given that our own findings show that violent campaigns can achieve their goals by means of a mix of effective strategy and aid from abroad. Although we could focus our efforts on why violent insurgency succeeds, other scholars have addressed this question (Arreguín-Toft 2005; Lyall 2010; Lyall and Wilson 2009; Merom 2003; Stoker 2007). Besides, our results are fairly consistent with the prevailing research, which suggests that violent campaigns that receive external state support are more likely to succeed than violent campaigns that do not receive such support. As we identified in chapter 2, half of the violent campaigns that received direct material support from other states succeeded, without accounting for covert aid or support from nonstate actors. But what others have just begun to study is how the success of violent insurgency may have negative impacts on the societies and polities in which they operate (Collier 2009, 75–100; Collier, Hoeffler, and Söderbom 2008; Elbawadi, Hegre, and Milante 2008; Fortna and Huang 2009).

In this chapter, we address these issues by comparing the *relative* consequences of nonviolent and violent campaigns for two particular outcomes: democracy and the recurrence of violent civil conflict.[1]

In cases where violent insurgents have succeeded at coming to power, expelling foreign occupations, or seceding, we find that democracy is less likely to develop than in similar cases where nonviolent resistance succeeded.[2] Thus, the case of Iran, where an autocratic government came to power following a mass nonviolent campaign, is not representative of most nonviolent campaigns.

Second, the success of violent campaigns is likely to lead to the recurrence of civil war within ten years of the end of the campaign. Nonviolent campaigns, on the other hand, are much less likely to be succeeded by violent civil wars, at least in the ten years following the end of the campaign. The probability of civil war recurrence is heightened, however, when violent campaigns exist alongside nonviolent insurgencies, which suggests that maintaining nonviolent discipline has advantages both in terms of winning the war and securing the peace.[3]

Our central contention, then, is that short-term strategic victories achieved by violent campaigns usually do not translate into democracy or civil peace. Success of a nonviolent campaign, on the other hand, is more likely to produce these long-term outcomes. In fact, strikingly, the long-term effects of *failed* nonviolent campaigns are more favorable to democracy and civil peace than the long-term effects of successful violent campaigns. We do not mean to suggest that successful nonviolent campaigns are never followed by sociopolitical polarization or intense political competition—the aftermath of the Orange Revolution in Ukraine is a case in point—but we do suggest that the postvictory competition is more likely to manifest itself in nonviolent, rather than violent, contestation.

This chapter proceeds as follows. First, we discuss the current literature on the requirements for democracy and civil peace. We then briefly review the literature on the social and political consequences of insurgency. We then theorize why the success of violent insurgencies might be problematic for democratic transition and recurrent civil war compared with transitions driven by nonviolent resistance. We offer statistical evidence to support these explanations and explore several illustrative cases on how violent resistance can lead to new regimes that replicate the nondemocratic and repressive structures of the insurgency. We conclude by outlining the implications of these findings for our understanding of democratic transition, civil war recurrence, and the efficacy of insurgency.

THE REQUIREMENTS FOR DEMOCRACY

In this study, we are interested in how insurgency affects the probability that a country will be a democracy after a campaign ends.[4] In defining democracy, while we recognize that there is no such thing as a one-size-fits-all democratic structure, we rely on the standard description in political science: the country has developed a set of institutions in which political leaders are chosen through free, fair, and competitive elections; citizens enjoy protection from unwarranted intrusions by the government (such as enforceable civil liberties); and the judiciary, legislature, and executive are separated by checks and balances.[5] Note that our definition corresponds with the notion of *liberal* democracy, whereas *illiberal* democracy would share many of the procedural elements of democracy but without human rights or minority protections (Zakaria 2007).

Despite decades of excellent research, scholars are still debating the conditions under which democracies emerge (Diamond 2008; Geddes 1999; McFaul and Stoner-Weiss 2004; McFaul, Stoner-Weiss, and Bunce 2009; Putnam 1993; and Zakaria 2007).[6] Some scholars assert that statistical studies on pathways to democracy or its durability have been inconclusive, such that generalizations about democracy are difficult to make (Karl 2005, 26; Kitschelt et al. 1999; O'Donnell and Schmitter 1986; and Teorell and Hadenius 2004). Other prominent scholars argue that "there is simply too much inherent contingency and uncertainty in transition to permit the utilization of the full range of social science tools" (Karl 2005, 25).

A number of scholars argue, however, that some general observations are possible. For example, many scholars agree that wealthier countries tend to become democracies more often than poor countries (Przeworski et al. 2000). Although disputed in recent scholarship, others have argued in favor of modernization theory, which posits that democracy requires a liberal political culture (Almond and Verba 1963; Dahl 1989; Huntington 1984; Inglehart and Baker 2000; Lipset 1959; and Przeworski and Limongi 1997).[7] Other scholars have argued that the nature of the pretransition regime shapes the dynamics and nature of the new regime (Bratton and van de Walle 1994, 454). For instance, Geddes has argued that the pretransition regime classification (personalistic, military, single party, and so on) helps to determine the ease with which the democratic transition proceeds. Specifically, military regimes will be more likely to fall to democratic reformers than personalistic regimes because of the military's premium on unity (1999). Bratton and van de Walle develop this theme further by arguing, similar to our own contention in this study, that the way a transition occurs predicts the way the new regime will rule (1994).

Terry Lynn Karl identifies four such "modes of transition," including "pacted, imposed, reformist, and revolutionary" (2005, 26). For the purposes of this study, our interest lies with the revolutionary mode of transition in which violent and nonviolent resistance campaigns seek to displace the existing order entirely. At the same time, we recognize that revolutionary modes are not necessarily mutually exclusive with the pacted or reformist modes. Indeed, revolutionary transitions are often resolved through pacts or reforms.

Without rejecting the notion that environmental factors, such as the level of economic development, domestic political culture, and other factors influence regime type, we nevertheless argue that nonenvironmental factors, notably the forces driving the transition, are equally (if not more) important than the conditions in which they emerge in influencing postconflict governance. Much of the literature eschews this more agency-focused perspective, favoring instead a top-down approach that emphasizes pacts between regime elites and members of the middle class as the main drivers of democratic transitions (see, e.g., Geddes 1999; Karl 2005; Moore 1993). Broad-based nonviolent movements that arise at the peak of the transition (or that precede the transition) may be considered less significant than the activities of elites or outside forces.

Alternatively, we take the approach that democratic transitions are often driven by an interactive process involving elites and grassroots civic elements. Central to this approach is the notion that elite preferences and proclivities are influenced by the strength and nature of the resistance—violent or nonviolent. In this way, a resistance campaign often serves as the catalyst for such a transition rather than as a sideshow. We also argue that nonviolent and violent insurgencies have systematic, observable, varying effects on the transition's trajectory.

THE REQUIREMENTS FOR CIVIL PEACE

The literature on the requirements for civil peace is equally inconclusive.[8] For our purposes, civil peace refers to the absence of violent internal conflict above the thresholds commonly associated with civil war.[9] Just as many different factors can lead to civil war, peace seems to have many causes. However, the civil war literature identifies several factors that may be particularly important.

First, as conflict scholars often note, civil wars often "beget" subsequent civil wars—the so-called conflict trap (Collier and Sambanis 2002; Walter

2004). Countries such as Sri Lanka, Cambodia, and Colombia have experienced multiple civil wars, and many other states experience smaller conflicts that seem to hold over from previous wars. In fact, some scholars argue that a history of violent conflict is one of the most important factors determining whether a country will revert to internal war (Doyle and Sambanis 2000; Hartzell, Hoddie, and Rothchild 2001; Licklider 1995; and Walter 2004). Barbara Walter takes issue with this approach, however, arguing that a higher quality of life and greater access to political participation reduce the likelihood of renewed war, regardless of whether the country has experienced a previous conflict (2004). Other factors, such as the issues at stake, the identity of the major actors, the level and extent of outside intervention, and the stabilization of the security sector after the conflict may also be critical variables (Toft 2003, 2009).

Regardless of whether one agrees or disagrees with the idea of a conflict trap, most conflict scholars agree that a peaceful postwar society requires basic, fundamental institutions by which to establish and enforce the rule of law and provide basic goods and services to the population (Paris 2005). Moreover, Walter argues that countries that experience higher levels of economic success and create open political systems are less likely to experience multiple civil wars, regardless of whether and how the previous conflict was resolved (2004). Other scholars argue that democratic regime type in a postwar context is often a prerequisite for the duration of civil peace (Hegre et al. 2001).

Of particular interest to us are the conditions under which violent insurgencies lead to internally stable, democratic regimes compared with nonviolent campaigns. The next section discusses the consequences of violent insurgency for postconflict societies.

THE CONSEQUENCES OF VIOLENT INSURGENCIES

Many scholars have discussed the effects of violent insurgencies, revolutions, civil wars, and other types of civil conflicts on regime type and the renewal of conflict. However, very few have compared the effects of nonviolent and violent insurgencies on the postconflict political milieu.

Although seldom compared with the consequences of nonviolent resistance, violent conflict typically produces negative long-term social, economic, and political consequences in the polities where it occurs.[10] Postwar societies must rebuild infrastructure destroyed during the conflict and develop confidence in the financial and political systems to attract foreign investment and tourism (Collier 1999, 2009). Additionally, civil wars tend to impose major public-health crises upon societies, even after the conflicts have ended. Hazem Adam Ghobarah, Paul Huth, and Bruce Russett have found that those most victimized by civil war are women and children in terms of long-term health impacts (2003).

Several historical examples seem to substantiate the conventional wisdom that successful violent insurgencies will result in stunted economic and political development because of recurring civil war. For instance, after the 1917 Revolution, Russia immediately became embroiled in a protracted civil war. In Afghanistan, after a violent insurgency ousted Soviet forces in 1989, a brutal civil war ensued, creating a political vacuum filled by the Taliban. The 1994–2001 Taliban regime never had a full monopoly on the use of force but rather bullied tribal factions into compliance and assassinated members of its main rival, the Northern Alliance. The Maoist Revolution in China was followed by the bloody Cultural Revolution, while the Cuban Revolution was followed by violent class wars. And, as evidenced throughout medieval European history, the successful violent overthrow of one monarchy was often followed by an armed uprising against the victors. Thus, there are multiple examples in which civil wars have immediately succeeded insurgent victories.[11]

Successful nonviolent campaigns can also impose costs on society, but they are typically not as devastating in social, political, and economic terms as those produced by violent conflicts. Potentially adverse effects of a nonviolent resistance include property damage that may have occurred during the regime's attempts to repress the movement or during the transition itself. Economic growth may also be slow to get off the ground, depending on the ability of the new leadership to inspire confidence in domestic and foreign investors. Sociopolitical cleavages may result following a successful nonviolent revolution, which may deepen if the popular uprising was less broadly based. In general, however, we would not expect to see the same devastation of the physical infrastructure or long-term casualties that trouble societies emerging from civil wars.

Besides economic and health impacts, violent insurgencies may be problematic from the perspective of producing a stable and reliable political order. In particular, studies have found that civil wars create weak governance and civil-society institutions, increase the probability of international conflict, and create more "specialists in violence than in politics" (Licklider 2003, 1). Successful resistance movements create windows of opportunity during which expectations are shaped regarding the postconflict order. A critical factor determining how those expectations are shaped is the nature of the insurgency itself, notably, the nature of the participation in that insurgency and the primary method of opposition mobilization. Political recoveries from insurgencies conducted by a relatively small number of armed fighters, we argue, are more difficult than those from insurgencies driven by large and unarmed segments of the population.

Moreover, developing societal expectations of peaceful conflict resolution, institutionalizing the rule of law, and establishing a reliable security-enforcement apparatus are especially difficult tasks following conflicts in which people have been "'killing one another with considerable enthusiasm and success'" because of the high stakes of a false sense of security among former belligerents (Hartzell, Hoddie, and Rothchild 2001, 183). The larger the number of deaths that occur during a violent insurgency, "the more likely it is that feelings of insecurity will prevail given the fears, memories, and sunk costs associated with high levels of casualties" (190). In particular, high levels of violence "foster particularly acute concerns by adversaries about the future" and make them "ready to interpret seemingly innocuous moves by their opponent as a violation of the terms of the settlement and, through responses of their own, contributing to the breakdown of the settlement" (190). In other words, the inculcation of a winner-take-all political culture, rather than one based on negotiation and compromise, is the likely result of political transitions driven by high levels of violence.

Constructing reliable, legitimate, and accountable democratic institutions is easier when the conflict has been primarily nonviolent for three reasons. First, the active participation of large numbers of citizens in the process of democratic change, through their involvement in campaigns of nonviolent resistance, enhances the prospect that the citizenry will remain politically engaged after the transition. Of course, there are no guarantees that this will happen, and often there is popular disillusionment with the state of governance following certain nonviolent transitions (as witnessed in Iran and more recently in Georgia and Ukraine). However, mass participation in nonviolent political change, we suggest, encourages the development of democratic skills and fosters expectations of accountable governance, both of which are less likely when transitions are driven by opposition violence.

Second, in countries where nonviolent resistance has succeeded in removing entrenched power, the victorious party has demonstrated that nonviolent means can be effective in winning power. Such victories become part of the collective memory. Furthermore, transitions driven by nonviolent movements may strengthen citizen expectations that the postconflict political regime will also be nonviolent in its relationship with constituents. In a country that has just witnessed the triumph of mass, nonviolent resistance, leaders may attempt to bolster their legitimacy by swearing off violence toward the very civilians that put them in power. For example, today in Thailand, a country with a rich history of nonviolent popular movements challenging authoritarianism, police are not permitted to carry firearms when responding to nonviolent rallies and demonstrations. During the February–May 2010 "red shirt" nonviolent protests, Thai security forces reacted to these protestors with remarkable restraint, resorting to violent repression only when provoked by violent "black shirt" oppositionists (Ruiz and Sarbil 2010). But once this conflict became violent, the repression was overwhelming.

Often the opposite occurs following successful violent insurgencies. As Karl argues, "in the context of high violence, this window of opportunity is very short-lived," as "war transitions threaten to produce failed states or democracies that are so perilous that many of their citizens long for a return to authoritarian rule" (2005, 19–20). Indeed, in many cases, we see the new governments scrambling to establish hegemony over the new polity, often using violence to do so.

Third, successful campaigns that rely primarily on violent methods are more likely to operate by means of secrecy and martial values.[12] Such values tend to reinforce themselves in the new regime, leaving little room for dissent or the establishment of consensual institutions that are necessary to manage conflicts and power relationships nonviolently. Armed insurgents in Cuba and Afghanistan installed closed and secretive dictatorships following their victories, for example. Conversely, campaigns that rely on a nonviolent strategy are more likely to use consent, leading to the establishment of more democratically oriented parallel institutions that might aid in the transition to a democratic system when the conflict has ended. In South Africa, for example, the nonviolent antiapartheid campaign coincided with popularly elected local governments and people's courts in black townships, which usurped the authority of apartheid regime-appointed administrators and judges long before majority rule came to the country as a whole (Zunes 2009b). And, strikingly, the postapartheid milieu has featured a Truth and

Reconciliation Commission, whose very charge was to encourage transparency regarding past and continuing government and social abuses (for a description, see Bouraine 2001).

Of course, this does not mean that governments and rulers who come to power following nonviolent revolutions will never resort to violence when challenged by nonviolent protest movements. Mikhail Saakashvili, the charismatic leader of Georgia's 2003 Rose Revolution, came under heavy domestic and international criticism for his heavy-handed response to nonviolent government challengers in November 2007. At the same time, the very fact that Saakashvili was severely criticized for the violent government response, compelling him to acknowledge wrongdoing, suggests that a country's experience with popular nonviolent struggle constrains postconflict regime behavior.

The Georgian and Iranian cases suggest that the level and degree of citizen participation in nonviolent campaigns—and how prominent a role charismatic leaders have—may influence the prospect of democracy afterward. The greater the reliance on charismatic leaders, the more difficult the transition to democracy, because politics tends to become personalized rather than institutionalized. Further research is required to shed light on the impact, positive and negative, of charismatic leadership in nonviolent movements.

The Effects of Successful Violent Insurgency on Democracy

Pundits often suggest that violent insurgent victories will cause the countries to backslide into authoritarianism.[13] This prediction is certainly intuitive given prominent historical cases. Well-known successful revolutions—such as the Russian Revolution, the Chinese Revolution, the North Vietnamese revolution, the Cuban Revolution, and the Taliban's rise to power—appear to substantiate the expectation that successful insurgents engage in strong-arm rule and rely extensively on their security apparatus (army, police, paramilitaries, intelligence) to maintain effective control over the population once they come to power. As Ackerman and Karatnycky have found, 67 percent of states designated as "Not Free" in 2005 had undergone recent transitions marked by violence (2005, 8).[14]

In the case of the Costa Rican Revolution, the victorious insurgents voluntarily held free and fair elections and even disbanded the state's military upon coming to power. But in reality, such developments are rare. In our data set of 218 violent insurgencies since 1900, democratic governments succeeded only about 5 percent of victorious insurgencies.[15]

According to Linz and Stepan, the way civil war affects the probability for democracy depends on the nature of civil and political society (cited in Bermeo 2003, 162–63). During the transition, elites must raise the costs of violent competition and lower the costs of nonviolent competition (163–65). The costs of violent competition must increase through strict enforcement mechanisms that are both legitimate and credible to the constituents. Bermeo argues that "elites must make every effort to neutralize violent groups of all sorts . . . the state must ensure that its police and judiciary take swift action against individuals who engage in political violence—regardless of ideology or social identity" (164).

This will be difficult to accomplish in a new state where the violent overthrow of the incumbent power has just occurred. The new government may be tempted to continue to use violence to purge remaining members of the old guard. While such purges could occur following transitions driven by nonviolent resistance, this is less likely because often a sizable part of the old guard has already shifted its allegiance and joined the opposition during the transition process. The co-optation of regime supporters by nonviolent oppositionists, including the nonviolent fraternization with members of the regime's security forces, are, as our case studies show, common facets of nonviolent resistance campaigns. The likelihood of the posttransition government unleashing its armed elements against the civilian population is further lowered, we argue, when there are no remaining nonstate armed factions following the transition. In other words, the greater the level of nonviolent discipline exemplified by the opposition prior to the transition, the lower the chances of violent purging following the transition.

Instead, for democracy to take hold, the successful insurgents must "distance themselves from the purveyors of violence" (Bermeo 2003, 165). The consequences of maintaining alliances with such perpetrators can be high and negative for democracy:

> Politicians have often failed to condemn violence perpetrated by groups who locate themselves on the same end of the political spectrum or who act against the politicians' own political enemies. This failure exaggerates the image of the violent group's support, sows panic in the minds of enemy groups, provides another rationale for counter-violence, and contributes to the likelihood of military intervention. Politicians who remain silent in an effort to maintain or

expand their vote base should be made to realize that their actions jeopardize voting itself. (165)

Opportunities and incentives for nonviolent competition can be created through elections and other forms of organization, as well as by means of measures to ensure government accountability and responsiveness.[16] Encouraging nonviolent competition is bolstered by the activities of civil society. Bermeo argues that groups in "civil society can raise the costs of violent competition through defensive but lawful mass mobilizations" (2003, 165).

In sum, nonviolent transitions that have succeeded contain inherent potential to continue to maintain accountability of the new state through civil society using nonviolent means, whereas successful violent insurgencies have premade violent civil society norms and organizations that are antithetical to democratic practices and the nonviolent resolution of inevitable conflicts.

In addition, the new elites likewise learn that successful nonviolent campaigns can recur if they fail to deliver public goods. Shared expectations between rulers and ruled in the new regimes enhance certainty about laws and institutions. As Bernhard and Karakoc note, shared attitudes and expectations about the new governing order are necessary for democracy (2007). Successful democracies require commitments to resolve domestic conflicts using nonviolent, institutional mechanisms, which may be undermined if a violent group seizes power (Diamond 1977, 2008). Civic engagement—including civil resistance—enhances government accountability and responsiveness, according to Putnam (1993). Campaigns that involve diverse groups in society may provide especially potent checks on the new government's power, since diverse campaigns expand the number of potential voters engaged in the political process.

At the same time, the frequent recurrence of people power campaigns involving large-scale protests and demonstrations in countries such as the Philippines and Thailand, and more recently in Lebanon, suggests inherent institutional weaknesses in those countries. The fact that large numbers of people feel the need to regularly circumvent normal institutional channels to voice grievances and resolve conflicts highlights the weakness of power-sharing arrangements and democracy in those countries. Whereas nonviolent protests and civil disobedience are fairly routine activities in mature democracies, popular reliance on extra-institutional and extra-legal means to resolve conflicts may be emblematic of democratic weakness.

From the success of violent insurgencies, on the other hand, different expectations emerge. Insurgents, deposed elites, and emerging elites may perceive that violence is an effective means of expressing political preferences and gaining political power. For the losers in the conflict, who see the conflict in zero-sum terms, violence is therefore likely to remain the tactical method of choice. In other words, the constant threat of violence from all sides of the previous conflict exacerbates uncertainty rather than reducing it, thereby undermining Bernhard and Karakoc's essential element of democracy. Under such conditions, reaching mutually agreeable power-sharing arrangements and building democratic institutions are highly problematic.

In the scholarly literature, therefore, the assumption that successful violent insurgencies will be undemocratic, thereby decreasing the state's likelihood of becoming a democracy, is based on two key observations: that the insurgents' violent methods of taking power will cause them to embrace authoritarianism once they achieve power, and that the violence used by many insurgents requires and legitimizes fundamentally antidemocratic means of political contestation. Thus, the outcomes of resistance campaigns generate citizen expectations about the new order. We argue that the main form of resistance driving the transition—violent or nonviolent—can influence the degree to which parties to the conflict share mutual expectations and certainty about postconflict governing relationships. If we are correct, violent insurgent success should reduce the probability of becoming a democracy relative to nonviolent campaigns.

Testing the Effects of Resistance Type on Postconflict Democracy

Our first set of tests analyzes the consequences of primary resistance type on postconflict regime type at different intervals after the end of the conflict. To those ends, we used our data set of insurgencies and their outcomes from 1900 to 2006. The resistance type (nonviolent or violent) is the main independent variable in these tests. The specific outcomes in question are postconflict regime type, the probability of a democratic regime type, and the probability of postconflict civil war, and we developed separate models for each.[17]

Next, we introduced a number of control variables, which vary according to each model. In all models, we controlled for the level of democracy at the end of the conflict, as this may affect the level of democracy after the conflict has ended. In each model, we also controlled for the duration of the conflict (the logged conflict duration in days), because duration may affect the degree of certainty about the conflict outcome after the conflict has ended (Fearon 1995). Moreover, longer conflicts may have afforded the campaign more opportunity to develop the institutions necessary for postconflict state building.[18] Additional control variables are discussed in the appendix.

Table 8.1 reports the results of an ordinary-least-squares regression (Model 1) and two logistic regressions (Models 2 and 3) on the effects of resistance type on the probability of achieving a democratic regime type five years after the end of an insurgency.

We can see from Model 1 that among all insurgencies, a nonviolent campaign is much more likely to have a higher level of postconflict democracy than a violent insurgency. This is true even when we control for the level of democracy the year before the conflict has ended, which is also positive and significantly correlated to the level of democracy five years after the end of the conflict. The duration of the conflict is insignificant, which suggests that the duration of the conflict has no effect on the level of democracy after a conflict ends. Nonviolent resistance has a positive and significant effect on the postconflict level of democracy, which suggests that our suspicions are correct. The Philippines, Serbia, and many other Eastern European countries are all cases where the type of campaign likely improved the odds that those countries would be democracies after the conflict ended.

Model 2 reports that the probability of democratic regime type within five years increases when the resistance is nonviolent, holding other factors constant.[19] In Model 2, we use the strict test of democracy—the dichotomous measure of whether the polity is democratic five years after the end of the conflict.[20] Again, we can see a confirmation of our argument. Figure 8.1 demonstrates the substantive effects of these findings.

Among countries with average levels of democracy at the end of the conflict, a nonviolent resistance campaign made the country over 40 percent likelier to be democratic five years after the conflict than countries in which the primary resistance type was violent.[21] When we restrict the sample to include only successful campaigns, the results are even more striking. Successful nonviolent campaigns increase the probability of democratic regime type by over 50 percent compared with successful violent insurgencies. Holding other variables constant, the probability that a country will be a democracy

TABLE 8.1 **THE EFFECT OF RESISTANCE TYPE ON POSTCONFLICT DEMOCRACY**

	MODEL 1	MODEL 2		MODEL 3	
	LEVEL OF DEMOCRACY (CONTINUOUS), ALL CAMPAIGNS[†]	DUMMY VARIABLE FOR DEMOCRACY (DICHOTOMOUS), ALL CAMPAIGNS[§]	MARGINAL EFFECTS PER ONE-UNIT INCREASE	DUMMY VARIABLE FOR DEMOCRACY (DICHOTOMOUS), FAILED CAMPAIGNS ONLY[§]	MARGINAL EFFECTS PER ONE-UNIT INCREASE
PRIMARY RESISTANCE TYPE IS NONVIOLENT	6.58*** (.90)	2.83*** (.57)	+45%	2.88** (1.11)	+35%
POLITY SCORE(T-1)	.61*** (.07)	.23*** (.05)	+3%	.33*** (.08)	+2%
DURATION OF CONFLICT	.03 (.29)	.16 (.20)	--	-.16 (.28)	--
CONSTANT	-1.33 (2.12)	-3.17* (1.43)	15%	-3.50* (2.03)	7%
N	195	195		131	
	F = 66.52	WALD CHI² = 29.43		WALD CHI² = 17.50	
	PROB > F =.0000	PROB > CHI² =.0000		PROB>CHI² =.0006	
	R² = .4123	PSEUDO R² = .2707		PSEUDO R² =.3639	

SIGNIFICANCE LEVELS: ***P<.01; **P<.05; *P<.1. [†]ORDINARY LEAST SQUARES REGRESSION WITH ROBUST STANDARD ERRORS CLUSTERED AROUND TARGET COUNTRY CODE. [§]LOGISTIC REGRESSION WITH ROBUST STANDARD ERRORS CLUSTERED AROUND TARGET COUNTRY CODE.

FIGURE 8.1 **THE EFFECT OF RESISTANCE TYPE ON PROBABILITY OF DEMOCRACY**

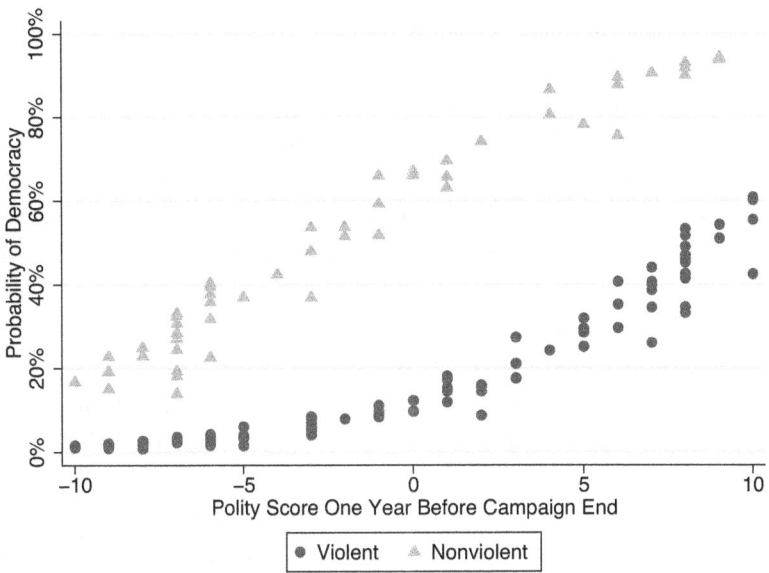

five years after a campaign ends is 57 percent among successful nonviolent campaigns but less than 6 percent for successful violent campaigns, corroborating Ackerman and Karatnycky's findings (2005). Among countries that are already democratic when the resistance campaign is occurring, a country with a successful nonviolent campaign is about 82 percent likely to remain a democracy after the campaign ends.

The Active Voices campaign in Madagascar fits this description. The nonviolent campaign, which occurred in the nominally democratic Madagascar from 1991 to 1993, sought to force President Didier Ratsiraka from power. When Ratsiraka stripped himself of his powers and named the opposition leader head of state, the resultant regime remained a stable democratic one. Strikingly, a democracy that succumbs to a violent insurgency, however, is less than 17 percent likely to remain a democracy after the campaign has ended. The Spanish civil war demonstrates this point, as the Republican government lost to fascist insurgents, who replaced the regime with an authoritarian one.

In Model 3, we report the effects of failed nonviolent campaigns on the probability of postconflict democracy. Holding all other variables constant, the average country with a failed nonviolent campaign has over a 35 percent chance of becoming a democracy five years after a conflict's end. This figure contrasts with failed violent campaigns, which have less than a 4 percent chance of being succeeded by democratic regimes. Among robust democracies, a country that defeats a nonviolent campaign is still 98 percent likely to remain a democracy. The anti-Calderón resistance in Mexico in 2006, for example, was a nonviolent campaign that occurred against a democracy, but the presence of the campaign did not reduce the level of democracy in Mexico.

A democracy that defeats a violent insurgency, however, is only 70 percent likely to remain a democracy. Imagine, for instance, if the anti-Calderón resistance had been a violent insurgency. The Mexican government may have felt compelled to circumvent civil liberties and repress the campaign violently. Mexico may have chosen to place restrictions on electoral politics to prevent the insurgents from becoming emboldened. All this may have reduced Mexico's overall level of democracy. Thus the type of resistance campaign has profound consequences for the postconflict political order.

These results suggest that regardless of whether the violent insurgency succeeds or fails, the level of democracy five years after the end of the conflict is lower than the levels succeeding a nonviolent campaign. Moreover, this is true whether the nonviolent campaign succeeds or fails. As Sidney Tarrow argued twenty years ago, nonviolent political action is good for democracy: it forces governments to comply with citizens' demands and forces citizens to participate in the political process (1989).

Testing the Effects of Resistance Type on Postconflict Civil War

The second set of tests concerns the relationship between resistance type and postwar violent conflict. As we argued above, we expect nonviolent resistance to reduce the likelihood that a country will experience a civil war after the conflict has ended. In this set of tests, the dependent variable is a dichotomous indicator of civil war onset ten years after the conflict.[22]

Next, we introduced a number of control variables. In all models, we controlled for the level of democracy ten years after the conflict, as previous research has shown that democracy can reduce civil war in the long run (Hegre et al. 2001). We used the typical indicator of government capabilities, the CINC score from the Correlates of War data set, to control for the effects of state capacity on the likelihood of an outbreak of violence. Finally, we also included a dichotomous variable for simultaneous violent movements, which is coded as 1 if the nonviolent or violent campaign coexisted with any rival violent groups during the course of the conflict, and 0 if otherwise. Consistent with Cunningham, we expected this variable to have a positive effect on the onset of civil war because of the tendency of such groups to act as spoilers (2006). The results appear in table 8.2.

Countries in which a violent campaign has occurred have a 42 percent chance of experiencing a recurrence of civil war within ten years, compared with 28 percent for countries in which a nonviolent campaign has occurred. Peru, for instance, faced the Sendero Luminoso (Shining Path) insurgency from 1980 to 1995. When this campaign was defeated, another violent campaign emerged: the Túpac Amaru Revolutionary Movement (MRTA). On the other hand, Argentina, which experienced a nonviolent campaign that ousted a military junta in 1977, did not experience violent civil conflict fol-

TABLE 8.2 **THE EFFECT OF RESISTANCE TYPE ON PROBABILITY OF POSTCONFLICT CIVIL WAR ONSET**

	PROBABILITY OF POSTCONFLICT CIVIL WAR ONSET§	MARGINAL EFFECTS PER ONE-UNIT INCREASE
PRIMARY RESISTANCE TYPE IS NONVIOLENT	−.62*** (.38)	−14%
POLITY SCORE (T+10)	.00 (.03)	--
SIMULTANEOUS VIOLENT CAMPAIGN	.94*** (.41)	+22%
GOVERNMENT CAPABILITIES, LOGGED	10.79** (5.37)	+49%
CONSTANT	−.89*** (.34)	36%
N	158	
WALD CHI²	11.83	
PROB > CHI²	.0187	
PSEUDO R²	.0620	

SIGNIFICANCE LEVELS: ***P<.01; **P<.05; *P<.1; LOGISTIC REGRESSION WITH ROBUST STANDARD ERRORS CLUSTERED AROUND TARGET COUNTRY CODE.
§ NONVIOLENT RESISTANCE AND LOGGED PARTICIPANTS ARE JOINTLY SIGNIFICANT AT P = .01.

lowing the regime's ouster. Even when an attempted coup occurred in 1986, civilians resorted to nonviolent resistance to force the coup plotters to restore democracy to the country.

The likelihood of civil war recurrence is heightened by the existence of spoilers during the campaigns. Nonviolent and violent campaigns that coexisted with armed groups had a 49 percent chance of experiencing a recurrence of civil war within ten years, compared with a 27 percent chance for campaigns that did not coexist with armed campaigns. In the Palestinian case, for example, the presence of multiple competing, armed factions predisposed the Palestinian Territories to a relapse into violent conflict. The nonviolent campaign that brought democracy to Slovenia, on the other hand, was relatively free from a contemporaneous violent insurgency. The absence of an organized, armed group left unsatisfied by the transition may have helped stave off future violence, whereas Slovenia's neighbors in the former Yugoslavia became embroiled in violent conflict.

These cumulative findings shed light on both the consequences and dynamics of civil war. Controlling for the effects of postconflict regime type and government capabilities, we still see the positive and significant effect that a history of violence has on the likelihood of a recurrent civil war. Moreover, the presence of a simultaneous violent campaign increases the probability for renewed violence, which lends support to the idea that a key challenge for nonviolent campaigns is to ensure nonviolent discipline throughout the campaign (Ackerman and Kruegler 1994). Although there are exceptions, the general pattern is clear. When nonviolent campaigns fail to remain disciplined in the exclusive use of nonviolent methods, or when they coexist with violent competitors in the political environment, we are more likely to see recurrent violent conflict between the government and insurgents.

IMPLICATIONS

In this chapter, we have examined the consequences of the success of violent insurgencies relative to the success of nonviolent insurgencies. We have found strong empirical support for the notion that successful nonviolent resistance is much likelier to lead to democracy and civil peace, whereas violent insurgent success prohibits or reverses democracy while increasing the likelihood for recurrent civil war.

In the theoretical portion of this chapter, we argued that uncertainty and the reinforcement of violent rules of political contestation exacerbate the security dilemma after the conflict has ended. Violent conflicts will likely result in rulers and regimes that hesitate to adopt democratic values and ideals that reverse the norms they have established during the course of their violent struggles. Conversely, the participants in successful nonviolent conflicts are more likely to codify emerging norms of nonviolent contestation into domestic institutions, thus encouraging nonviolent bargaining and conflict resolution after the dispute has ended.

The findings in this chapter and the additional findings reported in the appendix are broadly supportive of our argument. When violent insurgencies succeed, the country that hosts the insurgency is much less likely to become democratic. Countries in which nonviolent resistance movements succeed have a much better chance of becoming democratic within five years, particularly if the nonviolent campaign has succeeded. But even when nonviolent resistance campaigns fail, we see potential for democracy over time. This is not the case with violent insurgencies.

These outcomes are generalizable but not necessarily universal. In the case of Iran, for instance, a mass, primarily nonviolent struggle succeeded in ousting the Shah of Iran, replacing him with a violent regime within a year.[23] Conversely, three successful violent insurgencies were succeeded by democratic regimes: the National Liberation Army's 1948 victory in Costa Rica, the Jewish resistance in British-occupied Palestine, and the 1971 Bengali self-determination campaign against Pakistan. However, these instances represent only three cases out of fifty-five successful insurgencies in the twentieth century. They are as rare as authoritarian regimes that succeed victorious nonviolent campaigns.

This variation points to a potentially fruitful avenue of future research; namely, exploring the conditions under which violent insurgency leads to democracy and the conditions under which nonviolent insurgency leads to authoritarianism. Although a full inquiry into these puzzles is beyond the scope of this study, answers to these questions will allow us to further understand the long-term consequences of violent and nonviolent resistance campaigns.

CHAPTER NINE **CONCLUSION**

▬▬▬▬▬▬

Nonviolence is a flop. The only bigger flop is violence.
JOAN BAEZ

In this book, we have advanced several major arguments. First, we have argued that historically, nonviolent resistance campaigns have been more effective in achieving their goals than violent resistance campaigns. This has been true even under conditions in which most people would expect nonviolent resistance to be futile, including situations in which dissent is typically met with harsh regime repression. The only exception is secession campaigns, which have been historically ineffective whether nonviolent or violent and about which scholars have written extensively (Fuhrmann and Tir 2009; Toft 2003; Walter 2009).

Second, we have argued that the historical success of nonviolent campaigns is explained by the fact that the physical, moral, and informational barriers to participation in nonviolent campaigns are substantially lower than in violent campaigns given comparable circumstances. The lower barriers to participation translate into a higher degree of more diverse membership in nonviolent campaigns, which proves to be a critical factor in explaining the outcomes of resistance campaigns in five keys ways. First, mass, diverse participation tends to result in higher levels of civic disruption through mass noncooperation, which causes erstwhile regime supporters, including the security forces, to reevaluate their interests and preferences and become more willing to shift loyalties to the resistance. At the end of the day, most people want to survive and to be on the winning side of a conflict, so nonviolent contestation increases the incentives for loyalty shifts. Second, regime repression against large, nonviolent campaigns is more likely to backfire against the perpetrator than when repression is used against large, violent campaigns. Backfiring, whose effects are amplified for reasons described earlier, often results in even greater mobilization, shifts in loyalty among erstwhile regime elites, and sanctions against the offending regime. Third, campaigns that exhibit large-scale civilian participation are more likely than small campaigns to win meaningful support for their cause in the international community and to cause their opponent regimes to lose support among important regional or international powers. Fourth, large nonviolent campaigns tend to be better at evading and remaining resilient in the face of regime repression. Fifth, large nonviolent campaigns tend to be more adept at developing tactical innovations than small campaigns, allowing them to maneuver and adapt to conditions more easily than small campaigns.

Nevertheless, we have also shown that just because a campaign is nonviolent does not guarantee its success. Campaigns do not succeed simply because they have won the moral high ground, as some may suggest. Rather, the ability of the campaign to make strategic adjustments to changing conditions is crucial to its success, whether it is nonviolent or violent. But it is very difficult to predict or generalize which campaigns will be strategically competent until after some visible gains have been made. Because strategic ability is not observable at the outset of a campaign, we downplay its significance as a statistical pattern; however, the actual significance of the ability to outthink and outmaneuver one's adversary is obvious to anyone who has studied conflict.[1]

What we can say, though, is that there appears to be no general trend indicating that there are types of opponents against whom such strategic maneuvering is impossible. Contrary to theorists who emphasize structural factors in determining whether a conflict will succeed or fail, we find no such patterns. Nonviolent campaigns succeed against democracies and non-democracies, weak and powerful opponents, conciliatory and repressive regimes. Thus conditions shape—but do not predetermine—the capacity for a nonviolent resistance to adapt and gain advantage under even the direst of circumstances. While we do not wish to suggest that nonviolent resistance could always succeed against an opponent committed to genocide—an argument often put forward by those who doubt the efficacy of civil resistance when used against those committed to annihilation—we do wish to suggest that factors other than the opponent's willingness to use brutal force, such as the ability to achieve leverage and resiliency vis-à-vis the adversary, are just as important in determining conflict outcomes. Genocidaires are only as powerful as the henchman and underlings who carry out their orders (Summy 1994).

Statistical tests and congruence testing through four case studies support the notion that nonviolent campaigns are superior at inflicting considerable costs on the adversary in ways that divide the regime from its critical pillars of support. Conversely, violent campaigns tend to unify the regime, reinforcing its pillars and causing it to double down against violent insurgents—legitimately, in the eyes of many spectators. Thus, over 75 percent of violent insurgencies end up suppressed or engaged in protracted stalemates with state adversaries, whereas the majority of nonviolent campaigns ultimately succeed in achieving their objectives.

Although violent campaigns do succeed from time to time, they often do so only with the help of a foreign sponsor, which helps them to demonstrate credibility to potential recruits, elevate their material capabilities against the opponent, and evade authorities through foreign sanctuary. Half the successful violent insurgencies received overt support from state sponsors, whose support sometimes attempted to supplement the shortfall of willing recruits.

In countries in which violent insurgencies have been victorious, we find, however, that the country is much less likely to become a peaceful democracy after the conflict has ended. On the other hand, in analogous countries where mass, nonviolent campaigns have occurred, we see a much higher rate of postconflict democracies and a much lower rate of relapse into civil war. This does not mean that there will not be any sharp political contention or democratic backsliding following a successful nonviolent transition. But it does mean that political contention is more likely to transpire through nonviolent channels.

Some may cite the American Revolution against the British as a counterexample to the above assertion. It should be remembered, however, that the armed insurgency against British forces, notably in the form of guerrilla warfare, was preceded by a decade of parallel institution building, nonviolent boycotts, civil disobedience, noncooperation, and other nation-building methods (Conser et al. 1986).

Our study therefore concludes that nonviolent civil resistance works, both in terms of achieving campaigns' strategic objectives and in terms of promoting the long-term well-being of the societies in which the campaigns have been waged. Violent insurgency, on the other hand, has a dismal record on both counts.

SIGNIFICANCE FOR POLICY

Research regarding the successes and failures of nonviolent campaigns can provide insight into the most effective ways for governmental and nongovernmental actors to aid such movements. Our study suggests that nonviolent campaigns do not necessarily benefit from material aid from outside states, though relatively small sums of money for items including cell phones, computers, radios, fax machines, T-shirts, office space, and other items that nonviolent activists use for recruitment purposes can go a long way. Nonviolent campaigns can, furthermore, benefit from sanctions, diplomatic support, and allies in international civil society, who can strengthen and diversify the membership base that is so critical to success.

For instance, although there is no evidence that mass nonviolent mobilization can be successfully begun or sustained by external actors, targeted forms of external support were useful in a number of cases, like the international boycotts targeting the apartheid regime in South Africa. The existence of organized solidarity groups that maintained steady pressure on governments allied with the target regimes proved to be very helpful, suggesting that "extending the battlefield" is sometimes necessary for opposition groups to enhance their leverage over the target. Lending diplomatic support to human rights activists and democratic opposition leaders while penalizing regimes (or threatening penalties) that target unarmed activists with violent repression may be another way that governments can improve the probability of nonviolent campaign success.

These and other "tools" that diplomats and embassies have used to support human rights and democracy activists, including in some of the most repressive countries in the world, are captured in a recent publication by the Council for a Community of Democracies entitled *A Diplomat's Handbook for Democracy Development Support* (http://www.diplomatshandbook.org). The *Handbook* offers an extensive catalog of resources and assets that diplomats can draw from to support civil society and individuals and groups committed to nonviolent change. These include offering visas to threatened dissidents, providing the public with pertinent objective information (particularly useful in closed societies), engaging with governments managing democratic transitions, using official channels to identify emerging or actual problems involving local authorities, protesting human rights violations, seeking removal of restrictions to reformers and NGOs, connecting opposition leaders with moderate reformers within the government, providing nonviolent activists safe spaces for meetings, offering small-grant seed money for grassroots organizations, and attending in-country trials of dissidents.

The *Handbook* features a number of case studies (e.g., South Africa, Chile,

Zimbabwe, Cuba, China, and Egypt) and contains the international legal framework of agreements that allows democracy advocates to seek external support abroad and democratic governments to provide such assistance. The authors of the *Handbook* make very clear, however, that these forms of support should come at the behest of, and in support of, those leading nonviolent movements for change. Local legitimacy is a prerequisite for successful nonviolent change.

Facilitating the creation and maintenance of independent sources of media and technology that allow nonviolent actors to communicate internally and with the outside world—another tool featured in the *Handbook*—is another way that governmental and nongovernmental actors can support nonviolent campaigns and movements. Supporting traditional forms of communication, including radio, is particularly useful in countries, like Afghanistan, where the information technology sector is not as strong and literacy rates are low. However, even in developing countries like Afghanistan, cell-phone usage and SMS text messaging have become a critical means of sharing information and mobilization.

Technical capacity building in elections monitoring and human rights documentation are other useful tools for nonviolent activists. Nonviolent campaigns can feature their participation and generate greater leverage when they are able to maintain the attention of actors that are critical to the conflict, as scholars of transnational solidarity activism have shown (Keck and Sikkink 1998). The New Tactics in Human Rights project developed by the Center for Victims of Torture highlights innovative recent tactics employed by activists engaged in nonviolent struggles around the world; the online resource contains blogs and discussion boards that activists can use to gain information and learn from one another (http://www.newtactics.org). Online information sharing through YouTube and Facebook has been particularly useful for civic groups around the world—most recently in Tunisia and Egypt—that are using pressure from below to challenge corruption and promote government accountability. Other grassroots social networking initiatives, including DigiActive, offer online resources and communications tools for activists, particularly those living in repressive societies where firewalls and severe censorship pose obstacles to communicating with the outside world (http://www.digiactive.org).

The provision of educational materials that highlight lessons learned from other historical nonviolent movements in multiple languages is another possible contributor to nonviolent mobilization. For example, the Serbian opposition movement used the writings of Gene Sharp while conducting trainings of nonviolent activists in the period leading up to the 2000 ouster of Milosevic. The documentary film *Bringing Down a Dictator*, produced by York Zimmerman Inc., about the Serbian nonviolent movement was shown on public television in Georgia and Ukraine before and during the Rose and Orange revolutions in those countries. Introducing activists engaged in current nonviolent struggles to nonviolent conflict "veterans" from earlier nonviolent campaigns, thereby encouraging the exchange of lessons and skill building, is another important form of outside support. The effects of the level and type of training received by members of violent and nonviolent resistance campaigns and their trajectories and outcomes could be tested in a future study.

Thus, our study suggests that sanctions and state support for nonviolent campaigns work best when they support the activities of local opposition groups; but they are never substitutes for local participation. At the same time, outside support for local nonviolent groups is a double-edged sword that is often used by regimes to delegitimize local nonviolent groups and movements. Local actors must therefore be savvy about how they engage with external actors and be prepared to counter their opponents' propaganda. It may be the case that external support to nonviolent campaigns that is applied multilaterally (by the United Nations, European Union, OAS, or other regional bodies), rather than by single states, is more effective because it is seen to be more legitimate and less politicized. Further research into the types and timing of external assistance to civil resistance campaigns would enhance our understanding of when and how outside support either complements or diminishes the activities of local nonviolent activists.

Regimes that face resistance campaigns are undoubtedly interested in the ways that these campaigns can be disrupted. We have mentioned some of the ways that nonviolent campaigns have failed—through the inability to galvanize broad, diverse membership, the inability to adjust strategically to the opponent's counterattacks, and the inability to divide the adversary from its main pillars of support. Some regimes may try to use this information to make themselves more resilient against nonviolent campaigns; indeed, evidence suggests that the Russian, Chinese, and Zimbabwean regimes actively attempt to learn about how nonviolent mass movements operate in order to disrupt them (Spector 2006).

Such regimes use a predictable tool to disrupt mass resistance: repression. And what our findings suggest is that repression of a nonviolent campaign does not necessarily doom it to failure. On the contrary, mass campaigns are sometimes effective at causing regime repression to backfire, in which case the regime may begin to show its internal divisions and external pressures. Thus regime elites should not be so confident that indefinitely repressing nonviolent campaigns can bring a favorable result. Research has shown, in fact, that regimes that combine repression with co-optation and positive sanctions are generally more effective in suppressing challenge groups than those that rely on repression alone (Ackerman and Kruegler 1994, 15). Thomas Schelling captures the essence of this response and counterresponse dynamic inherent in civil resistance campaigns:

> [The] tyrant and his subjects are in somewhat symmetrical positions. They can deny him most of what he wants—they can, that is, if they have the disciplined organization to refuse collaboration. And he can deny them just about everything they want—he can deny it by using the force at his command . . . They can deny him the satisfaction of ruling a disciplined country, he can deny them the satisfaction of ruling themselves . . . It is a bargaining situation in which either side, if adequately disciplined and organized, can deny most of what the other wants, and it remains to see who wins. (1969, 351–52)

Implications for Insurgents

Another set of conclusions is meant for insurgents themselves. Violent insurgents often justify their use of violence as a method of last resort. Many academics agree that violence happens only when it is necessary, as a last resort when other options have been exhausted. An entire research program in international politics—the bargaining model of war—assumes that actors would not fight if they could settle their disputes using nonviolent methods.

This study challenges these claims. The argument that using violent resistance is the only effective way to win concessions from a repressive adversary simply does not stand up to the evidence. Nonviolent resistance has the strategic edge. The evidence presented also rejects the claim that there are some types of states against which only violence will work. We were able to discern no such states in this study.

Insurgents who claim that violent resistance is necessary are probably always wrong. In fact, we conjecture that many of the groups that claim violence as a last resort may have never attempted strategic nonviolent action, judging it to be too difficult at the outset. Max Abrahms identifies multiple terrorist groups, for instance, that elected to use violence as a first resort despite using a last resort rhetoric (2008, 84–85).

Groups that seek to challenge oppressive regimes or foreign occupations with nonviolent resistance have much better odds than those fighting with asymmetrical violence. The main mechanisms by which resistance campaigns extract major concessions from regimes are much likelier to occur when a campaign is nonviolent. And, although our book focuses on state opponents, civil resistance may effectively confront violent nonstate actors as well. As Merriman and DuVall write, "When civilian-based, nonviolent forces are able to come to the fore and produce decisive change in a society, the demand for terrorism as a form of struggle will subside" (2007, 223).

We do not intend to downplay the risks of nonviolent action or suggest that nonviolent campaigns are immune from setbacks or defeat. We furthermore concede that violent insurgencies and guerrilla campaigns sometimes succeed, often by securing outside sponsorship and winning wars of attrition. But we do want to convey that nonviolent resistance has the potential to succeed in nearly all situations in which violent resistance is typically used, and to more favorable ends in the longer term. Civil resistance enhances citizenship skills and societal resilience in ways that elude armed campaigns.

The historical record clearly shows that civil resistance is an enduring force for change in the international system. Civilian populations will continue to challenge repressive governments, occupiers, and even terrorists with collective action and noncooperation that deny formidable opponents the quiet and submission they need to maintain power. It behooves scholars, policy makers, resistance leaders, and the media to increase their understanding of how, when, and why nonviolent campaigns achieve goals that have eluded armed fighters for decades.

EPILOGUE

Just before this book went to press, a wave of "people power" movements toppled authoritarian regimes in Tunisia and Egypt. After completing this research, we both had confidence that nonviolent resistance was not only possible but also perfectly viable as a strategy for removing authoritarian regimes and achieving self-determination almost anywhere in the world. We even chose two case studies—the Palestinian Territories and Iran—in part to demonstrate how popular nonviolent uprisings had changed the political landscape of two societies in the Middle East, which many people associate with violence. Nevertheless, neither us of could have predicted the fury and speed with which nonviolent resistance has spread through the Middle East during the first months of 2011. On January 15, 2011, President Zine el-Abidine Ben Ali fled Tunisia and surrendered power to a new regime, succumbing to the force of massive civil resistance. Then, on January 24, 2011, hundreds of thousands of Egyptians gathered for nearly three weeks of organized demonstrations against Hosni Mubarak's decades-old dictatorship, ultimately forcing him to step down. Mass protests have since spread to Algeria, Bahrain, Iran, Iraq, Jordan, Libya, Morocco, Oman, the Palestinian Territories, Saudi Arabia, and Yemen. Perhaps by the time the book hits the shelf, several other Middle Eastern dictatorships will have collapsed.

The Egyptian uprising stands out as a particularly stunning example of why civil resistance works. Participants in this campaign were generally well organized, extremely disciplined, and well prepared for a weeks-long nonviolent fight. The campaign featured massive participation from diverse segments of Egyptian society—Muslims and Coptic Christians, tech-savvy youth and elderly, women and men, judges and trade unionists. The campaign did not over-rely on any one form of communication, although YouTube, Facebook, and Twitter helped activists to plan contingencies and coordinate mobilization before the major activities had begun. Once

Mubarak's regime shut down the Internet, activists who had been inspired by successful nonviolent revolutions in other countries, including Serbia, and immediately beforehand by the successful uprising in Tunisia, distributed pamphlets encouraging protestors to refrain from violence and appeal to security forces.

Despite days of violent repression, mobilization increased in Tahrir Square and in other parts of Egypt. Security forces stopped obeying the regime's orders to crack down on the protestors. Laborers coordinated strikes and boycotts in solidarity with the opposition. In a last-gasp effort to maintain power, Mubarak's regime unleashed a wave of armed *agents provocateurs*, attempting to intimidate the opposition into either leaving Tahrir Square or responding with violence, which would have undermined their domestic and international legitimacy and given Mubarak's security forces the pretext to repress them. Instead, the repression backfired. The protestors avoided the use of retaliatory violence. The combination of Mubarak's repression and the opposition's commitment to nonviolent methods, not to mention the active recruitment of diverse segments of society, inspired ever more committed mobilization by prodemocracy protestors. External support for the Egyptian opposition did not appear to play a significant role in the successful revolution, though foreign government pressure on Mubarak to step down intensified as the opposition demonstrated irreversible momentum.

Mubarak ultimately stepped down as the military assumed power in something of a bloodless coup—an outcome that would have been nearly unfathomable without the pressure caused by the civilian-led nonviolent resistance. Moreover, the protestors continue to occupy Tahrir Square to ensure that the military government maintains its commitment to return power to civilian control.

Casting off the legacy of decades of authoritarianism is a difficult task, and Egypt will not be an exception. But because the vast majority of opposition activity in Egypt was nonviolent, the prospects are far better than if the revolution was a violent one. In chapter 8, we use statistics to estimate the probability that different countries will be democratic five years after the end of a campaign. Controlling for other factors, if Egypt follows the pattern of other successful nonviolent campaigns, our estimates indicate that it has more than a 30 percent chance of being a democracy. Although that figure may sound uninspiring, the probability would be much closer to zero percent if the revolution had been violent or if it had not occurred at all. Meanwhile, the nonviolent ouster of ex-President Mubarak showed the Egyptian people that they could raise their voices and exert tremendous influence on the political process using nonviolent means of contestation.

In truth, Egypt has a long history of nonviolent resistance, with one of the most recent episodes being the failed 2005 Kefaya campaign, which is among the cases in our data set. The same is true for other countries in the Middle East and North Africa, as demonstrated in *Civilian Jihad: Nonviolent Struggle, Democratization, and Governance in the Middle East* (Stephan 2010). It is notable that the NAVCO data only documents campaign outcomes through 2006, and so suggests that nonviolent resistance campaigns have been less successful in the Middle East than elsewhere. But recent events may change that finding. If these last several months have taught us anything, it is that nonviolent resistance can be a near-unstoppable force for change in our world, even in the most unlikely circumstances.

APPENDIX

The online appendix introduces and discusses the data compiled for this book and the various robustness checks performed to test the findings reported in the text. It also contains brief narratives of each of the campaigns. It can be found at Erica Chenoweth's Web site. The cases of nonviolent and violent campaigns are listed in tables A.1 and A.2, respectively.

TABLE A.1 **NONVIOLENT CAMPAIGNS**

CAMPAIGN	LOCATION	TARGET	START	END	OUTCOME
	SUDAN	JAAFAR NIMIERY	1985	1985	SUCCESS
INTIFADA	PALESTINE	ISRAELI OCCUPATION	1987	1990	PARTIAL SUCCESS
	ZAMBIA	BRITISH RULE	1961	1963	SUCCESS
CARNATION REVOLUTION	PORTUGAL	MILITARY RULE	1974	1974	SUCCESS
	GREECE	MILITARY RULE	1974	1974	SUCCESS
	SOUTH KOREA	MILITARY JUNTA	1979	1980	FAILURE
PRODEMOCRACY MOVEMENT	PAKISTAN	ZIA AL-HUQ	1983	1983	FAILURE
	MALI	MILITARY RULE	1989	1992	SUCCESS
	SLOVENIA	COMMUNIST REGIME	1989	1990	SUCCESS
THE STIR	NEPAL	MONARCHY/PANCHAYAT REGIME	1989	1990	PARTIAL SUCCESS
STRIKE OF FALLEN ARMS	EL SALVADOR	MARTÍNEZ DICTATORSHIP	1944	1944	SUCCESS
	POLAND	COMMUNIST REGIME	1956	1956	PARTIAL SUCCESS
	ARGENTINA	ATTEMPTED COUP	1986	1986	SUCCESS
	CHILE	IBÁÑEZ REGIME	1931	1931	SUCCESS
	SOUTH KOREA	MILITARY GOVERNMENT	1987	1987	PARTIAL SUCCESS
DEFIANCE CAMPAIGN	SOUTH AFRICA	APARTHEID	1952	1961	FAILURE
	PANAMA	NORIEGA REGIME	1987	1989	FAILURE
SINGING REVOLUTION	ESTONIA	COMMUNIST REGIME	1989	1989	SUCCESS
	DENMARK	NAZI OCCUPATION	1944	1944	PARTIAL SUCCESS

HUNDRED FLOWERS MOVEMENT	CHINA	COMMUNIST REGIME	1956	1957	FAILURE
DIRETAS JÁ	BRAZIL	MILITARY RULE	1984	1985	SUCCESS
	KENYA	DANIEL ARAP MOI	1989	1989	PARTIAL SUCCESS
CONVENTION PEOPLE'S PARTY MOVEMENT	GHANA	BRITISH RULE	1951	1957	SUCCESS
ROSE REVOLUTION	GEORGIA	SHEVARDNADZE REGIME	2003	2003	SUCCESS
PRODEMOCRACY MOVEMENT	THAILAND	SUCHINDA REGIME	1992	1992	PARTIAL SUCCESS
KIFAYA	EGYPT	MUBARAK REGIME	2000	2005	PARTIAL SUCCESS
PEOPLE POWER	PHILIPPINES	FERDINAND MARCOS	1983	1986	SUCCESS
	TAIWAN	AUTOCRATIC REGIME	1979	1985	PARTIAL SUCCESS
	MALAWI	BANDA REGIME	1992	1994	SUCCESS
STUDENT PROTESTS	THAILAND	MILITARY DICTATORSHIP	1973	1973	SUCCESS
	POLAND	COMMUNIST REGIME	1968	1970	PARTIAL SUCCESS
	CROATIA	SEMIPRESIDENTIAL SYSTEM	1999	2000	SUCCESS
RUHRKAMPF RESISTANCE	GERMANY	FRENCH OCCUPATION	1923	1923	SUCCESS
	SENEGAL	DIOUF GOVERNMENT	2000	2000	PARTIAL SUCCESS
PRODEMOCRACY MOVEMENT	TANZANIA	MWINYI REGIME	1992	1995	PARTIAL SUCCESS
	GREECE	KARAMANLIS REGIME	1963	1963	SUCCESS
DEMOCRACY MOVEMENT	CHINA	COMMUNIST REGIME	1976	1979	FAILURE
PRODEMOCRACY MOVEMENT	EAST GERMANY	COMMUNIST REGIME	1989	1989	SUCCESS
	PERU	FUJIMORI GOVERNMENT	2000	2000	SUCCESS
MAY FOURTH MOVEMENT	CHINA	JAPANESE OCCUPATION	1919	1919	PARTIAL SUCCESS
PRODEMOCRACY MOVEMENT	BURMA	MILITARY JUNTA	1988	1988	FAILURE
	ZAMBIA	ONE-PARTY RULE	1990	1991	PARTIAL SUCCESS
	CZECHO-SLOVAKIA	SOVIET OCCUPATION	1968	1968	FAILURE
ANTIAPARTHEID	SOUTH AFRICA	APARTHEID	1984	1994	SUCCESS
TULIP REVOLUTION	KYRGYZSTAN	AKAYEV REGIME	2005	2005	SUCCESS
ACTIVE VOICES	MADAGASCAR	DIDIER RADSIRAKA	1991	1993	SUCCESS
	CHILE	AUGUSTO PINOCHET	1983	1989	SUCCESS
CEDAR REVOLUTION	LEBANON	SYRIAN FORCES	2005	2005	SUCCESS
	BOLIVIA	MILITARY JUNTAS	1977	1982	SUCCESS
	INDONESIA	SUHARTO RULE	1997	1998	SUCCESS
PRODEMOCRACY MOVEMENT	HUNGARY	COMMUNIST REGIME	1989	1989	SUCCESS
	THAILAND	THAKSIN REGIME	2005	2006	SUCCESS
	CHINA	COMMUNIST REGIME	1989	1989	FAILURE

	PAKISTAN	KHAN REGIME	1968	1969	PARTIAL SUCCESS
	HUNGARY	SOVIET OCCUPATION	1956	1956	FAILURE
	ZAMBIA	CHILUBA REGIME	2001	2001	SUCCESS
	ALBANIA	COMMUNIST REGIME	1989	1989	PARTIAL SUCCESS
ANTICOUP	VENEZUELA	ANTI-CHAVEZ COUP	2002	2002	SUCCESS
	VENEZUELA	JIMÉNEZ DICTATORSHIP	1958	1958	SUCCESS
	TIBET	CHINESE OCCUPATION	1987	1989	FAILURE
	GUYANA	BURNHAM/HOYTE AUTOCRATIC REGIME	1990	1992	SUCCESS
PEOPLE AGAINST VIOLENCE	SLOVAKIA	CZECH COMMUNIST GOVERNMENT	1989	1992	SUCCESS
IRANIAN REVOLUTION	IRAN	SHAH REZA PAHLAVI	1977	1979	SUCCESS
	NIGERIA	MILITARY RULE	1993	1999	SUCCESS
PRODEMOCRACY MOVEMENT	ARGENTINA	MILITARY JUNTA	1977	1981	SUCCESS
	NORWAY	NAZI OCCUPATION	1944	1944	PARTIAL SUCCESS
OCTOBER REVOLUTION-ARIES	GUATEMALA	UBICO DICTATORSHIP	1944	1944	SUCCESS
	MONGOLIA	COMMUNIST REGIME	1989	1990	PARTIAL SUCCESS
	YUGOSLAVIA	MILOSEVIC REGIME	2000	2000	SUCCESS
NYASALAND AFRICAN CONGRESS	MALAWI	BRITISH RULE	1958	1959	SUCCESS
SECOND PEOPLE POWER MOVEMENT	PHILIPPINES	ESTRADA REGIME	2001	2001	SUCCESS
	BULGARIA	COMMUNIST REGIME	1989	1989	SUCCESS
VELVET REVOLUTION	CZECHO-SLOVAKIA	COMMUNIST REGIME	1989	1989	SUCCESS
	HAITI	JEAN-CLAUDE DUVALIER	1985	1985	SUCCESS
	MEXICO	CALDERÓN REGIME	2006	2006	FAILURE
	BENIN	COMMUNIST REGIME	1989	1990	PARTIAL SUCCESS
DRUZE RESISTANCE	ISRAEL	ISRAELI OCCUPATION OF GOLAN	1981	1982	PARTIAL SUCCESS
	BANGLADESH	MILITARY RULE	1989	1990	PARTIAL SUCCESS
	BELARUS	COMMUNIST REGIME	1989	1989	PARTIAL SUCCESS
SOLIDARITY	POLAND	COMMUNIST REGIME	1981	1989	SUCCESS
	GHANA	RAWLINGS GOVERNMENT	2000	2000	SUCCESS
	ROMANIA	CEAUŞESCU REGIME	1987	1989	FAILURE
	NEPAL	NEPALESE GOVERNMENT, MARTIAL LAW	2006	2006	PARTIAL SUCCESS
KOSOVO ALBANIAN NATIONALIST MOVEMENT	YUGOSLAVIA	YUGOSLAV GOVERNMENT	1981	1981	FAILURE
KOSOVO ALBANIAN	YUGOSLAVIA	SERBIAN RULE	1989	1999	FAILURE

CAMPAIGN	LOCATION	TARGET	START	END	OUTCOME
PRODEMOCRACY MOVEMENT/SAJUDIS	LITHUANIA	LITHUANIAN REGIME	1989	1991	SUCCESS
PRODEMOCRACY MOVEMENT	MADAGASCAR	RADSIRAKA REGIME	2002	2003	SUCCESS
STUDENT REVOLUTION	SOUTH KOREA	RHEE REGIME	1960	1960	SUCCESS
PRODEMOCRACY MOVEMENT	LATVIA	COMMUNIST REGIME	1989	1989	SUCCESS
ORANGE REVOLUTION	UKRAINE	KUCHMA REGIME	2001	2004	SUCCESS
	MEXICO	CORRUPT GOVERNMENT	1987	2000	SUCCESS
	BELARUS	BELARUS GOVERNMENT	2006	2006	FAILURE
CROATIAN NATIONALISTS	YUGOSLAVIA	YUGOSLAV GOVERNMENT	1970	1971	FAILURE
	WEST PAPUA	INDONESIAN OCCUPATION	1964	2006	FAILURE
KYRGYZSTAN DEMOCRA-TIC MOVEMENT	KYRGYZSTAN	COMMUNIST REGIME	1989	1989	SUCCESS
	URUGUAY	MILITARY RULE	1984	1985	SUCCESS
TIMORESE RESISTANCE	EAST TIMOR	INDONESIAN OCCUPATION	1988	1999	SUCCESS
	EAST GERMANY	COMMUNIST REGIME	1956	1956	FAILURE
OGONI MOVEMENT	NIGERIA	NIGERIAN GOVERNMENT AND CORPORATE EXPLOITATION	1990	1995	FAILURE
	NIGER	MILITARY RULE	1991	1992	FAILURE
INDEPENDENCE MOVEMENT	NIGERIA	BRITISH OCCUPATION	1945	1950	PARTIAL SUCCESS
PRODEMOCRACY MOVEMENT	RUSSIA	ANTICOUP	1990	1991	SUCCESS
	EAST GERMANY	COMMUNIST REGIME	1953	1953	FAILURE
	INDIA	BRITISH RULE	1919	1945	PARTIAL SUCCESS
STUDENT PROTESTS	YUGOSLAVIA	COMMUNIST REGIME	1968	1968	PARTIAL SUCCESS
	EL SALVADOR	MILITARY/CIVILIAN JUNTA	1979	1981	FAILURE

TABLE A.2 **VIOLENT CAMPAIGNS**

CAMPAIGN	LOCATION	TARGET	START	END	OUTCOME
CLAN FACTIONS; SNM	SOMALIA	SIAD BARRE REGIME	1982	1997	SUCCESS
GAM	INDONESIA	INDONESIAN OCCUPATION	1976	2005	SUCCESS
FRETILIN	EAST TIMOR	INDONESIAN OCCUPATION	1974	1977	FAILURE
GREEK COMMUNISTS	GREECE	BRITISH AND U.S. OCCUPATION	1944	1949	FAILURE
RIFIAN REBELLION	MOROCCO	FRANCO-SPANISH OCCUPATION	1921	1926	FAILURE
DARUL ISLAM	INDONESIA	INDONESIAN GOVERNMENT	1953	1953	FAILURE
LTTE	SRI LANKA	SRI LANKAN OCCUPATION	1972	2006	FAILURE
TUNISIAN INDEPENDENCE MOVEMENT	TUNISIA	FRENCH OCCUPATION	1952	1954	SUCCESS
GREEK RESISTANCE	GREECE	NAZI OCCUPATION	1943	1945	FAILURE
KLA	SERBIA	SECESSION	1994	1999	PARTIAL SUCCESS
FSLN	NICARAGUA	NICARAGUAN REGIME	1978	1979	FAILURE
PHILIPPINE-MALAYAN INSURGENCY	PHILIPPINES	JAPANESE OCCUPATION	1941	1945	FAILURE
DRUZE REVOLT	LEBANON	FRENCH OCCUPATION	1925	1927	FAILURE

SOCIALISTS	AUSTRIA	DOLFUSS GOVERNMENT	1934	1934	FAILURE
CRISTEROS REBELLION	MEXICO	MEXICAN REGIME	1926	1930	FAILURE
ASTURIAN MINERS	SPAIN	RIGHT-WING GOVERNMENT	1934	1934	FAILURE
NORTH VIETNAM (NATIONAL LIBERATION FRONT)	VIETNAM	U.S. OCCUPATION	1958	1975	SUCCESS
PATHET LAO	LAOS	LAOTIAN GOVERNMENT	1960	1975	SUCCESS
KHMER ROUGE	CAMBODIA	CAMBODIAN GOVERNMENT	1970	1975	SUCCESS
HEZBOLLAH	LEBANON	ISRAELI OCCUPATION OF SOUTHERN LEBANON	1982	2000	SUCCESS
NAGA REBELLION	INDIA	INDIAN OCCUPATION	1955	1964	FAILURE
MANCHURIAN GUERRILLAS	CHINA	JAPANESE OCCUPATION	1931	1940	SUCCESS
MUSLIM FUNDAMENTALISTS	NIGERIA	NIGERIAN GOVERNMENT	1980	1984	FAILURE
MOLUCCANS	INDONESIA	INDONESIAN GOVERNMENT	1950	1950	FAILURE
CHECHEN SEPARATISTS	RUSSIA	RUSSIAN OCCUPATION	1994	2006	FAILURE
PHILIPPINE NATIONALISTS	PHILIPPINES	U.S. OCCUPATION	1899	1902	FAILURE
UKRAINIAN REBELLION	USSR	COMMUNIST REGIME	1946	1953	FAILURE
ARMED FORCES FOR NATIONAL LIBERATION (FALN)	VENEZUELA	BETANCOURT REGIME	1958	1963	FAILURE
DNIESTR	MOLDOVA	MOLDOVAN REGIME	1992	1992	PARTIAL SUCCESS
RWANDAN INDEPENDENCE	RWANDA	BELGIAN OCCUPATION	1956	1961	SUCCESS
HUKBALAHAP REBELLION	PHILIPPINES	PHILIPPINE GOVERNMENT	1946	1954	FAILURE
PALESTINIAN LIBERATION	PALESTINIAN TERRITORIES	ISRAELI OCCUPATION	1973	2006	FAILURE
INDIAN RESISTANCE	GUATEMALA	GOVERNMENT OF GUATEMALA	1966	1972	FAILURE
ESCOBAN-LED REBELLION	MEXICO	CALLES GOVERNMENT	1929	1929	FAILURE
WESTERN SAHARA FREEDOM MOVEMENT (POLISARIO)	WESTERN SAHARA	MOROCCAN OCCUPATION	1975	1991	PARTIAL SUCCESS
COMMUNIST REBELS	THAILAND	THAI GOVERNMENT	1970	1973	FAILURE
ANYA NYA	SUDAN	SUDANESE GOVERNMENT	1962	1973	PARTIAL SUCCESS
CONSTITUTIONALISTS	IRAN	SHAH REGIME	1908	1909	SUCCESS
ALGERIAN REVOLT/ NATIONAL LIBERATION FRONT	ALGERIA	FRENCH OCCUPATION	1952	1962	SUCCESS
LEFTISTS	LEBANON	LEBANESE GOVERNMENT	1975	1975	FAILURE
VMRO REBELS (MACEDONIANS) IN ILINDEN UPRISING	OTTOMAN EMPIRE	OTTOMAN RULE	1903	1903	FAILURE
CENTRAL ASIAN REBELS	USSR	SOVIET POLICIES OF CONSCRIPTION	1930	1935	FAILURE
ANTI-CEAUȘESCU REBELS	ROMANIA	CEAUȘESCU REGIME	1989	1989	SUCCESS
MORO ISLAMIC LIBERATION FRONT	PHILIPPINES	PHILIPPINE GOVERNMENT	1970	1980	FAILURE
FARABUNDO MARTÍ NATIONAL LIBERATION FRONT (FMLN)	EL SALVADOR	EL SALVADORAN GOVERNMENT	1979	1991	PARTIAL SUCCESS
AFGHAN RESISTANCE	AFGHANISTAN	SOVIET OCCUPATION	1979	1988	SUCCESS
FRANCO-SYRIAN WAR	SYRIA	FRENCH OCCUPATION	1920	1920	FAILURE
BIAFRANS	NIGERIA	NIGERIAN GOVERNMENT	1967	1970	FAILURE
TALIBAN	AFGHANISTAN	AFGHAN GOVERNMENT	2001	2006	FAILURE

RED GUARD	CHINA	ANTI-MAOISTS	1967	1968	FAILURE
ARMENIANS IN NAGORNO-KARABAKH	AZERBAIJAN	AZERI OCCUPATION	1991	1994	PARTIAL SUCCESS
ANTIREFORMIST MOVEMENT	AFGHANISTAN	AMANULLAH KHAN REGIME	1924	1929	FAILURE
COMMUNIST REBELS	FINLAND	FINNISH GOVERNMENT	1918	1918	FAILURE
SINO-TIBETAN WAR	TIBET	CHINESE OCCUPATION	1950	1951	FAILURE
NORTH VIETNAM (NATIONAL LIBERATION FRONT)	VIETNAM	GOVERNMENT OF SOUTH VIETNAM	1958	1975	SUCCESS
AFAR INSURGENCY	DJIBOUTI	DJIBOUTI REGIME	1991	1994	FAILURE
ITALIAN RESISTANCE	ITALY	NAZI OCCUPATION	1943	1945	FAILURE
TIBETAN RESISTANCE	CHINA	CHINESE OCCUPATION	1956	1959	FAILURE
POPULAR DEMOCRATIC ARMY (UTO)	TAJIKISTAN	RAKHMANOV REGIME	1992	1997	PARTIAL SUCCESS
IRAQI REBELS	IRAQ	BRITISH OCCUPATION	1920	1920	PARTIAL SUCCESS
PALESTINIAN ARAB REVOLT	PALESTINE	PRO-JEWISH BRITISH POLICIES	1936	1939	PARTIAL SUCCESS
JEWISH RESISTANCE	PALESTINIAN TERRITORIES	BRITISH OCCUPATION	1945	1948	SUCCESS
ARAB REVOLT	TURKEY	OTTOMAN RULE	1916	1918	PARTIAL SUCCESS
ISLAMIC SALVATION FRONT	ALGERIA	ALGERIAN GOVERNMENT	1992	2006	FAILURE
INDONESIAN REVOLT	INDONESIA	DUTCH OCCUPATION	1945	1949	SUCCESS
INDOCHINA REVOLT	VIETNAM	FRENCH OCCUPATION	1945	1954	SUCCESS
MULTIPLE FACTIONS	CENTRAL AFRICAN REPUBLIC	CAR REGIME	1994	1997	SUCCESS
POPULAR FRONT FOR THE LIBERATION OF OMAN AND THE ARAB GULF (PFLOAG)	OMAN	OMAN GOVERNMENT	1964	1976	PARTIAL SUCCESS
NICARAGUAN GUERRILLAS	NICARAGUA	U.S.-BACKED CONSERVATIVE GOVERNMENT/U.S. INTERVENING TROOPS	1925	1932	SUCCESS
REPUBLICANS	CHINA	IMPERIAL REGIME, MILITARY DICTATORSHIP	1911	1913	FAILURE
NATIONAL PATRIOTIC FORCES	LIBERIA	LIBERIAN GOVERNMENT	1996	1996	FAILURE
IKHWAN REBELLION	SAUDI ARABIA	IBN SAUD REGIME	1929	1930	FAILURE
KOCHKIRI REBELLION KURDISTAN (KTC)	TURKEY	KURDISH SECESSION	1920	1922	FAILURE
THIRD ANGLO-AFGHAN WAR	AFGHANISTAN	BRITISH OCCUPATION	1919	1919	SUCCESS
AGRARIAN LEAGUE MOVEMENT	BULGARIA	MILITARY REGIME	1923	1923	FAILURE
KDP KURDS	IRAQ	IRAQI GOVERNMENT	1996	1996	FAILURE
KDPI	IRAN	IRANIAN REGIME	1979	1996	FAILURE
HUTU REBELLION	BURUNDI	TUTSI HEGEMONY IN GOVERNMENT	1972	2002	FAILURE

IRAQI INSURGENCY	IRAQ	IRAQI GOVERNMENT	2003	2006	FAILURE
CPN-M/UPF	NEPAL	NEPALESE GOVERNMENT	1996	2006	FAILURE
SPLA-GARANG FACTION	SUDAN	SUDANESE GOVERNMENT	1983	2005	PARTIAL SUCCESS
LRA	UGANDA	MUSEVENI GOVERNMENT	1996	2006	FAILURE
SHIFTA INSURGENCY	ERITREA	BRITISH OCCUPATION	1945	1952	FAILURE
CONSERVATIVE MOVEMENT	COLOMBIA	LIBERAL GOVERNMENT	1948	1949	SUCCESS
SENDERISTA INSURGENCY (TÚPAC AMARU REVOLUTIONARY MOVEMENT (MRTA))	PERU	PERUVIAN GOVERNMENT	1996	1997	FAILURE
RENAMO	MOZAMBIQUE	MOZAMBIQUEAN GOVERNMENT	1979	1992	FAILURE
IFNI WAR	MOROCCO	SPANISH OCCUPATION	1957	1958	FAILURE
MOROCCAN INDEPENDENCE WAR	MOROCCO	FRENCH/SPANISH OCCUPATION	1953	1956	SUCCESS
WARS OF INDEPENDENCE	MOROCCO	FRENCH OCCUPATION	1911	1917	FAILURE
MOPLAH REBELLION	INDIA	LOCAL HINDU LEADERS	1921	1922	FAILURE
ITALO-LIBYAN WAR (SANUSI)	LIBYA	ITALIAN OCCUPATION	1920	1932	FAILURE
MUSLIM BROTHERHOOD	SYRIA	SYRIAN REGIME	1980	1982	FAILURE
POLISH RESISTANCE	POLAND	GERMAN OCCUPATION	1944	1944	FAILURE
MUJAHEDIN	IRAN	KHOMEINI REGIME	1981	1982	FAILURE
PF-ZAPU GUERRILLAS	ZIMBABWE	MUGABE REGIME	1983	1987	PARTIAL SUCCESS
FASCISTS	SPAIN	REPUBLICAN GOVERNMENT	1936	1939	SUCCESS
ANTI-DOE REBELS	LIBERIA	DOE REGIME	1989	1990	SUCCESS
SOMALI REBELS (OGADEN)	ETHIOPIA	ETHIOPIAN OCCUPATION OF OGADEN	1976	1983	FAILURE
HYDERABAD ACTIVISTS	INDIA	INDIAN ANNEXATION	1948	1948	FAILURE
SERB MILITIAS	BOSNIA-HERZEGOVINA	BOSNIAN GOVERNMENT	1991	1995	FAILURE
NEW PEOPLE'S ARMY	PHILIPPINES	PHILIPPINE GOVERNMENT	1972	2006	FAILURE
AFGHANS	AFGHANISTAN	AFGHAN GOVERNMENT	1978	1979	SUCCESS
ANTICOLONIALIST MOVEMENT	CAMEROON	FRENCH OCCUPATION	1955	1960	SUCCESS
POPULAR MOVEMENT FOR THE LIBERATION OF ANGOLA	ANGOLA	PORTUGUESE OCCUPATION	1961	1974	SUCCESS
LEFTISTS	BOLIVIA	MILITARY JUNTA	1952	1952	SUCCESS
LIBERALS OF 1949	COLOMBIA	CONSERVATIVE GOVERNMENT	1949	1949	FAILURE
UNITA	ANGOLA	ANGOLAN GOVERNMENT	1975	2001	PARTIAL SUCCESS
CHINESE REBELS	CHINA	JAPANESE OCCUPATION	1937	1945	FAILURE
KABILA-ADFL	ZAIRE/DRC	MOBUTU REGIME	1996	1997	SUCCESS
FORMER REBEL LEADERS	ALGERIA	BEN BELLA REGIME	1962	1963	FAILURE
LEFTISTS	DOMINICAN REPUBLIC	LOYALIST REGIME	1965	1965	FAILURE
BLANCO REBELLION	URUGUAY	ORDÓÑEZ REGIME	1904	1904	FAILURE
MAU MAU REBELLION	KENYA	BRITISH OCCUPATION	1952	1956	FAILURE
ETA	SPAIN	SPANISH OCCUPATION	1968	2006	FAILURE

	KENYA	BRITISH RULE	1938	1938	FAILURE
WATUSI	RWANDA	HUTU REGIME	1963	1964	FAILURE
YUNNAN REBELLION	CHINA	CHINESE OCCUPATION	1917	1918	PARTIAL SUCCESS
BUGANDA TRIBE	UGANDA	UGANDAN GOVERNMENT	1966	1966	FAILURE
DENIS SASSOU NGUEMO	CONGO-BRAZZAVILLE (ROC)	LISSOUBA REGIME	1997	1999	SUCCESS
FRONT FOR THE LIBERATION OF MOZAMBIQUE	MOZAMBIQUE	PORTUGUESE OCCUPATION	1963	1972	SUCCESS
FEZ CAIDS REBELLION	MOROCCO	FRENCH OCCUPATION	1907	1908	FAILURE
DOMINICAN INSURGENCY	DOMINICAN REPUBLIC	U.S. OCCUPATION	1916	1924	FAILURE
MOHAJIR	PAKISTAN	PAKISTANI GOVERNMENT	1994	1995	FAILURE
BOER SEPARATISTS	SOUTH AFRICA	BRITISH OCCUPATION	1899	1902	FAILURE
ROYALISTS	YEMEN ARAB REPUBLIC	AL-SALLAL REGIME	1962	1969	PARTIAL SUCCESS
LEFTISTS	LEBANON	SHAMUN REGIME	1958	1958	FAILURE
FIRST WAR OF INDEPENDENCE	TIBET	CHINESE OCCUPATION	1912	1913	PARTIAL SUCCESS
APRISTA REBELS	PERU	CERRO REGIME	1932	1932	FAILURE
PMIC	IVORY COAST	INCUMBENT REGIME	2002	2005	FAILURE
BOUGAINVILLE REVOLT	PAPUA NEW GUINEA	PAPUAN REGIME	1988	1998	FAILURE
TUTSI REBELS	RWANDA	HUTU REGIME	1990	1993	PARTIAL SUCCESS
BALUCHI REBELS	PAKISTAN	PAKISTANI RULE	1973	1977	FAILURE
IRA	NORTHERN IRELAND	BRITISH OCCUPATION	1968	2006	PARTIAL SUCCESS
KASHMIRI MUSLIM SEPARATISTS	INDIA	INDIAN OCCUPATION	1988	2006	FAILURE
HUERTA-LED REBELS	MEXICO	OBREGÓN REGIME	1923	1924	FAILURE
REBELS	CHAD	CHADIAN REGIME	1994	1998	FAILURE
KURDISH REBELLION	IRAQ	IRAQI GOVERNMENT	1961	1975	FAILURE
ACRE REBELLION	BOLIVIA	SECESSION FROM BOLIVIA	1902	1903	FAILURE
CROATS	YUGOSLAVIA	SERBIAN GOVERNMENT	1991	1992	SUCCESS
PALESTINIAN ACTIVISTS	JORDAN	JORDANIAN RULE	1970	1970	FAILURE
MIZO REVOLT	INDIA	INDIAN OCCUPATION	1966	1986	PARTIAL SUCCESS
KACHIN REBELS	BURMA	BURMESE GOVERNMENT	1983	1995	FAILURE
LEFTISTS	INDONESIA	SUKARNO REGIME	1956	1960	FAILURE
FRANCO-MADAGASCAN CONFLICT	MADAGASCAR	FRENCH OCCUPATION	1947	1948	FAILURE
LA REVOLUCIÓN LIBERTADOR	VENEZUELA	VENEZUELAN GOVERNMENT	1901	1903	FAILURE
YEMENI INSURGENCY	YEMEN	BRITISH AND ADEN ADMINISTRATION	1955	1957	FAILURE
SOMALIA MILITIA INSURGENCIES	SOMALIA	U.S. AND UN RELIEF MISSIONS	1992	1994	SUCCESS
PATRIOTIC FRONT	RWANDA	HUTU REGIME AND GENOCIDE	1994	1994	SUCCESS
NPFL AND ULIMO	LIBERIA	JOHNSON REGIME	1992	1995	PARTIAL SUCCESS

REVOLUTIONARY ARMED FORCES OF COLOMBIA AND NATIONAL LIBERATION ARMY	COLOMBIA	COLOMBIAN GOVERNMENT AND U.S. INFLUENCE	1964	2006	FAILURE
SWAPO	NAMIBIA	SOUTH AFRICAN OCCUPATION	1976	1988	SUCCESS
KATANGA-LED LEFTISTS	ZAIRE/DRC	SECESSION FROM DRC	1960	1965	FAILURE
FLOSY, NLF IN ADEN	YEMEN	BRITISH OCCUPATION	1963	1967	SUCCESS
RUF	SIERRA LEONE	REPUBLICAN GOVERNMENT	1991	1996	PARTIAL SUCCESS
NATIONAL UNION PARTY	COSTA RICA	CALDERÓN REGIME	1948	1948	SUCCESS
SOUTH WEST AFRICAN REVOLT (HERERO REVOLT)	NAMIBIA/SOUTH WEST AFRICA	GERMAN OCCUPATION	1904	1905	FAILURE
BALKAN RESISTANCE	SERBIA	GERMAN OCCUPATION	1940	1945	PARTIAL SUCCESS
NFDLM SECESSIONISTS	KENYA	SECESSION	1964	1969	FAILURE
SECRET ARMY ORGANIZATION	FRANCE	FRENCH WITHDRAWAL FROM ALGERIA	1958	1962	FAILURE
SHEIKH SAID INSURGENCY	TURKEY	KEMAL REGIME	1924	1927	FAILURE
SHIITE REBELLION	IRAQ	HUSSEIN REGIME	1991	1991	FAILURE
CONTRAS	NICARAGUA	SANDINISTA REGIME	1980	1990	FAILURE
TUTSI SUPREMACISTS	BURUNDI	HUTU REGIME	1991	1992	FAILURE
KURDISH REBELLION	TURKEY	TURKISH GOVERNMENT	1991	1997	FAILURE
SENDERISTA INSURGENCY (SENDERO LUMINOSO)	PERU	PERUVIAN GOVERNMENT	1980	1995	FAILURE
JVP	SRI LANKA	SRI LANKAN GOVERNMENT	1971	1971	FAILURE
GAMSAKURDIA AND ABKAZ	GEORGIA	GEORGIAN OCCUPATION	1991	1994	FAILURE
TUPAMAROS	URUGUAY	URUGUAYAN GOVERNMENT	1963	1972	FAILURE
PAOLISTAS	BRAZIL	BRAZILIAN REGIME	1932	1932	FAILURE
ZULU REBELLION (NATAL REBELLION)	NATAL	BRITISH OCCUPATION	1906	1906	FAILURE
TALIBAN	AFGHANISTAN	AFGHAN REGIME	1992	1996	SUCCESS
FRENCH RESISTANCE	FRANCE	GERMAN OCCUPATION	1940	1945	PARTIAL SUCCESS
CHINESE COMMUNIST MOVEMENT	CHINA	KUOMINTANG REGIME	1922	1949	SUCCESS
JEM/SLA	SUDAN	JANJAWEED MILITIA	2003	2006	FAILURE
CONSERVATIVE MOVEMENT	HONDURAS	CARÍAS REGIME	1924	1924	FAILURE
LEFTIST REBELLION	PARAGUAY	MORÍNIGO REGIME	1947	1947	FAILURE
YAHYA FAMILY REVOLT	YEMEN ARAB REPUBLIC	COUNTERCOUP	1948	1948	SUCCESS
BENGALIS	PAKISTAN	PAKISTANI RULE	1971	1971	SUCCESS
ETHNIKI ORGANOSIS KYPRIOS AGONISTON	CYPRUS	BRITISH OCCUPATION	1954	1959	SUCCESS
PINOCHET-LED REBELS	CHILE	ALLENDE REGIME	1973	1973	SUCCESS
ZIMBABWE AFRICAN PEOPLE'S UNION	ZIMBABWE	SMITH/MUZORENA REGIME	1974	1980	SUCCESS
TIGREAN LIBERATION FRONT	ETHIOPIA	ETHIOPIAN GOVERNMENT	1978	1991	SUCCESS
CONSERVATIVE MOVEMENT	GUATEMALA	ARBENZ LEFTIST REGIME	1954	1954	SUCCESS
MARXIST REBELS (URNG)	GUATEMALA	GOVERNMENT OF GUATEMALA	1961	1996	PARTIAL SUCCESS
NAXALITE REBELLION	INDIA	INDIAN REGIME	1967	1971	FAILURE
ERITREAN-LED REBELS	ETHIOPIA	ETHIOPIAN GOVERNMENT	1974	1991	SUCCESS

SIKH INSURGENCY	INDIA	SEPARATISM	1984	1994	FAILURE
TAIWANESE REVOLT	CHINA	CHINESE OCCUPATION	1947	1947	FAILURE
KURDISH REBELLION	IRAQ	SECESSION	1985	1993	FAILURE
SHAMMAR TRIBE AND PRO-WESTERN OFFICERS	IRAQ	QASSIM REGIME	1959	1959	FAILURE
SAYA SAN'S REBELLION	BURMA	BRITISH OCCUPATION	1930	1932	FAILURE
ERP/MONTENEROS	ARGENTINA	ARGENTINIAN REGIME	1973	1977	FAILURE
ANTI-BOLSHEVIKS	RUSSIA	BOLSHEVIK REGIME	1917	1921	FAILURE
KIRGHIZ AND KAZABLES REBELS	RUSSIA	ROMANOV REGIME	1916	1917	SUCCESS
DERVISH RESISTANCE	SOMALIA	BRITISH AND ETHIOPIAN OCCUPATION	1899	1905	FAILURE
LEFTIST REBELLION	EL SALVADOR	AUTHORITARIAN MARTÍNEZ REGIME	1932	1932	FAILURE
PAIGC	GUINEA-BISSAU	PORTUGUESE OCCUPATION	1963	1974	SUCCESS
LIBERALS AND RADICALS REBELLION	MEXICO	DÍAZ REGIME	1910	1920	SUCCESS
MAJI MAJI REVOLT	TANZANIA/ GERMAN EAST AFRICA	GERMAN COLONIZERS	1905	1906	FAILURE
LURD	LIBERIA	TAYLOR REGIME	2003	2003	SUCCESS
PEASANT/WORKER REBELLION	RUSSIA	ROMANOV DYNASTY	1905	1906	PARTIAL SUCCESS
FROLINAT	CHAD	CHADIAN GOVERNMENT	1966	1990	SUCCESS
MALAYAN EMERGENCY	MALAYSIA	BRITISH OCCUPATION	1948	1960	PARTIAL SUCCESS
FLNC	ZAIRE/DRC	DRC/ZAIREAN REGIME	1977	1978	FAILURE
KARENS	BURMA	BURMESE GOVERNMENT	1948	2006	FAILURE
NATIONAL RESISTANCE ARMY	UGANDA	OKELLO REGIME	1980	1988	SUCCESS
KHMER ROUGE	CAMBODIA	CAMBODIAN GOVERNMENT	1978	1997	FAILURE
CUBAN REVOLUTION	CUBA	BATISTA REGIME	1956	1959	SUCCESS
LEFTISTS	YEMEN PEOPLE'S REPUBLIC	ALI NASIR REGIME	1986	1986	PARTIAL SUCCESS
ANTICOMMUNIST MOVEMENT(WHITES)	HUNGARY	COMMUNIST REGIME	1919	1920	SUCCESS
SHANTI BAHINI	BANGLADESH	AUTONOMY FROM BANGLADESH REGIME	1976	1997	FAILURE
PEASANTS IN TA (TAMBOV REBELLION)	USSR	SOVIET REGIME	1920	1921	FAILURE
CACO REVOLT	HAITI	U.S. OCCUPATION	1918	1920	FAILURE
PEASANT REBELLION	ROMANIA	LAND-DISTRIBUTION SYSTEM	1907	1907	FAILURE
BELARUS RESISTANCE	USSR	NAZI OCCUPATION	1941	1945	FAILURE
REBELS (PEOPLE'S REVOLUTIONARY PARTY)	ZAIRE/DRC	MOBUTU REGIME	1993	1993	FAILURE

NOTES

1. THE SUCCESS OF NONVIOLENT RESISTANCE CAMPAIGNS

1. East Timor is a former Portuguese colony.
2. Indonesian forces killed most of the Falintil commanders, eliminated approximately 80 percent of their bases, and assumed control over approximately 90 percent of the East Timorese population. Most of the East Timorese died from starvation following forced displacement (Taur Matan Ruak, interview by Maria J. Stephan, Dili, East Timor, January 11, 2005).
3. "Clinton Demands Indonesia Accept International Force," Agence France Press, September 9, 1999; "US Cuts Military Ties with Indonesia," Reuters, September 9, 1999; Sanders Thoenes, "What Made Jakarta Accept Peacekeepers," *Christian Science Monitor*, September 14, 1999.
4. Fr. Jovito, interview by Maria J. Stephan, Dili, East Timor, on December 29, 2004.
5. When we use the term *violent resistance*, we are referring to nonstate armed opposition campaigns. This includes campaigns associated with insurgencies (Lyall and Wilson 2009), guerrilla warfare, nonstate combatants in civil wars (Gleditsch 2004), and terrorist campaigns (Pape 2005). Nonviolent resistance refers to nonstate unarmed opposition campaigns. We use the terms *nonviolent resistance* and *civil resistance* interchangeably. See also Carter, Clarke, and Randle (2006) and their supplement, available online at http://www.civilresistance.info (accessed December 19, 2009). For more information, see the online appendix at http://echenoweth.faculty.wesleyan.edu/wcrw/.
6. See the online appendix for a discussion of the NAVCO data set and coding rules.
7. The loss or gain of regime capabilities may be causally related to the campaign. Resistance campaigns may be partly responsible for degrading regime capabilities, or regimes may increase their capabilities to respond to a campaign. In chapter 3, however, we find such endogenous processes to be relatively unimportant. Even when aggregate government capabilities fluctuate in a country, such fluctuations are not systematically related to the outcomes of the campaigns.
8. To clarify the distinction between "normal" political action and nonviolent action, Schock uses this example: The display of antiregime posters in democracies would be considered a low-risk and regular form of political action, whereas the same activity in nondemocracies would be considered irregular and involve significant risk. Because of this difference in context and intention, the latter would be considered a form of nonviolent action, whereas the former would not. Similarly, strikes that occur in democratic societies within the normal bounds of institutionalized labor relations, writes Schock, cannot be considered nonviolent action, since they are not noninstitutional or indeterminate. On the other hand, most strikes in nondemocracies would be considered nonviolent action because of their indeterminate, noninstitutionalized, high-risk features (Schock 2003, 705).

9. In vol. 2, Sharp lists 198 methods of nonviolent action and cites at least one historical example of each method's application.
10. In acts of omission participants refuse to perform acts that they usually perform, are expected by custom to perform, or are required by law or regulation to perform; in acts of commission participants perform acts that they usually do not perform, are not expected by custom to perform, or are forbidden by law or regulation to perform; this method of resistance may involve a combination of acts of omission and commission (Sharp 2005, 41, 547).
11. For general literature on insurgency and counterinsurgency, see Beckett (2007), Joes (2007), Fishel and Manwaring (2006), Greskovits (1998), Chaliand (1982), Laqueur (1976).
12. The online appendix defines and discusses different types of unconventional asymmetrical warfare types, including guerrilla warfare, insurgency, insurrections, coups, revolutions, and terrorism. For a succinct review, see Galula (2006, 1–10).
13. Baldwin (2000) critiques the success/failure dichotomy, arguing that policy makers must use more nuanced gradations and evaluations of effectiveness. Although we agree that the subject is complex, such methods prohibit comparison across a large number of cases, which is our primary aim here. Thus, we simply use a high bar to evaluate whether a campaign has succeeded or failed, requiring the campaigns to have achieved their goals and to have had a distinguishable effect on the outcome. When we include counts of "limited success," the results are even more sympathetic toward nonviolent campaigns. See the online appendix for details.
14. Other scholars often use campaigns as their units of analysis, such as Pape (2005) and Horowitz and Reiter (2001). McAdam, Tarrow, and Tilly argue that social scientists should consider examining movement behavior as "episodes" rather than as individual events (2001).
15. There are some difficulties with this method. First, it is difficult to gather the strength of the movement and its activities over time (i.e., escalation or deescalation). Second, without specific events data, it is theoretically difficult to compare all campaigns as equal when we know that some are much more disruptive than others. However, there are good reasons to analyze campaigns rather than events. First, events data are so difficult to gather—especially nonviolent events data—that making generalizations about nonviolent conflict is virtually impossible. By analyzing campaigns rather than individual events, we are able to make some general observations about campaigns that can be explored further through in-depth case studies. Moreover, resistance campaigns involve much more than just events; they involve planning, recruiting, training, intelligence, and other operations besides their most obvious disruptive activities. Using events as the main unit of analysis ignores these other operations, whereas analyzing campaigns allows us to consider the broader spectrum of activities as a whole.
16. Moreover, his characterization of the main forms of resistance used in the United States may not be correct.
17. Sharp's minimalist definition of violence is that which inflicts or threatens to inflict bodily harm on another human being (Sharp 2003, 38).
18. See also Simon (1992, 77).
19. The Program on Nonviolent Sanctions and Cultural Survival at Harvard combined the quantitative study of nonviolent direct action with anthropological insights from 1972 to 2005 under the headship of David Maybury-Lewis. Doug Bond has continued the collection of events data on nonviolent action in both the Protocol for the Assessment of Nonviolent Direct Action project and the Integrated Data

for Events Analysis project. Neither of these data sets, however, has been used to systematically test the effectiveness of nonviolent vs. violent resistance, at least in publicly available material.
20. Robert Pape (2005), Max Abrahms (2006), and Mia Bloom (2005) have led the debate with regard to terrorism, and Pape (1996, 1997) and Horowitz and Reiter (2001) have debated the effectiveness of aerial bombing, economic sanctions, and other tactics of persuasion or coercion. Others, such as Liddell Hart (1954), Andre Beufre (1965), Colin Gray (1999), Gil Merom (2003), Jason Lyall and Isaiah Wilson (2009), and Ivan Arreguín-Toft (2001, 2005), have made contributions to our understanding of why certain strategies succeed and others fail in unconventional warfare.
21. See also Arjomand (1998) and Skocpol (1979).
22. See especially chapter 5, "Denmark, the Netherlands, the Rosenstraße: Resisting the Nazis."
23. Our statistics remain similar, however, when we exclude ongoing campaigns from our analysis.
24. See Chenoweth and Lawrence (2010) for an argument on why comparing the relative effectiveness of nonviolent and violent strategies is necessary to determine success.

2. THE PRIMACY OF PARTICIPATION IN NONVIOLENT RESISTANCE

1. Our theory is based on truly voluntaristic bottom-up civic mobilization; we do not include paid crowds that come out to support different politicians for compensation ("rent-a-crowds," as some call them).
2. We relied on countless encyclopedic and open sources to generate these figures. Please see the online appendix for details.
3. We were unable to find reliable participation figures for about 20 percent of the observations. We conducted a series of tests to determine whether there were systematic conditions that caused the data to be unavailable, and we found no significant evidence of that. We also used multiple imputation techniques to reestimate our analyses using imputed membership figures. We found no significant difference in any of the results reported throughout this book. See the online appendix for more information.
4. Fanon, influenced by a Marxist paradigm that equates violence with power, probably did not consider that nonviolent resistance could engender similarly intense feelings of individual and collective empowerment and meaning.
5. Martyrdom, of course, does not necessarily entail killing another person while struggling and dying for a cause. Here, cultural interpretations are critical.
6. About 40 percent of the campaigns in the data set boast over twenty-five thousand participants.
7. In nearly all models, we control for population size for several reasons. First, multiple authors have found that countries with large populations are more difficult for leaders to control (Fearon and Laitin 2003; Herbst 2000; Smith 2007, 26). Second, one of our primary explanatory variables—the number of campaign participants—is not as meaningful without taking into account the total population size of the country. One hundred thousand participants in a country of 1 million people is much more meaningful than one hundred thousand participants in a country of 30 million people.
8. Sharp (1973) identifies over 198 nonviolent tactics (including strikes, boycotts, sit-ins, and occupations), and scholars have since expanded the list to include many more because of advances in communications technology (Martin 2001).

9. At the same time, satellite television and the Internet have made it easier for armed resistance groups to communicate their goals, attract recruits, and exaggerate their membership. This is also true for nonviolent resistance campaigns.
10. See Boserup and Mack (1974) on the advantages and disadvantages of underground and aboveground activity.
11. When the regime responds to the insurgency with indiscriminate violence, Matthew Kocher and Stathis Kalyvas (2007) argue that incentives to join or support the insurgency increase. However, they do not compare how those incentives might be different with nonviolent campaigns vs. violent ones.
12. Thanks to Hardy Merriman for this insight.
13. Other times, however, simple acts of nonviolent defiance can result in imprisonment, unemployment, and the threatening or disappearance of loved ones. However, as we argue, such repressive regime actions are likelier to backfire when used against nonviolent campaigns than when applied against violent campaigns.
14. Marginal effects identify the percentage change per single unit increase in the independent variable. By a "single unit" increase, we mean a single standard deviation for continuous variables, and a change from 0 to 1 for the dummy variables.
15. A potential concern is that of reverse causation: that large membership is what permits nonviolent campaigns to remain nonviolent, whereas violent campaigns adopt violence precisely because they cannot attract large numbers of participants. If this argument is correct, we should expect to see two things. First, we should expect to see large numbers of people spontaneously hitting the streets, followed by a decision on the part of the campaign leadership to commit to nonviolent resistance. Second, we should expect to see large campaigns abandon violence when it is clear that the membership is sufficient to win the day using nonviolent resistance. In general, we are dubious of this argument. We conducted a test to determine whether the relationship between the choice of violent resistance was endogenous to membership and found no statistical support for this claim (see the online appendix). Second, in several of the cases we examine in part 2, it is clear that the nonviolent campaigns experienced a gradual increase in membership over time. Moreover, some violent campaigns that achieved large memberships, such as the Chinese Revolution or the Russian Revolution, did not abandon nonviolent resistance once they obtained a critical mass. Instead, they used their membership to wage wars to the death against the incumbent regimes. In reality, it is difficult to disentangle these relationships and virtually impossible to do so using statistical analysis with the data in its current form. In the case studies, though, it is possible to see that the campaigns' commitment to nonviolent resistance is one factor that encouraged large-scale mobilization, whereas the use of violent methods discouraged participation.
16. Arreguín-Toft (2005) argues that during strategic interactions between stronger and weaker conflict parties, the use of opposite tactics (indirect-direct) against a stronger adversary can translate into victory for the weaker power. Others have argued that continual and escalating disruption is the key variable determining success (Wood 2000).
17. For figures of attacks perpetrated by the communist insurgency in Nepal, see START/CETIS (2008).
18. For applications of the positive radical flank effect, see Barkan (1979); Gamson (1990); Haines (1984); Jenkins and Eckert (1986); Marger (1984); and McAdam (1999).
19. For different viewpoints on this topic, see Button (1989); Colby (1985); Gamson (1990); Haines (1988); Jenkins and Eckert (1986); McAdam (1999); Mueller (1978); Piven and Cloward (1979); Schumaker (1975); Schock (2005, 47–49); and Sharp

(1973). While the concept of radical flank effects is interesting and important, we do not take on simultaneity of violent and nonviolent resistance campaigns, since we are dealing primarily with ideal types. Empirical studies could help shed light on the different effects of radical flanks.
20. Robert Helvey defines "pillars of support" as "the institutions and sections of society that supply the existing regime with the needed sources of power to maintain and expand its power capacity" (2004, 160).
21. International actions can complement these domestic actions, such as when the international divestment campaign targeting the apartheid regime created significant economic pressure, which was an important factor in the regime's ultimate decision to negotiate with the ANC. In another example of complementary internal and external actions, the withholding of loans and economic assistance by international financial institutions to the Suharto regime in Indonesia (against the backdrop of the 1998 Asian financial crisis) combined with a mass popular uprising in that country led to Suharto's ouster. The withdrawal of external financial support to the Marcos regime in the Philippines similarly coincided with an economic crisis in the early 1980s combined with a broadening anti-Marcos movement inside the country that enjoined the support of moderate reformers, church leaders, and businesspeople, a move toward the center by the opposition that would have been unlikely had the resistance been confined to communist and Muslim guerrillas.
22. For example, the junta in El Salvador was able to survive a wave of strikes from 1979 to 1981 because of the junta's strong support from the United States. Thanks to Stephen Zunes for this point.
23. For an elaboration on the notion of extending the nonviolent battlefield to address the challenge of inverse dependency relationships in the context of civil resistance campaigns, see Stephan (2006); Stephan and Mundy (2006); Stephan (2005); Galtung (1989, 19); and Schock (2005).
24. Data are gleaned from multiple sources listed in the online appendix.
25. In an additional model reported in the online appendix, we generated an interaction term, which combines the membership and nonviolent resistance variables, to estimate the probability that a combination of high membership in a nonviolent resistance has on the probability of inducing loyalty shifts. A joint significance test reveals that the model including all three independent variables is jointly significant (Prob > chi^2 = 0.07), and multiple bivariate regressions reveal a positive relationship between nonviolent resistance and security-force defections.
26. Brian Martin emphasizes the important role played by media coverage of contentious interaction involving unarmed protestors and security forces. Furthermore, regimes have developed their own strategies to inhibit the effects of backfiring (2007). Martin's concept of backfiring is a more nuanced approach to what Gene Sharp first described as "political jiu-jitsu" (Sharp 1973).
27. A combination of sustained confrontation with the adversary, the maintenance of nonviolent discipline, and the existence of a sympathetic audience may be necessary conditions for triggering jujitsu. See Martin (2007) and Martin and Varney (2003).
28. This is not to suggest that it is necessarily strategically wise for nonviolent campaigns to purposefully evoke repression from their adversaries. On the contrary, many nonviolent campaigns have succeeded without relying on the backfire backfiring process.
29. There is an entire body of literature about sanctions, including work by David Cortright, Daniel Drezner, and others. For an example of an applied work on sanctions, see Cortright (2001).

30. On the role of international sanctions in the South African antiapartheid struggle, see Ackerman and DuVall (2000); Schock (2005); Zunes, Kurtz, and Asher (1999). On the role of democratic embassies in the antiapartheid struggle, see the Community of Democracies' *A Diplomat's Handbook*, available at http://www.diplomatshandbook.org.
31. The relative importance of the armed and nonviolent resistances in the antiapartheid struggle is controversial. Some have argued that the violent and nonviolent resistances were complementary (Lodge 2009). Others have argued that these forms of resistance were not complementary, and that the ANC-led armed struggle played a far less important role than the mass nonviolent resistance in ending apartheid (Barrel 1993; Lodge 2009).
32. We created a dichotomous variable, which is coded 1 if there were economic sanctions launched against a country in response to its treatment of a resistance campaign and 0 if otherwise. See the online appendix for details. A joint significance test reveals that the interaction term and its two components are jointly significant (Prob > chi^2 = 0.02).
33. On NGO support and global civil society, see Bob (2005) and Schock (2005), respectively. On the role of transnational advocacy networks in supporting local nonviolent movements, see Keck and Sikkink (1998).
34. Clifford Bob writes a more careful exegesis on the conditions under which rebel groups are able to secure foreign sponsorship (2005), which is not necessarily our aim here.
35. State sponsorship of insurgencies and terrorist groups has been an ongoing foreign policy dilemma for decades (Byman 2005).
36. Schock argues that the more broad based participation is, the more likely that tactical innovations will occur (2005, 144).
37. Thanks to Kurt Schock for this point. For more information on the importance of sanctuary for insurgencies, see Salehyan (2007, 2008, 2009).
38. We need to give a caveat for Model 2(b), because it contains fewer than one hundred observations. Long (1997) suggests that researchers avoid sample sizes of less than a hundred when using maximum likelihood estimation, since the results tend to be unstable. We reestimated the model without the membership variable, which contains missing data. The results were the same when N = 106, although the significance of violent regime repression increases.
39. Mao Zedong's writings on revolutionary warfare emphasize the importance of building oppositional consciousness, winning broad-based support, and achieving mass mobilization. The creation of parallel structures and institutions—a form of nonviolent intervention—is another critical component of successful revolutionary warfare. See Chaliand (1982); Laqueur (1977); Sun-Tzu (1963).
40. In some cases, like the Philippines and Thailand, major disputes continue to be resolved in the streets via people power movements rather than through normal political channels.
41. Thanks to Hardy Merriman for this insight.

3. EXPLORING ALTERNATIVE EXPLANATIONS FOR THE SUCCESS OF CIVIL RESISTANCE

1. Of course, domestic and international factors are not completely isolated from one another. Local forces influence and are influenced by international pressures. We oversimplify these dynamics in the NAVCO data set and in our discussion here for theoretical and empirical purposes. However, much research remains to be done on the interaction between domestic and international support of resistance campaigns.

2. We consider these three factors independently of one another. The reason is that testing them all together causes a reduction in the sample size (because of missing data in many observations) such that accurate inferences are unlikely.
3. The CINC score is the most common indicator of power in international relations scholarship. But because this index measure does not take into account factors such as oil production, trade, and alliances as contributors to national strength, these figures should be taken as suggestive.
4. Please see the online appendix for more information about these variables and statistics. We also considered the possibility that changes in the opponent's regime type or capabilities over the course of the campaign may affect the probability of success. Skeptics may argue that nonviolent campaigns gather steam as the state enters a period of decline, that the success of nonviolent campaigns is more a function of external changes in the opponent government and that nonviolent campaigns emerge as a *response* to these changes. Thus, we consider the effects of nonviolent resistance, this time controlling for *changes* in the polity score, GDP, and capabilities of the target country. The skeptic's expectation would be that significant decreases in these areas would make a campaign more likely to succeed. Our tests reveal that none of these factors significantly affected the odds of success, but the use of a nonviolent strategy improved the odds of success by 25 percent, even when accounting for changes in the opponent's regime type, a change in economic conditions, or a change in the target's military capabilities. Because of the small number of observations, the results are unstable, so we do not report them here.
5. We present these three maximalist goals as if they were either static or uniformly pursued by all factions in a resistance campaign. In practice, the classification of these campaigns was not clear-cut and required us to make judgment calls, where we attempted to characterize each campaign according to these broad categories. For an excellent analysis challenging the unitary-actor model, see Pearlman (2010).
6. Partial success indicates that the campaign achieved significant concessions short of our strict criterion of 100 percent success of stated objectives.
7. Eleven campaigns (seven violent, four nonviolent) do not fall into any of these three categories and are listed as "Other" campaigns. Among these campaigns, all seven violent campaigns failed, one nonviolent campaign failed, and three nonviolent campaigns succeeded. Thus, these campaigns also reflect the trends reported in table 3.2 (p = .007).
8. Estimating the model using random effects shows no difference in the results (see the online appendix). Because this finding contradicts previous research on contagion effects or "waves" of democratization, further research on the subject is necessary (Huntington 1991; Kurzman 1998; Midlarsky, Crenshaw, and Yoshida 1980; Way 2008).
9. In the two-stage model, the first stage generates an instrumental variable that estimates the predicted probability that a campaign is violent. The second stage substitutes the instrument for the main independent variable to determine whether the instrument continues to predict the campaign outcome. The automatic model uses the ivprob estimator in Stata, which applies Amemiya's generalized least squares estimator with endogenous regressors using Newey's equations (1987); see Gartzke and Jo (2009, 220n16).
10. Because secession may be correlated with failure, we construct instruments with and without this indicator. The results are not substantially different. The model with secession is a better instrument because it is more highly correlated with violent resistance than the model without secession.

11. We also construct several additional variations on the construction of the instruments and the covariates included in the exogenous model, and the results remain roughly the same.
12. Even after using an instrumental approach, endogeneity problems are very difficult to overcome. All social science questions face problems of endogeneity and selection bias, which are nearly impossible to resolve. Structural conditions and strategic choices are iterative. Key events, such as economic crises and regime-sponsored massacres undoubtedly influence the trajectories of opposition movements, though not always in obvious ways. What we find, though, is that contrary to much social science research, few aggregate conditions (i.e., regime type, repression, and so on) inhibit a movement's growth or success. Instead, political opportunities occur below these aggregate levels, where campaigns respond with what they view as the best methods to advance their ultimate goals. Interestingly, though, it seems that given similar sets of opportunities, some campaigns choose to rely on violent methods whereas others rely on nonviolent methods, so even at the more granular levels of analysis, conditions do not predetermine the choice to use violent or nonviolent methods. This chapter finds that endogeneity is not a statistical concern, but scholars should apply formal models, agent-based models, and experimental designs to further inquire about which external forces determine the choice to use nonviolent resistance.

4. THE IRANIAN REVOLUTION, 1977-1979

1. Portions of this chapter also appear in Sazegara and Stephan (2010).
2. Additional sources consulted for this chapter include Afshar (1985); Albert (1990); Amuzegar (1991); Daneshvar (1996); Farhi (1990); Ganji (2002); Keddie (2003); Milani (1994); Naraghi (1994); Parsons (1984); Pollack (2004); Ramazani (1990); Salehi (1988); Wright (2000).
3. One of these groups, the Coalition of Islamic Associations (Hey'atha-ye Mo'talefeh-ye Islami) was created in 1963 as a merger between three smaller groups with close links to the bazaar and Ayatollah Khomeini–led ulema. After 1963, the group focused on using political violence as a means to confront the Shah. Its high point was the January 1965 assassination of Prime Minister Hasan Ali Mansour by Muhammad Bukhara'i. The clandestine group was discovered after the plot, and some of its key members were executed. The group acknowledged that its activities had come to a halt by 1971, and a number of its members joined the Mujahedin. Another group, the Revolutionary Organization of the Tudeh Party of Iran (ROTPI), was established in February 1964 as a Maoist offshoot of the Tudeh (Communist) Party that was largely decimated by the Shah in the late 1950s. ROTPI militants participated in a rebellion in south-central Iran that was small and easily crushed in 1965; that same year a member attempted to assassinate the Shah and was killed in the process; members sought to join a rebellion in Iranian Kurdistan in 1967, but the rebellion was crushed and its leaders killed before ROTPI guerrillas arrived. "As with the Tudeh and the Islamic Coalition, all attempts by the ROTPI to establish a network inside the country were frustrated by the end of the 1960s" (Behrooz 2004).
4. Some of its prominent members were Mohammad Hanifnejad, Mohsen Sadegh, Mohammad Bazargani, Sa'id Mohsen, Ali Asghar Badizadegan, and Massoud Rajavi.
5. Some of the main personalities of the organization were Mohammad Taghi Shahram, Bahram Aram, Hossein Rouhani, and Torab Haghshenas.
6. Similar backfiring has occurred in many other cases. See Martin (2007).

7. The organization claimed credit for a small number of attacks—one in the summer 1977, two in early 1978, and five in the summer of 1978, according to the group's pronouncements (Kurzman 2004, 146).
8. The leftists joined the masses in a march to the air force base, where they joined thousands in resisting the Imperial Guards' attempts to retake the base (Abrahamian 1989, 171–72; Behrooz 2000, 68; Hegland 1987, 206; Kurzman 2004, 147).
9. Kurzman nevertheless notes, "The rhythm of the revolution was set by clerical revolutionaries rather than students. Students joined in clerical-led protests but not vice-versa . . . The clerics largely commandeered the universities in late 1978 just as they had commandeered the mosque network earlier in the year" (2004, 148–49).
10. Secular Iranian women eventually became threatened when some refused to wear the *hejab*; they were harassed and rumors circulated that women who did not wear the *hejab* would have acid thrown at them (Kurzman 2004).

5. THE FIRST PALESTINIAN INTIFADA, 1987-1992

1. Additional sources consulted for this chapter include Cordesman and Moravitz (2005); Farsoun and Zacharia (1997); Fernea and Hocking (1992); Gelvin (2005); Gordon, Gordon, and Shriteh (2003); Hudson (1990); Jamal (2005); King (2007); Lockman and Beinin (1989); Lukacs (1992); Pearlman (2008); Peretz (1990); Rothstein, Maoz, and Shikaki (2002); and Tessler (1995).
2. For a discussion of the Israeli occupying authorities' dual policy of dependency and integration vis-à-vis the West Bank and Gaza, see Ayyash (1981) and Ryan (1974).
3. An English translation can be found in Leila S. Kadi, *Basic Political Documents of the Armed Palestinian Resistance Movement*, Palestine Research Centre (1969).
4. Some refer to the UNLU as the United National Command; see King (2007).
5. One UNLU leader from Nablus, Radi Jraey, was simultaneously the editor of the *Al-Fajr* newspaper in Jerusalem, a student at Bir Zeit University, and the district coordinator of the northern district. "I was constantly moving around to prevent the Israeli intelligence from arresting me," he said. Organizationally, the West Bank was divided into three districts. The northern district consisted of Jenin, Tulkarem, Nablus, and Qalqilya. The central district consisted of Ramallah, Jericho, and Jerusalem. The southern district consisted of Bethlehem and Hebron. During the intifada, the West Bank district coordinators coordinated their efforts with the leaders from the Gaza districts (Radi Jraey, interview by Maria Stephan, Ramallah, September 5, 2004).
6. Ahmad Hanoun, ex–political prisoner from Balata Camp, Nablus, interview by Maria Stephan, Ramallah, September 4, 2004.
7. Arafat and Abu Jihad issued orders through a coordinating committee based in Amman, Jordan, and the PLO's European offices, which sent faxes to East Jerusalem newspapers and trade unions.
8. Schiff and Ya'ari write that Arafat and the PLO originally considered the Arab population of Israel to be a small and insignificant minority living in enemy territory and incapable of advancing the Palestinian cause. After 1973, however, links were established between the PLO and the Arab-Israeli community through non-Zionist political parties like the Rakah Israeli Communist Party and the Progressive List for Peace as well as through the traditional Arab parties in the Knesset. The PLO funneled money to Israeli-Arab institutions and organizations in order to expand its base of support inside Israel (1989, 173).
9. "Crippled Ship of Return a Focus of Hopes and Fears," *Athens News*, February 18, 1988.

10. "PLO's Ship of Return Hits a Raw Nerve in Israel," *International Herald Tribune*, February 12, 1988.
11. "Mine Rips Vessel Hired for PLO Trip," *Philadelphia Inquirer*, February 16, 1988.
12. After the ship was blown up and three PLO leaders were assassinated by Israeli intelligence, Yasser Arafat made a declaration from Kuwait saying that he might reconsider his Cairo Declaration, that terrorist activities would be carried out only against targets in Israel and the occupied territories (O'Ballance 1998, 37)
13. For a detailed discussion of the Islamist movement inside the Palestinian Territories, see Robinson (1997, 132–77). See also Mishal and Mishal (2000); Litvak (2003); and Ahmad (1994).
14. Article 11 of Hamas's Mithaq reads, "The Islamic Resistance Movement believes that the land of Palestine is an Islamic waqf land consecrated for future Muslim generations until Judgement Day. It, or any part of it, should neither be squandered nor relinquished. No Arab country, no king or president, no organization—Palestinian or Arab—possesses that right" (Robinson 1997, 151).
15. M. Sela, *Jerusalem Post*, May 26, 1989, 9.
16. Mark Bowden, "Live Burial of Arabs Is Horror to Israelis," *Philadelphia Inquirer*, February 2, 1988.
17. On the extent of the Israeli government's attempt to prevent media coverage of the intifada, see Rigby (1991, chap. 6, "The Role of the Media").
18. In June 1988, four members of a group of Israeli leftists who met with the PLO in Romania were convicted of violating the Prevention of Terror Law, sentenced to six months in prison, and forced to pay $2,500 each. In 1990 the Israeli peace activist Abie Nathan was sentenced to a six-month prison term for meeting with members of the PLO. Right-wing Knesset members also began meeting with PLO officials. See Nunn (1993).
19. These more radical groups criticized the mainstream peace movement, led by Peace Now, for its "refusal to transgress boundaries deemed permissible by the occupation regime." For example, Peace Now refused to engage in any form of civil disobedience or to actively confront the Israeli government over specific policies. The more mainstream peace groups criticized the military refuser movement and refused to support it in any way. Peace Now officials refused to meet with PLO representatives until other Israeli peace groups made it a mainstream practice (Kaminer 1989).
20. The number of reservists who refused to serve in the occupied territories rose from 160 (in January 1988) to more than 600 by the seventh month of the intifada. In signing their declaration, the refusers referred to the "absence of a political solution" and not simply the degree of violence as the reason for their refusal. By March 1988, some 2,000 reserve officers were urging Prime Minister Shamir to "favor the way of peace." A petition was sent by 1,250 army officers and commanders to Shamir calling for "territories in exchange for peace." At that time, the Israeli organization Peace Now found that "90% of the senior officers in the Israeli army are in favor of territorial compromise and the return of the territories in exchange for peace." The Council for Peace and Security was established in May 1988 by former Israeli generals to convince the public of the need to negotiate directly with the PLO and withdraw from the occupied territories to improve Israeli security (Cited in the *Jerusalem Post International Edition*, June 11, 1988; in Dajani [1994, 80–82]).
21. Israeli organizations, including Parents Against Moral Erosion, established by parents of Israel Defense Force soldiers, focused on pressuring the Israeli government to start negotiations and end the occupation.

22. E. Farjoun, quoted in Ertugul (1987, 15–16).
23. Mubarak Awad, interview by Maria Stephan, Washington D.C., March 24, 2004.
24. "The indigenous Palestinian leadership (i.e. the new generation of leaders who had led the *Intifada*) would be given the task of governing, while the 'outsiders' would continue to represent and guide, with the country's delegation to the inevitable negotiations with Israel being composed of people from both categories. Beyond that, the document spoke explicitly of making peace with Israel" (Schiff and Ya'ari 1989, 279).
25. A 1975 pact between the United States and Israel stipulated that the United States would not recognize or negotiate with the PLO unless it recognized Israel's right to exist, accepted UN Resolutions 242 and 338, and renounced terrorism.
26. For further description and analysis of U.S. diplomacy during the intifada, see Pollock (1991).
27. Shamir later acknowledged that his intentions were to stall the creation of a Palestinian state for up to ten years. He conceded that his peace plan had been intended to remove the PLO from the picture.
28. Dole pointed out that Israel was the only country to receive U.S. aid without having to pay interest. In a *New York Times* article he said that Israel had received $40 billion in U.S. aid in the last ten to twelve years, adding that "Black Africans get $1 per person, while Israel got $10,000 per head" (Dole cited in O'Ballance [1998, 75–76]).
29. Gruen writes, "Even those American Jews who favored additional settlements in principle were critical of the prime minister [Shamir] for his public confrontational stance. They were also concerned that Shamir's words would not only endanger prospects of Israel's request for the $400 million in housing loan guarantees but would also strengthen the hands of Chief of Staff John Sununu and other administration officials who wanted to subject all American aid to Israel to the same close scrutiny and line-by-line supervision given to other aid recipients to make sure that Israel could not, in the words of a *Washington Post* editorial, 'Pay West Bank bills from another account'" (1991, 257).
30. They issued this statement: "We, the people of Beit Sahour, being an integral part of the Palestinian people and its intifada, refuse to pay taxes to the occupiers of our land, considering such payment to be a symbol of slavery and oppression. We consider the occupation of one people by another to be a clear violation of all international laws and religions, and it is in violation of the most basic human rights and democratic principles. We strongly believe that every citizen has to pay taxes to his national government in order to enable it to perform its duties and obligations. No taxation without representation."
31. The leader of the PLF, Abu Abbas, was on the PLO Executive Committee.
32. Ghassan Andoni, interview by Maria Stephan, Beit Sahour, West Bank, August 23, 2004.
33. Ibid.
34. Meanwhile, inside the occupied territories, members of the PFLP, DFLP, Hamas, and Islamic Jihad all opposed the conference and called for an escalation of the intifada in protest. The PFLP suspended its membership in the PLO. At the same time, inside Jericho leaflets were being circulated that announced that the popular committees would become local forums for the new peace process. Nationalist leaders from Gaza won local elections for the local chamber of commerce (the only elections allowed in the occupied territories) and openly supported the Madrid talks (O'Ballance 1998, 111–12).
35. After his election defeat, Shamir revealed his policy intentions vis-à-vis settlements in an interview with the *Maariv*: "I would have carried on the autonomy

talks for ten years, and meanwhile we would have reached half-a-million souls in Judea and Samaria ... I don't believe there was a majority in favor of a Greater Israel, but it could be attained over time." Shamir went on to say that after half a million settlers had established residence in the occupied territories, it would make "land for peace" an impossibility (O'Ballance 1998, 127).

36. The Oslo Accords included the 1994 Gaza-Jericho Agreement (Oslo I), the 1995 Interim Agreement on the West Bank and Gaza Strip (Oslo II, or the Taba agreement), the January 1997 Hebron Protocol, the October 1998 Wye River Memorandum, and the 1999 Sharm el-Sheikh Memorandum.

37. The accords established direct PA control over most of Gaza and Jericho, direct control over an additional 7 percent of the West Bank (designated area A), and shared control with Israel over another 24 percent (area B). Israel retained absolute control over approximately 69 percent of the West Bank (area C), with three future undefined withdrawals from area C anticipated (Robinson 1997, 175).

38. According to Israeli Maj. Gen. (ret.) Shlomo Brom, "The U.S. government has always been rhetorically opposed to the settlements. But this has never translated into concrete actions. Settlements were the main problem then and are the main problem now" (Maj. Gen. Shlomo Brom, interview by Maria Stephan, Jaffee Center for Strategic Studies, Tel Aviv University, August 18, 2004).

39. Haitham Arar, interview by Maria Stephan, Ramallah, West Bank, September 5, 2004.

40. Comparative analyses of the two Palestinian uprisings can be found in Andoni (2001) and Beitler (2004).

41. Ghassan Andoni, interview by Maria Stephan, Beit Sahour, West Bank, August 30, 2004.

42. The results were strongly conditioned by age, with older respondents opposing armed action at higher rates. Moreover, support for armed action was much higher in the Gaza Strip than in the West Bank, and much higher among Palestinians who opposed the peace process with Israel.

43. Randi Jo Land, "A Separate Peace?" *Jerusalem Post*, June 29, 1989.

44. Miriam Jordan, "Palestinian Children Pay Big Psychological Price in Uprising," Reuters News, July 20, 1990.

45. Maj. Gen. Shlomo Brom, interview by Maria Stephan, Jaffee Center for Strategic Studies, Tel Aviv University, August 18, 2004.

46. Radwan Abu Ayyash, interview by Maria Stephan, Ramallah, West Bank, September 5, 2004.

47. "The worst mistake we can make is to burden the uprising with tasks it cannot handle, for if it fails to fulfill them, it will be deemed a failure ... The best aid to the intifada is to clarify that it cannot achieve strategic objectives, such as ending the occupation ... We must strive to escalate the uprising as long as that is possible; but the command must be prepared to retreat, when conditions demand it, so as to advance again later on" (Palestinian leader cited in Schiff and Ya'ari 1989, 259).

48. Ghassan Andoni, interview by Maria Stephan, Beit Sahour, West Bank, August 30, 2004.

49. For a detailed analysis of the role of collaborators in the First Intifada, see Rigby (1997).

50. Radwan Abu Ayyash, interview by Maria Stephan, Ramallah, West Bank, September 5, 2004.

51. Adam Keller, interview by Maria Stephan, Hoblon, near Tel Aviv, June 8, 2003.

52. Mubarak Awad, remarks made during the National Conference on Nonviolent Sanctions in Conflict and Defense, Washington, D.C., February 1990.

53. Dr. Azmi Bishara, interview by Maria Stephan, East Jerusalem, September 4, 2004.

54. Mark Lance, interview by Maria Stephan, Washington, D.C., June 7, 2004.
55. Lance described the major weakness with the global solidarity movement: "There were major problems of coordination. There was little coordination between activists on the outside and Palestinians in the occupied territories. Prominent Palestinians like Edward Said and J. Ahmad met with Arafat starting in the '60s to convince him to support a global nonviolent strategy. But Arafat didn't support it. It was a control thing. Arafat wanted to be regarded as the head of a militant movement. This was very different from the African National Congress (ANC), which sent representatives to visit university campuses in the U.S. The PLO did none of this—it never reached out to the grassroots in the U.S. Furthermore, the United Leadership of the Uprising (UNLU) was not a visible face in the international community. Because it was forced to organize clandestinely nobody knew anything about it. UNLU was seen as a voice of the PLO" (ibid.).
56. Ghassan Andoni, interview by Maria Stephan, Beit Sahour, West Bank, August 23, 2004.

6. THE PHILIPPINE PEOPLE POWER MOVEMENT, 1983-1986

1. Additional sources consulted for this chapter include Boudreau (2004); Davis (1989); Johnson (1987); Komisar (1987); Mendoza (2009); Reid and Guerrero (1995); and Thompson (1995).
2. See also Staff Report Prepared for the U.S. Senate Committee on Foreign Relations, *Korea and the Philippines: November 1972*, Committee Print, 93rd Cong., 1st sess., February 18, 1973, p. 32;
3. The CPP was founded December 26, 1968 (Mao's birthday) by Jose Maria Sison and others who had grown disillusioned with its communist precursor, the PKP, which had been operating inside the country since 1930.
4. This Mabuhay Philippines Movement, scholars note, was not the Social Democrats' first attempt at building an armed movement. In the mid-1970s, the Philippine Social Democratic Party began training a small army in Sabah, Malaysia, with the help of the Moro National Liberation Front, with which it had established ties starting at the beginning of martial law. After the army failed to grow, it turned to arson and bombing to force Marcos to grant electoral concessions (Boudreau [2001]; Psinakis [1981]; and Thompson [1995]).
5. Thompson (1995) argues that the A6LM attack on the travel agent meeting compelled Marcos to accelerate the lifting of martial law, a move he was already considering. However, Mendoza (2009) notes that these small armed groups were crippled by arrests and failures, received no concessions from Marcos, and were blacklisted as terrorists by the U.S. government.
6. UNIDO was led by Eva Estrada Kalaw, Salvador Laurel, Gerardo Roxas, and, from the United States, Benigno Aquino and Raul Manglapus (Schock 2005, 70).
7. COMELEC announced that the Marcos-Tolentino ticket had won over 53 percent of the vote, while NAMFREL claimed that the Aquino-Laurel ticket had won 52 percent (Schock 2005, 77; Timberman 1991, 145–48).
8. Citing McCoy (1999), Boudreau writes that the Philippine field officers who would have been most useful against the demonstrators were the least likely to support General Ver and were the most likely to be members or supporters of RAM (2004, 183).
9. Boudreau notes that there was a great deal of sociological similarity between state defectors and movement leaders: they were graduates of the same universities, members of the same fraternities, and linked to the same families. This may have helped facilitate the loyalty shifts that occurred over the course of the anti-Marcos uprising (2004, 188).

10. See, for instance, Goodwin (2001, 298). The degree to which these radical flanks are effective remains the source of considerable debate. See, for example, McAdam (1996b); McAdam, Tarrow, and Tilly (2001); Schock (2003, 709–10); and Schock and Chenoweth (2010).

7. WHY NONVIOLENT CAMPAIGNS FAIL: THE BURMESE UPRISING, 1988-1990

1. This case study does not include the August–October 2007 Saffron Revolution. For information on this campaign, see Gamage (2008). The political repercussions of the so-called Saffron Revolution are undetermined. See International Federation for Human Rights, "Burma's 'Saffron Revolution' Is Not Over: Time for the International Community to Act," http://www.fidh.org/IMG/pdf/BURMA-DEC2007.pdf.
2. Burma's ethnic groupings had achieved different stages of political development before the eighteenth century. Some were independent kingdoms, while others were independent principalities. During the eighteenth century, the Burman feudal kings grew stronger than the other ethnic leaders and colonized the Mon and Arakan kingdoms, along with the Shan principalities. The Chin, Kachin, and Karenni peoples remained independent of Burman rule. When the British colonized the territory in 1885, all the ethnic groups fell under British control and the regions were united by the British into a single country by the name of Burma. Burma was incorporated in the British empire and became a province of India. The ethnic minorities are mainly concentrated in the seven states and divisions named after the Shan, Kayah, Karen, Mon, Chin, Kachin, and Rakhine ethnic groups.
3. The KNU has peaked at a membership of between four thousand and six thousand since its inception. But thousands of Karenni civilians have died and hundreds of thousands have been internally displaced since the Karen uprising began in 1949. KNU leaders have occasionally met with government officials to discuss a cease-fire, but negotiations have stalled over the government's demand that the insurgents lay down their weapons ("Burma Insurgency," Global Security report, http://www.globalsecurity.org/military/world/war/burma.htm)
4. These groups include the Shan State Army, which merged with the Shan State National Army in 2005, with about 10,000 members; the KNU, approximately 5,000 members; Karen National Liberation Army, 2,000 to 4,000 members; Kachin Independence Organization, approximately 8,000 members; Karenni National Progressive Party, 800 to 2,000 members; All Burma Students' Democratic Front, approximately 2,000 members; Democratic Karen Buddhist Army, 100 to 500 members; Mong Thai Army, approximately 3,000 members; Mon National Liberation Army, approximately 1,000 members; Myanmar National Democratic Alliance Army, approximately 1,000 members. Other smaller armed resistance groups include the Palung State Liberation Army, Arakan Liberation Party, Lahu Democratic Front, Wa National Army, Hongsawatoi Restoration Party, Mergui-Tavoy United Front, Lahu National Organization, National Socialist Council of Nagaland, Chin National Front, Arakan Rohingya National Organization, National Unity Party of Arakan. See Ploughshares' "Armed Conflicts Report," available at http://www.ploughshares.ca/libraries/ACRText/ACR-Burma.html (accessed October 3, 2009).
5. Boudreau cites an informant, who claimed that as the BCP murdered student recruits who were accused of counterrevolutionary activity, many students, while seeking to evade capture, joined one of the ethnic insurgencies. The BCP, for its part, continued to focus its recruitment efforts among the minority populations living in frontier areas (2004, 92).

6. As part of Ne Win's demonetization policy, only 45 and 90 kyat notes were kept in circulation. The reason: these amounts were divisible by nine, which Ne Win considered a lucky number. By canceling the other currency notes held by Burmese citizens, most people lost their savings overnight.
7. In an interview Boudreau conducted with a Burmese informant, it was revealed that by late August, in the middle of opposition demonstrations, members of the military intelligence had approached him and asked what the opposition wanted and proposed the formation of a coalition government. The students rejected their proposal outright (Boudreau 2004, 210).
8. New armed ethnic groups were formed during this time, including the Chin National Army (CNA), which was formed in November 1988 along the western border with India. Since its inception the five hundred members of the CNA have not controlled much territory; its main targets have been military and its main tactics have been ambushlike attacks against the Burma Army. Some Chin have criticized the CNA for inviting, through its armed actions, more government forces to Chin land (http://www.globalsecurity.org/military/world/war/burma.htm).
9. "Burma Insurgency," Global Security report, http://www.globalsecurity.org/military/world/war/burma.htm (accessed September 28, 2008). Armed groups that did not sign cease-fire agreements with the regime include the KNU and the Shin National Army.
10. Ibid.
11. Burma provides the bulk of the world's opium supply, more than 80 percent of the opium cultivated in Southeast Asia. Most of the illicit opium refinement and trade occur in the ethnic minority areas, notably in the Shan state. SLORC negotiated cease-fire deals with many of the ethnic drug-trafficking groups in these areas, offering them autonomy in exchange for putting down their weapons. Many insurgent leaders have exploited their relationship with SLORC to expand their business activities. The Wa insurgents have relied on Chinese-supplied weaponry (machine guns and mortars) to expand their military capabilities and areas of operation (ibid.).

8. AFTER THE CAMPAIGN: THE CONSEQUENCES OF VIOLENT AND NONVIOLENT RESISTANCE

1. Here we use *civil conflict*, *civil war*, and *violent insurgency* interchangeably.
2. Again, we deal with ideal types, so we treat nonviolent and violent campaigns as separate phenomena.
3. Scholars of nonviolent conflict have highlighted nonviolent discipline as a key variable in explaining the success of nonviolent campaigns. The presence of violent competitors, or the breakdown of nonviolent discipline when faced with opponent violence or agents provocateurs, can undermine the strategic advantages of this form of resistance because regimes often conflate the nonviolent resistance and acts of violence to justify repression. Such conflation makes the resistance less attractive to potential participants, makes it more likely that the regime will unify against the resistance rather than divide internally about how to respond to it, and reduces the legitimacy of the campaign in the eyes of the international community. See Ackerman and DuVall (2000); Ackerman and Kruegler (1994).
4. We are most interested in democracy as an outcome rather than in *democratic transitions*, *democratic consolidation*, or *democratization* writ large. These are distinct concepts in the democratization literature. The idea of "democratic consolidation" means that countries that are already democracies are trying to remain democracies. Democratic consolidation is a longer-term process involving many more

variables. For instance, Larry Diamond characterizes democratic consolidation as involving "a broad, deep national commitment to democracy as the best form of government" (2008, 295). According to Diamond's data, the vast majority of the eighty or so post-1974 democracies remain unconsolidated (see also Schleder [1998]). It could be that democratic consolidation is impacted as much by regional dynamics and demonstration effects as by the initial drivers of the transition. We do not attempt to answer this question in depth but instead seek to simply explain the likelihood of a democracy after the resistance campaign has ended.

5. In the political science literature, most scholars rely on the Polity IV data set, which we do here. In terms of Polity IV, a country is defined as a democracy if it scores above a 6 on the polity scale.

6. For a review, see Diamond (2008); Geddes (1999); McFaul and Stoner-Weiss (2004); and McFaul, Stoner-Weiss, and Bunce (2009).

7. For literature that challenges aspects of modernization theory, see Diamond (2008).

8. In the civil war literature, there is a vigorous debate concerning the definition of civil peace. Until now, most civil war databases have defined peace as the absence of civil war. James Fearon defines civil war as "violent conflict within a country fought by organized groups that aim to take power at the center or in a region, or to change government policies" (Fearon [2007]). The Correlates of War data set, used for this analysis, imposes a criterion of one thousand annual battle deaths for inclusion in the intrastate conflict data set. See Sarkees and Schafer (2000). For a critique of the dichotomous treatment of civil war, see Chenoweth and Lawrence 2010).

9. The conventional threshold in political science is one thousand battle deaths. See n. 8.

10. On the other hand, some scholars have hypothesized that war may be "good" for societies. For example, civil conflicts may generate stronger states in the long run in terms of centralized power and a monopoly on the use of force. Stronger states have higher capacities for reducing violent crime and maintaining order in society. See Licklider (2003). Strong states, however, are not necessarily democratic ones, as we know from the literature. See Huntington (1968). The long-term outcome of state building following violent conflict, therefore, may be stable but authoritarian regimes.

11. An additional perspective is that even after insurgencies "end," wars have negative effects on health and well-being, such that structural violence occurs even "after the shooting stops." See Ghobarah et al. (2003).

12. Stephen Zunes, pers. comm., August 28, 2009.

13. See, for instance, Associated Press, "McCain: U.S. Back from 'Abyss of Defeat' in Iraq," April 7, 2008.

14. The "Not Free" distinction is based on Freedom House ratings, which are available online at http://www.freedomhouse.org.

15. This statistic applies only until five years after the insurgency has ended.

16. Larry Diamond elaborates on this point, arguing that nonviolent regime change must be accompanied (or preceded) by the creation of institutional checks and balances, including explicit minority rights protection, so that there will be restraints on the posttransition government's ability to wield power (2008).

17. We measure these three variables separately for theoretical and methodological reasons. We introduced two indicators for regime type. The first indicator is a continuous variable that measures the Polity IV score five years after the end of the campaign. The second indicator is a dichotomous indicator measuring whether the country is classified as a democracy five years after the end of the campaign. The data are from the Polity IV data set, a widely used database of political insti-

stitutions that measures the regime type of each country in the world from 1800 to 2006. Polity IV ranks political regimes on a scale of -10 (totalitarian regime/absolute monarchy) to 10 (fully democratic) based on the country's commitment to civil liberties, constraints on executive power, and political competition.
18. Thanks to Maciej Bartkowski for this point.
19. Tables with tests of relevant control variables are available in the online appendix. In these tables, we control for other factors, such as urban growth, youth bulges, the presence of other competing insurgencies, GDP growth, and the country's Polity IV score at the end of the conflict.
20. The results in Model 2 do not significantly change when we restrict the sample to countries that are authoritarian at the end of the campaign. Nonviolent campaigns are over 35 percent likely to experience democracy after the campaign ends, compared with less than 4 percent for violent campaigns in authoritarian regimes.
21. This is true holding other variables at their means.
22. The data are from Kristian Gleditsch's (2004) modified list of intrastate wars, as well as from our own data set of violent insurgencies.
23. Our model predicts that Iran had only a 17 percent chance of being a democracy after the nonviolent campaign succeeded holding other factors constant; but this is better than the 1 percent chance it would have had if the campaign had been violent.

9. CONCLUSION
1. An important next step is to systematically observe and evaluate specific tactics and strategic decisions during the conflict.

REFERENCES

Abrahamian, Ervand. 1978. Iran: The political challenge. *MERIP Reports* 69 (July/August): 3–8.
——. 1989. *The Iranian Mojahedin.* New Haven: Yale University Press.
Abrahms, Max. 2006. Why terrorism does not work. *International Security* 31, no. 2 (fall): 42–78.
——. 2008. What terrorists really want: Terrorist motives and counterterrorist strategy. *International Security* 32, no. 4 (spring): 78–105.
Ackerman, Peter, and Jack DuVall. 2000. *A force more powerful.* London: St. Martin's Press/Palgrave Macmillan.
Ackerman, Peter, and Adrian Karatnycky, eds. 2005. *How freedom is won: From civic resistance to durable democracy.* Washington, D.C.: Freedom House.
Ackerman, Peter, and Christopher Kruegler. 1994. *Strategic nonviolent conflict: The dynamics of people power in the twentieth century.* Westport, Conn.: Praeger.
Afshar, Haleh, ed. 1985. *Iran: A revolution in turmoil.* Albany: SUNY Press.
Ahmad, Hisham. 1994. *Hamas.* Jerusalem: PASSIA.
Albert, David H., ed. 1980. *Tell the American people: Perspectives on the Iranian revolution.* Philadelphia: Movement for a New Society.
Almond, Gabriel A., and Sidney Verba. 1963. *The civic culture: Political attitudes and democracy in five nations.* Princeton: Princeton University Press.
Amuzegar, Jahangir. 1991. *The dynamics of the Iranian revolution: The Pahlavi's triumph and tragedy.* Albany: SUNY Press.
Anderson, Benedict. 1988. Cacique democracy in the Philippines. *New Left Review* 169 (May/June): 3–31.
Andoni, Gassan. 2001. A comparative study of intifada 1987 and intifada 2000. In *The new intifada: Resisting Israel's apartheid,* ed. Roane Carey, 209–18. New York: Verso.
Arjomand, Said Amir. 1988. *The turban for the crown.* Oxford: Oxford University Press.
Armed Conflict Events Database. 2007. Wars of the world: National military history index. http://www.onwar.com/aced/nation/index.htm.
Arreguín-Toft, Ivan. 2001. How the weak win wars: A theory of asymmetric conflict. *International Security* 26, no. 1 (summer): 93–128.
——. 2005. *How the weak win wars: A theory of asymmetric conflict.* New York: Cambridge University Press.
——. 2007. How a superpower can end up losing to the little guys. Commentary, Nieman Watchdog. http://www.niemanwatchdog.org/index.cfm?fuseaction=background.view&backgroundid=00163.
Ashraf, Ahmad, and Ali Banuazizi. 1985. The state, classes and modes of mobilization in the Iranian revolution. *State, Culture, and Society* 1 (spring): 3–40.
Ashworth, Scott, Joshua D. Clinton, Adam Meirowitz, and Kristopher W. Ramsay. 2008. Design, inference, and the strategy logic of suicide terrorism. *American Political Science Review* 102, no. 2 (May): 269–73.
Ayyash, Abdul-Ilah Abu. 1981. Israeli planning policy in the occupied territories. *Journal of Palestine Studies* 11, no. 1, 10th anniversary issue, Palestinians under Occupation (autumn): 111–23.
Bakhash, Shaul. 1984. *The reign of the ayatollahs.* New York: Basic Books.
Baldwin, David A. 2000. Success and failure in foreign policy. *Annual Review of Political Sci-*

ence 3:167–82.
Banks, Arthur, William Overstreet, and Thomas Muller. 2004. *Political handbook of the world, 2000–2002.* Washington, D.C.: CQ Press.
Barghouti, Husain Jameel. 1990. Jeep versus bare feet: The villages in the intifada. In *Intifada: Palestine at the crossroads*, ed. Jamal R. Nassar and Roger Heacock, 107–42. New York: Praeger.
Barkan, Steven E. 1979. Strategies, tactics and organizational dilemmas of the protest movements against nuclear power. *Social Problems* 27, no. 1 (October): 19–37.
Barrel, Howard. 1993. Conscripts to their age: African National Congress operational strategy, 1976–1986. Ph.D. diss., St. Anthony's College, Oxford University.
Barro, Robert J. 1999. Determinants of democracy. *Journal of Political Economy* 106, no. 6 (December): 158–83.
Bartkus, Viva Ona. 1999. *The dynamics of secession.* Cambridge: Cambridge University Press.
BBC News. 2007. Burma's 1988 protests. *BBC News: Asia-Pacific*, September 9.
Beckett, Ian, ed. 2007. *Modern counter-insurgency.* London: Ashgate.
Beer, Michael. 1999. Violent and nonviolent struggle in Burma: Is a unified strategy workable? In Zunes, Kurtz, and Asher, *Nonviolent social movements*, 174–85.
Behrooz, Maziar. 2000. *Rebels with a cause: The failure of the left in Iran.* New York: Taurus.
———. 2004. Iranian revolution and the legacy of the guerrilla movement. In *Reformers and revolutionaries in modern Iran: New perspectives on the Iranian left*, ed. Stephanie Cronin, 189–206. London: Routledge Curzon.
———. N.d. Iran's guerrillas: The legacy of Iran's guerrilla movement. *The Iranian.*
Beissinger, Mark. 2002. *Nationalist mobilization and the collapse of the Soviet state.* Cambridge,: Cambridge University Press.
Beitler, Ruth. 2004. *The path to mass rebellion: An analysis of two intifadas.* New York: Lexington Books.
Bennis, Phyllis. 1990. *From stones to statehood: The Palestinian uprising.* New York: Zed.
Benvenisti, Meron. 1987. *1987 report: Demographic, economic, legal, social, and political developments in the West Bank.* Jerusalem: West Bank Data Base Project, Jerusalem Post.
Bermeo, Nancy. 1990. Rethinking regime change. *Comparative Politics* 22, no. 3 (April): 359–77.
———. 2003. What the democratization literature says—or doesn't say—about postwar democratization. *Global Governance* 2, no. 9 (April–June): 159–77.
Bernhard, Michael. 1993. *The origins of democratization in Poland.* New York: Columbia University Press.
Bernhard, Michael, and Akrem Karakoc. 2007. Civil society and the legacies of dictatorship. *World Politics* 59, no 4 (July): 539–67.
Beufre, Andre. 1965. *Introduction to strategy.* New York: Praeger.
Binnendijk, Anika Locke, and Ivan Marovic. 2006. Power and persuasion: Nonviolent strategies to influence state security forces in Serbia (2000) and Ukraine (2004). *Communist and Post-Communist Studies* 39, no. 3 (September): 411–29.
Bleiker, Roland. 1993. *Nonviolent struggle and the revolution in East Germany.* Boston: Albert Einstein Institute.
Bloom, Mia. 2005. *Dying to kill: The allure of suicide terror.* New York: Columbia University Press.
Bob, Clifford. 2005. *The marketing of rebellion: Insurgents, media and international activism.* New York: Cambridge University Press.
Bob, Clifford, and Sharon Erickson Nepstad. 2007. Kill a leader, murder a movement? Leadership and assassination in social movements. *American Behavioral Scientist* 50, no. 10 (June): 1370–94.
Boserup, Anders, and Andrew Mack. 1974. *War without weapons.* London: Pinter.
Boudreau, Vincent. 2001. *Grassroots and cadre in the protest movement.* Quezon City: Ateneo de

Manila University Press.

———. 2004. *Resisting dictatorship: Repression and protest in Southeast Asia.* New York: Cambridge University Press.

Bouraine, Alex. 2001. *A country unmasked: Inside South Africa's Truth and Reconciliation Commission.* New York: Oxford University Press.

Brady, Henry E., and David Collier, eds. 2004. *Rethinking social inquiry: Diverse tools, shared standards.* Berkeley: University of California Press.

Bratton, Michael, and Nicolas van de Walle. 1994. Neopatrimonial regimes and political transitions in Africa. *World Politics* 46, no 4 (July): 453–89.

Breckenridge, Keith. 1998. The allure of violence: Men, race and masculinity on the South African goldmines, 1900–1950. *Journal of Southern African Studies* 24, no. 4 (December): 669–93.

Brooks, Risa. 2003. Making military might: Why do states fail and succeed; A review essay. *International Security* 28, no. 2 (fall): 149–91.

Brooks, Risa, and Elizabeth Stanley, eds. 2007. *Creating military power: The sources of military effectiveness.* Stanford, Calif.: Stanford University Press.

Brownlee, Jason. 2007. *Authoritarianism in an age of democratization.* New York: Cambridge University Press.

Burkhart, Russ E., and Michael Lewis-Beck. 1994. Comparative democracy: The economic development thesis. *American Political Science Review* 88, no. 4 (December): 111–31.

Burma Watcher. 1989. Burma in 1989: There came a whirlwind. *Asian Survey* 29, no. 2 (February): 174–80.

Burns, Gene. 1996. Ideology, culture, and ambiguity: The revolutionary process in Iran. *Theory and Society* 25, no. 3 (June): 349–88.

Burrowes, R. J. 1996. *The strategy of nonviolent defense: A Gandhian approach.* Albany: SUNY Press.

Button, James. 1989. *Blacks and social change.* Princeton: Princeton University Press.

Byman, Daniel. 2005. *Deadly connections: States that sponsor terrorism.* New York: Cambridge University Press.

Byman, Daniel, Peter Chalk, Bruce Hoffman, William Rosenau, and David Brannon. 2001. *Trends in outside support for insurgent movements.* Washington, D.C.: RAND.

Byman, Daniel, and Matthew Waxman. 1999. *Air power as a coercive instrument.* Washington, D.C.: RAND.

———. 2000. Kosovo and the great air power debate. *International Security* 24, no. 4 (spring): 5–38.

———. 2002. *The dynamics of coercion: American foreign policy and the limits of military might.* New York: Cambridge University Press.

Callahan, William A. 1998. *Imagining democracy: Reading "the events of May" in Thailand.* Singapore: Institute of Southeast Asian Studies.

Carothers, Thomas. 1999. *Aiding democracy abroad: The learning curve.* Washington, D.C.: Carnegie Endowment for International Peace.

Carothers, Thomas, and Marina Ottoway, eds. 2005. *Uncharted journey: Promoting democracy in the Middle East.* Washington, D.C.: Carnegie Endowment for International Peace.

Carter, April, Howard Clark, and Michael Randle. 2006. *People power and protest since 1945: A bibliography of nonviolent action.* London: Housmans.

Central Intelligence Agency. 2007. *The world factbook.* https://www.cia.gov/library/publications/the-world-factbook/.

Chaliand, Gerard, ed. 1982. *Guerrilla strategies: An historical anthology from the long march to Afghanistan.* Berkeley: University of California Press.

Chenoweth, Erica. 2006. The inadvertent effects of democracy on terrorist group emergence. Belfer Center for Science and International Affairs Discussion Paper 2006–06, John F. Kennedy School of Government, Harvard University.

Chenoweth, Erica, and Adria Lawrence, eds. 2010. *Rethinking violence: States and non-state actors in conflict.* Cambridge, Mass.: MIT Press.
Clark, Howard. 2000. *Civil resistance in Kosovo.* London: Pluto.
Clodfelter, Michael. 2002. *Warfare and armed conflicts: A statistical reference to casualty and other figures, 1500–2000.* New York: McFarland.
Coggins, Bridget. 2004. The withholding and granting of recognition to secessionist states. Paper presented at the annual meeting of the Midwest Political Science Association, Chicago.
Colby, David. 1985. Black power, white resistance, and public policy. *Journal of Politics* 47, no. 2 (June): 579–95.
Collier, Paul. 1999. On the economic consequences of civil war. *Oxford Economic Papers* 51:168–83.
———. 2009. *Wars, guns, and votes: Democracy in dangerous places.* New York: HarperCollins.
Collier, Paul, Anke Hoeffler, and Måns Söderbom. 2008. Post-conflict risks. *Journal of Peace Research* 45, no. 4 (July): 461–78.
Collier, Paul, and Nicholas Sambanis. 2002. Understanding civil war: A new agenda. *Journal of Conflict Resolution* 46, no. 3 (February): 3–12.
Collier, Ruth Berins. 1999. *Paths to democracy: The working class and elites in Western Europe and South America.* Cambridge: Cambridge University Press.
Collins, Randall. 2008. *Violence: A micro-sociological theory.* Princeton: Princeton University Press.
Conser, Walter H., Ronald McCarthy, David Toscano, and Gene Sharp, eds. 1986. *Resistance, politics, and the American struggle for independence, 1765–1775.* Boulder, Colo.: Rienner.
Cordesman, Anthony, with Jennifer Moravitz. 2005. *The Israeli-Palestinian war: Escalating to nowhere.* Westport, Conn.: Praeger.
Cortright, David. 2001. Powers of persuasion: Sanctions and incentives in the shaping of international society. *International Studies* 38, no. 2 (April): 113–25.
CPRS Survey Research Unit. Public opinion poll #13: Unemployment, Jordanian-Israeli treaty, armed operations, elections, and other issues, November 17–19, 1994. Palestinian Center for Policy and Survey Research.
Crenshaw, Martha. 1995. The effectiveness of terrorism in the Algerian war. In *Terrorism in Context*, ed. Martha Crenshaw, 473–513. University Park, Penn.: Penn State University Press.
Cronin, Audrey Kurth. 2009. *How terrorism ends.* Princeton: Princeton University Press.
Cunningham, David E. 2006. Veto players and civil war duration. *American Journal of Political Science* 50, no. 5 (October): 875–92.
Cunningham, David E., Kristian Skrede Gleditsch, and Idean Salehyan. 2009a. It takes two: A dyadic analysis of civil war duration and outcome. *Journal of Conflict Resolution* 53, no. 4 (August): 570–97.
———. 2009b. Codebook for the non-state actor data. http://privatewww.essex.ac.uk/~ksg/data/eacd_codebook.pdf.
Dahl, Robert A. 1989. *Democracy and its critics.* New Haven: Yale University Press.
Dajani, Souad. 1994. *Eyes without country: Searching for a Palestinian strategy of liberation.* Philadelphia: Temple University Press.
Daneshvar, Parviz. 1996. *Revolution in Iran.* New York: St. Martin's Press.
Daroy, Petronila B. N. 1988. On the eve of dictatorship and revolution. In *Dictatorship and revolution: Roots of people power*, ed. Aurora Javate–de Dios, Petronila B. N. Daroy, and Lorna Kalaw-Tirol, 1–25. Metro Manila: Conspectus.
Dashti-Gibson, Jalch, Patricia Davis, and Benjamin Radcliff. 1997. On the determinants of the success of economic sanctions: An empirical analysis. *American Journal of Political Science* 41, no. 2 (April): 608–18.
Davis, Leonard. 1989. *Revolutionary struggle in the Philippines.* New York: St. Martin's Press.

De Dios, Emmanuel. 1988. The erosion of dictatorship. In *Dictatorship and revolution: Roots of people power*, ed. Aurora Javate–de Dios, Petronila B. N. Daroy, and Lorna Kalaw-Tirol, 70–131. Metro Manila: Conspectus.
DeNardo, James. 1985. *Power in numbers*. Princeton: Princeton University Press.
Desch, Michael C. 2008. *Power and military effectiveness: The fallacy of democratic triumphalism*. Baltimore: Johns Hopkins University Press.
Diamond, Larry. 1977. Introduction: In search of consolidation. In *Consolidating the Third Wave democracies*, ed. Larry Diamond, Marc F. Plattner, Yunhan Chu, and Hung-mao Tien. Baltimore: Johns Hopkins University Press.
———. 2008. *The spirit of democracy: The struggle to build free societies throughout the world*. New York: Times Books.
Diamond, Larry, and Juan Linz. 1989. Introduction: Politics, society, and democracy in Latin America. In *Democracy and developing countries: Latin America*, ed. Larry Diamond, Juan Linz, and Seymour Martin Lipset. Boulder, Colo.: Rienner.
Diokno, Jose. 1982. US interventionism, the nuclear menace, and US bases. *Diliman Review* 30, no. 1:18–23.
Diokno, Maria Serena I. 1988. Unity and struggle. In *Dictatorship and revolution: Roots of people power*, ed. Aurora Javate–de Dios, Petronila B. N. Daroy, and Lorna Kalaw-Tirol, 136–37. Metro Manila: Conspectus.
Downes, Alexander B. 2008. *Targeting civilians in war*. Ithaca, N.Y.: Cornell University Press.
———. 2009. How smart and tough are democracies? Reassessing theories of democratic victory in war. *International Security* 33, no. 4 (spring): 9–51.
Doyle, Michael W., and Nicholas Sambanis. 2000. International peacebuilding: A theoretical and quantitative analysis. *American Political Science Review* 94, no. 4 (December): 779–801.
Drury, A. Cooper. 1998. Revisiting economic sanctions reconsidered. *Journal of Peace Research* 35, no. 4 (July): 497–509.
Eckstein, Susan, ed. 2001. *Power and popular protest: Latin American social movements*. Berkeley: University of California Press.
EDSA Revolution Website. n.d. http://library.thinkquest.org/15816/mainpage.html.
Eglitis, Olgerts. 1993. *Nonviolent action in the liberation of Latvia*. Boston: Albert Einstein Institute.
Elbadawi, Ibrahim, Håvard Hegre, and Gary J. Milante. 2008. The aftermath of civil war. *Journal of Peace Research* 45, no. 4 (July): 451–59.
Elwood, Donald J. 1986. *Philippine revolution 1986: Model of nonviolent change*. Quezon City: New Day.
Englebert, Pierre, and Rebecca Hummel. 2005. Let's stick together: Understanding Africa's secessionist deficit. *African Affairs* 104, no. 416:399–427.
Ertugul, I. 1987. Working together for peace. *Middle East International*. January 9.
Fanon, Frantz. 1961. *The wretched of the earth*. New York: Grove Press.
Farhi, Farideh. 1990. *States and urban-based revolutions: Iran and Nicaragua*. Urbana: University of Illinois Press.
Farsoun, Smith, and Christina E. Zacharia. 1997. *Palestine and the Palestinians*. Boulder, Colo.: Westview Press.
Fearon, James D. 1995. Rationalist explanations for war. *International Organization* 49, no. 3 (summer): 379–414.
———. 2007. Iraq's civil war. *Foreign Affairs* 86, no. 2 (March/April): 2–7.
Fearon, James D., and David Laitin. 2003. Ethnicity, insurgency, and civil war. *American Political Science Review* 97, no. 1 (February): 75–90.
Fernea, Elizabeth W., and Mary E. Hocking, eds. 1992. *The struggle for peace: Israelis and Palestinians*. Austin: University of Texas Press.
Fink, Christina. 2001. *Living silence: Burma under military rule*. London: Zed.

Fishel, John T., and Max G. Manwaring. 2006. *Uncomfortable wars revisited.* Norman: University of Oklahoma Press.
Fogarty, Philippa. 2008. Was Burma's 1988 uprising worth it? *BBC News*, June 8.
Fortna, Page, and Reyko Huang. 2009. Democratization after civil war. Paper presented at the annual meeting of the American Political Science Association, Toronto.
Francisco, Ronald. 2004. After the massacre: Mobilization in the wake of harsh repression. *Mobilization: An International Journal* 9, no. 2 (June): 107–26.
———. 2005. The dictator's dilemma. In *Repression and mobilization,* ed. Christian Davenport, Hank Johnston, and Carol Mueller, 58–83. Minneapolis: University of Minnesota Press.
Fuhrmann, Matthew. 2009. Spreading temptation: Proliferation and peaceful nuclear cooperation agreements. *International Security* 34, no. 1 (summer): 7–41.
Fuhrmann, Matthew, and Jaroslav Tir. 2009. Territorial dimensions of enduring internal rivalries. *Conflict Management and Peace Science* 26, no. 4 (September): 307–29.
Galtung, Johan. 1989. *Nonviolence in Israel/Palestine.* Honolulu: University of Hawai'i Press.
Galula, David. 2006. *Counterinsurgency warfare: Theory and practice.* Westport, Conn.: Praeger.
Gamage, Daya. 2008. Latest visit to Burma yielded no "immediate tangible outcome," Gambari tells UN security council. *Asian Tribune* 7, no. 1 (March). http://www.asiantribune.com/?q=node/10128.
Gamson, William A. 1990. *The strategy of social protest.* 2nd ed. Belmont, Calif.: Wadsworth.
Ganji, Manouchehr. 2002. *Defying the Iranian revolution: From a minister to the shah to a leader of resistance.* Westport, Conn.: Praeger.
Ganz, Marshall. 2010. *Why David sometimes wins: Leadership, organization, and strategy in the California farm worker movement.* Oxford: Oxford University Press.
Gartzke, Erik, and Dong-Joo Jo. 2009. Bargaining, nuclear proliferation, and interstate disputes. *Journal of Conflict Resolution* 53, no. 2 (April): 209–33.
Gause, F. Gregory. 1991. The Arab world and the intifada. In *The intifada: Its impact on Israel, the Arab world, and the superpowers,* ed. Robert O. Freedman. Miami: Florida International University Press.
Geddes, Barbara. 1999. What do we know about democratization after twenty years? *Annual Review of Political Science* 2:115–44.
Gelvin, James. 2005. *The Israeli-Palestine conflict: One hundred years of war.* New York: Cambridge University Press.
George, Alexander, and Andrew Bennett. 2005. *Case studies and theory development in the social sciences.* Cambridge, Mass.: MIT Press.
Ghobarah, Hazem Adam, Paul Huth, and Bruce Russett. 2003. Civil wars kill and maim people—long after the shooting stops. *American Political Science Review* 97, no. 2 (May): 189–202.
Gleditsch, Kristian. 2004. A revised list of wars between and within independent states, 1816–2002. *International Organization* 30, no. 3 (July): 231–62.
Golder, Matthew. 2005. Democratic electoral systems around the world, 1946–2000. *Electoral Studies* 24, no. 1:103–21.
Goldstone, Jack A. 1994. Is revolution really rational? *Rationality and Society* 6, no. 1 (January): 139–66.
———. 2002. Population and security: How demographic change can lead to violent conflict. *Journal of International Affairs* 56, no. 1 (fall): 3–22.
Goodno, James. 1991. *The Philippines: The land of broken promises.* London: Zed.
Goodwin, Jeff. 2001. *No other way out: States and revolutionary movement, 1945–1991.* New York: Cambridge University Press.
Gordon, Haim, Rivca Gordon, and Taher Shriteh. 2003. *Beyond intifada: Narratives of freedom fighters in the Gaza Strip.* Westport, Conn.: Praeger.
Graham, Robert. 1980. *Iran: The illusion of power.* Boston: St. Martin's Press.

Granovetter, Mark. 1978. Threshold models of collective behavior. *American Journal of Sociology* 83, no. 6 (May): 1420–43.
Grant, Philip. 1990. Nonviolent political struggle in the occupied territories. In *Arab nonviolent political struggle in the Middle East*, ed. Philip Grant, Ralph E. Crow, and Saad E. Ibrahim, 75–90. Boulder, Colo.: Rienner.
Gray, Colin. 1999. *Modern strategy.* Oxford: Oxford University Press.
Greene, Thomas H. 1974. *Comparative revolutionary movements.* Upper Saddle River, N.J.: Prentice Hall.
Greskovits, Bela. 1998. *The political economy of protest and patience: East European and Latin American transformations compared.* Budapest: Central European University Press.
Gruen, George. 1991. The impact of the intifada on American Jews. In *The intifada: Its impact on Israel, the Arab world, and the superpowers*, ed. Robert O. Freedman, 293–324. Miami: Florida International University Press.
Gugler, Josef. 1982. The urban character of contemporary revolutions. *Studies in Comparative International Development* 17, no. 2 (June): 60–73.
Haggard, Stephen, and R. R. Kaufman. 1995. *The political economy of democratic transitions.* Princeton: Princeton University Press.
Haines, Herbert. 1984. Black radicalization and the funding of civil rights: 1957–1970. *Social Problems* 32, no. 1 (October): 31–43.
———. 1988. *Black radicals and the civil rights mainstream.* Knoxville: University of Tennessee Press.
Harney, Desmond. 1998. *The priest and the king: An eyewitness account of the Iranian revolution.* London: Taurus.
Hart, Liddell. 1954. *Strategy: The indirect approach.* London: Faber and Faber.
Hartzell, Caroline, Matthew Hoddie, and Donald Rothchild. 2001. Stabilizing the peace after civil war: An investigation of some key variables. *International Organization* 55, no. 1 (February): 183–208.
Hathaway, Jane, ed. 2001. *Rebellion, repression, reinvention: Mutiny in comparative perspective.* Westport, Conn.: Praeger.
Hegland, Mary Elaine. 1987. Islamic revival or political and cultural revolution? An Islamic case study. In *The Islamic resurgence in comparative perspective*, ed. Richard Antoun and Mary Hegland, 194–219. Syracuse: Syracuse University Press.
Hegre, Håvard, Tanja Ellingsen, Scott Gates, and Nils Petter Gleditsch. 2001. Toward a democratic civil peace? Democracy, political change, and civil war, 1816–1992. *American Political Science Review* 95, no. 1 (March): 33–48.
Helvey, Robert. 2004. *On strategic nonviolent conflict: Thinking about fundamentals.* Boston: Albert Einstein Institute.
Heraclides, Alexis. 1990. Secessionist minorities and external involvement. *International Organization* 44, no. 3:341–78.
Herbst, Jeffrey. 2000. *States and power in Africa: Comparative lessons in authority and control.* Princeton: Princeton University Press.
Heston, Alan, Robert Summers, and Bettina Aten. 2006. Penn world table version 6.2. Center for International Comparisons of Production, Income and Prices, University of Pennsylvania. http://pwt.econ.upenn.edu/php_site/pwt_index.php.
Horowitz, Donald L. 1981. Patterns of ethnic separatism. *Comparative Studies in Society and History* 23, no. 2 (April): 165–95.
———. 2000. *Ethnic groups in conflict.* Berkeley: University of California Press.
Horowitz, Michael, and Dan Reiter. 2001. When does aerial bombing work? Quantitative empirical tests, 1917–1999. *Journal of Conflict Resolution* 45, no. 2 (April): 147–73.
Howes, Dustin. 2009. *Toward a credible pacifism: Violence and the possibilities of politics.* Albany: SUNY Press.

Hudson, Michael C., ed. 1990. *The Palestinians: New directions.* Washington, D.C.: Center for Contemporary Arab Studies.
Hufbauer, Gary Clyde, Kimberley Ann Elliott, and Jeffrey J. Schott. 2007. Summary of economic sanctions episodes. Peterson Institute for International Economics. http://www.iie.com/research/topics/sanctions/sanctions-timeline.cfm.
Hufbauer, Gary Clyde, Jeffrey J. Schott, and Kimberly Ann Elliott. 1992. *Economic sanctions reconsidered: Theory, history, and current policy.* Washington, D.C.: Institute of International Economics.
Hunter, F. Robert. 1991. *The Palestinian uprising: A war by other means.* 2nd ed. Berkeley: University of California Press.
Huntington, Samuel P. 1968. *Political order in changing societies.* New Haven: Yale University Press.
——. 1984. Will more countries become democratic? *Political Science Quarterly* 99, no. 2 (summer): 193–218.
——. 1991. *The third wave: Democratization in the late twentieth century.* Norman: University of Oklahoma Press.
Huxley, Steven Duncan. 1990. *Constitutionalist insurgency in Finland: Finnish "passive resistance" against Russification as a case of nonmilitary struggle in the European resistance tradition.* Helsinki: Finnish Historical Society.
Ibrahim, Hassanein Tawfiq. 2008. Social and political change in the wake of the oil boom. *Arab Insight* 2, no. 3 (fall): 112–20.
Inglehart, Ronald, and Wayne E. Baker. 2000. Modernization, cultural change, and the persistence of traditional values. *American Sociological Review* 65, no. 1 (February): 19–52.
Jaafar, Rudy, and Maria J. Stephan. 2010. Lebanon's independence intifada: How unarmed insurrection expelled Syrian forces. In *Civilian Jihad: Nonviolent struggle, democratization, and governance in the Middle East*, ed. Maria J. Stephan, 169–84. New York: Palgrave Macmillan.
Jamal, Amal. 2005. *The Palestinian national movement: Politics of contention, 1967–2005.* Bloomington: Indiana University Press.
Jarbawi, Ali. 1990. Palestinian elites in the occupied territories: Stability and change through the intifada. In *Intifada: Palestine at the crossroads*, ed. Jamal R. Nassar and Roger Heacock, 287–307. New York: Praeger.
Jenkins, J. Craig, and C. M. Eckert. 1986. Channeling the black insurgency: Elite patronage and professional social movement organizations in the development of the black movement. *American Sociological Review* 51, no. 6 (December): 812–29.
Jervis, Robert. 1984. *The illogic of American nuclear strategy.* Ithaca, N.Y.: Cornell University Press.
Joes, Anthony James. 2007. *Urban guerrilla warfare.* Lexington: University Press of Kentucky.
Johnson, Bryan. 1987. *The four days of courage: The untold story of the people who brought Marcos down.* New York: Free Press.
Johnson, Dominic D. P., and Dominic Tierney. 2006. *Failing to win: Perceptions of victory and defeat in international politics.* Cambridge, Mass.: Harvard University Press.
Kadi, Leila S., ed. 1969. *Basic political documents of the armed Palestinian resistance movement.* Beirut: Palestine Research Centre.
Kagian, Jules. 1988. The United Nations: The four resolutions. *Middle East International* 317, no. 9:8–10.
Kalyvas, Stathis N. 2006. *The logic of violence in civil war.* Cambridge: Cambridge University Press.
Kaminer, Reuven. 1989. The protest movement in Israel. In *Intifada: The Palestinian uprising against Israeli occupation*, ed. Zachary Lockman and Joel Beinin, 231–49. Boston: South End Press.

———. 1996. *The politics of protest: The Israeli peace movement and the Palestinian intifada*. Brighton, U.K.: Sussex Academic Press.

Karl, Terry Lynn. 2005. From democracy to democratization and back: Before transitions from authoritarian rule. CDDRL Working Papers, no. 45. Stanford, Calif.: Stanford University Press.

Keck, Margaret E., and Kathryn Sikkink. 1998. *Activists beyond borders: Advocacy networks in international politics*. Ithaca, N.Y.: Cornell University Press.

Keddie, Nikki R. 2003. *Modern Iran: Roots and results of revolution*. New Haven: Yale University Press.

Keshk, Omar. 2003. CDSIMEQ: A program to implement two-stage probit least squares. *Stata Journal* 3 (June): 157–67.

Keshk, Omar, Brian Pollins, and Rafael Reuveny. 2004. Trade still follows the flag: The primacy of politics in a simultaneous model of interdependence and armed conflict. *Journal of Politics* 66, no. 4 (November): 1155–79.

Khawaja, Marwan. 1993. Repression and popular collective action: Evidence from the West Bank. *Sociological Forum* 8, no. 1 (March): 47–71.

Kim, Hyung Min, and David Rousseau. 2005. The classical liberals were half right (or half wrong): New tests of the liberal peace, 1960–1988. *Journal of Peace Research* 42, no. 5 (September): 523–43.

King, Mary E. 2007. *A quiet revolution: The first Palestinian intifada and nonviolent resistance*. New York: Nation Books.

Kishtainy, Khalid. 2010. Humor and resistance in the Arab world and greater Middle East. In *Civilian jihad: Nonviolent struggle, democratization, and governance in the Middle East*, ed. Maria J. Stephan, 53–64. New York: Palgrave Macmillan.

Kitschelt, Herbert, Zdenka Mansfeldova, Radoslaw Markowski and Gabor Toka. 1999. *Post-communist party systems: Competition, representation, and inter-party cooperation*. New York: Cambridge University Press.

Kocher, Matthew Adam, and Stathis N. Kalyvas. 2007. How free is free riding in civil wars? Violence, insurgency, and the collective action problem. *World Politics* 59, no. 2 (January): 177–219.

Kohen, Arnold S. 1999. *From the place of the dead: The epic struggles of Bishop Belo of East Timor*. New York: St. Martin's Press.

Komisar, Lucy. 1987. *Corazon Aquino: The story of a revolution*. New York: Braziller.

Koopmans, Ruud. 1993. The dynamics of protest waves: West Germany, 1965 to 1989. *American Sociological Review* 58, no. 5 (October): 637–58.

Kreager, Philip. 1991. Aung San Suu Kyi and the peaceful struggle for human rights in Burma. In Aung San Suu Kyi, *Freedom from fear and other writings*, ed. Michael Aris, 318–59. New York: Penguin.

Kull, Steven, Clay Ramsay, Phillip Warf, and Monica Wolford. The potential for a nonviolent intifada: Study of Palestinian and Jewish public attitudes (August 28, 2002). World Public Opinion, Program on International Policy Attitudes. http://www.pipa.org/OnlineReports/IsPal_Conflict/Intifada1_Aug02/Intifada1_Aug02_rpt.pdf.

Kuran, Timur. 1989. Sparks and prairie fires: A theory of unanticipated political revolution. *Public Choice* 61, no. 1 (April): 41–74.

Kurzman, Charles. 1996. Structural opportunity and perceived opportunity in social-movement theory: The Iranian revolution of 1979. *American Sociological Review* 61, no. 1 (February): 153–70.

———. 1998. Waves of democratization. *Studies in Comparative International Development* 33, no. 1 (1998): 42–64.

———. 2004. *The unthinkable revolution in Iran*. Cambridge, Mass.: Harvard University Press.

Lande, Carl. 1978. The April 7th election in Manila: A brief report. *Philippine Studies Newsletter* (June).

Lane, Max. 1990. *The urban mass movement in the Philippines, 1983–87*. Canberra: Department of Political and Social Change, Australian National University.

Laqueur, Walter. 1976. *Guerrilla: A historical and critical study*. Boston: Little, Brown.

———, ed. 1977. *The guerrilla reader: A historical anthology*. Philadelphia: Temple University Press.

Lichbach, Mark. 1994. Rethinking rationality and rebellion: Theories of collective action and problems of collective dissent. *Rationality and Society* 6, no. 1 (January): 8–39.

Licklider, Roy. 1995. The consequences of negotiated settlement in civil wars, 1945–1993. *American Political Science Review* 89, no. 3 (September): 681–90.

———. 2003. The consequences of civil wars: Correlation and counterfactual. Paper presented at the annual meeting of the American Political Science Association, Philadelphia.

Lieberman, Evan S. 2005. Nested analysis as a mixed-method strategy for cross-national research. *American Political Science Review* 99 (August): 435–52.

Lindsey, Charles. 1984. Economic crisis in the Philippines. *Asian Survey* 24, no. 12 (December): 1201–4.

Lintner, Bertil. 1990. *The rise and fall of the communist party of Burma (CPB)*. Ithaca, N.Y.: Cornell University Press.

———. 1994. *Burma in revolt: Opium and insurgency since 1948*. Boulder, Colo.: Westview Press.

Lipset, Seymour Martin. 1959. Some social requisites of democracy: Economic development and political legitimacy. *American Political Science Review* 53, no. 1 (March): 69–105.

Litvak, Meir. 2003. The Islamization of Palestinian identity: The case of Hamas. Tel Aviv: Moshe Dayan Center for Middle Eastern Studies, Tel Aviv University.

Lockman, Zachary, and Joel Beinin, eds. 1989. *Intifada: The Palestinian uprising against Israeli occupation*. Boston: South End Press.

Lodge, Tom. 2009. The interplay of violence and nonviolence in the movement against apartheid in South Africa, 1983–94. In Roberts and Garton Ash, *Civil resistance and power politics*, 213–30.

Londregan, J. B., and K. Poole. 1990. Poverty, the coup trap, and the seizure of executive power. *World Politics* 42, no. 2 (January): 151–83.

———. 1996. Does high income promote democracy? *World Politics* 49, no. 1 (October): 1–30.

Long, J. Scott. 1997. *Regression models for categorical and limited dependent variables*. Thousand Oaks, Calif.: Sage.

Long, J. Scott, and Jeremy Freese. 2005. *Regression models for categorical dependent variables using Stata*. College Station, Tex.: Stata Press.

Lukacs, Yehuda, ed. 1992. *The Israeli-Palestinian conflict: A documentary record*. New York: Cambridge University Press.

Lyall, Jason K. 2009. "Does indiscriminate violence incite insurgent attacks? Evidence from Chechnya." *Journal of Conflict Resolution*, 53, no. 3 (June): 331–62.

———. 2010. Do democracies make inferior counterinsurgents? Reassessing democracy's impact on war outcomes and duration. *International Organization* 64, no. 1 (January): 167–92.

Lyall, Jason K., and Isaiah Wilson. 2009. Rage against the machines: Explaining outcomes in counterinsurgency wars. *International Organization* 63, no. 1 (winter): 67–106.

Macaranza, Bach. 1988. *Workers participation in the Philippine people power revolution: An examination of the roles played by trade unions in the Philippine people power movement*. Manila: Ebert.

Mackey, Sandra. 1998. *The Iranians: Persia, Islam, and the soul of a nation*. New York: Plume.

Maddala, G. S. 1983. *Limited dependent and qualitative variables in econometrics*. Cambridge: Cambridge University Press.

Manning, Robert. 1984/1985. The Philippines in crisis. *Foreign Affairs* 63, no. 2 (winter): 392–410.

Marchant, Eleanor, Adrian Karatnycky, Arch Puddington, and Christopher Walter. 2008. Enabling environments for civic movements and the dynamics of democratic transition. Freedom House special report. July 18.
Marger, Martin N. 1984. Social movement organizations and response to environmental change: The NAACP, 1960–1973. *Social Problems* 32, no. 1 (October): 16–27.
Marinov, Nikolay. 2005. Do economic sanctions destabilize country leaders? *American Journal of Political Science* 49, no. 3 (July): 564–76.
Marshall, Monty, Keith Jaggers, and Ted Robert Gurr. Polity IV project: Regime transitions and characteristics, 1800–2007. Center for Systemic Peace.
Martin, Brian. 2001. *Technology for nonviolent struggle*. London: War Resisters' International.
———. 2007. *Justice ignited: The dynamics of backfire*. Lanham, Md.: Rowman and Littlefield.
Martin, Brian, and Wendy Varney. 2003. Nonviolence and communication. *Journal of Peace Research* 40, no. 2 (March): 213–42.
Martin, Brian, Wendy Varney, and Adrian Vickers. 2001. Political jiu-jitsu against Indonesian repression: Studying lower-profile nonviolent resistance. *Pacifica Review* 13, no. 2 (June): 143–56.
Martin, Ian. 2000. The popular consultations and the United Nations mission in East Timor: First reflections. In *Out of the ashes: The destruction and reconstruction of East Timor*, ed. James J. Fox and Dionisio Babo Soares, 126–40. Adelaide: Crawford House.
Martin, Lisa L. 1992. *Coercive cooperation: Explaining multilateral sanctions*. Princeton: Princeton University Press.
Marwell, Gerald, and Pamela Oliver. 1993. *The critical mass in collective action: A micro-social theory*. Cambridge: Cambridge University Press.
Maung, Mya. 1992. *Totalitarianism in Burma: Prospects for economic development*. New York: Paragon House.
Maung Than, Tin Maung. 2007. Myanmar: Challenges galore but opposition failed to score. In *Southeast Asian Affairs 2006*, ed. Daljit Singh and Lorraine C. Salazar, 186–207. Singapore: Institute of Southeast Asian Studies.
Mazower, Mark. 2008. *Hitler's empire: How the Nazis ruled Europe*. New York: Penguin.
McAdam, Doug. 1996a. Political opportunities: Conceptual origins, current problems, future directions. In McAdam, McCarthy, and Zald, *Comparative perspectives on social movements*, 23–40.
———. 1996b. The framing function of movement tactics: Strategic dramaturgy in the American civil rights movement. In McAdam, McCarthy, and Zald, *Comparative perspectives on social movements*, 338–54.
———. 1999. *Political process and the development of black insurgency, 1930–1970*. 2nd ed. Chicago: University of Chicago Press.
McAdam, Doug, John D. McCarthy, and Mayer N. Zald. 1996. *Comparative perspectives on social movements: Political opportunities, mobilizing structures, and political framing*. Cambridge: Cambridge University Press.
McAdam, Doug, Sidney Tarrow, and Charles Tilly. 2001. *Dynamics of contention*. New York: Cambridge University Press.
McCarthy, Ronald, and Gene Sharp. 1997. *Nonviolent resistance: A research guide*. New York: Garland.
McCoy, Alfred W. 1989. Quezon's commonwealth: The emergence of Philippine authoritarianism. In *Philippine colonial democracy*, ed. Ruby Paredes, 114–60. New Haven: Southeast Asian Studies, Yale University.
———. 1999. *Closer than brothers: Manhood at the Philippine military academy*. New Haven: Yale University Press.
McFaul, Michael. 2007. Ukraine imports democracy: External influences on the Orange Revolution. *International Security* 32, no. 2 (fall): 45–83.

McFaul, Michael, and Kathryn Stoner-Weiss. 2004. *After the collapse of communism: Comparative lessons of transitions.* Cambridge: Cambridge University Press.

McFaul, Michael, Kathryn Stoner-Weiss, and Valerie Bunce, eds. 2009. *Waves and troughs of democratization in the post-communist world.* Cambridge: Cambridge University Press.

Mendoza, Amado, Jr. 2009. "People power" in the Philippines, 1983–86. In Roberts and Garton Ash, *Civil resistance and power politics*, 179–96.

Merom, Gil. 2003. *How democracies lose small wars: State, society, and the failures of France in Algeria, Israel in Lebanon, and the United States in Vietnam.* New York: Cambridge University Press.

Merriman, Hardy, and Jack DuVall. 2007. Dissolving terrorism at its roots. In *Nonviolence: An alternative for defeating global terrorism*, ed. Senthil Ram and Ralph Summy, 221–34. New York: Nova Science.

Midlarsky, Manus I., Martha Crenshaw, and Fumihiko Yoshida. 1980. Why violence spreads: The contagion of international terrorism. *International Studies Quarterly* 24, no. 2 (June): 262–98.

Milani, Mohsen M. 1994. *The making of Iran's Islamic revolution: From monarchy to Islamic republic.* 2nd ed. Boulder, Colo.: Westview Press.

Miniotaite, Grazina. 2002. *Nonviolent resistance in Lithuania: A story of peaceful liberation.* Boston: Albert Einstein Institute.

Mishal, Shaul, and Avraham Sela Mishal. 2000. *The Palestinian Hamas: Vision, violence and coexistence.* New York: Columbia University Press.

Moin, Baqer. 2000. *Khomeini: The life of the ayatollah.* London: Taurus.

Moksha, Yitri. 1989. The crisis in Burma: Back from the heart of darkness? *Asian Survey* 29, no. 6 (June): 543–58.

Molloy, E. Ivan. 1985. Revolution in the Philippines: The question of an alliance between Islam and communism. *Asian Survey* 25, no. 8 (August): 822–33.

Montiel, Cristina Jayme. 2006. Political psychology of nonviolent democratic transitions in Southeast Asia. *Journal of Social Issues* 62, no. 1 (March): 173–90.

Moore, Barrington, Jr. 1993. *The social origins of dictatorship and democracy: Lord and peasant in the making of the modern world.* Boston: Beacon Press.

Moore, Will H. 1998. Repression and dissent: Substitution, context, and timing. *American Journal of Political Science* 42, no. 3 (July): 851–73.

Mueller, Carol McClug. 1978. Riot violence and protest outcomes. *American Journal of Sociology* 105:697–735.

Naraghi, Ehsan. 1994. *From palace to prison: Inside the Iranian revolution.* Trans. Nilou Mobasser. Chicago: Dee.

Neher, Clark D. 1981. The Philippines in 1980: The gathering storm. *Asian Survey* 21, no. 2 (February): 263–65.

Newey, Whitney. 1987. Efficient estimation of limited dependent variable models with endogenous explanatory variables. *Journal of Econometrics* 36, no. 3 (November): 231–50.

Nunn, Maxine Kaufman. 1993. *Creative resistance: Anecdotes of nonviolent action by Israel-based groups.* Jerusalem: Alternative Information Center.

O'Ballance, Edgar. 1998. *The Palestinian intifada.* New York: St. Martin's Press.

Oberschall, Anthony. 1994. Rational choice in collective protests. *Rationality and Society* 6, no. 1 (January): 79–100.

O'Donnell, Guillermo, and Philippe C. Schmitter. 1986. *Transitions from authoritarian rule: Tentative conclusions about uncertain democracies.* Baltimore: Johns Hopkins University Press.

Olson, Mancur. 1965. *The logic of collective action.* Cambridge, Mass.: Harvard University Press.

Oo, May. 2007. Plausible dialogue in Burma. *Foreign Policy in Focus*, October 22. http://www.fpif.org/articles/plausible_dialogue_in_burma.

Overholt, William H. 1986. The rise and fall of Ferdinand Marcos. *Asian Survey* 26, no. 11

(November): 1147–48.
Pape, Robert A. 1996. *Bombing to win: Air power and coercion in war*. Ithaca, N.Y.: Cornell University Press.
———. 1997. Why economic sanctions do not work. *International Security* 22, no. 2 (autumn): 90–136.
———. 2003. The strategic logic of suicide terrorism. *American Political Science Review* 97, no. 3 (August): 343–61.
———. 2005. *Dying to win: The strategic logic of suicide terrorism*. New York: Random House.
Paris, Roland. 2005. *At war's end*. New York: Cambridge University Press.
Parkman, Patricia. 1988. *Nonviolent insurrection in El Salvador*. Tucson: University of Arizona Press.
———. 1990. *Insurrectionary civic strikes in Latin America, 1931–1961*. Boston: Albert Einstein Institute.
Parsons, Anthony. 1984. *The pride and the fall: Iran 1974–1979*. London: Cape.
Pearlman, Wendy. 2008. Spoiling from the inside out: Internal political contestation and the Middle East peace process. *International Security* 33, no. 3 (winter): 79–109.
———. 2009. Precluding nonviolence, propelling violence: The effect of internal fragmentation on movement behavior. Paper presented at Comparative-Historical Social Science Workshop, April 10, 2010, Northwestern University.
———. 2010. A composite-actor approach to conflict behavior. In *Rethinking violence: States and non-state actors in conflict*, ed. Erica Chenoweth and Adria Lawrence, 197–220. Cambridge, Mass: MIT Press.
People Power in the Philippines. 1997. Fragments. http://www.fragmentsweb.org/TXT2/philiptx.html.
Peretz, Don. 1990. *Intifada: The Palestinian uprising*. Boulder, Colo.: Westview Press.
Peterson, Roger D. 2001. *Resistance and rebellion*. New York: Cambridge University Press.
Piven, Frances Fox, and Richard A. Cloward. 1979. *Poor people's movements: Why they succeed, how they fail*. New York: Vintage.
Pollack, Kenneth M. 2004. *The Persian puzzle: The conflict between Iran and America*. New York: Random House.
Pollock, David. 1991. The American response to the intifada. In *The intifada: Its impact on Israel, the Arab world, and the superpowers*, ed. Robert O. Freedman, 109–35. Miami: Florida International University Press.
Popovic, Srdja. 2009. On strict policy with the police and with the wider audience considering the problem of the police. Canvasopedia: Nonviolent Struggle Multimedia Library. http://www.canvasopedia.org/.
Popovic, Srdja, Slobodan Djinovic, Andrej Milivojevic, Hardy Merriman, and Ivan Marovic. 2007. *CANVAS Core Curriculum: A guide to effective nonviolent struggle, students book*. Belgrade: CANVAS.
Przeworski, Adam, Michael Alvarez, Jose Cheibub, and Fernando Limongi. 2000. *Democracy and development: Political institutions and well-being in the world, 1950–1990*. Cambridge: Cambridge University Press.
Przeworski, Adam, and Fernando Limongi. 1997. Modernization: Theories and facts. *World Politics* 49, no. 2 (January): 155–83.
Psinakis, Steve. 1981. *Two "terrorists" meet*. San Francisco: Alchemy.
Putnam, Robert. 1993. *Making democracy work*. Princeton: Princeton University Press.
Rabinovich, Itamar. 2004. *Waging peace: Israel and the Arabs, 1948–2003*. Princeton: Princeton University Press.
Rafael, Vincent. 1990. Patronage and pornography: Ideology and spectatorship in the early Marcos years. *Comparative Studies in History and Society* 32, no. 2 (April): 282–304.
Ramazani, R. K., ed. 1990. *Iran's revolution: The search for consensus*. Bloomington: Indiana University Press.

Rasler, Karen. 1996. Concessions, repression, and political protest in the Iranian revolution. *American Sociological Review* 61, no. 1 (February): 132–52.
Record, Jeffrey. 2006. External assistance: Enabler of insurgent success. *Parameters* 36, no. 3 (autumn): 36–49.
Reid, Robert H., and Eileen Guerrero. 1995. *Corazon Aquino and the brushfire revolution.* Baton Rouge: Louisiana State University Press.
Rigby, Andrew. 1991. *Living the intifada.* London: Zed.
———. 1997. *Legacy of the past: The problem of collaborators and the Palestinian case.* Jerusalem: PASSIA.
Roberts, Adam, ed. 1969. *Civilian resistance as a national defence: Nonviolent action against aggression.* New York: Penguin.
Roberts, Adam, and Timothy Garton Ash, eds. 2009. *Civil resistance and power politics: The experience of non-violent action from Gandhi to the present.* Oxford: Oxford University Press.
Robinson, Glenn E. 1997. *Building a Palestinian state: The incomplete revolution.* Bloomington: Indiana University Press.
Ross, Lauren G., and Nader Izzat Sa'id. 1995. "Palestinians: Yes to negotiations, yes to violence; Polling Arab views on the conflict with Israel. *Middle East Quarterly* 2, no. 2 (June): 15–23.
Rothstein, Robert L., Moshe Maoz, and Khalil Shikaki. 2002. *The Israeli-Palestinian peace process: Oslo and the lessons of failure.* Brighton, U.K.: Sussex Academic Press.
Roy, Sara. 2001. Decline and disfigurement: The Palestinian economy after Oslo. In *The new intifada: Resisting Israel's apartheid*, ed. Roane Carey, 91–109. New York: Verso.
Ruiz, Kenneth Todd, and Olivier Sarbil. 2010. Unmasked: Thailand's men in black. *Asia Times Online*, May 29.
Ryan, Sheila. 1974. Israeli economic policy in the occupied territories. *MERIP Reports*, no. 24:3–24.
Sagan, Scott. 1989. *Moving targets: Nuclear strategy and national security.* Princeton: Princeton University Press.
Saleh, Abdul Jawad. 2002. The Palestinian nonviolent resistance movement. Alternative Palestinian Agenda. http://www.ap-agenda.org/11-02/asaleh.htm.
Salehi, M. M. 1988. *Insurgency through culture and religion.* Westport, Conn.: Praeger.
Salehyan, Idean. 2007. Transnational rebels: Neighboring states as sanctuary for rebel groups. *World Politics* 59, no. 2 (January): 217–24.
———. 2008. No shelter here: Rebel sanctuaries and international conflict. *Journal of Politics* 70, no. 1 (January): 54–66.
———. 2009. *Rebels without borders: Transnational insurgencies in international politics.* Ithaca, N.Y.: Cornell University Press.
Sarkees, Meredith Reid, and Paul Schafer. 2000. The correlates of war data on war: An update to 1997. *Conflict Management and Peace Science* 18, no. 1:123–44.
Sazegara, Mohsen, and Maria J. Stephan. 2010. Iran's Islamic revolution and nonviolent struggle. In *Civilian jihad: Nonviolent struggle, democratization, and governance in the Middle East*, ed. Maria J. Stephan, 185–204. New York: Palgrave Macmillan.
Schelling, Thomas C. 1969. Some questions on civilian defence. In Roberts, *Civilian resistance as a national defence*, 351–52. .
———. 1978. *Micromotives and macrobehavior.* New York: Norton.
Schiff, Ze'ev, and Ehud Ya'ari. 1989. *Intifada: The Palestinian uprising—Israel's third front*, ed. and trans. Ina Friedman. New York: Simon and Schuster.
Schleder, Andreas. 1998. What is democratic consolidation? *Journal of Democracy* 9, no. 2 (April): 91–107.
Schock, Kurt. 2003. Nonviolent action and its misconceptions: Insights for social scientists. *PS: Political Science and Politics* 36, no. 4 (October): 705–12.

———. 2005. *Unarmed insurrections: People power movements in nondemocracies*. Minneapolis: University of Minnesota Press.
Schock, Kurt, and Erica Chenoweth. 2010. The impact of violence on the outcome of nonviolent resistance campaigns: An examination of intermovement radical flank effects. Paper presented at the annual meeting of the International Peace Research Association, Sydney, Australia.
Schumaker, Paul. 1975. Policy responsiveness to protest group demands. *Journal of Politics* 37, no. 2 (May): 488–521.
Scipes, Kim. 1992. Understanding the New Labor Movement in the "Third World": The emergence of social movement unionism. *Critical Sociology* 19:81–101.
Seekins, Donald M. 2005. Burma and US sanctions: Confronting an authoritarian regime. *Asian Survey* 45, no. 3 (May/June): 437–52.
Semelin, Jacques. 1993. *Unarmed against Hitler: Civilian resistance in Europe, 1939–1943*. Westport, Conn.: Praeger.
Sepp, Kalev. 2005. Best practices in counterinsurgency. *Military Review* 85, no. 3 (May/June): 8–12.
Seymour, Lee. 2006. The surprising success of "separatist" groups: The empirical and juridical in self-determination. Paper presented at the International Studies Association annual convention, San Diego, Calif.
Sharp, Gene. 1973. *The politics of nonviolent action*. 3 vols. Boston: Sargent.
———. 1990. *Civilian-based defense: A post-military weapons system*. Princeton: Princeton University Press.
———. 1999. Nonviolent action. In *Encyclopedia of violence, peace, and conflict*, ed. Lester Kurtz and Jennifer E. Turpin, 2:567–74. New York: Academic Press.
———. 2003. *There are realistic alternatives*. Boston: Albert Einstein Institution.
———, ed. 2005. *Waging nonviolent struggle: 20th century practice and 21st century potential*. Boston: Sargent.
Shaykhutdinov, Renat. 2010. Give peace a chance: Nonviolent protest and the creation of territorial autonomy arrangements. *Journal of Peace Research* 47, no. 2 (March): 179–91.
Simon, Jeffrey. 1992. The changing low-intensity environment. In *Transforming struggle: Strategy and the global experience of nonviolent direct action*, Program on Nonviolent Sanctions in Conflict and Defense, Center for International Studies, Harvard University. Boston: Albert Einstein Institute.
Singer, J. David. 1988. Reconstructing the correlates of war dataset on material capacities of states, 1816–1985. *International Interactions* 14, no. 2 (May): 115–32.
Singer, J. David, Stuart Bremer, and John Stuckey. 1972. Capability, distribution, uncertainty, and major power war, 1820–1965. In *Peace, war, and numbers*, ed. Bruce Russett, 19–48. Beverly Hills: Sage.
Skocpol, Theda. 1979. *States and social revolutions: A comparative analysis of France, Russia, and China*. New York: Cambridge University Press.
Smith, Benjamin. 2007. *Hard times in the lands of plenty: Oil politics in Iran and Indonesia*. Ithaca, N.Y.: Cornell University Press.
Smith, Martin. 1999. *Burma: Insurgency and the politics of ethnicity*. London: Zed.
Snyder, Richard. 1992. Explaining transitions from neopatrimonial dictatorships. *Comparative Politics* 24, no. 4 (July): 379–400.
———. 1998. Paths out of sultanistic regimes: Combining structural and voluntaristic perspectives. In *Sultanistic regimes*, ed. H. E. Chehabi and Juan J. Linz, 49–81. Baltimore: Johns Hopkins University Press.
Spector, Regine. 2006. The anti-revolutionary toolkit. *Central Asia–Caucasus Analyst* 8, no. 24 (December): 3–4.

START/CETIS. 2010. The global terrorism database. The National Consortium for the Study of Terrorism and Responses to Terrorism. http://www.start.umd.edu/gtd/.

Stephan, Maria J. 2005. Nonviolent insurgency: The role of civilian-based resistance in the East Timorese, Palestinian, and Kosovo Albanian self-determination movements. Ph.D. diss., Tufts University.

———. 2006. Fighting for statehood: The role of civilian-based resistance in the East Timorese, Palestinian, and Kosovo Albanian self-determination struggles. *Fletcher Forum on World Affairs* 30, no. 2 (summer): 57–80.

——— ed. 2010. *Civilian jihad: Nonviolent struggle, democratization, and governance in the Middle East.* New York: Palgrave Macmillan.

Stephan, Maria J., and Erica Chenoweth. 2008. Why civil resistance works: The strategic logic of nonviolent conflict. *International Security* 33, no. 1 (summer): 7–44.

Stephan, Maria J., and Jacob Mundy. 2006. A battlefield transformed: From guerilla resistance to mass nonviolent struggle in the Western Sahara. *Journal of Military and Strategic Studies* 8, no. 3 (spring): 1–32.

Stoker, Donald. 2007. Insurgents rarely win—and Iraq won't be any different (maybe). *Foreign Policy*, no. 158 (January). http://www.foreignpolicy.com/articles/2007/01/14/insurgencies_rarely_win_ndash_and_iraq_wont_be_any_different_maybe.

Stoltzfus, Nathan. 1996. *Resistance of the heart: Intermarriage and the Rosenstrasse protest in Nazi Germany.* New York: Norton.

Summy, Ralph. 1994. Nonviolence and the case of the extremely ruthless opponent. *Pacifica Review* 6, no. 1 (May/June): 1–29.

Sun-Tzu. 1963. *The art of war.* Trans. Samuel B. Griffith. Oxford: Oxford University Press.

Suu Kyi, Aung San. 1995. Speech to a mass rally at the Shwedagon Pagoda, August 26, 1988. In *Freedom from fear and other writings*, 192–98. Rev. ed. New York: Penguin.

Tarrow, Sidney. 1989. *Democracy and disorder.* Oxford: Clarendon.

———. 1998. *Power in movement.* New York: Cambridge University Press.

Tarrow, Sidney, and Tsveta Petrova. 2007. Transactional and participatory activism in the emerging European polity: The puzzle of east central Europe. *Comparative Political Studies* 40, no. 1 (January): 74–94.

Taylor, Robert H. 1987. *The state in Burma.* Honolulu: University of Hawai'i Press.

———. Change in Burma: Political demands and military power. *Asian Survey* 22, no. 2 (June): 131–41.

Teorell, Jan, and Axel Hadenius. 2004. Global and regional determinants of democracy: Taking stock of large-N evidence. Paper presented at the 100th annual meeting of the American Political Science Association, Chicago.

Tessler, Mark. 1995. *A history of the Israeli-Palestinian conflict.* Bloomington: Indiana University Press.

Thompson, Mark R. 1991. Searching for a strategy: The traditional opposition to Marcos and the transition to democracy in the Philippines. Ph.D. diss., Yale University.

———. 1995. *The anti-Marcos struggle: Personalistic rule and democratic transition in the Philippines.* New Haven: Yale University Press.

———. 1996. Off the endangered list: Philippine democratization in comparative perspective. *Comparative Politics* 28, no. 2 (January): 179–205.

Tiglao, Rigoberto. 1988. The consolidation of the dictatorship. In *Dictatorship and revolution: Roots of people power*, ed. Aurora Javate–de Dios, Petronila B. N. Daroy, and Lorna Kalaw-Tirol, 34–49. Metro Manila: Conspectus.

Tilly, Charles. 1978. *From mobilization to revolution.* Reading, Mass.: Addison-Wesley.

Timberman, David. 1991. *A changeless land: Continuity and change in Philippine politics.* Singapore: Institute of Southeast Asian Studies.

Toft, Monica Duffy. 2003. *The geography of ethnic violence: Identity, interests, and the indivisibility of territory*. Princeton: Princeton University Press.
———. 2009. *Securing the peace: The durable settlements of civil wars*. Princeton: Princeton University Press.
Toye, Jeremy. 1980. Subversion trial opens. *Asia Record*, July, 7–14.
Tullock, Gordon. 1971. The paradox of revolution. *Public Choice* 11, no. 1 (September): 89–99.
Urdal, Henrik. 2006. A clash of generations? Youth bulges and political violence. *International Studies Quarterly* 50, no 3 (September): 607–30.
U.S. Department of State. 2004. Report on U.S. trade sanctions against Burma. U.S. Department of State. http://www.america.gov/st/washfile-english/2004/May/20040506115321ASesuarKo.1069605.html.
van der Kroef, Justus. 1973. Communism and reform in the Philippines. *Pacific Affairs* 46, no. 1 (spring): 29–58.
Villegas, Bernardo. 1985. The Philippines in 1985: Rolling with the political punches. *Asian Survey* 26, no. 2 (February): 127–40.
Walter, Barbara F. 2004. Does conflict beget conflict? Explaining recurring civil war. *Journal of Peace Research* 41, no. 3 (May): 371–88.
———. 2009. *Reputation and civil war: Why separatist conflicts are so violent*. New York: Cambridge University Press.
Walzer, Michael. 2001. Excusing terror: The politics of ideological apology. *American Prospect*, October 22, 16.
Way, Lucan. 2008. The real causes of the Color Revolutions. *Journal of Democracy* 19, no. 3 (July): 55–69.
Wehr, Paul, Heidi Burgess, and Guy Burgess, eds. 1994. *Justice without violence*. Boulder, Colo.: Rienner.
Weinstein, Jeremy. 2007. *Inside rebellion: The politics of insurgent violence*. New York: Cambridge University Press.
White, Robert. 1989. From peaceful protest to guerrilla war: Micromobilization of the Provisional Irish Republican Army. *American Journal of Sociology* 94, no. 6 (May): 1277–1302.
Wickham-Crowley, Timothy. 1992. *Guerrillas and revolution in Latin America: A comparative study of insurgents and regimes since 1956*. Princeton: Princeton University Press.
Wood, Elisabeth Jean. 2000. *Forging democracy from below: Insurgent transitions in South Africa and El Salvador*. New York: Cambridge University Press.
———. 2003. *Insurgent collective action and civil war in El Salvador*. New York: Cambridge University Press.
World Bank. 2003. *World development indicators*. CD-ROM. Washington, D.C.: World Bank.
Wright, Robin. 2000. *The last great revolution: Turmoil and transformation in Iran*. New York: Knopf.
Wurfel, David. 1977. Martial law in the Philippines: The methods of regime survival. *Pacific Affairs* 50, no. 1 (spring): 5–30.
———. 1988. *Filipino politics: Development and decay*. Quezon City: Ateneo de Manila University Press.
Yawnghwe, Chao-Tzang. 1995. Burma: The depoliticization of the political. In *Political legitimacy in Southeast Asia*, ed. Muthiah Alagappa, 170–92. Stanford, Calif.: Stanford University Press.
Zakaria, Fareed. 2007. *The future of freedom: Illiberal democracy at home and abroad*. New York: Norton.
Zia-Zarifi, Abolhassan. 2004. *The biography of Hassan Zia-Zarifi: From Tehran University to the Evin killing fields*. Tehran: Amindezh.
Zones, Marvin. 1983. Iran: A theory of revolution from accounts of the revolution. *World Politics* 35, no. 4 (July): 586–606.

Zunes, Stephen. 1994. Unarmed insurrections against authoritarian governments in the third world: A new kind of revolution. *Third World Quarterly* 15, no. 3 (September): 403–26.

———. 1999. The origins of people power in the Philippines. In Zunes, Kurtz, and Asher, *Nonviolent social movements*, 129–57.

———. 2009a. Iran's history of civil insurrections. *Huffington Post*, June 19. http://www.huffingtonpost.com/stephen-zunes/irans-history-of-civil-in_b_217998.html.

———. 2009b. Weapons of mass democracy: Nonviolent resistance is the most powerful tactic against oppressive regimes. *Yes! Magazine*, September 16. http://www.yesmagazine.org/issues/learn-as-you-go/weapons-of-mass-democracy.

Zunes, Stephen, Lester Kurtz, and Sarah Beth Asher, eds. 1999. *Nonviolent social movements: A geographical perspective*. Malden, Mass.: Blackwell.

INDEX

Abdel Shafi, Haidar, 135
ABFSU. *See* All Burma Federation of Student Unions
Abrahms, Max, 25, 227
Abu Ayyash, Radwan, 140, 142
Abu Jihad, 121–22, 124
Ackerman, Peter, 14, 22, 60, 209, 215
Active Voices campaign (Madagascar), 215
Afghanistan, 42, 54, 56, 65, 206, 208
AFPLF. *See* Anti-Fascist People's Freedom League
Africa: anticolonial campaigns, 69; nonviolent campaigns listed, 233–42; rates of campaign success, 74(fig.). *See also specific countries*
African National Congress (ANC), 247n21, 248n31, 255n55
Ahmad, J., 255n55
Algeria, 122, 229; Algerian Revolution (1954–1962), 59
All Burma Federation of Student Unions (ABFSU), 183
All Burma Students' Democratic Front, 187
All Burma Young Monks' Union, 186
American Revolution, 222
Americas: nonviolent campaigns listed, 233–42; rates of campaign success, 74(fig.), 81(table). *See also specific countries*
ANC. *See* African National Congress
Andoni, Ghassan, 145
antiapartheid campaigns, 7, 27, 53, 223, 247n21. *See also* South Africa
Anti-Fascist People's Freedom League (AFPLF; Burma), 173
antioccupation campaigns, 6, 13, 45, 69, 70(table), 73. *See also* First Intifada; Palestinian Territories
antiregime campaigns. *See* Burmese uprising; Egypt; Iranian Revolution; People Power revolution; Tunisia
April 6 Liberation Movement (Philippines), 154, 255n5
Al-Aqsa Intifada, 26, 137

Aquino, Benigno, 150, 155–57, 171
Aquino, Cory, 5; and commitment to nonviolent discipline, 160, 167–68; consolidation of Aquino government, 170; and EDSA Revolution, 163; and elections of 1986; sworn in as president, 163; "triumph of the people" speech of February 16, 1986, 160–61
Arafat, Yasser, 121–22; and Gulf War, 134; and PLO declaration of independence, 132–33; and reasons for eventual failure of First Intifada, 145, 195, 197–98, 255n55; recognition of Israel's right to exist and renunciation of terrorism, 132; and Ship of Return incident (1988), 252n12
Armed Forces of the Philippines (AFP), 147
Arreguín-Toft, Ivan, 24, 65, 67, 246n16
arson, 154
Ash, Timothy Garton, 22
Ashwari, Hanan, 135
Asia, 88; nonviolent campaigns listed, 233–42; rates of campaign success, 74(fig.), 81(table). *See also specific countries*
assassinations, 35; Afghanistan, 42; Burma, 173; Iran, 92, 97–98, 250n3; Philippines, 147, 150, 155–57, 171
Aung Din, 183
Aung Gyi, 181
Aung San, 172–73
Aung San Suu Kyi, 189, 190, 201; explicit avoidance of attempts to divide the military, 189, 196, 197; house arrest, 183–84, 196; rise to power, 181–82
authoritarian regimes: as difficult opponents, 66–67; as most common regime type following violent campaigns, 60, 201, 205–16, 258n10; as most common regime type targeted by nonviolent campaigns, 66, 67(fig.); and political opportunity approach, 64; repressive theocracy following Iranian Revolution, 110, 116–18, 202, 219; and war as

authoritarian regimes *(continued)*
"good" for societies, 258n10. *See also* regime type
Awad, Mubarak, 131, 143–44

backfiring of repression. *See* repression, backfiring of
Bahrain, 229
Baker, James, 133, 196
Bakhtiar, Shapour, 108, 111
Baldwin, David, 26–27, 244n13
Ba Maw, 172–73
BANDILLA (Philippines umbrella group), 159
Barak, Ehud, 78
Barghouti, Husain, 126
BAYAN (Philippines umbrella organization), 158–59
Bayat, Asef, 104
Bazargan, Mehdi, 94, 102, 109, 117
BCP. *See* Burmese Communist Party
Behrooz, Maziar, 97
Beit Sahour village, 133–34, 253n30
Ben Ali, Zine el-Abidine, 229
Bengali self-determination campaign, 219
Benigno, Teodoro, 165
Bermeo, Nancy, 210–11
Bernhard, Michael, 211, 212
Birzeit Solidarity Committee (BSC), 130, 139
Bishara, Azmi, 144
Black Friday (September 8, 1978; Iran), 102–4
Black September (1970; Palestinian Territories), 122
Bloody Friday massacre (March 13, 1988; Burma), 177–78
Bob, Clifford, 54
bombings, 13, 35, 42, 56, 110
Bond, Doug, 244n19
Boudreau, Vincent: on Benigno Aquino, 155; on insurgencies in the Philippines, 149; on loyalty shifts and diverse participation, 165–66, 168–70, 189, 255nn8,9; on outcomes of prodemocracy movements in Asia, 23; on student exodus to join insurgencies, 256n5
boycotts, 6, 12, 31–32, 35, 44; Burma, 186, 190; Egypt, 230; Palestinian Territories, 119, 125, 138; Philippines, 161; South Africa, 27, 223
Bratton, Michael, 203
Brazil, 33(table)

Bringing Down a Dictator (film), 225
Brom, Shlomo, 254n37
BSC. *See* Birzeit Solidarity Committee
BSPP. *See* Burma Socialist Program Party
Buddhist monks' participation in Burmese uprising, 179, 180, 182, 186–87, 191
Bukhara'i, Muhammad, 250n3
Burma, 172–97; backfiring of repression, 187; and Bloody Friday massacre (1988), 177–78; cease-fire agreements with insurgent groups, 183–84; drug trafficking, 183, 257nn8,11; economic crisis of 1987, 177, 257n6; economic grievances and protests in the 1970s, 176; elections of 1990 and SLORC's refusal to honor results, 183–84; end of British rule, 173; ethnic divisions, 172–73, 256n2; external aid to insurgents, 175–76; general strike of August 1988, 180–82; history, 172–73; internecine violence among insurgents, 176; isolation of, 177, 185, 190; and lack of diplomatic pressure, 53; Maung Maung presidency, 181–82; National Democratic Front, 177; Ne Win's military coup and martial law, 174–77; Panglong Agreement, 173; protests in the 1960s, 175; Rangoon Spring period (June to September 1988), 179–82, 187; regime capabilities, 186, 188; regime censorship and elimination of independent media, 187; repression of activists, 175, 176, 180–84, 185(table), 186, 187; rise of Aung San Suu Kyi, 181–82; SLORC coup of September 1988, 182–84; statistics on outcomes and number of members in resistance campaigns, 33(table); student activism, 174–80, 186, 191, 197, 256n5; student exodus to rural insurgent groups, 175, 186, 196, 256n5; support form regional powers, 196; transition from democracy to dictatorship, 172–77; travel restrictions, 190; urban protest groups, 175; violent insurgencies, 57, 173–76, 183–84, 256nn3,4, 257n8. *See also* Burmese uprising; Ne Win; State Law and Order Restoration Council
Burma Socialist Program Party (BSPP), 174–75, 179, 186
Burmese Communist Party (BCP), 173, 175–76
Burmese uprising (1988–1990), 172, 177–91; analysis of case study, 184–91; Bud-

dhist monks' participation, 179, 180, 182, 186–87, 191; case study summary, 192–97, 194(table); coexistence with multiple armed factions, 184–88; communication, 178; contrast to armed struggle, 185(table); diversity of participants, 181, 185(table), 191; and 8-8-88 general strike, 180–82; explicit avoidance of attempts to divide the military, 189, 196, 197; and isolation of Burma, 185, 190; leadership, 182, 195–96; and media attention, 196; organization, 178–80; Rangoon Spring period (June to September 1988), 179–82, 187; reasons for failure, 184–91, 185(table), 195–97; repression of, 180–83, 185(table), 186–87; and SLORC coup of September 1988, 182–84; statistics on outcomes and number of members in resistance campaigns, 33(table); student activism, 177–80, 182, 186, 191, 197; tactics, 180–82, 190, 196–97; triggers to popular uprising, 177–79; turn toward violence, 182

Burns, Gene, 95

Bush, George H. W., 133, 134

business and professional classes, participation in resistance campaigns: Burma, 180, 191; Iran, 92, 94, 100, 103, 110–11, 113–14, 116; Palestinian Territories, 121, 145(table); Philippines, 154, 156, 157(table), 160, 162, 165, 166, 170, 247n21

Cambodia, 205

Carter, April, 13, 15

Carter, Jimmy, 98

Catholic Church (Philippines), 151–52, 160, 167, 195

CCIF. *See* Committee Confronting the Iron Fist

Cedar Revolution (Lebanon), 26, 56

Center for Victims of Torture, 224

Central America: nonviolent campaigns listed, 233–42

Chechen rebels, 24

children, 47, 129, 139, 142, 144, 162, 165, 206

Chile, 33(table), 38, 44, 56

China: aid to Burmese insurgents, 175–76; Chinese Revolution (1946–1950), 59, 65, 206, 209, 246n15; Cultural Revolution, 176, 206; and difficulties of inverse economic dependency relationship between citizens and state for Tibetans, 45; disruption of nonviolent campaigns, 225; and economic dependence of Tibet, 45; failure of anti-Japanese insurgency (1930s and '40s), 39; and lack of diplomatic pressure on Burma, 53; statistics on outcomes and number of members in resistance campaigns, 33(table); support for Kim Jong Il regime, 53; Tiananmen Square massacre, 39; ties to SLORC (Burma), 190, 196

Chin National Army (CNA; Burma), 257n8

CINC score (Composite Index of National Capabilities), 67, 68, 217, 249n3

civil disobedience. *See* nonviolent resistance tactics

civil resistance. *See* nonviolent resistance campaigns

civil society: and expectations of citizens shaped by nature of transition, 207–8, 211–12; and quality of democracy, 61; requirements for emergence of civil peace, 204–5; requirements for emergence of democracy, 202–4, 210–11, 258n16; shared expectations between rulers and ruled, 211; weak governments and civil-society institutions resulting from violent conflicts, 206–7. *See also* participation in resistance campaigns

civil wars in the postcampaign era, 201–8, 216–18, 217(table); and coexistence of violent and nonviolent campaigns, 202, 218; conflict trap, 204–5; definition of civil war, 258n8

Clandestine Front (East Timor), 3, 78

Clark, Howard, 13, 15

CNA. *See* Chin National Army

Coalition of Islamic Associations (Iran), 250n3

coercion, and leverage of violent campaigns, 42–46

Cold War, 75

Colombia, 57, 205, 206

commitment issues for resistance participants, 37–39

Committee Confronting the Iron Fist (CCIF; Palestinian Territories), 131, 139

communication within resistance campaigns: and barriers to participation, 35–36; Burma, 178; Egypt, 229; Iran, 100–102, 108, 111, 113–14, 116; Palestinian Territories, 125–28, 131; Philippines, 160, 161; and policy recommendations for ex

communication within resistance campaigns *(continued)*
 ternal actors, 223, 224; and satellite TV/Internet, 246n9
Communist Party of Burma, 173
Communist Party of the Philippines (CPP), 4, 148, 150, 151, 158, 255n3
concentration methods of resistance, 55–56, 193. *See also* Burmese uprising; First Intifada; Iranian Revolution; People Power revolution; protests; sit-ins
conflict trap, 204–5
contentious politics approach to explaining outcomes of resistance campaigns, 10, 17–18, 21, 23, 64, 66–69
Correlates of War (COW) database, 13, 67, 217, 258n8
Costa Rican Revolution (1948), 209, 210, 219
Council for a Community of Democracies, 223–24
Council of Peace and Security (Israel), 252n20
coups d'état, 13; Burma, 174–77, 182–84
COW. *See* Correlates of War (COW) database
CPP. *See* Communist Party of the Philippines
critical mass theories of collective action, 36, 114
Cuban Revolution (1953–1958), 39, 42, 59, 206, 208
Cultural Revolution (1966–1976; China), 176, 206
Cunningham, David E., 217
Czechoslovakia, 33(table)

DAB. *See* Democratic Alliance of Burma
Defiance Campaign (South Africa), 79
Democratic Alliance of Burma (DAB), 183, 187
Democratic Front for the Liberation of Palestine (DFLP), 121, 253n34
democratic regimes: and charismatic leaders, 209; democratic consolidation, 257n4; democratic regimes more likely to result from nonviolent transitions, 60–61, 201–16, 214(table), 215(fig.), 218–19; effect of successful violent insurgencies on probability of postconflict democracy, 209–12; effects of defeated violent insurgencies on democratic regimes, 216; effects of failed nonviolent campaigns on probability of postconflict democracy, 216; exceptional cases of democracies following violent campaigns, 209–10, 219; and expectations of citizens shaped by nature of transition, 207–8; fate of democracies that succumb to violent insurgencies, 215–16; frequent recurrence of people power campaigns as evidence of inherent institutional weaknesses, 211–12; and misperceptions about success of resistance campaigns in different regime types, 19; and political opportunity approach, 64; requirements for emergence of democracy, 202–4, 210–11, 258n16; scholars' expectations about, 66; stability of democratic regimes following successful nonviolent campaigns, 10, 29; and terrorism, 25–26; violent insurgencies' effectiveness against, 25, 64. *See also* regime type
DeNardo, James, 18
Denmark, 20
DFLP. *See* Democratic Front for the Liberation of Palestine
Diamond, Larry, 258n16
DigiActive, 224
diplomatic support, 223
A Diplomat's Handbook for Democracy Development Support, 223–24
direct defense (Arreguín-Toft's concept), 24
dispersion methods of resistance, 38, 56, 193. *See also* boycotts; Burmese uprising; First Intifada; Iranian Revolution; noise-making tactic; People Power revolution; stay-aways; strikes
Disraeli, Benjamin, 63
diversity of participants in resistance campaigns, 39–41; Burma, 181, 185(table), 191; Iran, 110, 112; Palestinian Territories, 136, 145(table), 146; Philippines, 157(table), 165, 168, 192
Dole, Robert, 133, 253n28
domestic mobilization. *See* participation in resistance campaigns
drug trafficking, 183, 257n11
Dumas, Alexander, 63
DuVall, Jack, 22, 227

Eastern Europe, 44
East Germany, 33(table), 39
East Timor, 3–4, 47, 53, 78, 243n1. *See also* Falintil

economic sanctions. *See* international sanctions
EDSA Revolution (Philippines), 161–64, 170, 255nn8,9
Egypt, 6, 36, 53, 56, 229–31
Elliott, Ann, 53
El Salvador, 47, 247n22
endogeneity, as possible explanation for outcomes of campaigns, 28, 63–64, 76–82, 246n15, 250n12
Enrile, Juan Ponce, 150, 156, 161–64, 166–67
ethnic factionalism, 63–64, 80, 172–73
Europe: nonviolent campaigns listed, 233–42; rates of campaign success, 74(fig.), 81(table). *See also specific countries*
external actors, 52–55, 61, 193; and anti-apartheid campaign in South Africa, 27, 53, 223, 247n21; and Burma's isolation, 185(table), 190; Chinese support for Burma's insurgents, 175–76; decline in U.S. support for Marcos regime, 159, 163, 168, 196, 247n21; and delegitimization of movements, 55, 197, 225; diplomatic support, 27, 53–54, 185, 223; effects of persistent support for opponent regime, 197; external support leading to insurgents' mistreatment of civilian population, 55; fickleness of state sponsors, 54; foreign state support and success of violent campaigns, 10, 11, 53–54, 59, 202, 222; foreign state support not correlated with outcomes of nonviolent campaigns, 59; free-rider problem of state support, 54; greater international support for non-violent campaigns, 53; international actions complementing domestic actions, 247n21; international repercussions of crackdowns on terrorists vs. nonviolent civilians, 53; and leverage in times of economic crisis, 247n21; nuclear weapons and international conflict, 63–64; percentage of nonviolent vs. violent campaigns receiving diplomatic support, 53; percentage of nonviolent vs. violent campaigns receiving material support from external states, 54; perception of First Intifada as violent, 119–20, 142–45; policy recommendations, 27, 222–26; response to PLO declaration of independence, 132–33; and secession campaigns, 69; statistics, 49(table). *See also* international sanctions

Facebook, 224, 229
failed campaigns, 11, 39, 53; effects of failed nonviolent vs. failed violent campaigns on probability of postconflict democracy, 216; emergence of nonviolent campaigns from failed violent campaigns, 78; and endogeneity problem, 63; likelihood of democracy greater following failed nonviolent campaigns than successful violent campaigns, 202; rates of success, partial success, and failure, 9(table); reasons for eventual failure in Palestinian Territories, 120, 140–44, 146, 195, 197, 255n55; reasons for failure in Burma, 184–91, 185(table), 195–97; successful and failed nonviolent campaigns compared, 193–97; violent campaigns as possible failed nonviolent campaigns, 76–77
Falintil, 3–4, 42, 78, 243n2
Fanon, Frantz, 32, 245n4
FARC insurgency (Colombia), 57
Fatah, 121, 141, 142
Fearon, James, 258n8
fedayeen (Iran), 96, 97, 108, 112, 116
First Intifada (1987–1992), 26, 119–46; and Arab population of Israel, 127–28, 251n8; and backfiring of regime violence, 145(table), 146; Beit Sahour village's civil disobedience, 133–34, 253n30; case study summary, 192–97, 194(table); and change in status quo, 135–36; and civil disobedience among security forces, 130, 252n20; communication, 125–28, 131; contrast to armed struggle, 26, 119, 138, 145(table), 192; and deportation of Mubarak Awad, 131; diversity of participants, 134, 145(table), 146; effectiveness lost when violence introduced, 77, 119–20, 134, 137; and election of 1992, 135–36; emergence of, 119, 123; external perceptions of, 119–20, 142–45; impact of Gulf War and Madrid Conference, 134–35; impact of mass participation on perceptions of resistance legitimacy, 47; impact on Israeli society and the region, 139–40; and international sanctions, 145(table); and Islamist groups, 128–29; Israel and PLO surprised by, 123–25; leadership, 120, 124–27, 132, 138, 140–41, 195–97; and loyalty shifts of regime supporters, 130, 145(table), 252n20; and media attention,

First Intifada (1987–1992) *(continued)* 119, 129, 134, 142; media censorship, 127, 129–30; and modification of Palestinian goals, 132; nonviolent nature of, 119, 120(table); organization of, 124–25, 251n5, 255n55; and Oslo Accords (1993), 136–37, 254nn36,37; overreliance on Arafat, 197–98; as partial success, 131–32, 138, 145(table); and PLO, 122–27, 132–33, 136–37; reasons for eventual failure, 120, 134, 137, 140–44, 146, 195, 197, 255n55; repression of, 127, 129–31, 133–34, 146; and stone-throwing, 119, 120, 143; and tactical diversity and innovation, 119, 125, 138, 145(table); and U.S. policy, 140, 144. *See also* Palestinian Territories
A Force More Powerful (DuVall), 22
fraternization tactic, 107, 162, 166, 210
Freedom House, 258n14
free-rider problem of state support, 54
Fretilin, 3, 78

Gamson, William, 15
Gandhi, Mahatma, 56
Geddes, Barbara, 203
genocide, 20, 221
geographic region, as possible explanation for outcomes of campaigns, 63, 70(table), 73–74, 81(table)
Georgia, 6, 207, 209, 225
Germany, 20. *See also* Nazis
Ghobarah, Hazem Adam, 206
Gleditsch, Kristian, 13, 259n22
goals of resistance campaigns. *See* political objectives of resistance campaigns
go-slow workplace actions, 56
government capacity. *See* regime capabilities
Greece, 14, 33(table)
Gruen, George, 253n29
guerrilla warfare, 24–25; Iran, 42, 92, 95–98, 108, 111; and media attention, 42; Palestinian Territories, 122; Philippines, 149–50, 166; and physical abilities of participants, 35; and regime capabilities to combat unconventional, indirect tactics, 65; and resilience of opposition, 57; United States, 222. *See also* violent campaigns and insurgencies
Gulf War (1990–1991), 24, 134–35
Gush Emunim, 121
Habibie, B. J., 4

Hamas, 128–29, 141, 142, 253n34
Helvey, Robert, 21–22, 247n20
Hitler, Adolf, 20, 24
honking of horns, 38, 153
Horowitz, Donald, 69
How the Weak Win Wars (Arreguín-Toft), 24
Hufbauer, Gary Clyde, 53
Humor and satire, 36
Hussein, King of Jordan, 131–32
al-Husseini, Feisal, 135
Huth, Paul, 206
Hyderabad, 69

identity cards, burned, 133–34, 138
improvised explosive devices (IEDs), 42, 56
Independence Intifada (Lebanon). *See* Cedar Revolution
India, 56, 63–64, 69
Indochina, French attempts to regain control of, 65
Indonesia, 3–4, 247n21. *See also* East Timor
information, dissemination of. *See* communication within campaigns
insurgencies. *See* guerrilla warfare; nonviolent resistance campaigns compared to violent campaigns; violent campaigns and insurgencies
Integrated Data for Events Analysis, 244n19
international community. *See* external actors
international sanctions, 52–53; and East Timor, 53; lack of, and Burma, 185(table); not correlated with outcomes of nonviolent resistance campaigns, 59; and the Philippines, 157(table); and South Africa, 53; statistics, 49(table)
Internet, 224, 229–30, 246n9
Intifada. *See* Al-Aqsa Intifada; First Intifada
Iran: aftermath of revolution, 110, 116–18, 202, 207, 219; assassinations, 92, 97–98, 250n3; Bakhtiar government (caretaker government), 108, 111; and Carter administration, 98; demonstrations of 2011, 229; early opposition groups, 94–95; guerrilla resistance, 42, 92, 95–98, 108, 111; Islamist challenge to Shah, 94–95; lead-up to revolution, 92–98; media attention, 42; model predictions about posttransition regime type, 259n23; repressive Pahlavi regime, 93, 95, 98–107; secret police (SAVAK), 93, 97; Siahkal attack (1971), 97; statistics on outcomes

and number of members in resistance campaigns, 33(table); White Revolution (1963), 93, 95. *See also* fedayeen; Iranian Revolution; Khomeini, Ayatollah Ruhollah; Mujahedin; Pahlavi, Shah Reza

Iranian Revolution (1977–1979), 92–118, 192; aftermath as exceptional case, 110, 202, 219; and ambiguous ideology, 95, 112, 118; analysis of case study, 110–18; backfiring of repression, 108, 112; Black Friday (September 8, 1978), 102–4; case study summary, 192–97, 194(table); communication, 100–102, 108, 111, 113–14, 116; conscious refraining from use of violence, 115–16; contrast to armed struggle, 33(table), 34, 110–12, 117(table), 192; and death of Mostafa Khomeini, 98–99; diversity of participants, 110, 112; end of monarchy and return of Khomeini, 108–10; as example of successful nonviolent campaign, 116; impact of mass participation on perceptions of resistance legitimacy, 48; increase in commitment of population after advent of nonviolent campaign, 38; Islamist opposition, 101; leadership, 112–13, 195, 251n9; lead-up to revolution, 92–98; liberal opposition, 100, 110; and loyalty shifts of regime supporters, 92, 93, 107–8, 109–10, 112, 114; martial law and general strike, 103–7, 115; mobilization of Khomeini's supporters, 98–100; mutiny at Tehran air force base (February 1979), 109–10, 251n8; protests sparked by Abadan fire and Black Friday, 102–4; Qom massacre, 101, 115; and regime capabilities, 105–8, 114; as regime change case study, 92; repression of, 98–107, 109–10, 115; repressive theocracy following, 110, 116–18, 202, 219; resilience of movement, 114–15; Shah's offer of concessions, 102–3; struggles over meaning of revolution after fall of the monarchy, 95; tactics, 56, 99, 101–7, 110–13; ulema-bazaari network and 1978 mass mobilization, 100–102, 111, 113–14, 116; violent conflicts between Islamists and leftists, 110; and violent fringe groups, 118. *See also* Khomeini, Ayatollah Ruhollah

Iran-Iraq War, 117

Iraq, 42, 77, 229

Ireland, 77

Islam: Muslim insurgency in the Philippines, 149, 151; religious activism in Iran, 94, 98–102, 110–11, 113–14, 116, 195, 251n9; religious activism in the Palestinian Territories, 120, 128–29, 141, 145(table), 253n34

Islamic Government (Khomeini), 95

Islamic Jihad, 128–29, 141, 253n34

Israel, 136–37; and backfiring of repression, 129–31, 140; early definition of "terrorist activities," 120; and economic dependence of occupied territories, 121, 140; election of Rabin (1992), 135–36; impact of First Intifada, 130–31, 139–40, 252nn19,20; Jewish resistance to British occupation of Palestine, 219; Madrid Conference (1991), 134–35; media censorship, 127, 129–30; origins of resistance to occupation, 120–22; Oslo Accords (1993), 136–37, 195, 254nn36,37; perception of First Intifada as violent, 120, 142–45; and Prevention of Terror Law, 130, 252n18; reinvigoration of peace movement inside Israel, 130–31, 252nn19,20; repression in response to PLO violence, 122; repression of activism, 77, 127, 129–31, 133–34, 146; security forces' refusal to serve in the occupied territories, 130, 252n20; settlement movement, 121, 135–37, 140, 253nn27,29,35; Ship of Return incident (1988), 127–28, 144, 252n12; surprised by sudden onset of First Intifada, 123–25; U.S. pressure on, 133, 196; U.S. support for, 253n28. *See also* First Intifada; Palestinian Territories; Shamir, Yitzhak

Italy, 54

Japan, 190, 196

Jazani, Bizhan, 96

Jordan, 54, 122, 131–32, 140, 229

Jraey, Radi, 251n5

Kalyvas, Stathis, 246n11

Karakoc, Akrem, 211, 212

Karatnycky, Adrian, 60, 209, 215

Karen National Union (KNU; Burma), 57, 173, 256nn3,4

Karenni National Progressive Party (KNPP), 173

Karl, Terry Lynn, 208

Karzai, Hamid, 42
KBL. *See* Kusang Bagon Lipunan
Keller, Adam, 143
Khin Nyunt, 182
Khomeini, Ayatollah Ruhollah: background and rise to power, 94–95; call for calm and dispersion tactics, 101–2; conscious refraining from use of violence, 115–16; exile, 95; ideology and plan for government, 95; mobilization of supporters, 98–100; response to Shah's offer of concessions, 102; return from exile, 108–10
Khomeini, Mostafa, 98–99
kidnappings, 13
Kilusang Mayo Uno (KMU; Philippines), 152, 159
KMP. *See* Peasant Movement of the Philippines
KMU. *See* Kilusang Mayo Uno
KNPP. *See* Karenni National Progressive Party
KNU. *See* Karen National Union
Kocher, Matthew, 246n11
Kruegler, Christopher, 14, 22
Kurzman, Charles, 98, 105, 107, 112, 251n9
Kusang Bagon Lipunan (KBL; Philippines), 153

LAFM. *See* Light a Fire Movement
Lance, Mark, 144–45, 255n55
Laurel, Jose, 155
Laurel, Salvador, 155, 163, 167
leadership of resistance campaigns: Burma, 182, 195–96; consequences of lack of unity, 126, 132, 141, 182, 195–96; and importance of maintaining nonviolent discipline, 115–16, 120, 126, 160, 167–68, 218, 246n15, 247n27, 257n3; Iran, 112–13, 195, 251n9; Palestinian Territories, 120, 124–27, 132, 138, 140–41, 195–97; Philippines, 160, 166, 167–68, 195; and post-conflict regime type, 209; problems of reliance on single personality, 196–97; and success of nonviolent resistance campaigns, 195
Lebanon, 6; frequent recurrence of people power campaigns as evidence of inherent institutional weaknesses, 211; and PLO, 122–23; protests, 36; statistics on outcomes and number of members in resistance campaigns, 33(table); success of nonviolent resistance campaigns, 26; tent city in Beirut, 56
leverage, mechanisms of, 41–59; defined, 41; disruptive effects of organized noncooperation, 10, 41, 44–45, 82, 104, 115, 188, 220, 246n16; impact on target regime, 41–42, 44–47; international sanctions and external support, 52–55; loss of regime supporters, 44–53; and violence, 42–46. *See also* external actors; international sanctions; organized noncooperation; repression, backfiring of; security forces, defection of
Liberation Movement of Iran, 94
Libya, 149, 229
Light a Fire Movement (LAFM; Philippines), 154
Linz, Juan J., 210
Long, J. Scott, 248n38
loyalty shifts of security forces and other regime supporters, 10–11, 44–50, 58, 61, 82, 193, 220; and case study summary, 193; elite support, 46–50; Iran, 93, 107–8, 109–10; lack of, in Burma, 185(table), 188–89; and mass mobilization in some violent campaigns, 59; Palestinian Territories, 130, 145(table); Philippines, 157(table), 161–63, 165–66, 169, 255nn8,9. *See also* repression, backfiring of
LTTE. *See* Tamil Tigers
Lyall, Jason, 13, 25, 26

Mabuhay Philippines Movement, 255n4
Madagascar, 6, 33(table), 215
Madani, Ayatollah Asadollah, 116
Madrid Conference (1991), 134–35
Malaysia, 149
Malcolm X, 3
Maleki, Khalil, 94
Mansour, Hasan Ali, 250n3
Mao Zedong, 248n39
Marcos, Ferdinand, 5, 147, 255n5; counterinsurgency campaign, 149, 151, 155; declaration of martial law (September 1972), 148–50; decline in U.S. support for, 159, 163, 168, 196, 247n21; deteriorating health, 155; and economic crisis of early 1980s, 154–55; and EDSA Revolution, 163; and elections of 1978, 153; and elections of 1986, 159–61; loss of power, 163–64; martial law lifted (1981), 155, 255n5; "normalization" policies, 155; rise

to power, 147; strategic hamlet counterinsurgency technique, 151, 155
Martin, Brian, 50, 247n26
Maung Maung, 181–82
Maybury-Lewis, David, 244n19
McAdam, Doug, 19
media: Burma, 187, 196; importance of media coverage of interactions between unarmed protesters and security forces, 247n26; issues kept alive through terrorism and guerrilla violence, 42; and magnification of impact of protest activities, 36; Palestinian Territories, 119, 127, 129, 134, 142; Philippines, 160, 161, 162, 166, 196; and policy recommendations for external actors, 224
Mendoza, Amado, Jr., 255n5
Merriman, Hardy, 227
Mexico, 33(table), 216
Middle East, 88; nonviolent campaigns listed, 233–42; rates of campaign success, 74(fig.), 81(table); uprisings of 2011, 6. See also specific countries
Milhem, Mohammed, 127–28
military. See security forces; security forces, defection of
Milosevic, Slobodan, 77
Mindanao independence movement, 149
MKO (Iran), 96
Moaddel, Mansoor, 115
modernization theory, 203
Montiel, Cristina Jayme, 164
moral barriers to participation in resistance campaigns, 36–37
Morocco, 229
Moro National Liberation Movement, 149
mosque network (Iran), 100–102, 111, 113–14, 116, 195
Mossad, 128
Mossadegh, Mohammad, 93
mountainous terrain, 80
Mubarak, Hosni, 229–31
Mujahedin (Iran), 96, 112, 115
Muslim Brotherhood, 128
Myanmar National Democratic Alliance Army, 183

NAMFREL. See National Movement for Free Elections
Nashashibi, Rana, 139
Nathan, Abie, 252n18

National Citizens' Movement for Free Elections (Philippines), 5
National Coalition government of the Union of Burma (NCGUB), 187–88
National Democratic Front (NDF; Burma), 177
National Democratic Front (NDF; Philippines), 151
National League for Democracy (NLD; Burma), 172, 183–84
National Movement for Free Elections (NAMFREL; Philippines), 158, 160
National Unity Party (Burma), 184
NAVCO. See Nonviolent and Violent Campaigns and Outcomes (NAVCO) data set
Nazis: Danish resistance, 20; French resistance, 219; Greek resistance, 14; ineffectiveness of bombing British civilian targets, 24; and misperceptions about success of resistance campaigns in different regime types, 20; success of Rosenstraße protests, 20; support for Franco, 54
NCGUB. See National Coalition government of the Union of Burma
NDF. See National Democratic Front
negative radical flank effect, 43, 152
Nejat-hoseini, Mohsen, 96
Nepal, 6, 42, 43
Netanyahu, Benjamin, 135
Ne Win: and BSPP congress of 1988, 179; counterinsurgency campaign, 175; demonetization policy, 177, 257n6; military coup and martial law, 174–77; repression of activism, 175, 176, 180–81; and SLORC coup of September 1988, 182–84
New People's Army (NPA; Philippines), 4, 167
New Tactics in Human Rights project, 224
Nigeria, 33(table)
NLD. See National League for Democracy
noise-making tactic, 38, 56, 153
Nonviolent and Violent Campaigns and Outcomes (NAVCO) data set, 6, 231
nonviolent resistance campaigns: coexistence with violent campaigns, 78, 168–69, 184–88, 202, 218, 257n3; contrast to violent campaigns (see nonviolent resistance campaigns compared to violent campaigns); and credibility as negotiat-

nonviolent resistance campaigns *(continued)*
ing partners of nonviolent participants, 11; defined, 11–12, 243n5; emergence from failed violent campaigns, 78; failures *(see* failed campaigns); frequent recurrence of people power campaigns as evidence of inherent institutional weaknesses, 211–12; list of, 233–42; misperceptions about success in different regime types, 19–20; overview of civil resistance research, 21–25; policy implications, 27, 222–26; and postconflict regime type *(see* regime type); potential negative effects, 206; resilience of, 57–58, 114–15, 193, 221; scholarly implications of research, 18–27; successful and failed nonviolent campaigns compared, 193–97. *See also* leadership of resistance campaigns; nonviolent resistance tactics; organization of resistance campaigns; outcomes of resistance campaigns; participation in resistance campaigns; political objectives of resistance campaigns; research methodology; statistics on nonviolent vs. violent campaigns

nonviolent resistance campaigns compared to violent campaigns, 6–7, 215(fig.); Burma, 185(table); and case study summary, 192–93; commitment issues for participants, 37–39; difficulties of comparison studies, 15–17; and dissemination of information, 35–36; effectiveness of violence, 25–27; frequency, 7(table); greater international support for nonviolent campaigns, 53; Iran, 110–12, 117(table); likelihood of democracy greater following failed nonviolent campaigns than successful violent campaigns, 202; and moral barriers to participation, 36–37; number of civilian casualties, 60; outcomes and number of participants, 32–34; Palestinian Territories, 26, 119, 138, 145(table), 192; participation advantage of nonviolent campaigns, 10–11, 28, 30–62, 40(fig.), 82; Philippines, 157(table), 165–67, 192; physical risks and costs, 34–35; and postconflict civil wars, 201–8, 216–18; and postconflict regime type, 60–61, 201–16, 214(table), 215(fig.), 218–19; success rate of violent vs. nonviolent campaigns, 7, 9(table), 11, 73(table); violent insurgency more successful in secession cases, 7, 73(table), 220. *See also* statistics on nonviolent vs. violent campaigns

nonviolent resistance tactics: acts of omission/acts of commission, 12, 244n10; boycotts *(see* boycotts); candlelight vigils, 38; concentration methods, 55–56 *(see also* protests; sit-ins); contrast to "normal" political action, 12, 243n8; dispersion methods, 38, 55–56 *(see also* boycotts; stay-aways; strikes); fraternization tactic, 107, 111, 162, 166, 210; importance of maintaining nonviolent discipline, 115–16, 120, 126, 160, 167–68, 218, 246n15, 247n27, 257n3; list of, 6, 12, 38; low risk compared to violent methods, 38; mass protests *(see* protests); noise-making, 38, 56, 153; organized noncooperation *(see* organized noncooperation); sit-ins, 12, 31, 35, 56, 158; stay-aways, 12, 31, 38, 101, 104, 113 *(see also* strikes); strikes *(see* strikes); tactical diversity and innovation, 10–11, 39, 40, 55–56, 119, 125, 138, 145(table), 162, 166, 168, 193, 248n36; underground schools, 38; wearing of opposition insignia, 38. *See also* Burmese uprising; First Intifada; Iranian Revolution; People Power revolution

North America: nonviolent campaigns listed, 233–42

North Korea, 53

North Vietnamese Revolution, 206

NPA. *See* New People's Army

nuclear weapons, 63–64

objectives of resistance campaigns. *See* political objectives of resistance campaigns

occupations (nonviolent tactic), 31, 56

Oman, 229

Orange Revolution (Ukraine), 56, 202

Organization of People's Feda'i Guerrillas. *See* fedayeen

organization of resistance campaigns: Burma, 178–79, 180; Iran, 100–102, 111, 113–14, 116, 195; Palestinian Territories, 124–25, 251n5, 255n55; Philippines, 158–59, 195

organized noncooperation, 6, 12, 30, 38, 43, 227; and American Revolution, 222; Burma, 184; disruptive effects of, 10, 41,

44–45, 82, 104, 115, 188, 220, 246n16; Iran, 92, 103–7, 110, 115; and loyalty shifts, 46, 50; Palestinian Territories, 119, 133–34; Philippines, 44, 158–59; and violent insurgencies, 59

Oslo Accords (1993), 136–37, 195, 254nn36,37

Otpor, 46–47, 54, 77

outcomes of resistance campaigns, 63–91, 70–71(table); and backfiring of regime violence, 20, 50–53, 82 (*see also* repression, backfiring of); civil wars in the postcampaign era, 201–8n29, 216–18; comparison of successful and failed nonviolent campaigns, 193–97; contentious politics approach, 10, 17–18, 21, 64, 66–69; criteria for judging outcomes, 14; distribution of campaign outcomes by campaign objective, 73(table); effects of regime crackdowns on probability of success, 51, 51–52(tables); endogeneity issue, 76–82, 246n15, 250n12; and exceptionally difficult target regimes, 66–69; external support, 52–55, 59; factors found not to be significant, 63–64, 249n4; failed campaigns (*see* failed campaigns); and geographical region, 73–74, 81(table); importance of maintaining nonviolent discipline, 115–16, 120, 126, 160, 167–68, 218, 246n15, 247n27, 257n3; and international sanctions, 52–53, 59; and likelihood of victory, 76–81; list of campaigns and outcomes, 233–42; loyalty shifts of security forces and other regime supporters (*see* loyalty shifts of security forces and other regime supporters); most critical components of successful campaigns, 58–59, 61; need for both quantity and quality of participation, 39–40; negative effect of nonviolent resistance on likelihood of success in secession campaigns, 7, 73(table), 220; and negative radical flank effect, 43; overview of structural explanations, 63–69, 70–71(table); partial success, defined, 249n6; participation advantage of nonviolent campaigns, 10–11, 28, 30–62, 40(fig.), 82 (*see also* participation in resistance campaigns); perception of opposition's legitimacy as bargaining partner, 48; persistence necessary but not sufficient, 58; and political objectives, 69–73; political opportunity approach, 19, 64; and positive radical flank effect, 43; postconflict regime types, 29, 201–16, 218–19; and regime capabilities, 64, 67–68; and regime type, 64, 66, 67(fig.), 221; resilience of resistance movements, 57–58; resistance campaigns as competitions over who succeeds at dividing and ruling the opponent, 195; resource mobilization theory, 20–21; and reverse causation issue, 246n15; and stability of democratic regimes following successful nonviolent campaigns, 29; and strategic and tactical choices, 39–41, 55–56; strategic interaction thesis, 65; successful violent campaigns, 11, 59–61, 73, 219; and timing of campaigns, 70–71(tables), 75; voluntaristic features of campaigns (especially skills of resistors) as better predictors of success than structural determinants, 18–19

PA. *See* Palestinian Authority

Pahlavi, Shah Reza, 92; background and rise to power, 93; and Carter administration, 98, 100; counterinsurgency campaign, 97–98; economic policies, 94; illness, 105; martial law and general strike, 103–7; offer of concessions, 102–3; perceived as puppet of the West, 93–94; repression under regime, 93, 95, 98–107; signs of leniency, 98; unpopularity of, 93–94; White Revolution (1963), 93. *See also* Iranian Revolution

Pakistan, 42; Bengali self-determination campaign, 219; and Burma, 190; and nuclear weapons, 63–64; sanctuary for Al-Qaeda affiliates, 57; support for anti-Soviet insurgency in Afghanistan, 54

Palestine Communist Party (PCP), 141

Palestine Liberation Front (PLF), 134

Palestine Liberation Organization (PLO), 26, 141; and Arab population of Israel, 251n8; bases of operation, 122–23; contrast to First Intifada, 119, 138; declaration of independence, 132–33, 253n24; and fickleness of state sponsors, 54; and First Intifada, 122–27, 141, 145, 195; and Iran, 115; and media attention, 42; modification of political position due to First Intifada, 140; origins and composition,

Palestine Liberation Organization (PLO) *(continued)*
 121–22; and Oslo Accords (1993), 136–37, 195, 254nn36,37; and reasons for eventual failure of First Intifada, 120, 141, 145, 195; and Ship of Return incident (1988), 127–28, 144, 252n12; violent tactics, 121–22. *See also* Arafat, Yasser
Palestinian Authority (PA), 136–38, 140, 195, 254n37
Palestinian Communist Party (PCP), 121, 126
Palestinian Territories: as antioccupation campaign case study, 72; Al-Aqsa Intifada, 26, 137; choice of violence or nonviolent resistance, 77–78; coexistence of violent and nonviolent campaigns, 121–22, 137, 218; demonstrations of 2011, 229; early nonviolent direct action, 121; economic dependence on Israel, 45, 121, 140; effectiveness of First Intifada lost when violence introduced, 77; failure to achieve unified leadership, 141; Israeli repression, 77, 127, 143(table), 146; origins of resistance to Israeli occupation, 120–22; and Oslo Accords (1993), 136–37, 195; Palestinian Authority (PA), 136–38, 140, 195, 254n37; Palestinian issue kept alive through violence, 42; and PLO armed struggle, 121–22; PLO-led government-in-exile, 122; post-Oslo status, 136–37; public opinion on violent vs. nonviolent resistance, 138, 254n42; repression of activism, 127, 129–31, 133–34, 146; Ship of Return incident (1988), 127–28, 144, 252n12; success of First Intifada compared to PLO movement and Al-Aqsa Intifada, 26. *See also* First Intifada
Pape, Robert, 25–26
participation in resistance campaigns, 30–62; barriers to, 34–39; commitment issues for participants, 37–39; consequences of the nature of participation in violent vs. nonviolent campaigns, 207; correlation with success of nonviolent campaigns, 32–35, 33(table), 39–41, 40(fig.), 58, 61; critical-mass theories of collective action, 36; critiques of participation viewpoint, 63–64; defined, 30–32; diversity of participants, 39–41, 61; Egypt, 229; and enhanced resilience, 10; free-rider problem of state support, 54; greater appeal of nonviolent vs. violent campaigns, 32–33; and greater likelihood of links between elites/security forces and resistance in movements with mass participation, 47; impact of mass participation on perceptions of resistance legitimacy, 48; and information dissemination, 35–36; and loyalty shifts of security forces and regime supporters, 10, 44–53, 61; mass support for some violent campaigns (Russian Revolution, etc.), 59; mechanisms of leverage, 41–59; mobilization as necessary but not sufficient condition for success, 194; moral barriers, 36–37; need for quantity and quality of participation, 39–40; odds of success improved through greater participation, 39–59 *(see also specific mechanisms)*; participation advantage of nonviolent campaigns, 10–11, 28, 30–62, 40(fig.), 82; physical risks and costs of participation, 34–35, 37–39; and reasons for failure of nonviolent campaigns, 11 *(see also* failed campaigns); and research methodology, 245nn1,3,7; and resilience of opposition, 57–58; and reverse causation issue, 246n15; summary of conclusions, 220–26; and tactical diversity and innovation, 10–11, 55–56, 248n36. *See also* Burmese uprising; First Intifada; Iranian Revolution; People Power revolution
PCP. *See* Palestinian Communist Party
Peace Now (Israel), 130, 252nn19,20
Peasant Movement of the Philippines (KMP), 159
People Power revolution (1983–1986; Philippines), 147–71; analysis of case study, 164–71; Aquino's "triumph of the people" speech of February 16, 1986, 161; and assassination of Benigno Aquino, 155–57, 171; and backfiring of regime violence, 196; case study summary, 192–97, 194(table); and Catholic Church, 151–52, 154, 160, 167; coexistence with violent campaigns, 78, 167–69, 192; communication, 160, 161, 166; contrast to armed struggle, 157(table), 165–67, 192; and decline of U.S. support for Marcos regime, 159, 163, 168, 196, 247n21; diversity of participants, 157(table), 165, 168, 192; and

elections of 1984, 157–59; and elections of 1986, 159–61; increase in commitment of population after advent of nonviolent campaign, 38; leadership, 166, 195; and leadership's commitment to nonviolent discipline, 160, 167–68; low barriers to participation, 165; loyalty shifts of security forces and other regime supporters, 155, 157(table), 161–63, 165–66, 168, 169–70, 255nn8,9 (*see also* EDSA revolution); and media attention, 196; mobilization of business class and other mainstream elements, 156; nonviolent campaign compared to violent campaign, 192; number of participants, 164; organization of, 158–59; participants' motivations, 164; success of, 161–64; tactics, 156, 158–62, 166, 168

People's Volunteer Organization (Burma), 173

Peterson, Roger, 31

PFLP. *See* Popular Front for the Liberation of Palestine

Philippines, 4–5; assassination of Benigno Aquino, 155–57, 171; backfiring of repression, 157(table), 167; Catholic Church-supported activism, 148, 151–52, 154, 160, 167; coexistence of violent and nonviolent campaigns, 78, 168–69; consolidation of Aquino government, 170; costs to regime of nonviolent resistance, 44; counterinsurgency campaign, 149, 151, 155; declaration of martial law (September 1972), 148–50; decline in U.S. support for Marcos regime, 159, 163, 168, 196, 247n21; dispersed tactics of resistance following elections of 1978, 153; early protest activity, 148–49; and economic crisis of early 1980s, 154–55; EDSA Revolution, 161–64, 170; elections of 1978, 153; elections of 1984, 157–59; elections of 1986, 159–61; expansion of grassroots movement and trade union activism in the late 1970s–early 1980s, 152–54; "First Quarter Storm," 148; impact of mass participation on perceptions of resistance legitimacy, 47; impact of violent insurgency on nonviolent campaign, 168–69; increase in commitment of population after advent of nonviolent campaign, 38; Marcos's loss of power, 163–64; Marcos's rise to power, 147; martial law lifted (1981), 155; Mindanao independence movement, 149; Moro National Liberation Movement, 149; nonviolent and violent resistance campaigns compared, 157(table); recurrence of people power movements to resolve disputes, 211, 248n40; reformist and underground opposition in the 1970s, 150–51; repression of activism, 150–51, 155, 157, 157(table); statistics on outcomes and number of members in resistance campaigns, 33(table); strategic hamlet counterinsurgency technique, 151, 155; student activism, 148, 153; violent resistance to regime, 149–51, 153–54, 166, 167, 192, 255n5. *See also* Aquino, Cory; Marcos, Ferdinand; People Power revolution

Pinochet, Augusto, 38, 56

PLF. *See* Palestine Liberation Front

PLO. *See* Palestinian Liberation Organization

Poland, 33(table), 36

police. *See* security forces; security forces, defection of

policy implications of research on nonviolent resistance, 27, 222–26

"political jiu-jitsu," 247n26

political objectives of resistance campaigns, 9(table), 12, 69–73, 70(table), 73(table). *See also* secession campaigns

political opportunity approach, 19, 64

The Politics of Nonviolent Action (Sharp), 21

Popovic, Srdja, 46–47

Popular Front for the Liberation of Palestine (PFLP), 121, 142, 253n34

positive radical flank effect, 43, 169

pots and pans, banging on, 38, 56, 153

Pouyan, Amir Parviz, 96

poverty, 80

power of target regimes. *See* regime capabilities

process tracing, 88

Program on Nonviolent Sanctions and Cultural Survival, 244n19

protests, 6, 12, 31; Burma, 174–81; choice of slogans, 107, 112; Egypt, 229; festival-like atmosphere, 36, 162; fraternization tactic, 107, 111, 162, 166, 210; Iran, 99, 102–3, 110–13; Palestinian Territories, 119, 123; Philippines, 156, 162; and risks

protests *(continued)*
  of regime violence, 56; spontaneous emergence, 119, 123
Protocol for the Assessment of Nonviolent Direct Action project, 244n19
Putnam, Robert, 211

Al-Qaeda, 57
Qom massacre, 115

Rabin, Yitzhak, 135–36
radical flank effect, 152, 169
radio, 160, 161, 166, 224
RAM. *See* Reform the Armed Forces Movement
Ramos, Fidel, 161–63, 166–67
Randle, Michael, 13, 15
Rasler, Karen, 113
Ratsiraka, Didier, 215
Reagan, Ronald, 5, 163, 196
Reform the Armed Forces Movement (RAM; Philippines), 160
regime capabilities, 63, 243n7; Burma, 186, 188; exceptionally powerful regimes, 67–68; Iran, 105–8, 114; and political opportunity approach, 64; and unconventional, indirect tactics of violent insurgencies, 65; and war as "good" for societies, 258n10
regime change campaigns, 6, 9(table), 13, 70(table). *See also* Burmese uprising; Iranian Revolution; People Power revolution
regime features, as possible explanation for outcomes of campaigns. *See* regime capabilities; regime type; repression
regime type, 70(table); misperceptions about success of resistance campaigns in different regime types, 19–20, 221; and modes of transition, 204; and onset of violent campaigns, 80; and political opportunity approach, 64; regime type following nonviolent vs. violent transitions, 60–61, 201–16, 214(table), 215(fig.), 218–19, 222, 258n17, 259n20. *See also* authoritarian regimes; democratic regimes
regions. *See* geographic region, as possible explanation for outcomes of campaigns
religious activism: Burma, 179, 180, 182, 186–87, 191; Iran, 94, 98–102, 110–11, 113–14, 116, 195, 251n9; Palestinian Territories, 120, 128–29, 141, 145(table); Philippines, 148, 151–52, 154, 160, 167, 195
rentier states, 45
repression, 68–71, 226; backfiring of (*see* repression, backfiring of); Burma, 175, 176, 180–84, 185(table), 186, 187; effects of regime crackdowns on probability of success, 51, 51–52(tables); Egypt, 230; faced by most resistance campaigns, 51, 77; Iran, 93, 95, 98–110, 112–13, 115; iterative relationship between regimes and campaigns, 65; and mobilization, 68; and need for tactical diversity and innovation, 56; not correlated with outcomes of nonviolent resistance campaigns, 58; Palestinian Territories, 77, 122, 127, 129–31, 133–34, 140, 146; Philippines, 150–51, 155, 157, 157(table), 167, 196; possible impact on outcome of campaigns, 64–65; repressive/authoritarian nature of regimes following successful violent campaigns, 60, 201, 203–16, 258n10; repressive theocracy following Iranian Revolution, 110, 116–18, 202, 219; and resilience of opposition, 57–58. *See also* authoritarian regimes
repression, backfiring of, 10–11, 20, 58, 61, 82, 196, 220, 226, 246n13; and benefits of diversity of participants, 40; Burma, 187; East Timor, 3–4; Egypt, 230; and importance of maintaining nonviolent discipline, 247n27; importance of media coverage of interactions between unarmed protesters and security forces, 247n26; Iran, 108, 112; mechanisms of backfiring, 68; Palestinian Territories, 129–31, 140; Philippines, 157(table), 167, 196. *See also* loyalty shifts of security forces and other regime supporters
research methodology, 11–15, 87–91; case studies (*see* Burma; Iran; Palestinian Territories; Philippines); case study procedure, 88–90; criteria for judging outcomes, 14, 244n13; databases, 6, 13; data-collection strategy, 14–15; definition of terms, 12–14; difficulties of comparison studies, 15–17; overview of civil resistance research, 21–25; and participation measures, 245nn1,3,7; and policy objectives of campaigns, 12; reasons for judging campaigns rather than events, 244n15; and regime type following nonviolent vs. vio-

lent transitions, 258n17, 259n20; and relationship between nonviolent resistance and security-force defections, 247n25; scholarly implications of research, 18–27; selection effects, 14–15; testing effects of resistance type on postconflict civil war, 216–18; testing effects of resistance type on postconflict democracy, 212–16; testing for endogeneity, 79–81
resilience of resistance movements, 57–58, 114–15, 193, 221
resource mobilization theory, 20–21
Revolutionary Organization of the Tudeh Party of Iran (ROTPI), 250n3
Revolutionary War, 24
Rigby, Andrew, 131
risks and costs of participation in resistance campaigns, 34–35, 37–39
Roberts, Adam, 22
Robinson, Glenn, 136
Rosenstraße protests (Berlin), 20
ROTPI. *See* Revolutionary Organization of the Tudeh Party of Iran
rule of law, 207
Russett, Bruce, 206
Russia: and Chechen rebels, 24; disruption of nonviolent campaigns, 225; and lack of diplomatic pressure on Burma, 53; Russian Revolution (1917), 56, 59, 206, 209, 246n15; statistics on outcomes and number of members in resistance campaigns, 33(table)

Saakashvili, Mikhail, 209
sabotage, 13, 102, 154
Sadegh, Abolhassan, 98
Said, Edward, 255n5
Sai Yee, 189
sanctions. *See* international sanctions
Saudi Arabia, 53, 229
SAVAK (Iranian secret police), 93, 97
Saw Maung, 182
Schelling, Thomas, 226
Schiff, Ze'ev: on Arab population of Israel, 251n8; on backfiring of repression, 129; on Communist Party, 126; on First Intifada as a surprise to Israel and PLO, 123; on impact of First Intifada on Israeli society, 139; on nonviolent nature of First Intifada, 142; on PLO assumptions about Palestinians in the occupied territories, 122; on Ship of Return incident, 128
Schock, Kurt: distinction between "normal" political action and nonviolent action, 12, 243n8; on effectiveness of nonviolent resistance against repressive opponents, 19; on failure of Burmese uprising, 188; on leverage, 41; on Marcos regime, 150–51; on opposition to Marcos regime, 155; on Rangoon Spring, 187; on reasons for outcomes of resistance campaigns, 23; on success of People Power movement, 170; on tactical innovations, 55, 248n36
Schott, Jeffrey J., 53
secession campaigns, 13, 70(table); American Revolution, 222; criteria for identifying, 72; examples, 72; and external actors, 69; negative effect of nonviolent resistance on likelihood of success, 7, 73(table), 220
Second National Front (Iran), 94
security forces: Burma, 173–74, 176, 189, 196, 197; defection of (*see* security forces, defection of); and expectations of citizens, 208; Iran, 93, 97, 106–8; Palestinian Territories, 124, 128, 129–30; Philippines, 147, 166; support for regime reinforced by threat of violence ("rally around the flag" effect), 48
security forces, defection of, 46–50, 58, 247n25; and case study summary, 193; and First Intifada, 130, 252n20; and fraternization tactic, 107, 111, 162, 166, 210; and Iranian Revolution, 92, 107–8, 109–10, 112, 114; lack of defections in Burma, 188–89; and People Power movement (Philippines), 161–63, 165–66, 170; statistics, 48, 48(table), 50(fig.)
Sein Lwin, 179, 181, 184, 189
Sein Win, 187–88
selection effects, 14–15
self-determination campaigns. *See* secession campaigns
Sepp, Kalev, 13
Serbia, 6, 36, 46–47, 225, 230. *See also* Otpor
Shamir, Yitzhak: defeated in 1992 election, 135–36; Jewish settlement policy, 121, 133, 253nn27,29,35; and Madrid Conference (1991), 135, 140; and Ship of Return incident (1988), 128; and U.S. pressure, 133, 196

Shan State Army (SSA; Burma), 173
Sharon, Ariel, 137
Sharp, Gene, 12, 21–22, 225, 245n8, 247n26
Shi'a Islam, 115. *See also* Iranian Revolution
Shultz, George, 133
Siahkal attack (1971; Iran), 97
Sin, Cardinal Jaime, 152, 156, 160, 161, 167
Singapore, 190
Sison, Jose Maria, 255n3
sit-ins, 12, 31, 35, 56, 158
SLORC. *See* State Law and Order Restoration Council
Slovenia, 218
snap elections (Philippines election of 1986), 159–61
Social Democrats (SD; Philippines), 153–54, 156, 255n4
Socialist Party (Burma), 173
Sol Phryne (ship), 127–28, 144, 252n12
South Africa: antiapartheid campaign and external actors, 27, 53, 223, 249n21; debate over importance of armed vs. unarmed struggle, 248n31; Defiance Campaign, 79; economic costs of strikes and boycotts, 44, 47; and lack of diplomatic pressure on Zimbabwe, 53; and long-term consequences of nonviolent campaign, 208–9; and loyalty shifts of regime supporters, 47; and radical flank effect, 169
South America: nonviolent campaigns listed, 233–42. *See also specific countries*
Soviet Union, 33(table), 54, 65
Soviet Union, former states of, 75; rates of campaign success, 74(fig.), 81(table)
Spain, 54, 215–16
Sri Lanka, 72, 205. *See also* Tamil Tigers
SSA. *See* Shan State Army
Stalin, Joseph, 20
State Law and Order Restoration Council (SLORC; Burma), 182, 184, 187, 191, 196
statistics on nonviolent vs. violent campaigns: distribution of campaign outcomes by campaign objective, 73(table); effects of defeated violent insurgencies on democratic regimes, 216; effects of failed nonviolent vs. failed violent campaigns on probability of postconflict democracy, 216; effects of nonviolent resistance on number of participants, 34(table); effects of regime crackdowns on probability of success, 51, 51–52(tables); effects of resistance type on probability of postconflict civil war, 217(table), 218; failure rates, 9(table); frequency, 7(table); international sanctions, 49(table); involvement of external actors, 49(table); number of nonviolent campaigns and percentage of successes, 8(table); number of participants in largest resistance campaigns, 33(table); partial success rates, 9(table); percentage of campaigns in states of differing relative power, 72(fig.); percentage of campaigns meeting with regime violence, 51; percentage of campaigns receiving diplomatic support, 53; percentage of campaigns receiving material support from external states, 54; percentage of campaigns targeting different regime types, 67(fig.); percentage of states designated "not free" that have undergone recent violent transitions, 209; public opinion on violent vs. nonviolent resistance in the Palestinian Territories, 138; regime type following nonviolent vs. violent transitions, 60, 214(table), 215(fig.); and secession cases, 7, 73(table), 220; security forces defections, 48(table), 50(fig.); success rate, 7, 9(table), 11, 73(table), 222; success rate and participation, 33(table), 34–35, 39, 40(fig.); success rates by campaign objective, 9(table); success rates by decade, 8(table); success rates by region, 74(fig.), 81(table)
stay-aways, 12, 31, 38, 101, 104, 113. *See also* strikes
strategic interaction thesis, 65
strategic nonviolent action, 10
Strategic Nonviolent Conflict (Ackerman and Kruegler), 22
strikes, 6, 12, 35, 44; Burma, 180–82; Egypt, 230; Iran, 56, 99, 101, 103–7, 110, 115; Palestinian Territories, 119, 121, 125; Philippines, 158–59, 161
structural conditions as possible explanation for outcomes of resistance campaigns, 63–67, 70–71(table); authoritarian opponents, 66–67; and comparison of successful and failed nonviolent campaigns, 194; geographic region, 63; polit-

ical opportunity approach, 64; powerful opponents, 67–68; regime capabilities, 64, 67–68; regime type, 64, 66–67; repressive opponents, 68–71; timing of campaigns, 63. *See also* repression
student activism: Burma, 174–75, 177–80, 186, 191, 196, 256n5; Iran, 94, 96, 98–101, 104, 113, 114, 117(table), 251n9; Palestinian Territories, 121, 145(table); Philippines, 148, 153; Serbia, 46–47, 54, 77
successful nonviolent campaigns. *See* Iranian Revolution; Palestinian Territories (partially successful); Philippines
Suharto, 3–4, 247n21
suicide bombers, 36, 42, 137
Syria, 122

tactics. *See* nonviolent resistance tactics; violent resistance tactics
Taleqani, Ayatollah Mahmud, 94, 98
Taliban, 42, 56, 206
Tamil Tigers (LTTE), 57
Tarrow, Sidney, 17, 19, 55, 216
Tatmadaw (Burmese armed forces), 173–74, 176
Taylor, Robert, 176
terrorism, 25; and aftermath of Iranian Revolution, 110; effectiveness compared to other tactics, 25–26; implications of research, 226–27; international repercussions of crackdowns on terrorists, 53; and media attention, 42; and Palestinian Territories, 78, 120, 137; and the Philippines, 153–54; violence as a first resort, 227
Thailand, 190, 208, 211, 248n40
Thakin Kodaw Hmine, 177
Than Shwe, 182
Third Force (Iran), 94
Thompson, Mark R., 255n5
Tiananmen Square massacre, 39, 56
Tibet, 45
Tilly, Charles, 55
time, as possible explanation for outcomes of campaigns, 63, 70–71(table), 75
Tin Maung Oo, 177
Tin Oo, 181
Tunisia, 6, 123, 229, 230
Twenty-first Year (Israel), 130
Twitter, 229

Ukraine, 6, 207, 225; aftermath of Orange Revolution, 202; Maidan Square sit-in, 56; protests, 36; statistics on outcomes and number of members in resistance campaigns, 33(table)
Unarmed Insurrections (Schock), 23
United Democratic Organization (UNIDO; Philippines), 155, 159–61, 255n6
United Kingdom, 24
United Nationalist Democratic Organization (UNIDO; Philippines), 5
United Nationalist League for Democracy (UNLD; Burma), 184
United National Leadership of the Uprising (UNLU; Palestinian Territories), 125–27, 138, 140, 142, 195, 197, 255n55
United States: American Revolution, 222; and Burma, 190; civil rights movement and radical flank effect, 169; decline in U.S. support for Marcos regime, 159, 163, 168, 196, 247n21; and El Salvador, 247n22; and First Intifada, 140, 144; and Iran, 98; and Israel, 196, 253n28; and PLO declaration of independence, 133; Shah perceived as puppet of, 93–94; support for anti-Soviet insurgency in Afghanistan, 54; support for unpopular regimes in Saudi Arabia and Egypt, 53
United Wa State Army (Burma), 183
UNLD. *See* United Nationalist League for Democracy
UNLU. *See* United National Leadership of the Uprising
U Nu, 174, 181
U Thant, 176

van de Walle, Nicolas, 203
Ver, Fabian, 147, 163
Vietnam, 33(table), 42, 59, 65, 206
violent campaigns and insurgencies, 12–13; appeal of, 32; Burma, 57, 173–76, 183–84, 256nn3,4, 257nn8,11; Chechen rebels, 24; and civil wars in the postconflict era, 29, 201–8, 216–18, 217(table); coexistence with nonviolent campaigns, 78, 168–69, 184–88, 202, 218, 257n3; and commitment issues, 37–39; contrast to nonviolent campaigns (*see* nonviolent resistance campaigns compared to violent campaigns); defined, 11–13, 243n5; definition of "participation" in violent insurgencies,

violent campaigns and insurgencies *(continued)*
31; effectiveness of, 8–9(figs.), 11, 25–26, 59–61, 64, 73, 220; and ethnic factionalization, 80; exceptional cases of democracies following violent campaigns, 202, 219; and expectations of citizens shaped by nature of transition, 207–8, 212; and external allies, 10, 11, 59, 69, 175–76, 202, 222; external support leading to mistreatment of civilian population, 55; factors influencing onset of, 80; failure and endogeneity problem, 63; fate of democracies that succumb to violent insurgencies, 215–16; as first choice in many cases, 77–78, 227; high human costs of successful campaigns, 60; high risk of death, 38; implications of research, 226–27; Iran, 42, 92, 95–98, 111, 117(table), 192; Iraq, 77; and leverage, 42–46; and likelihood of victory, 76; longevity of insurgencies not indicative of success, 57; moral barriers to participation, 36–37; and mountainous terrain, 80; negative impacts on societies and polities, 202–19; and negative radical flank effect, 43, 152; number of participants, 32–34, 192; Palestinian Territories, 42, 121–22, 137, 218 *(see also* Palestine Liberation Organization); persistence of violence even when proven ineffective, 78; Philippines, 149–50, 153–54, 166–69, 192, 255n5; physical risks and costs of participation, 34–35; and positive radical flank effect, 43; as possible failed nonviolent campaigns, 76–77; and postconflict regime types, 29, 60, 201, 205–16, 222; and poverty, 80; recruitment issues, 35; reliance on underground activities, 35–36; resilience of, 57; and secession campaigns, 7, 69, 73, 220; secrecy and martial values, 208; Sri Lanka, 57; successful violent campaigns, 11, 59–61, 73, 219; support for regime reinforced by threat of violence ("rally around the flag" effect), 45–46; symbolic function, 42; tactics *(see* violent resistance tactics); and target regime type, 80; types of participation, 31. *See also* guerrilla warfare

violent resistance tactics, 12–13, 34–35, 56. *See also* assassinations; bombings; coups d'état; direct defense; guerrilla warfare; improvised explosive devices; sabotage; terrorism

Walter, Barbara, 205
Walzer, Michael, 77
war of attrition, 57
al-Wazir, Khalil (Abu Jihad), 121–22
Web sites, 223
Weinstein, Jeremy, 18, 55
welgang bayan (people's strikes; Philippines), 158–59
White Revolution (1963; Iran), 93, 95
Wilson, Isaiah, 13, 25, 26
women: and health impacts of violent insurgencies, 206; and *hejab* issue in Iran, 99, 114, 251n10; marginalized in post-Oslo Palestinian Territories, 137; participation in First Intifada, 129, 139, 145(table); participation in resistance campaign in Iran, 99, 114, 117(table); participation in resistance campaigns in the Philippines, 151, 157(table), 162, 165; participation in violent campaigns, 35; and physical capabilities for participation in resistance campaigns, 35; and Rosenstraße protests (Nazi Germany), 20
Wood, Elizabeth Jean, 18, 47
workers. *See* stay-aways; strikes
World War II, 14, 20, 24
Wurfel, David, 150

Ya'ari, Ehud: on Arab population of Israel, 251n8; on backfiring of repression, 129; on Communist Party, 126; on First Intifada as a surprise to Israel and PLO, 123; on impact of First Intifada on Israeli society, 139; on nonviolent nature of First Intifada, 142; on PLO assumptions about Palestinians in the occupied territories, 122; on Ship of Return incident, 128
Yemen, 229
Yesh Gvul Dai La'kibush (Israel), 130
YouTube, 224, 229

zero-sum perception of conflicts, 44, 207, 212
Zimbabwe, 53, 225
Zunes, Stephen, 22, 247n22

GPSR Authorized Representative: Easy Access System Europe, Mustamäe tee
50, 10621 Tallinn, Estonia, gpsr.requests@easproject.com

www.ingramcontent.com/pod-product-compliance
Lightning Source LLC
Chambersburg PA
CBHW021149260326
41798CB00029B/325